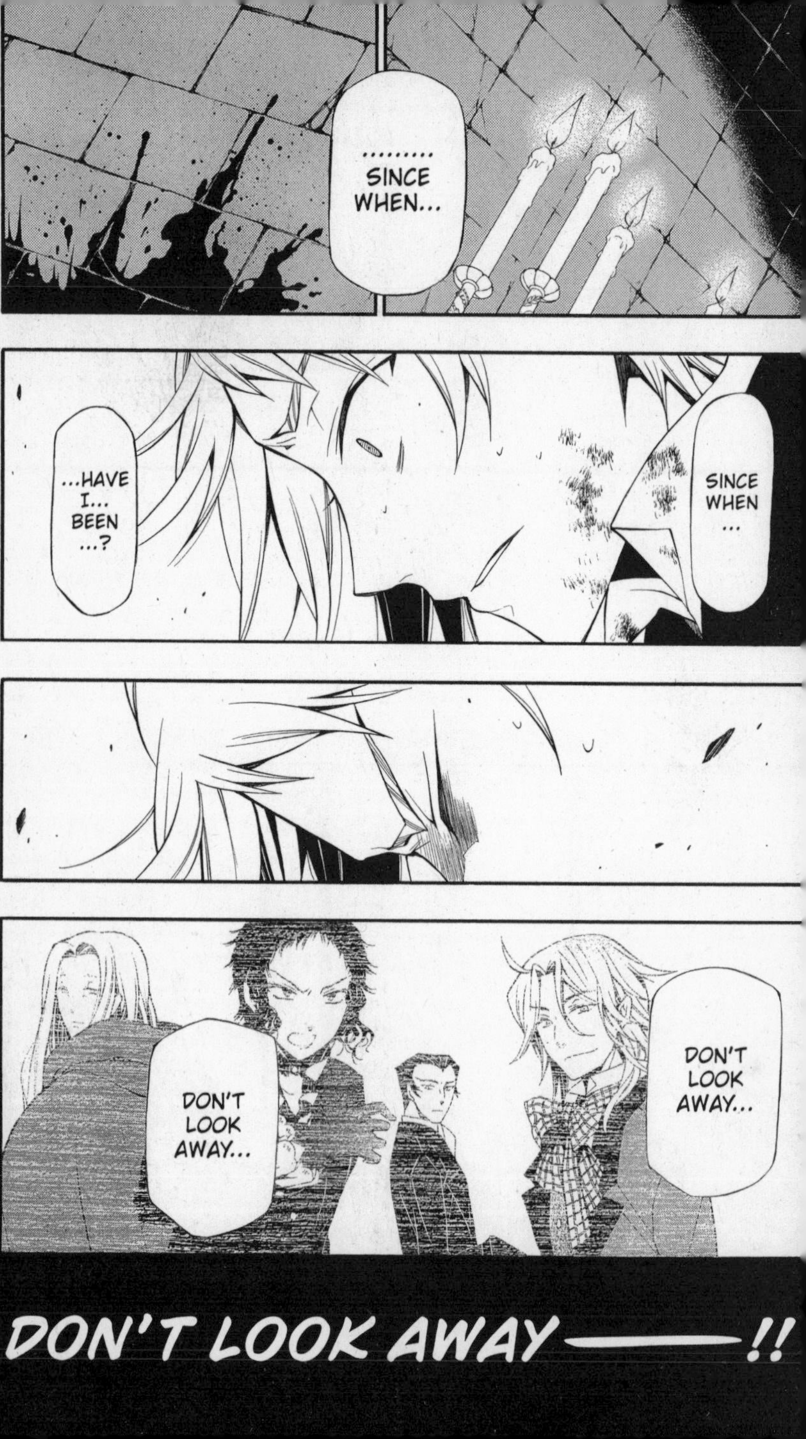
....
SINCE WHEN...
SINCE WHEN ...
...HAVE I... BEEN ...?
DON'T LOOK AWAY...
DON'T LOOK AWAY...
DON'T LOOK AWAY——!!

Retrace:LVIII Puddle of blood

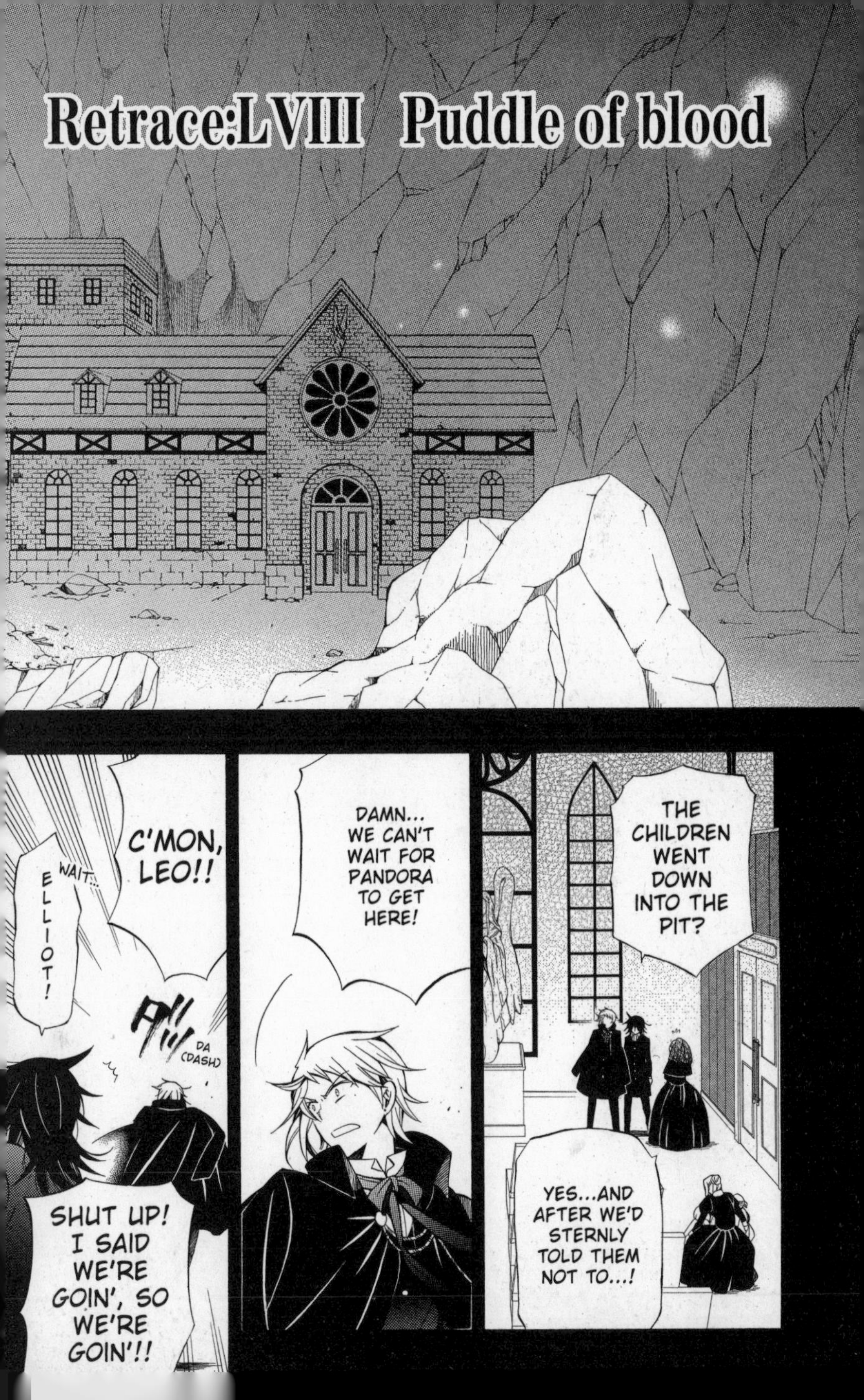
THE CHILDREN WENT DOWN INTO THE PIT?
YES...AND AFTER WE'D STERNLY TOLD THEM NOT TO...!
DAMN... WE CAN'T WAIT FOR PANDORA TO GET HERE!
C'MON, LEO!!
WAIT... ELLIOT!
DA (DASH)
SHUT UP! I SAID WE'RE GOIN', SO WE'RE GOIN'!!

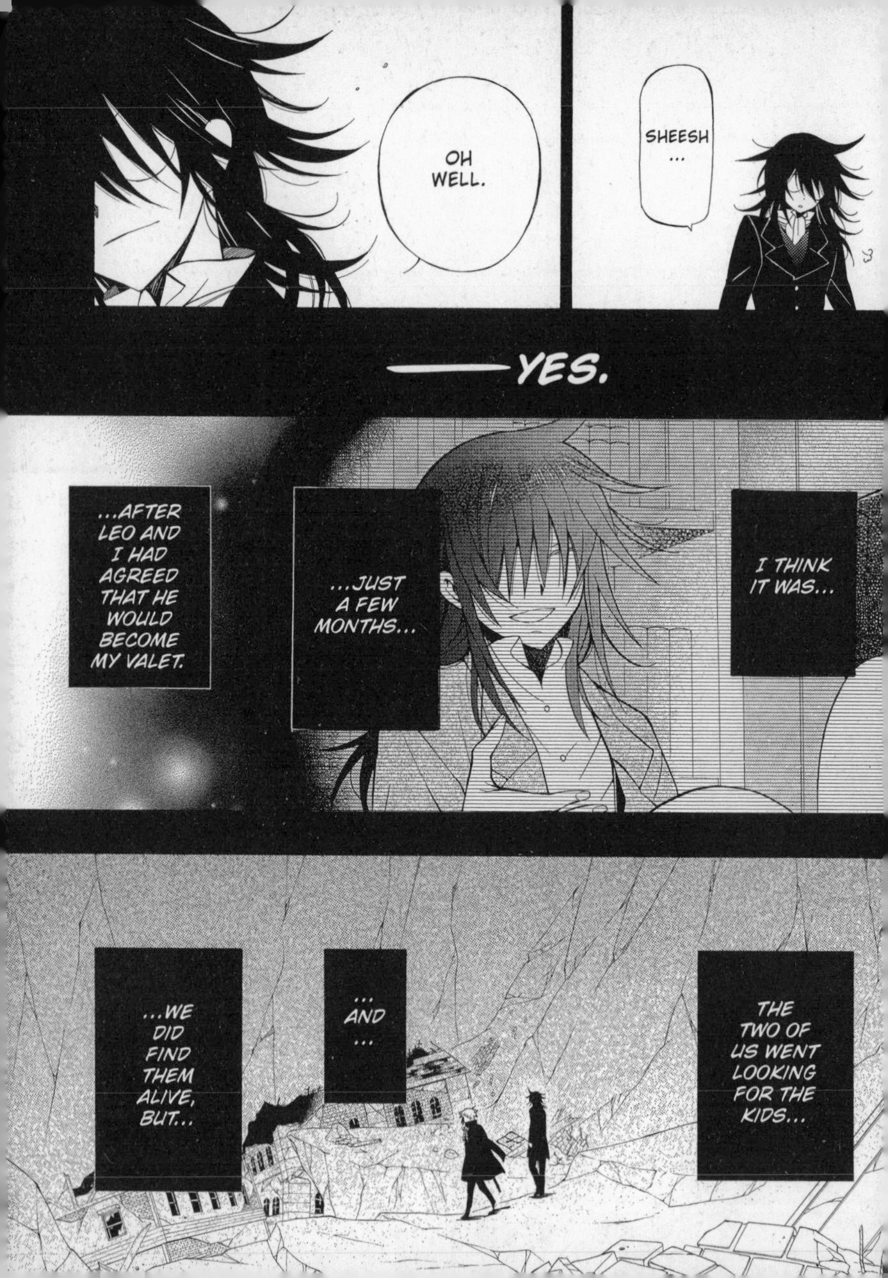
SHEESH ...
OH WELL.
—YES.
I THINK IT WAS...
...JUST A FEW MONTHS...
...AFTER LEO AND I HAD AGREED THAT HE WOULD BECOME MY VALET.
THE TWO OF US WENT LOOKING FOR THE KIDS...
... AND ...
...WE DID FIND THEM ALIVE, BUT...

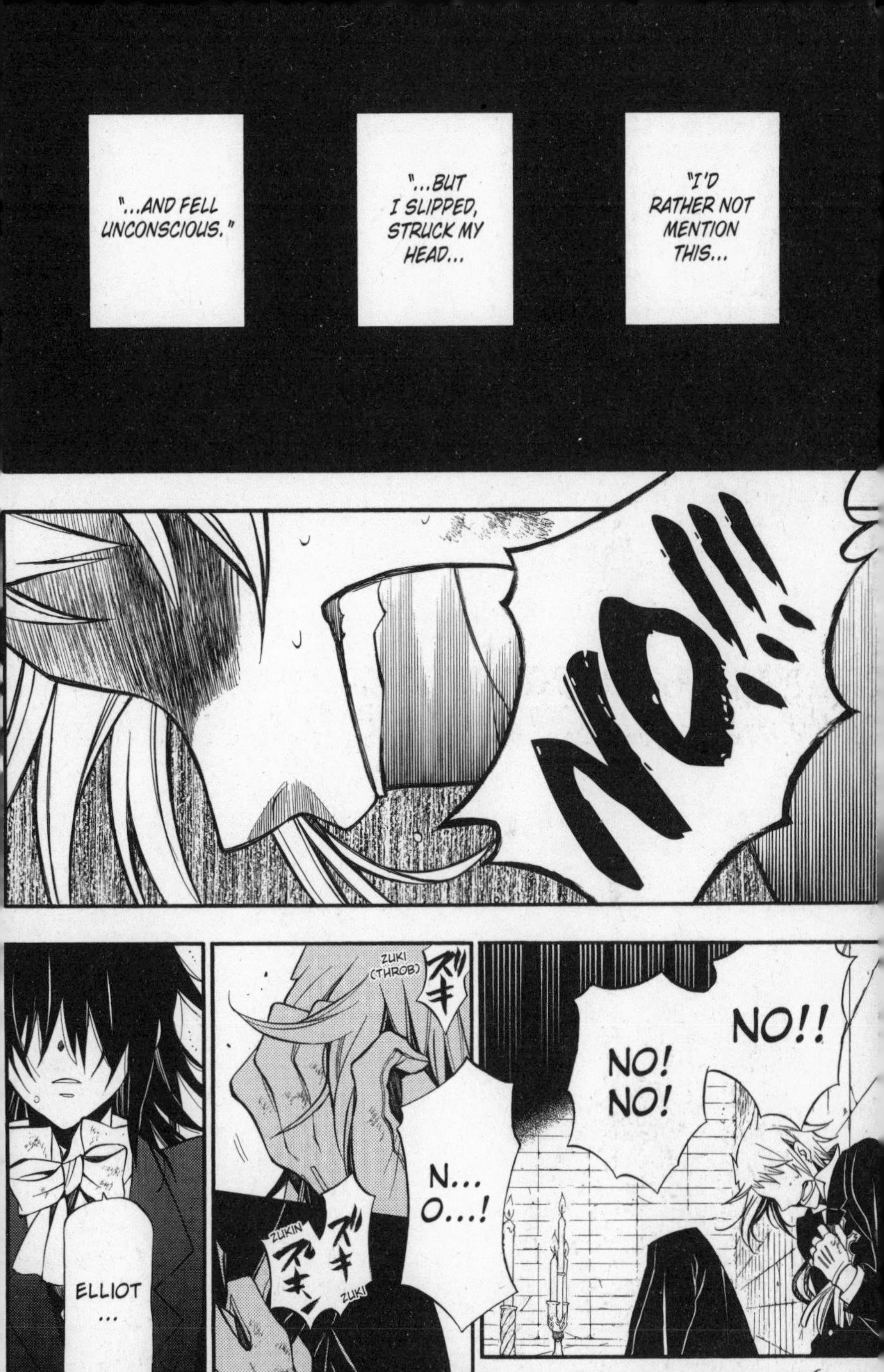
"I'D RATHER NOT MENTION THIS...
"...BUT I SLIPPED, STRUCK MY HEAD...
"...AND FELL UNCONSCIOUS."
NO!!!
NO!!
NO! NO!
ZUKI (THROB) ズキ
N... O...!
ズキン ZUKIN
ズキ ZUKI
ELLIOT...

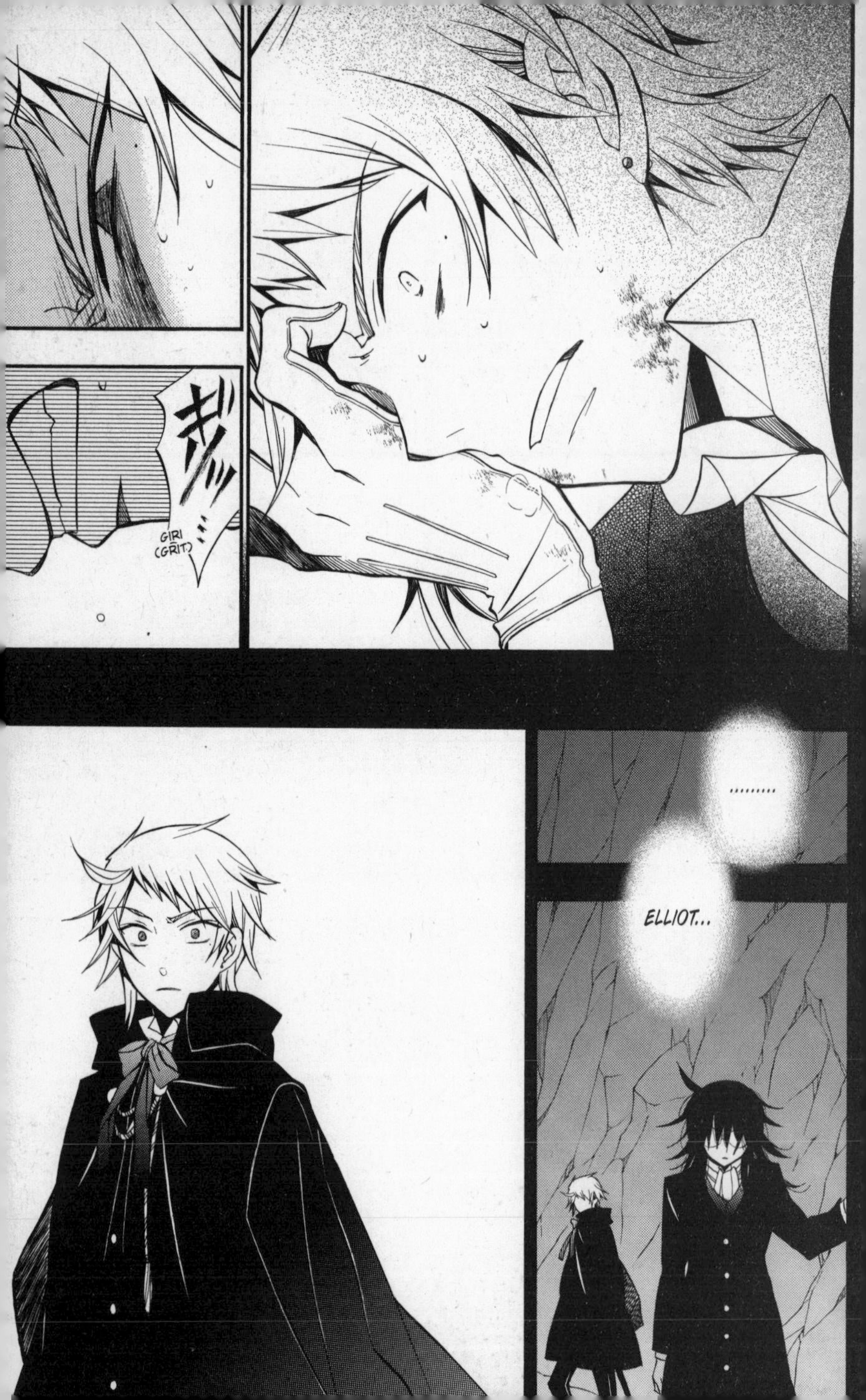
GIRI (GRIT)
....
ELLIOT...

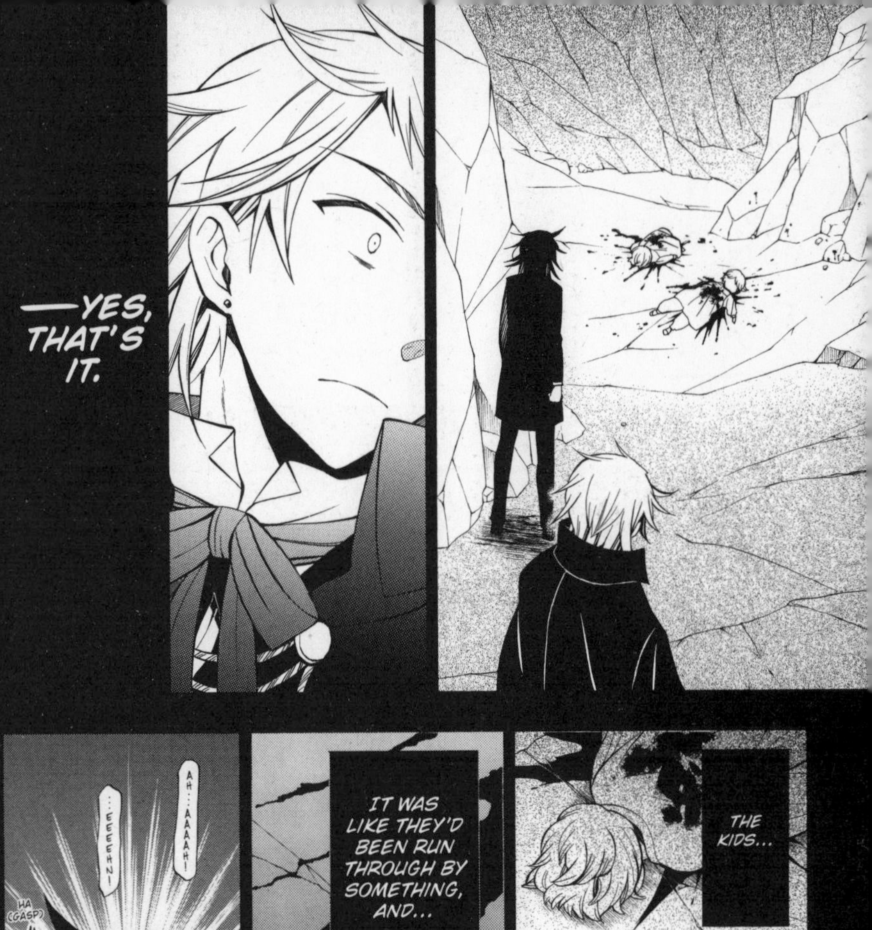
—YES, THAT'S IT.
THE KIDS...
...WEREN'T ALIVE.
IT WAS LIKE THEY'D BEEN RUN THROUGH BY SOMETHING, AND...
...THEY LAY DEAD IN A MASSIVE PUDDLE OF BLOOD.
AH...AAAAH!
...EEEEHN!
HA (GASP)

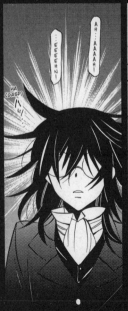

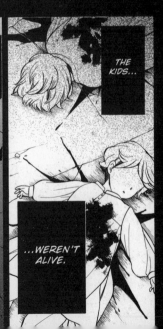

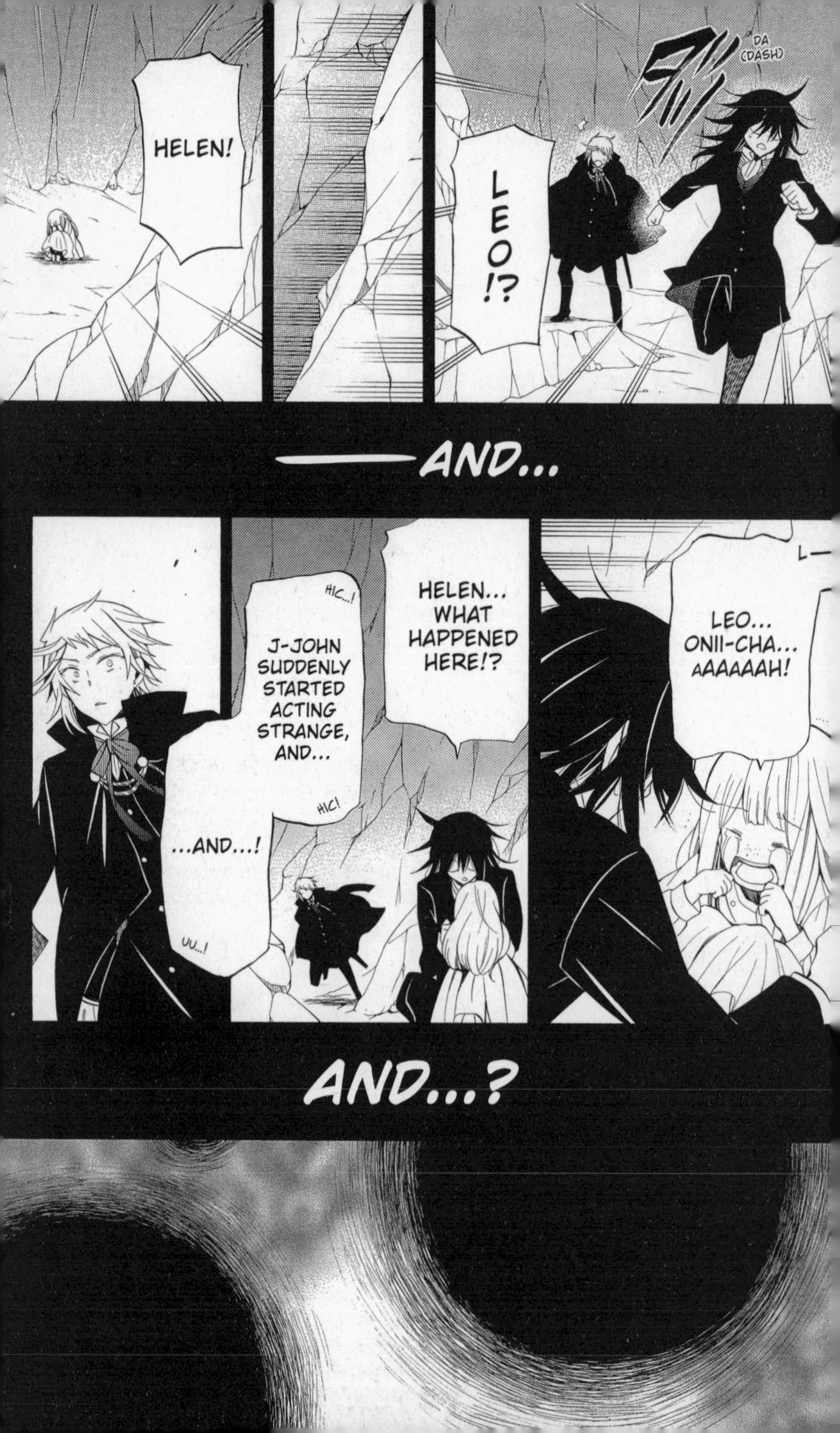
DA (DASH)
LEO!?
HELEN!
——AND...
L—
LEO... ONII-CHA... AAAAAAH!
...
HELEN... WHAT HAPPENED HERE!?
HIC...!
J-JOHN SUDDENLY STARTED ACTING STRANGE, AND...
HIC!
...AND...!
UU...!
AND...?

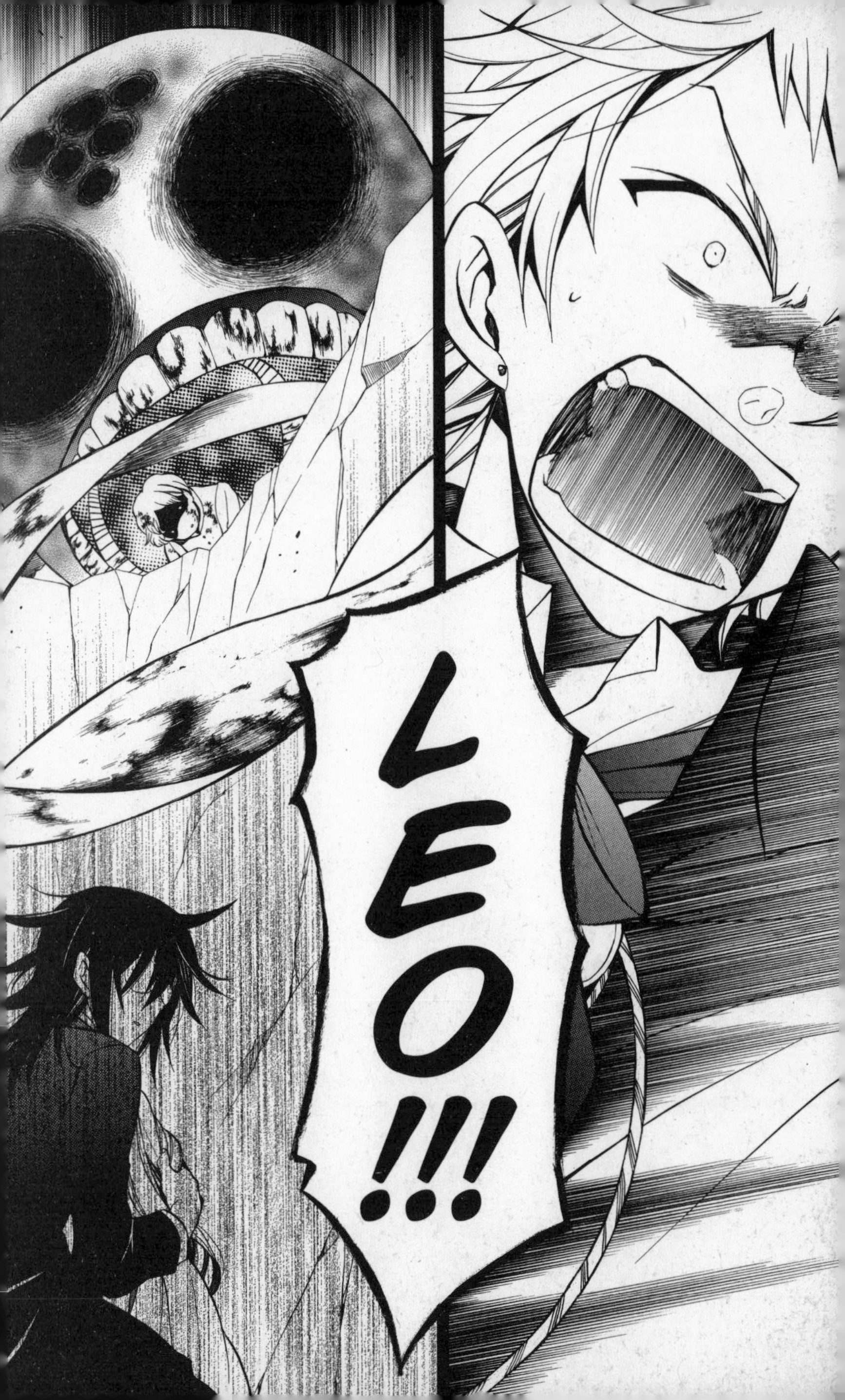
LEO!!!

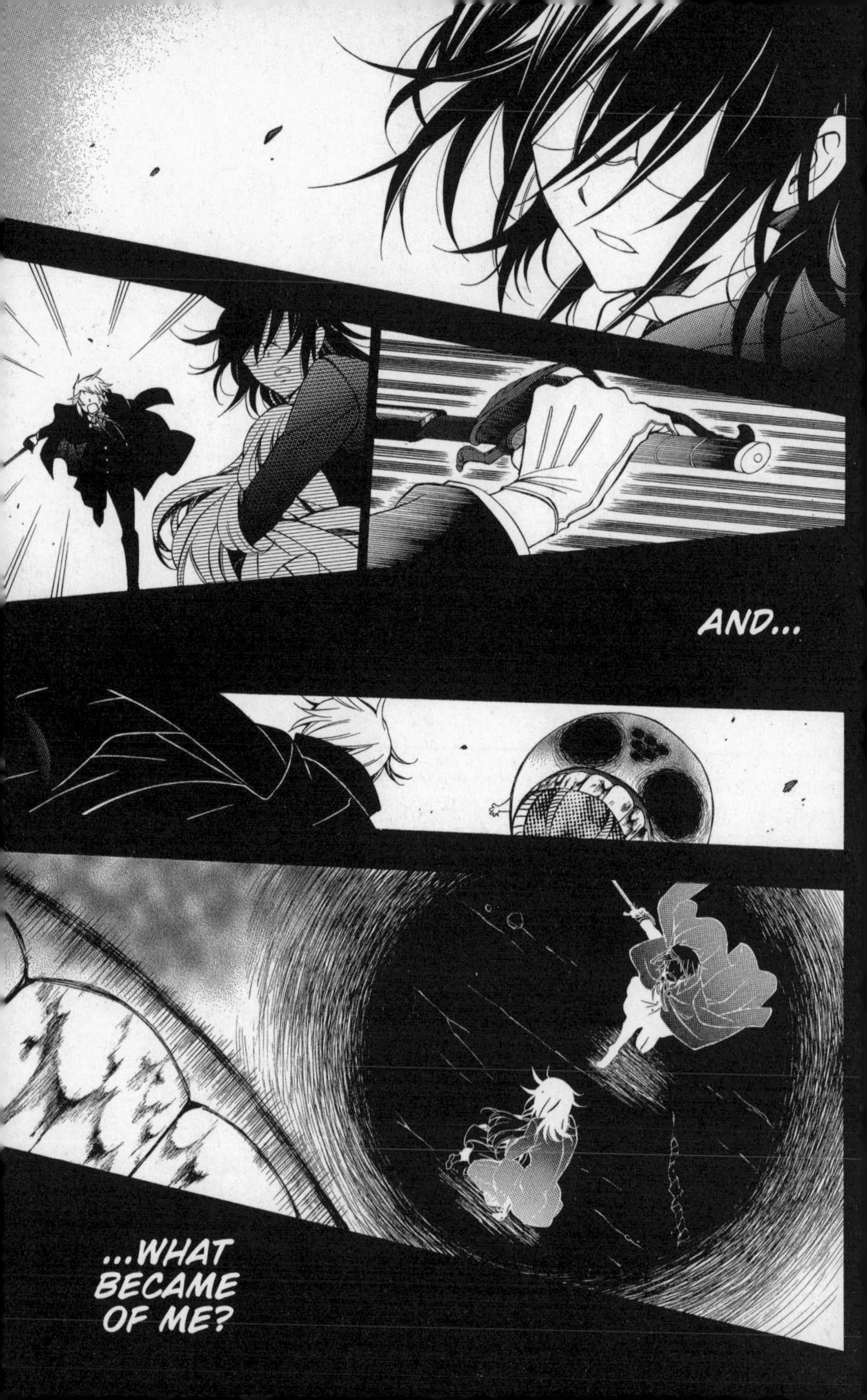
AND...
...WHAT BECAME OF ME?

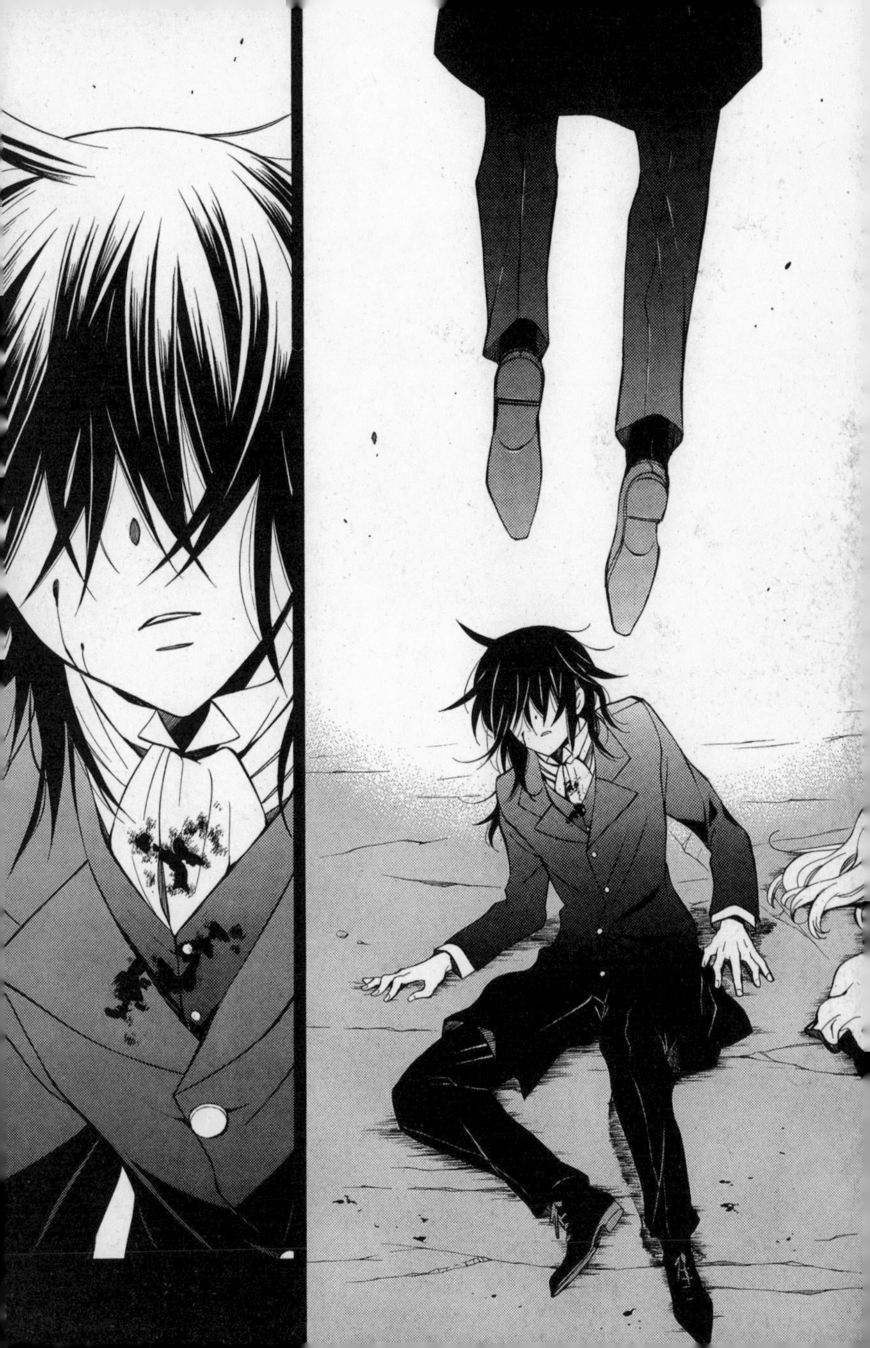

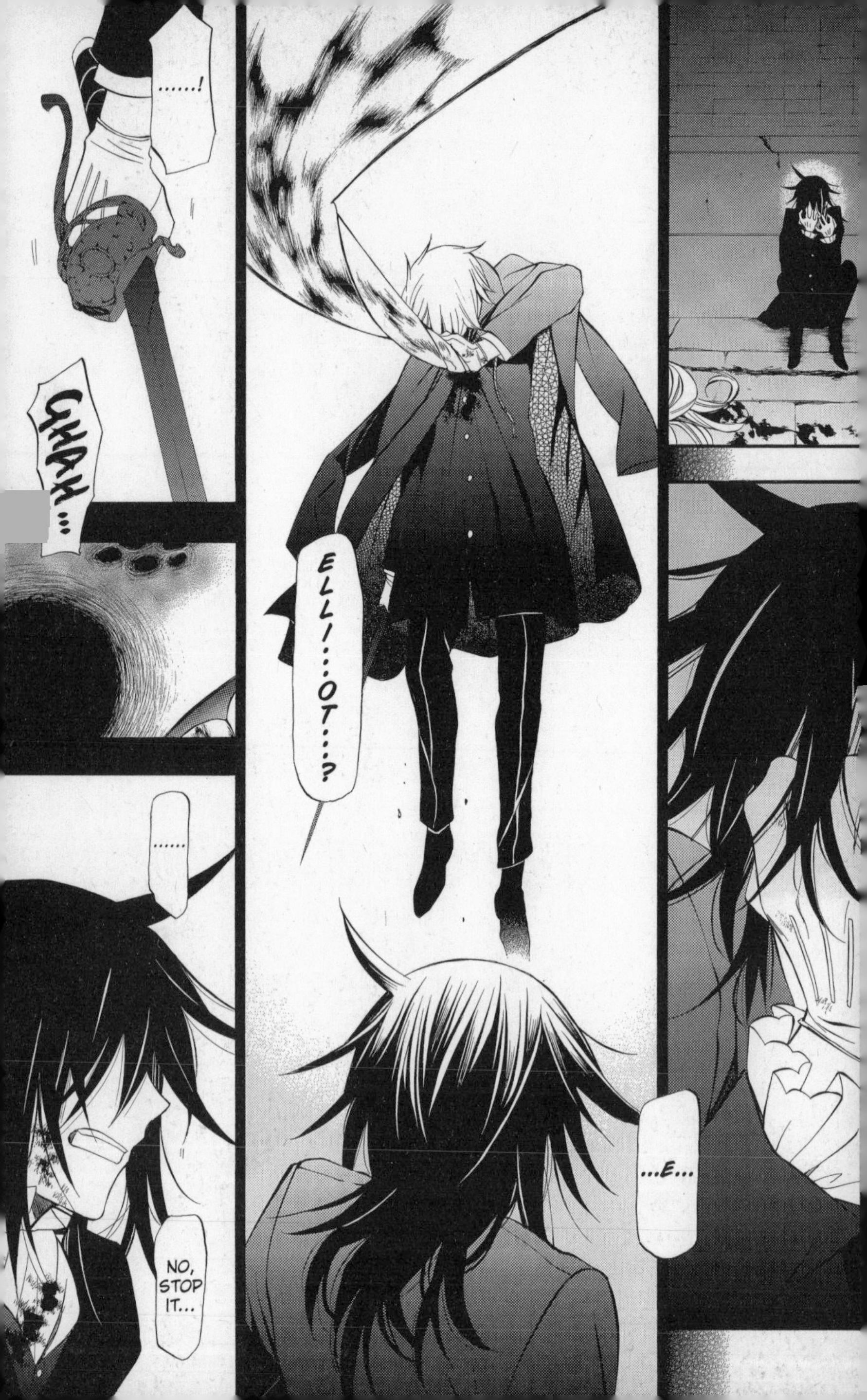

ELLI...OT...?
...E...
......!
GHAH...
......
NO, STOP IT...

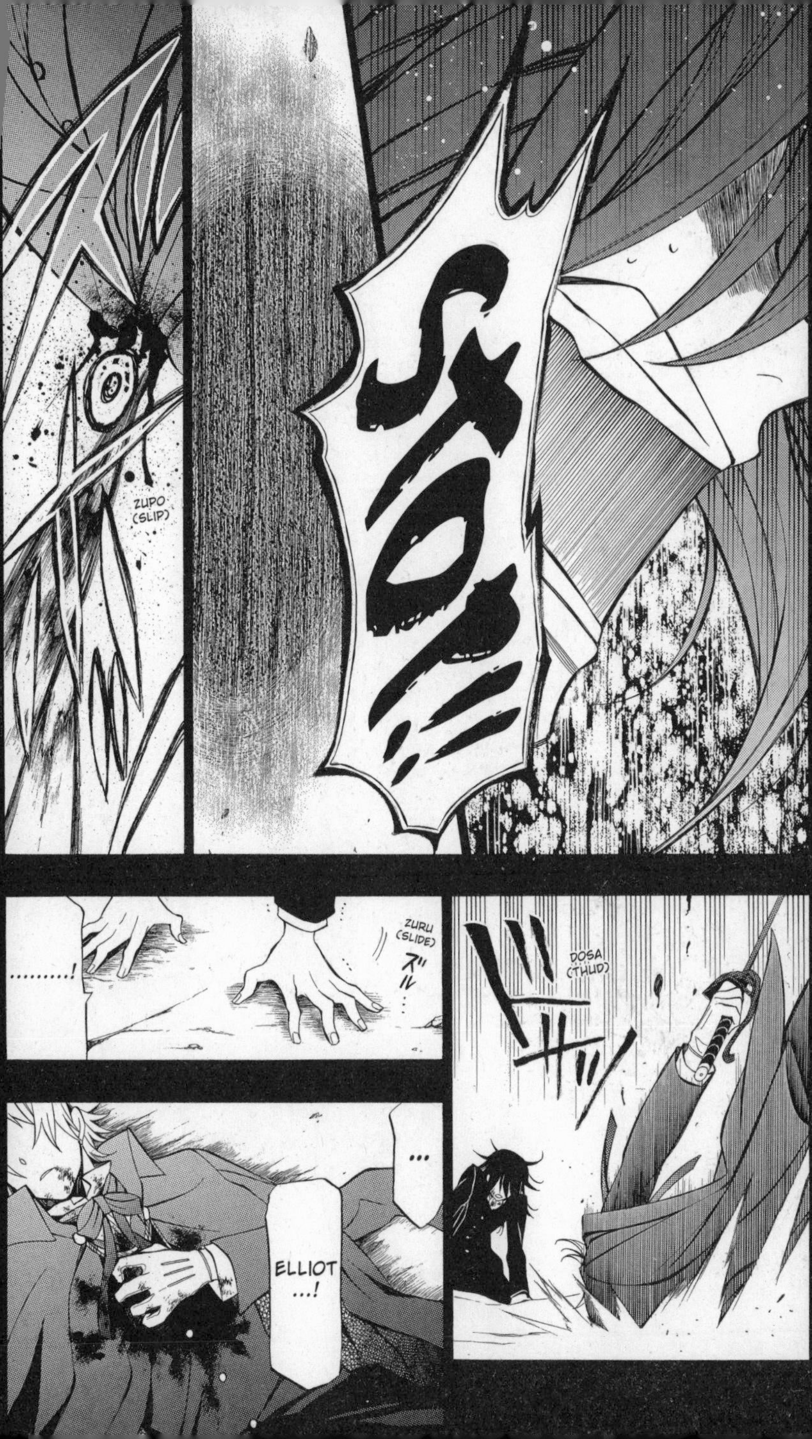
ZUPO (SLIP)
DOSA (THUD)
ドサッ
ZURU (SLIDE)
ズル…
..........!
...
ELLIOT ...!

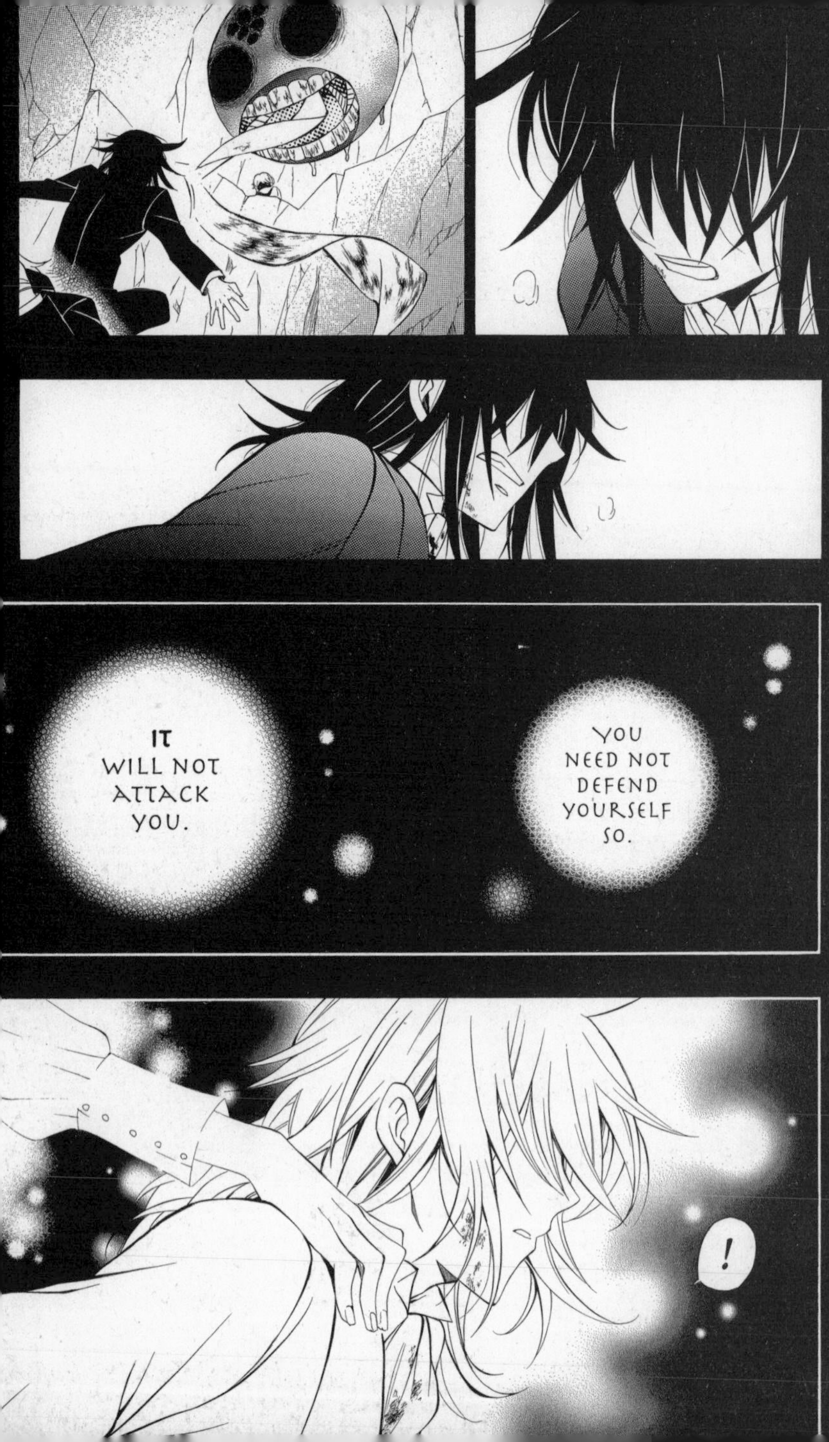
IT WILL NOT ATTACK YOU.
YOU NEED NOT DEFEND YOURSELF SO.
!

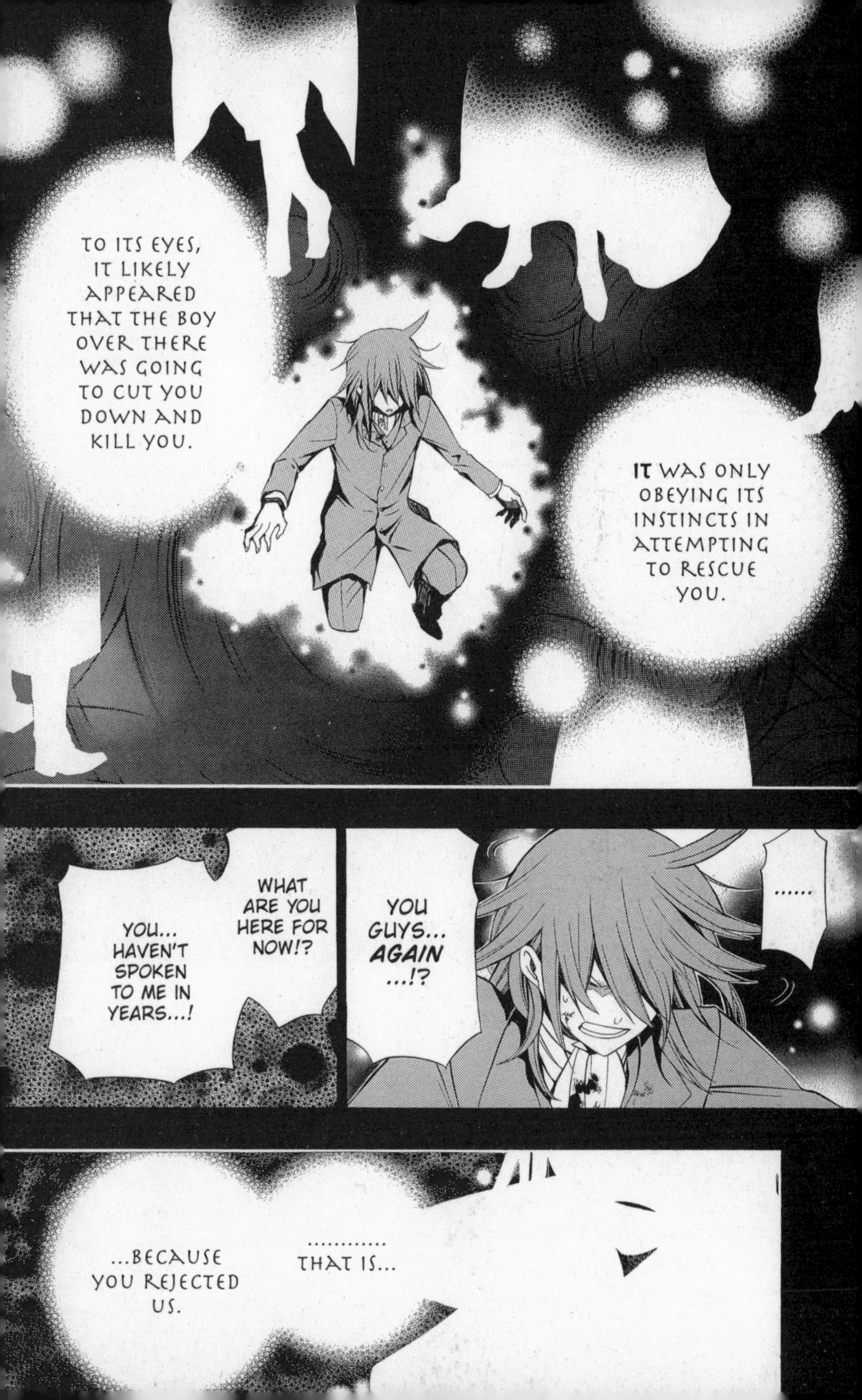
TO ITS EYES, IT LIKELY APPEARED THAT THE BOY OVER THERE WAS GOING TO CUT YOU DOWN AND KILL YOU.
IT WAS ONLY OBEYING ITS INSTINCTS IN ATTEMPTING TO RESCUE YOU.
......
YOU GUYS... AGAIN ...!?
WHAT ARE YOU HERE FOR NOW!?
YOU... HAVEN'T SPOKEN TO ME IN YEARS...!
.... THAT IS...
...BECAUSE YOU REJECTED US.

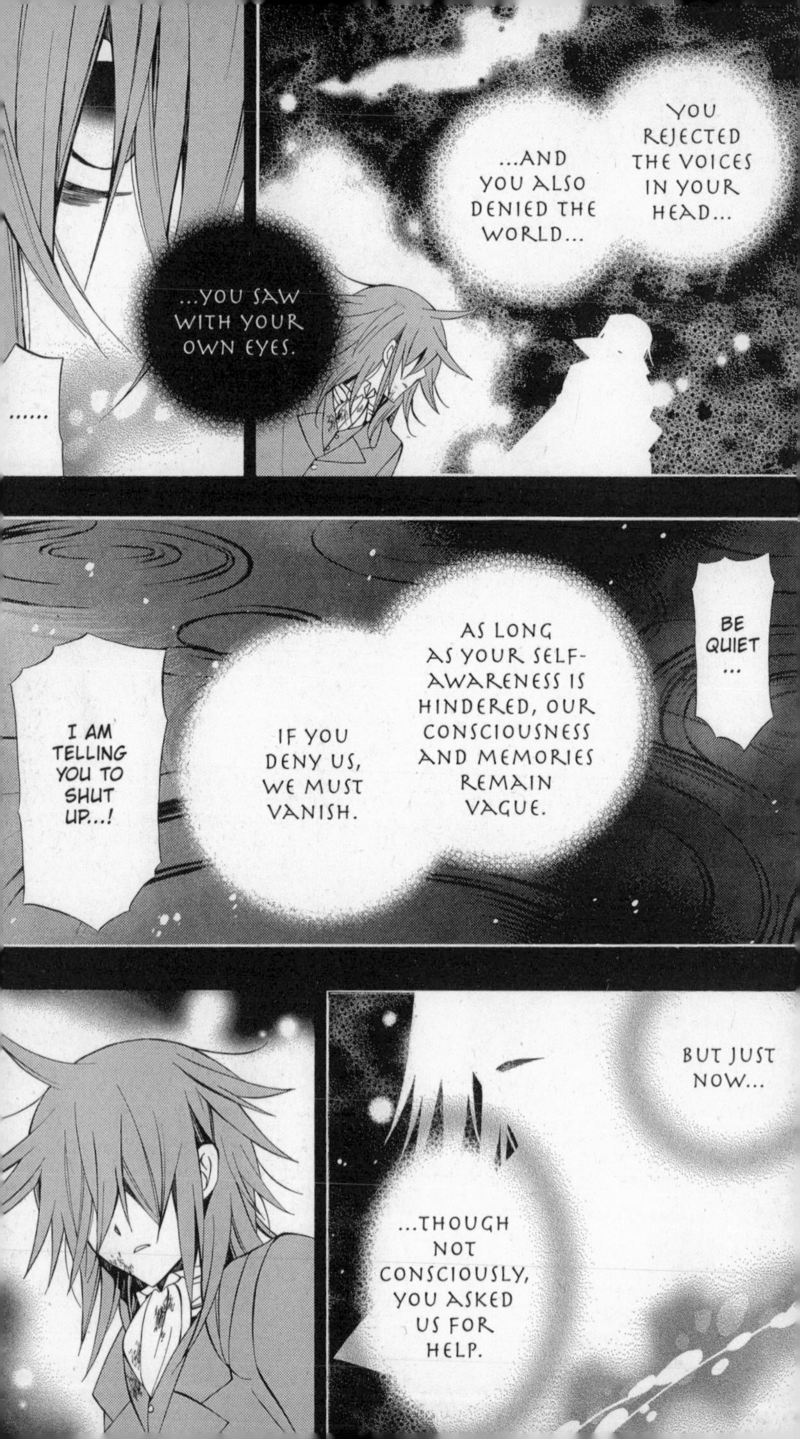
YOU REJECTED THE VOICES IN YOUR HEAD...
...AND YOU ALSO DENIED THE WORLD...
...YOU SAW WITH YOUR OWN EYES.
......
BE QUIET...
AS LONG AS YOUR SELF-AWARENESS IS HINDERED, OUR CONSCIOUSNESS AND MEMORIES REMAIN VAGUE.
IF YOU DENY US, WE MUST VANISH.
I AM TELLING YOU TO SHUT UP...!
BUT JUST NOW...
...THOUGH NOT CONSCIOUSLY, YOU ASKED US FOR HELP.

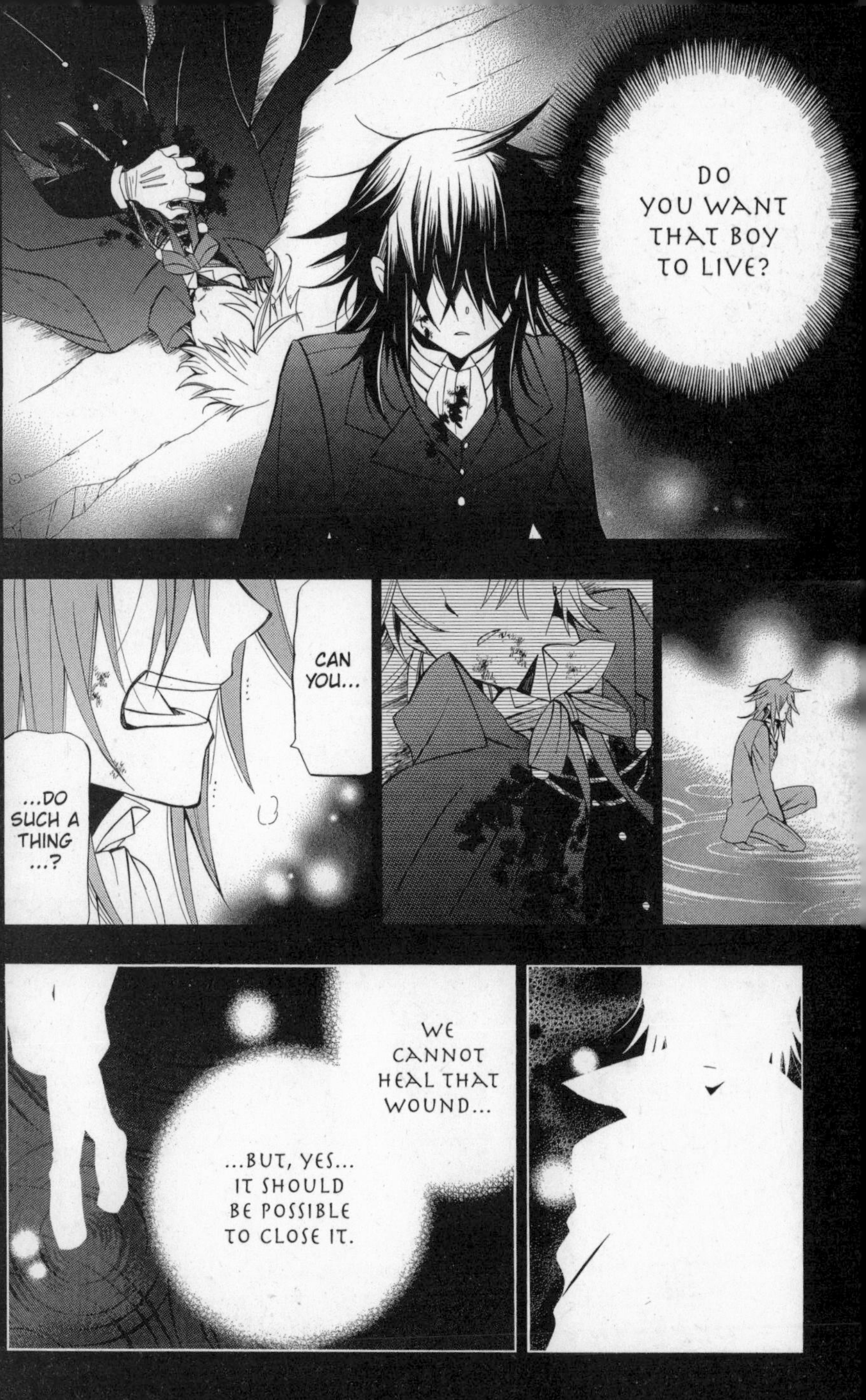
DO YOU WANT THAT BOY TO LIVE?
CAN YOU...
...DO SUCH A THING ...?
WE CANNOT HEAL THAT WOUND...
...BUT, YES... IT SHOULD BE POSSIBLE TO CLOSE IT.

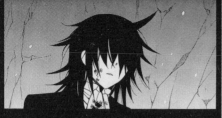

MAKE HIM DRINK ITS BLOOD...
...AND HAVE HIM CALL ITS NAME.
ITS... NAME ...?
YES. UNFORTUNATELY, IT IS NOT KNOWN TO US AS WE ARE NOW.
YOU MUST GAZE UPON IT FOR YOURSELF AND DECIPHER IT.
......
"HUMPTY... DUMPTY" ...?

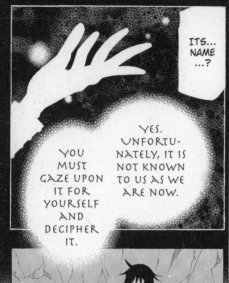

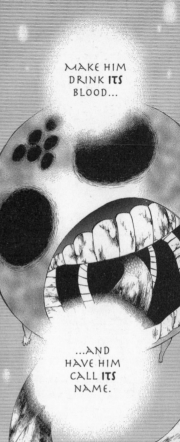

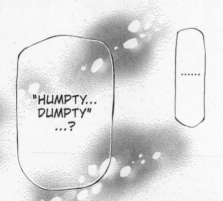

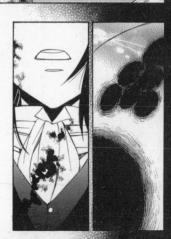

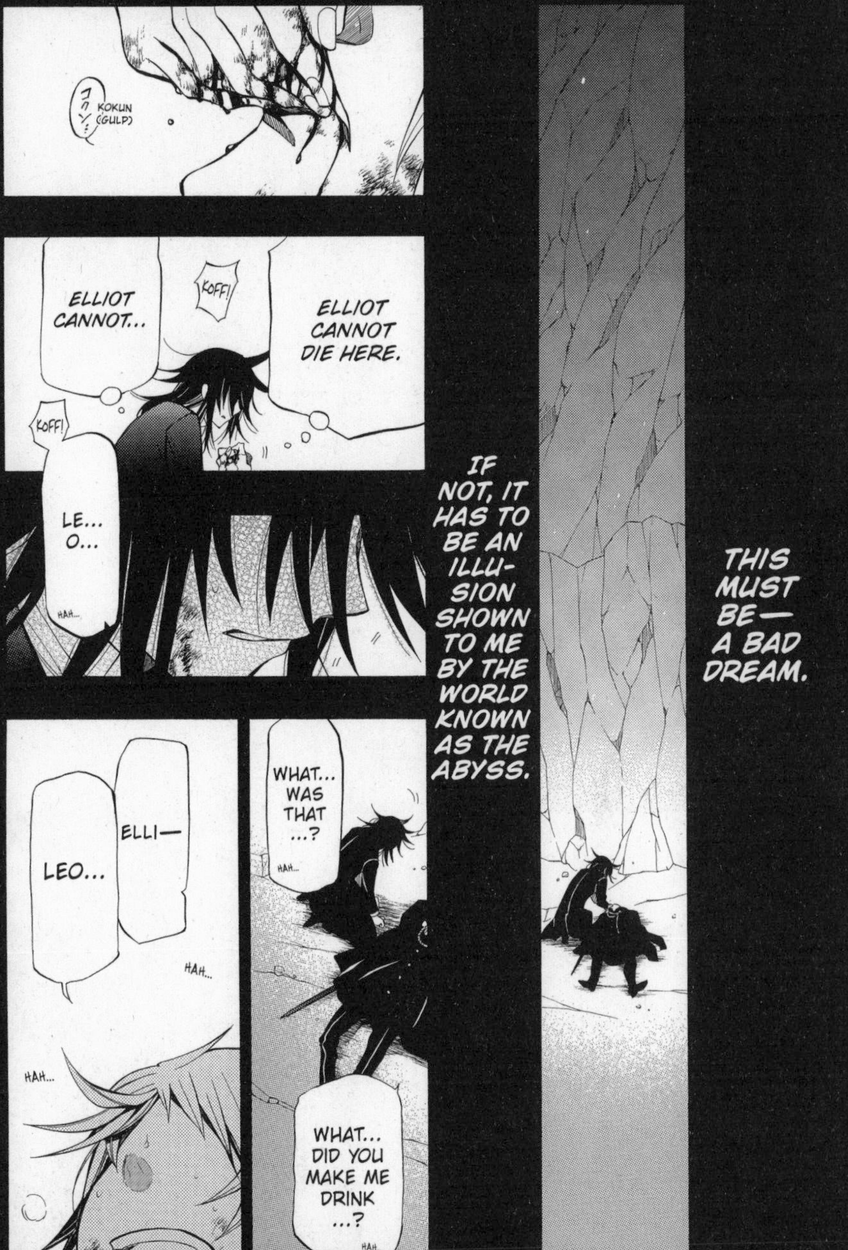
THIS MUST BE— A BAD DREAM.
IF NOT, IT HAS TO BE AN ILLUSION SHOWN TO ME BY THE WORLD KNOWN AS THE ABYSS.
コクン…
KOKUN (GULP)
ELLIOT CANNOT DIE HERE.
KOFF!
ELLIOT CANNOT...
KOFF!
LE... O...
HAH...
WHAT... WAS THAT ...?
HAH...
WHAT... DID YOU MAKE ME DRINK ...?
HAH...
ELLI—
LEO...
HAH...
HAH...

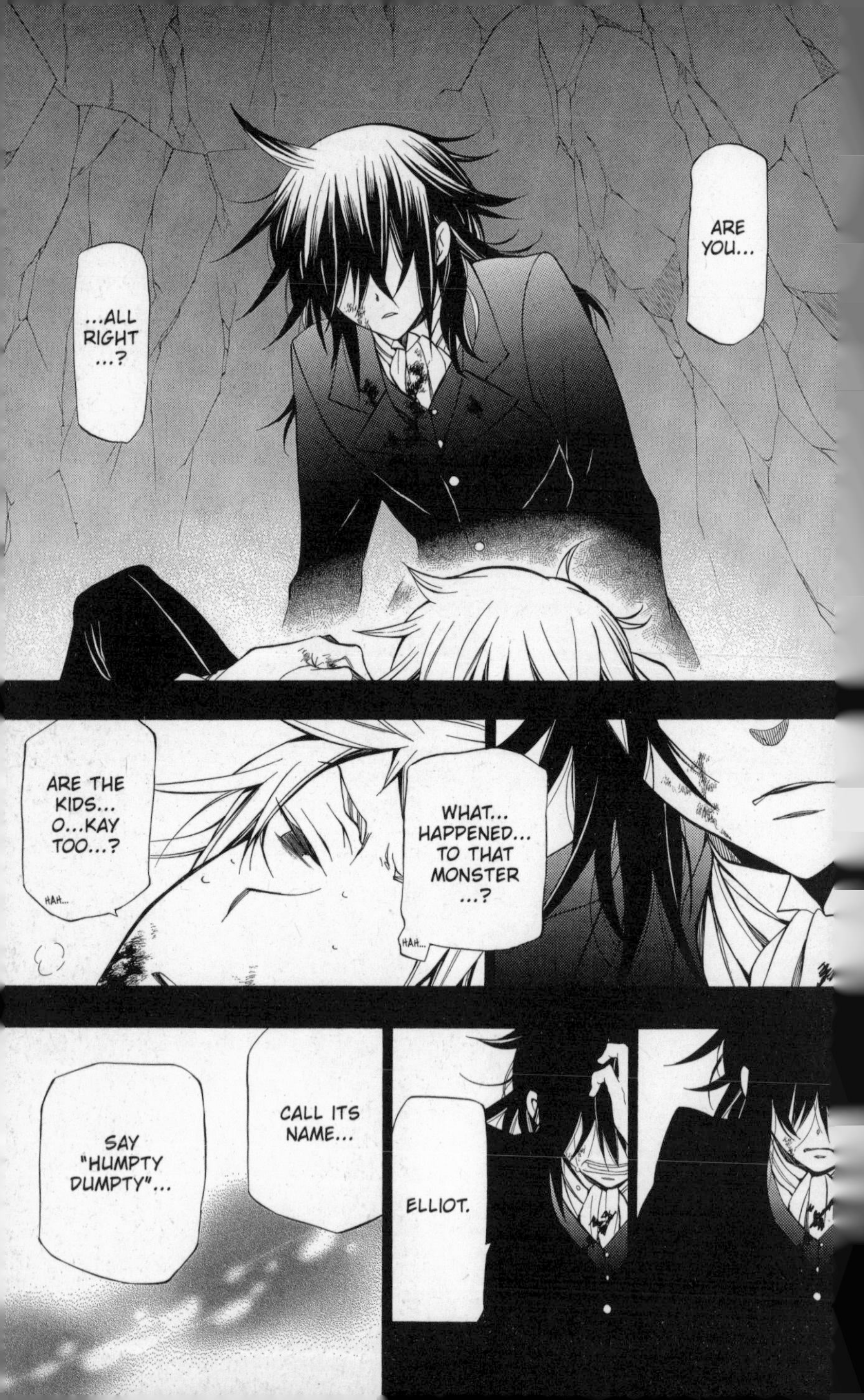
ARE YOU...
...ALL RIGHT ...?
WHAT... HAPPENED... TO THAT MONSTER ...?
HAH...
ARE THE KIDS... O...KAY TOO...?
HAH...
ELLIOT.
CALL ITS NAME...
SAY "HUMPTY DUMPTY"...

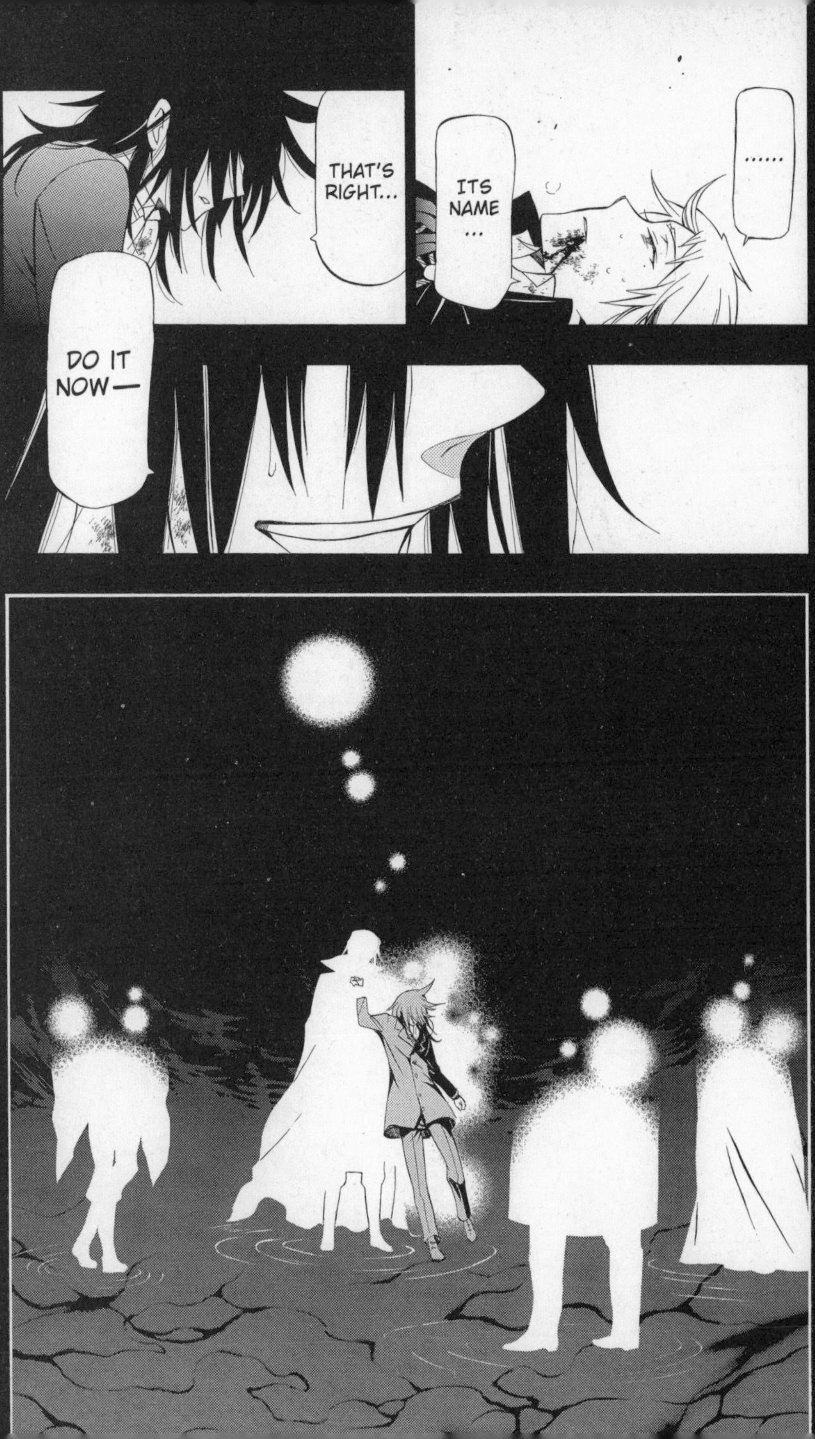
......
ITS NAME ...
THAT'S RIGHT...
DO IT NOW—

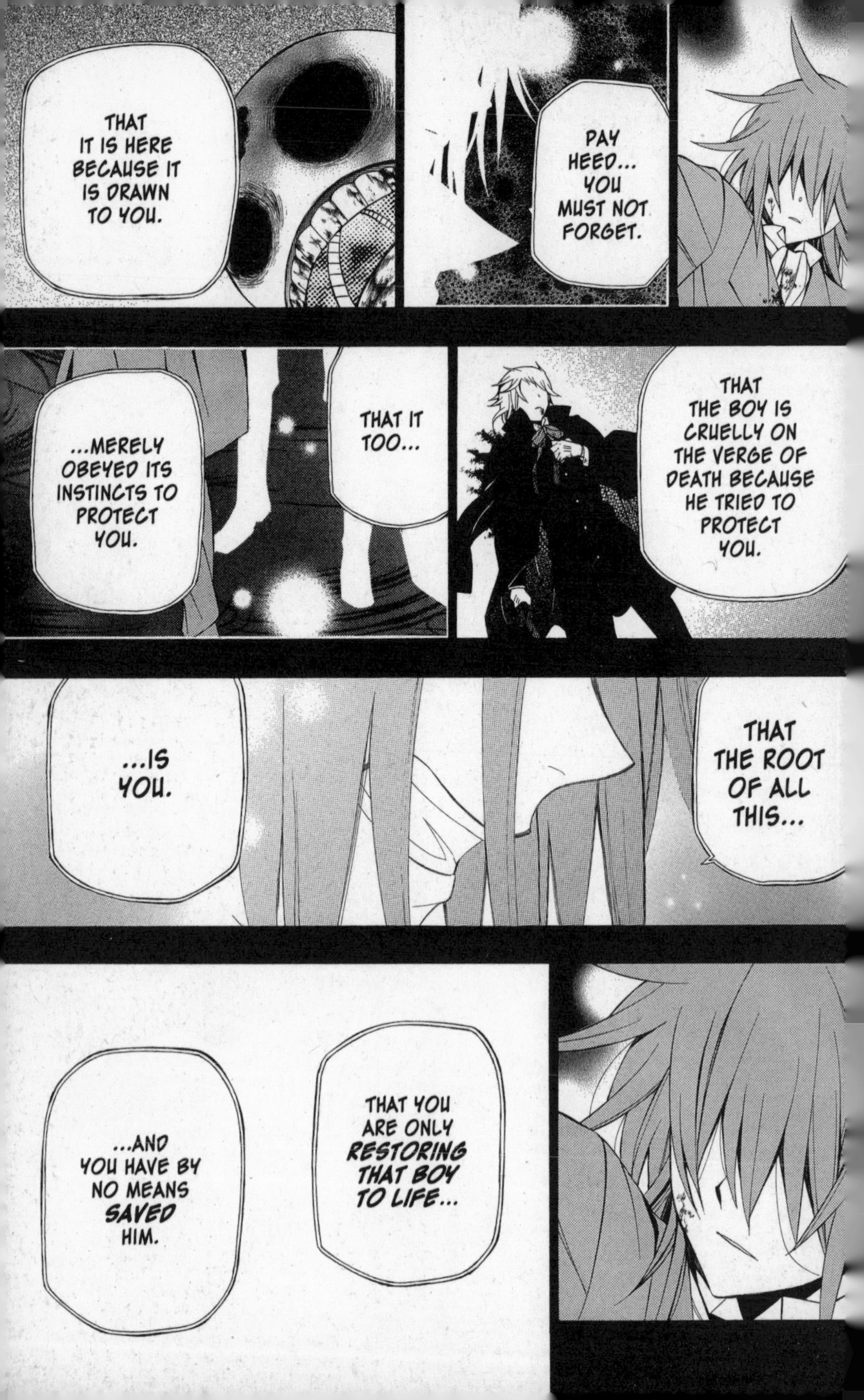
PAY HEED... YOU MUST NOT FORGET.
THAT IT IS HERE BECAUSE IT IS DRAWN TO YOU.
THAT THE BOY IS CRUELLY ON THE VERGE OF DEATH BECAUSE HE TRIED TO PROTECT YOU.
THAT IT TOO...
...MERELY OBEYED ITS INSTINCTS TO PROTECT YOU.
THAT THE ROOT OF ALL THIS...
...IS YOU.
THAT YOU ARE ONLY *RESTORING THAT BOY TO LIFE*...
...AND YOU HAVE BY NO MEANS *SAVED* HIM.

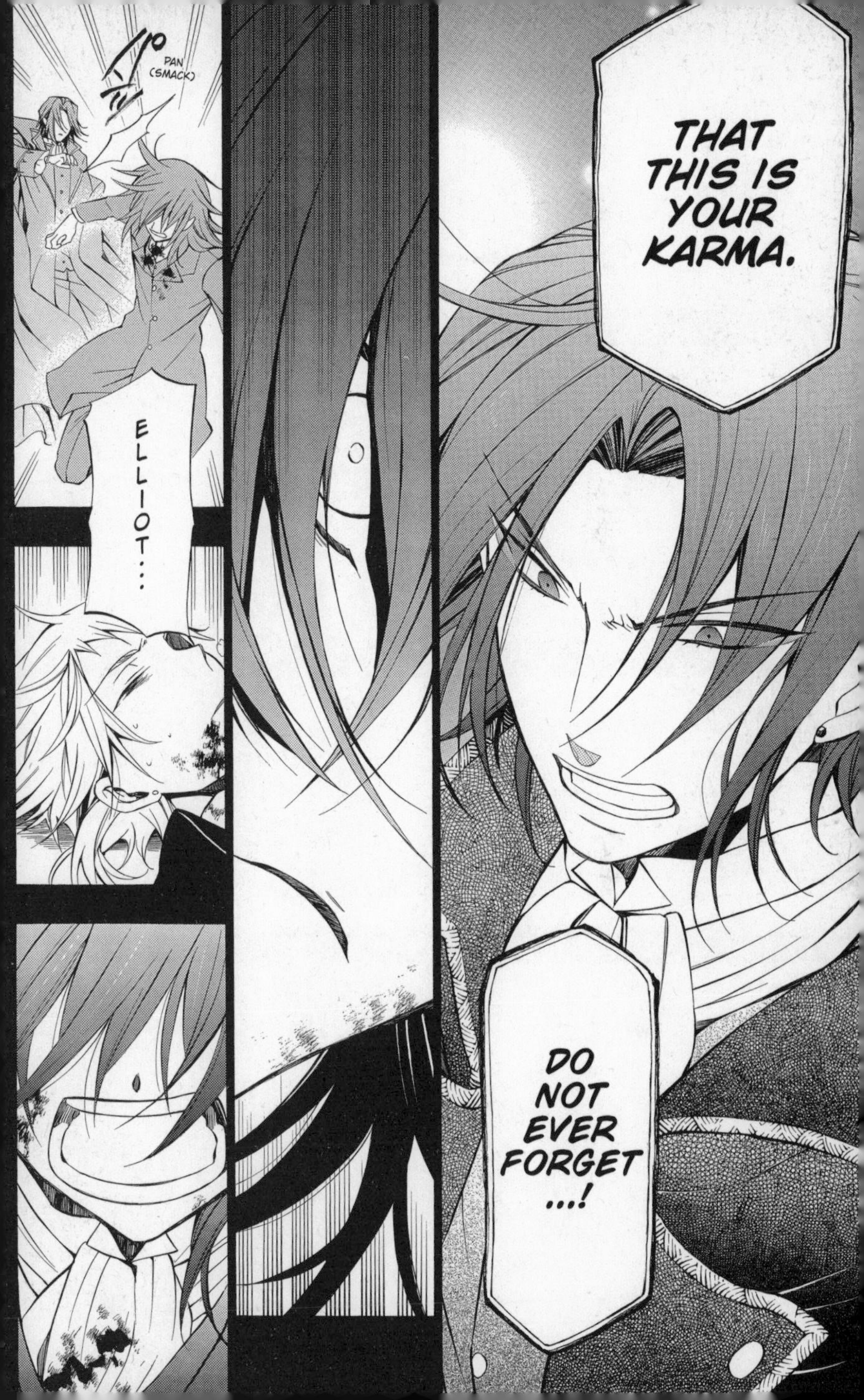
THAT THIS IS YOUR KARMA.
DO NOT EVER FORGET ...!
PAN (SMACK)
ELLIOT...

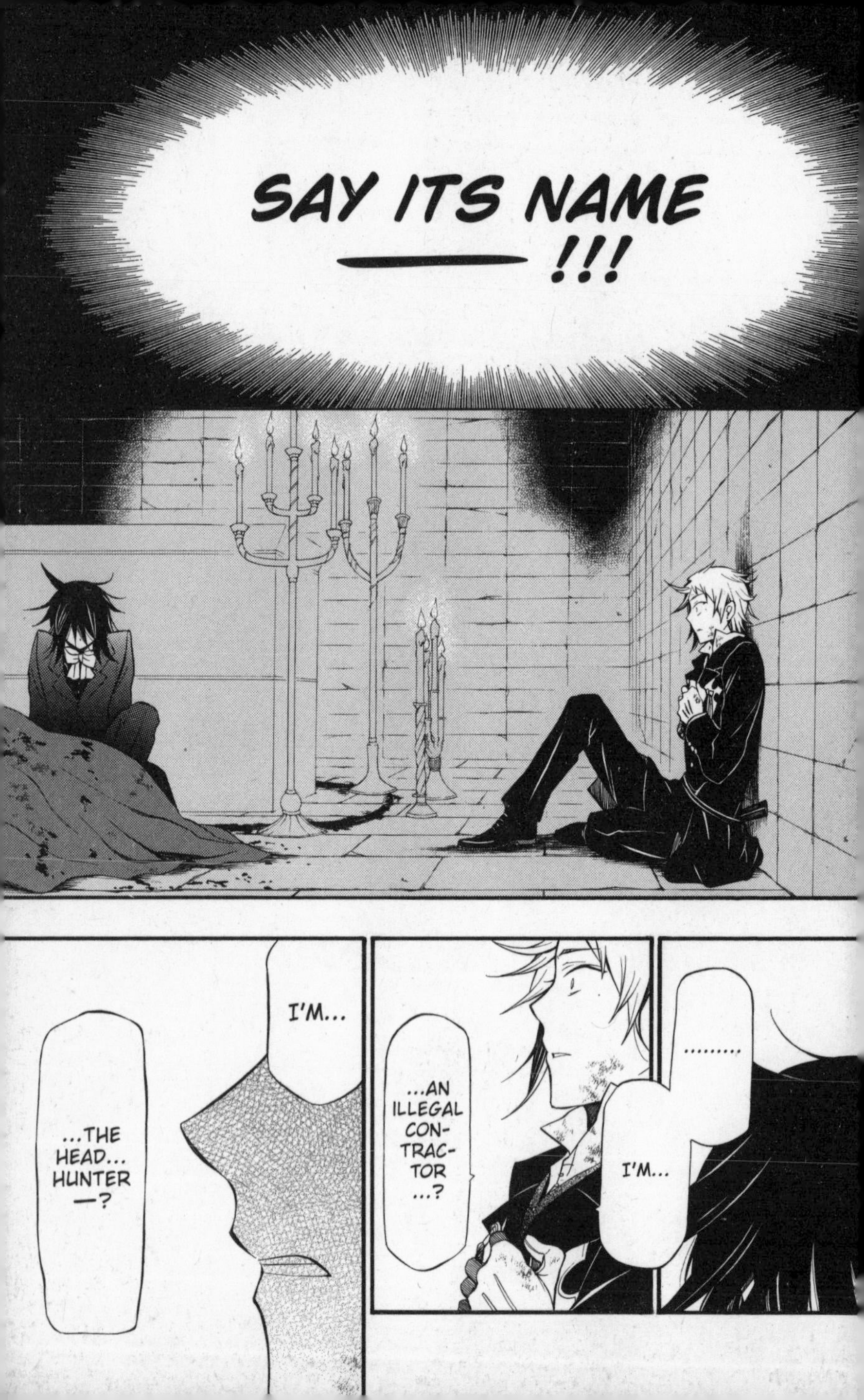
SAY ITS NAME —— !!!
....
I'M...
...AN ILLEGAL CON-TRACTOR ...?
I'M...
...THE HEAD... HUNTER —?

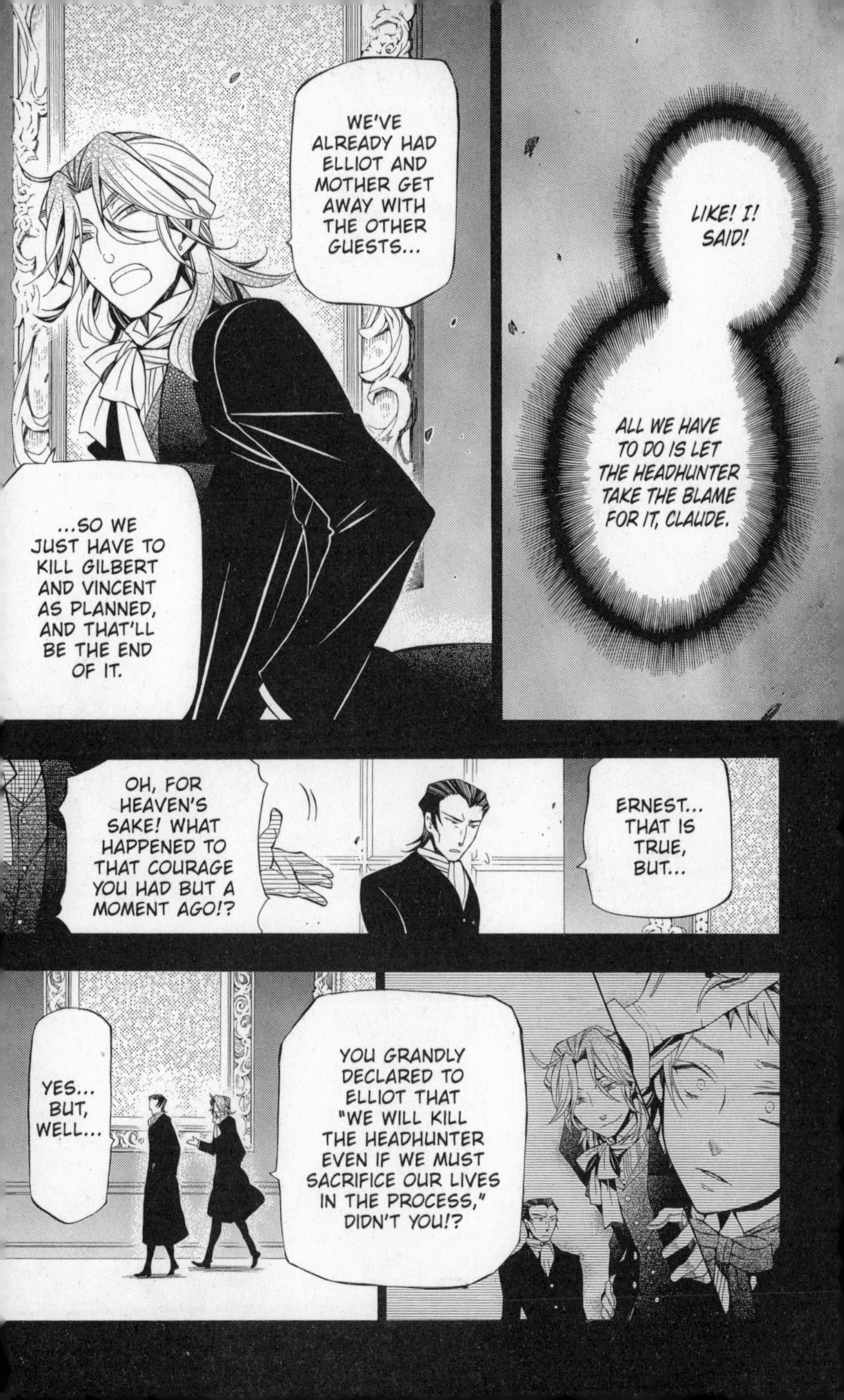
LIKE! I! SAID!
ALL WE HAVE TO DO IS LET THE HEADHUNTER TAKE THE BLAME FOR IT, CLAUDE.
WE'VE ALREADY HAD ELLIOT AND MOTHER GET AWAY WITH THE OTHER GUESTS...
...SO WE JUST HAVE TO KILL GILBERT AND VINCENT AS PLANNED, AND THAT'LL BE THE END OF IT.
ERNEST... THAT IS TRUE, BUT...
OH, FOR HEAVEN'S SAKE! WHAT HAPPENED TO THAT COURAGE YOU HAD BUT A MOMENT AGO!?
YOU GRANDLY DECLARED TO ELLIOT THAT "WE WILL KILL THE HEADHUNTER EVEN IF WE MUST SACRIFICE OUR LIVES IN THE PROCESS," DIDN'T YOU!?
YES... BUT, WELL...

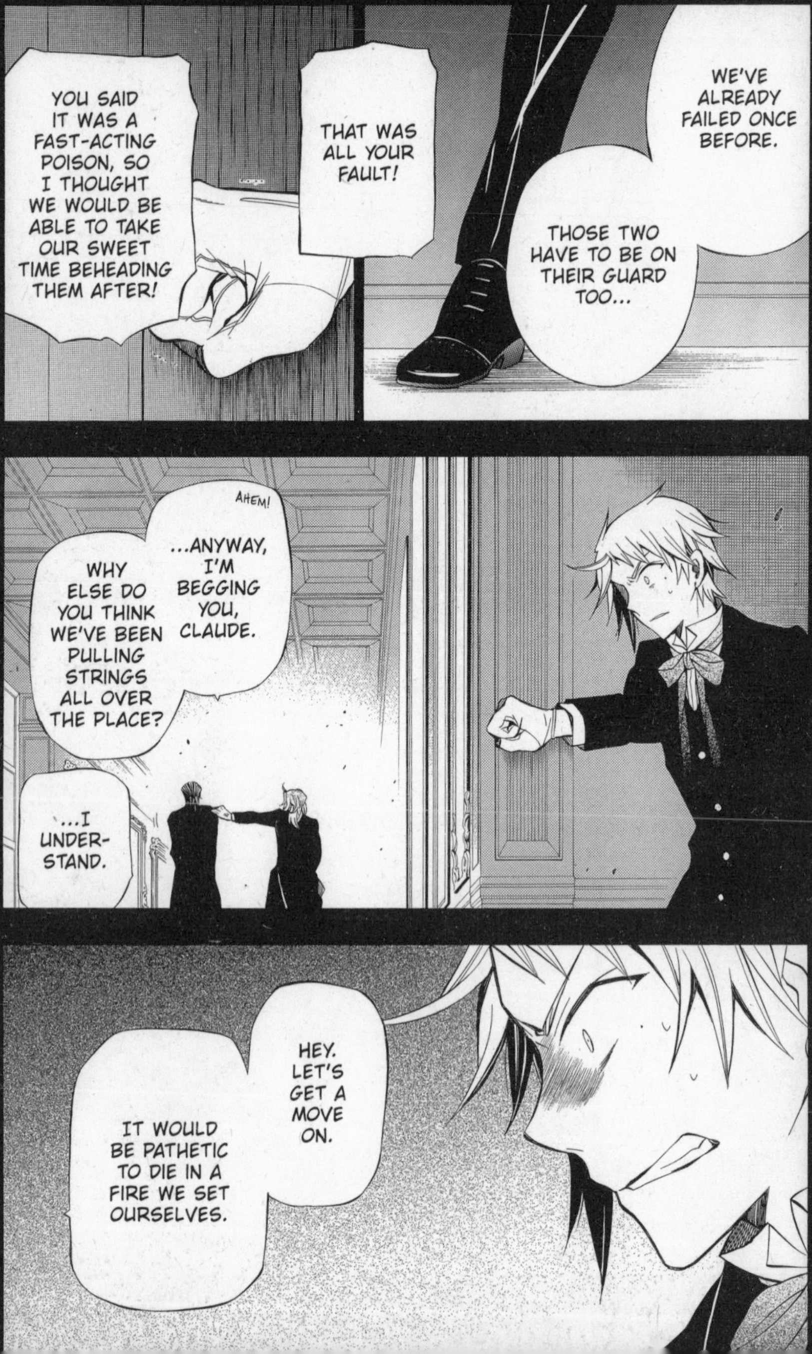
WE'VE ALREADY FAILED ONCE BEFORE.
THOSE TWO HAVE TO BE ON THEIR GUARD TOO...
THAT WAS ALL YOUR FAULT!
YOU SAID IT WAS A FAST-ACTING POISON, SO I THOUGHT WE WOULD BE ABLE TO TAKE OUR SWEET TIME BEHEADING THEM AFTER!
AHEM!
...ANYWAY, I'M BEGGING YOU, CLAUDE.
WHY ELSE DO YOU THINK WE'VE BEEN PULLING STRINGS ALL OVER THE PLACE?
...I UNDER-STAND.
HEY. LET'S GET A MOVE ON.
IT WOULD BE PATHETIC TO DIE IN A FIRE WE SET OURSELVES.

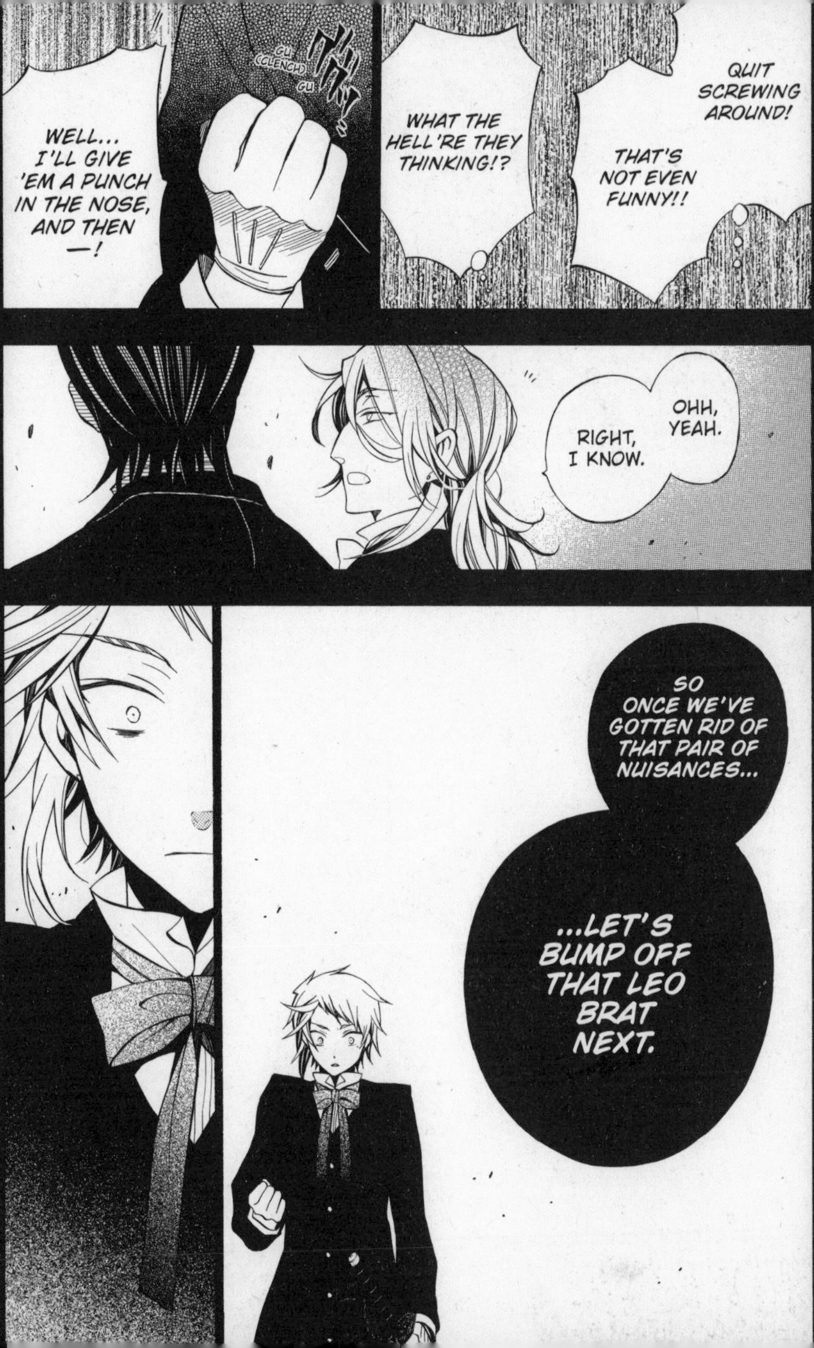
QUIT SCREWING AROUND!
THAT'S NOT EVEN FUNNY!!
WHAT THE HELL'RE THEY THINKING!?
GU (CLENCH) GU
WELL... I'LL GIVE 'EM A PUNCH IN THE NOSE, AND THEN —!
OHH, YEAH.
RIGHT, I KNOW.
SO ONCE WE'VE GOTTEN RID OF THAT PAIR OF NUISANCES...
...LET'S BUMP OFF THAT LEO BRAT NEXT.

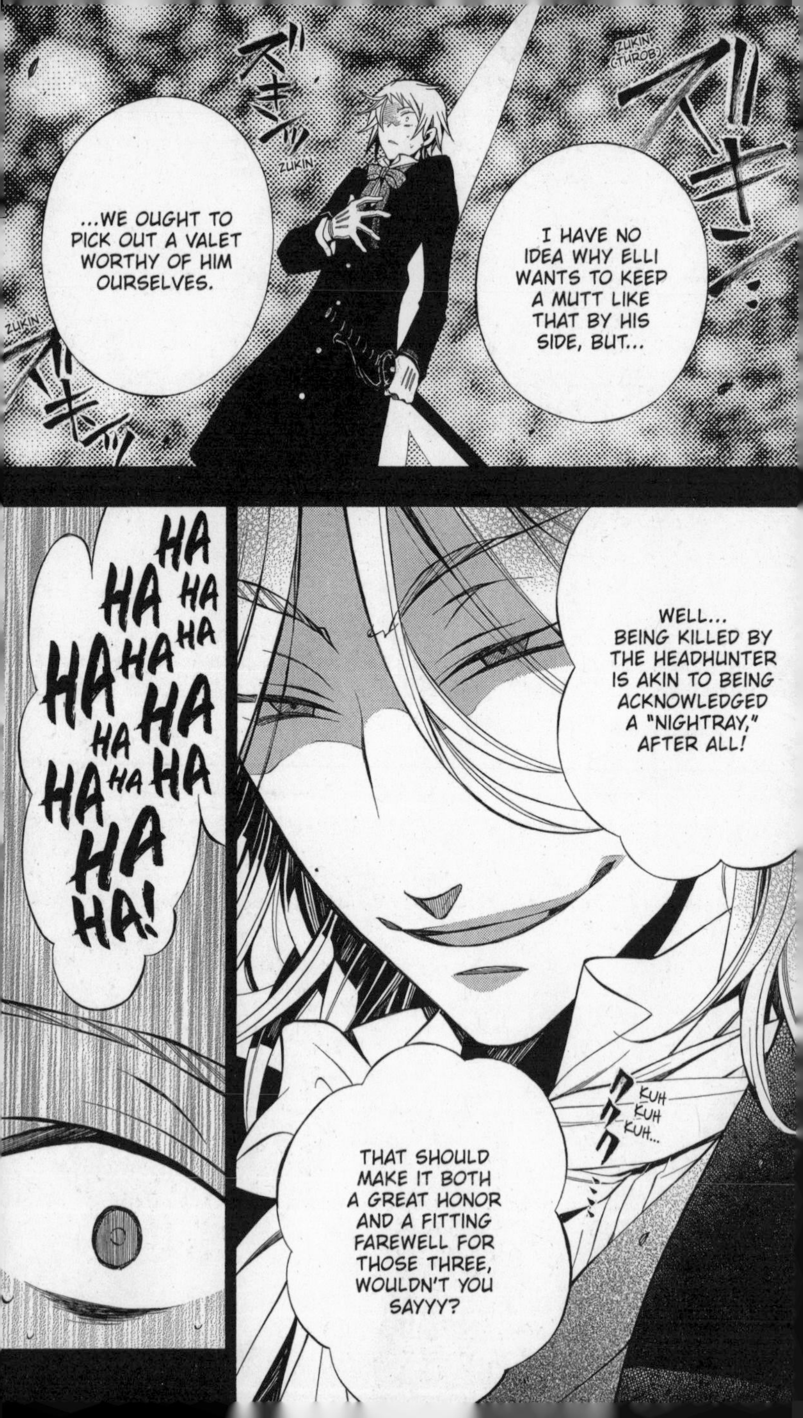
ZUKIN (THROB)
I HAVE NO IDEA WHY ELLI WANTS TO KEEP A MUTT LIKE THAT BY HIS SIDE, BUT...
ZUKIN
...WE OUGHT TO PICK OUT A VALET WORTHY OF HIM OURSELVES.
ZUKIN
WELL... BEING KILLED BY THE HEADHUNTER IS AKIN TO BEING ACKNOWLEDGED A "NIGHTRAY," AFTER ALL!
KUH KUH KUH...
THAT SHOULD MAKE IT BOTH A GREAT HONOR AND A FITTING FAREWELL FOR THOSE THREE, WOULDN'T YOU SAYYY?
HA HA HA HA HA HA HA HA HA HA HA HA HA HA HA HA HA!

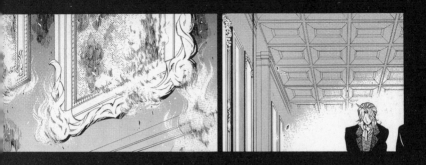

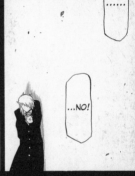

...OH, BUT YOU CAN.

NO! NO!

I CAN'T!

I CAN'T!

......

...NO!

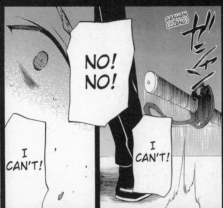

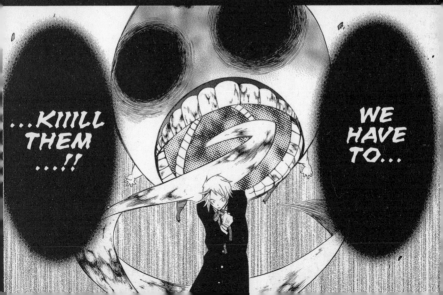

...KIIILL THEM ...!!

WE HAVE TO...

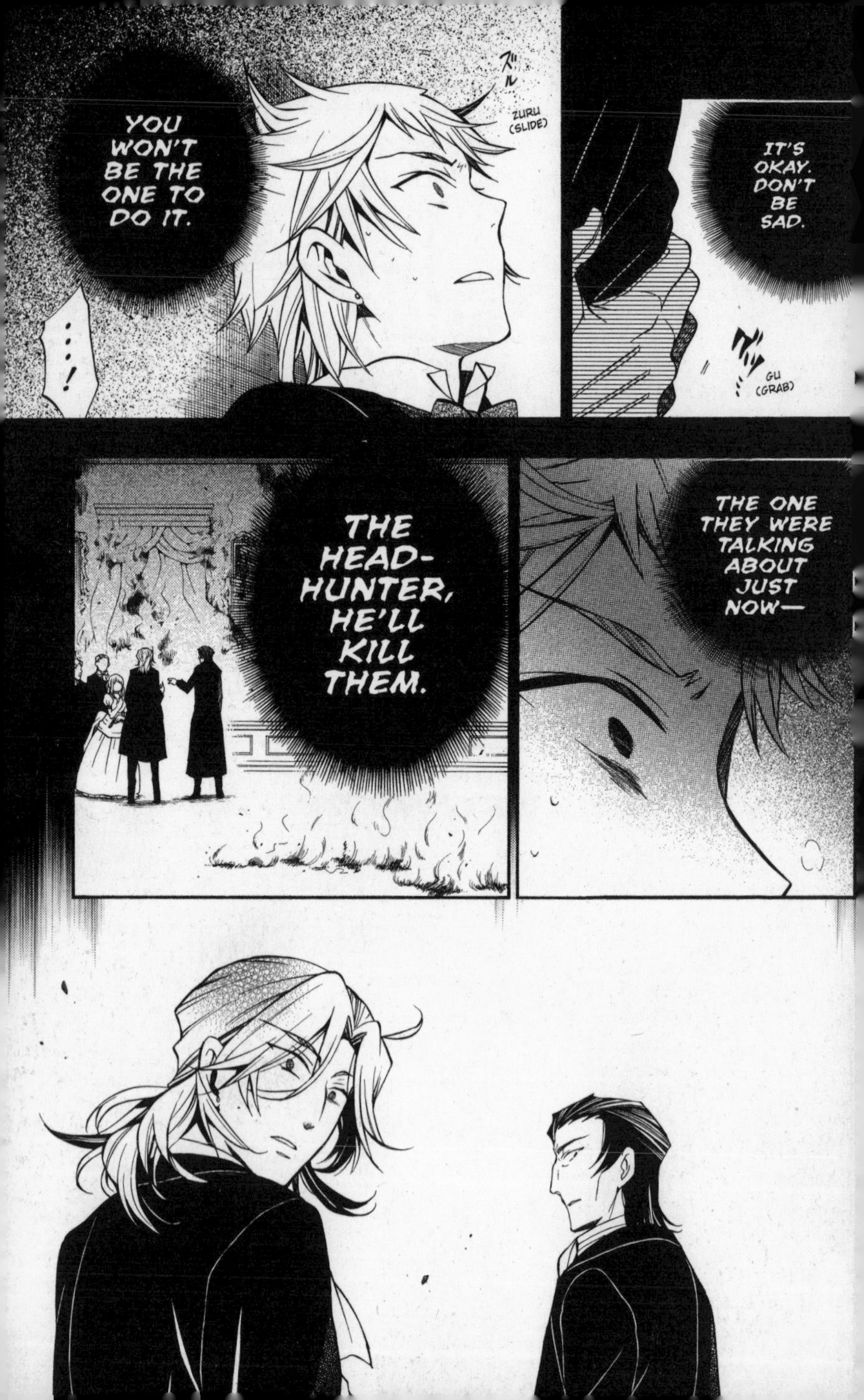

IT'S OKAY. DON'T BE SAD.
グッ
GU (GRAB)
YOU WON'T BE THE ONE TO DO IT.
ズル
ZURU (SLIDE)
...!
THE ONE THEY WERE TALKING ABOUT JUST NOW—
THE HEAD-HUNTER, HE'LL KILL THEM.

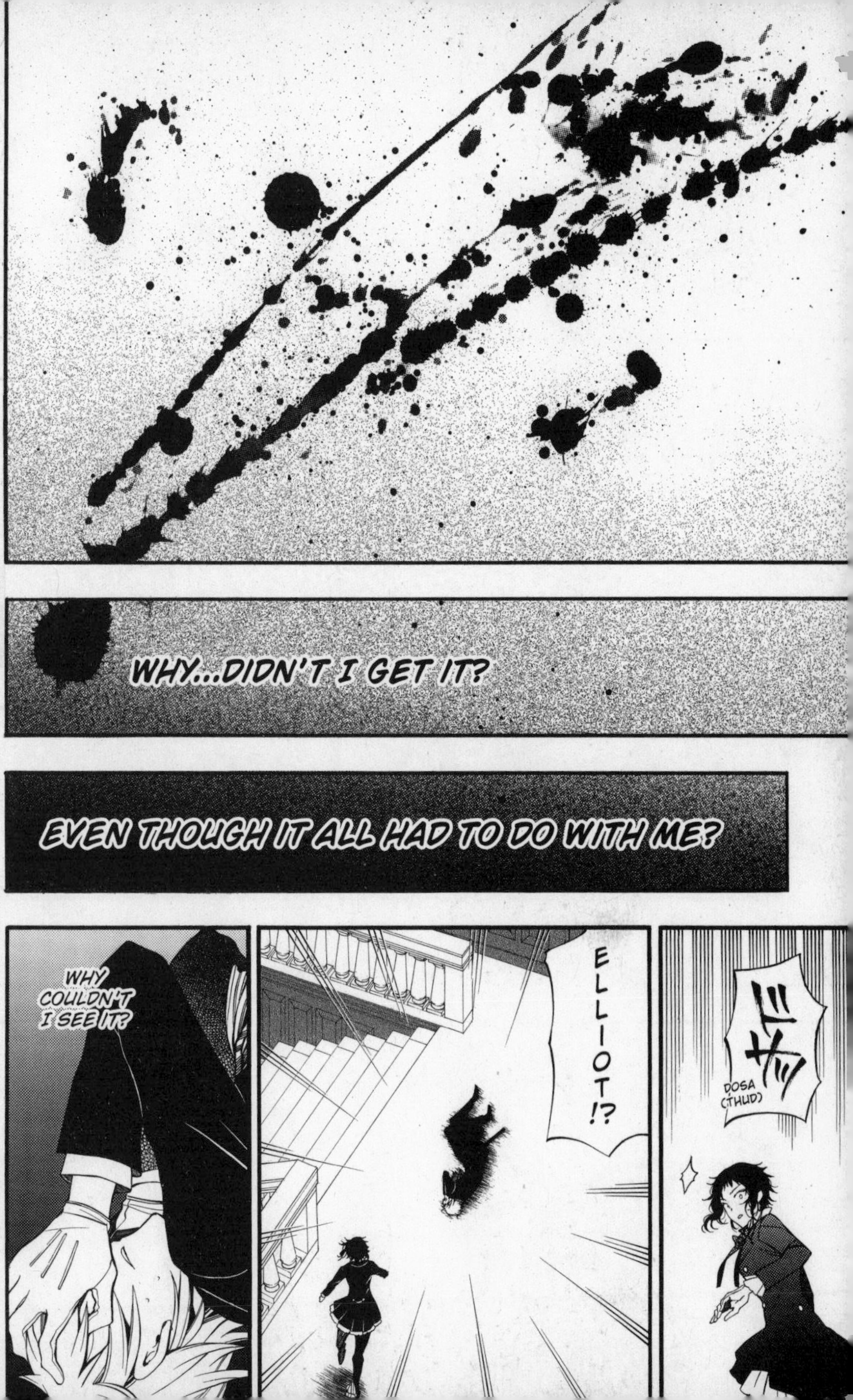
WHY...DIDN'T I GET IT?
EVEN THOUGH IT ALL HAD TO DO WITH ME?
ドサッ
DOSA (THUD)
ELLIOT!?
WHY COULDN'T I SEE IT?

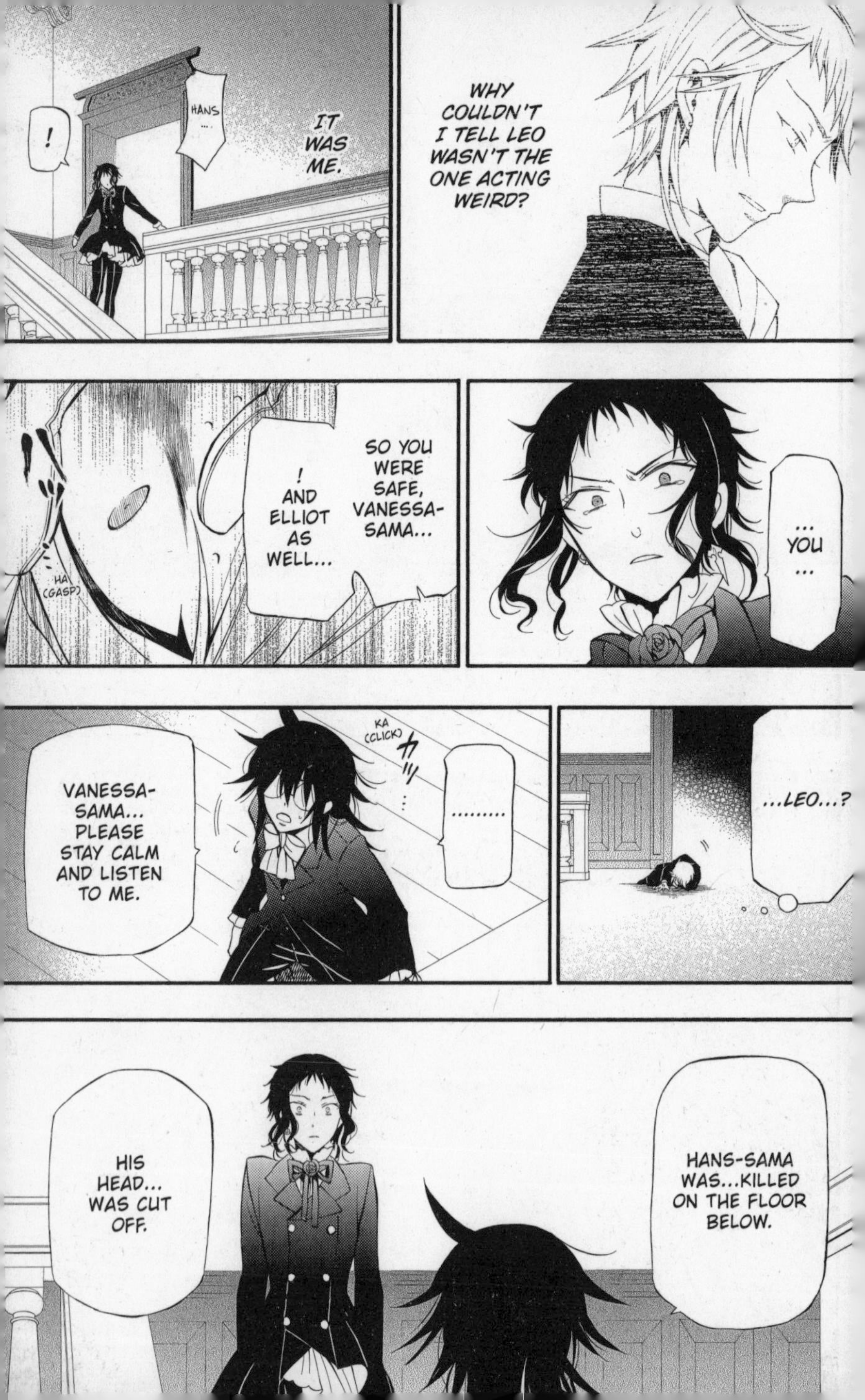
WHY COULDN'T I TELL LEO WASN'T THE ONE ACTING WEIRD?
IT WAS ME.
HANS ...
!
... YOU ...
SO YOU WERE SAFE, VANESSA-SAMA...
! AND ELLIOT AS WELL...
HA (GASP)
...LEO...?
KA (CLICK)
....
VANESSA-SAMA... PLEASE STAY CALM AND LISTEN TO ME.
HANS-SAMA WAS...KILLED ON THE FLOOR BELOW.
HIS HEAD... WAS CUT OFF.

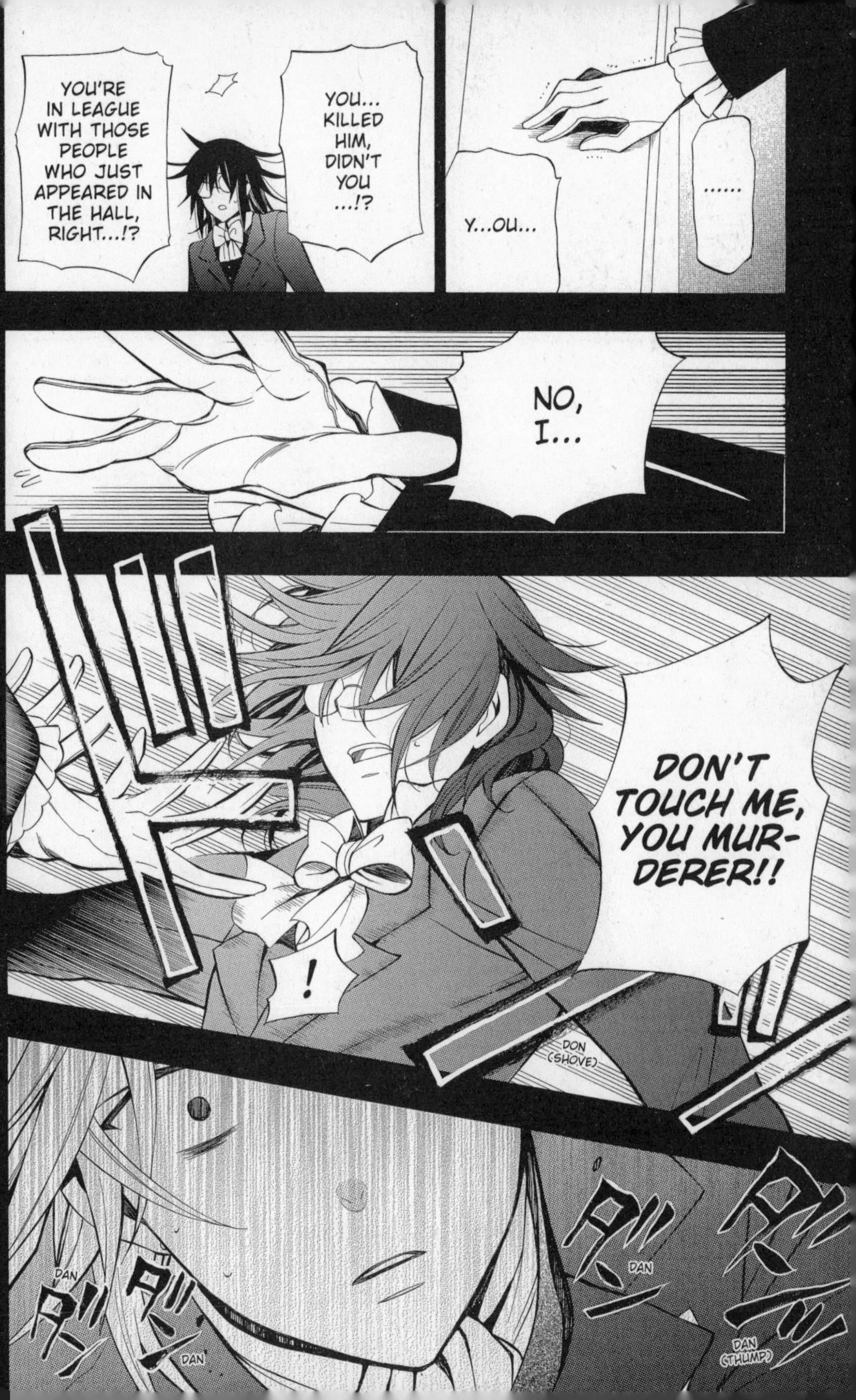
......
Y...OU...
YOU... KILLED HIM, DIDN'T YOU ...!?
YOU'RE IN LEAGUE WITH THOSE PEOPLE WHO JUST APPEARED IN THE HALL, RIGHT...!?
NO, I...
DON'T TOUCH ME, YOU MUR-DERER!!
!
DON (SHOVE)
DAN
DAN (THUMP)
DAN
DAN

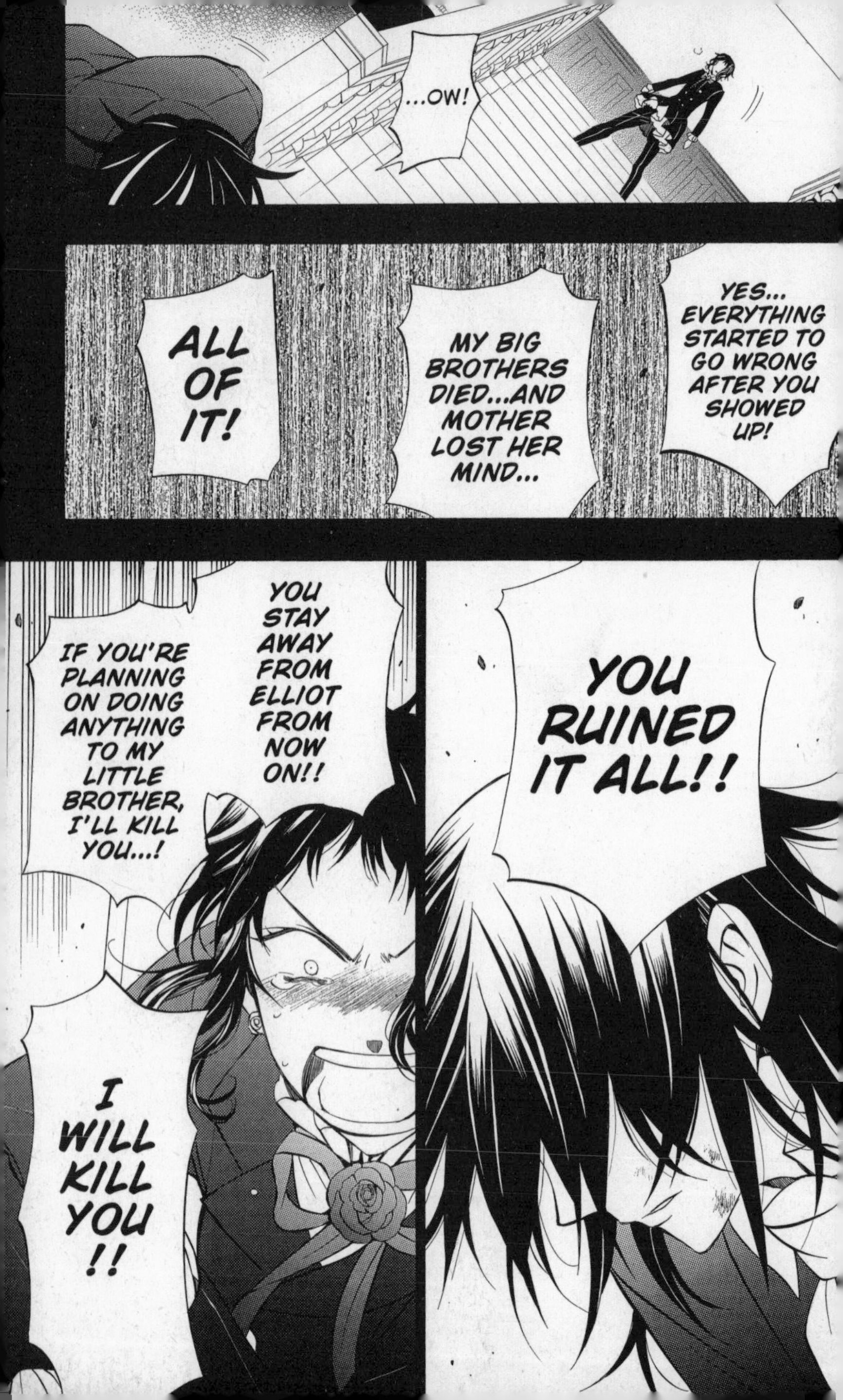
...OW!
YES... EVERYTHING STARTED TO GO WRONG AFTER YOU SHOWED UP!
MY BIG BROTHERS DIED...AND MOTHER LOST HER MIND...
ALL OF IT!
YOU RUINED IT ALL!!
YOU STAY AWAY FROM ELLIOT FROM NOW ON!!
IF YOU'RE PLANNING ON DOING ANYTHING TO MY LITTLE BROTHER, I'LL KILL YOU...!
I WILL KILL YOU!!

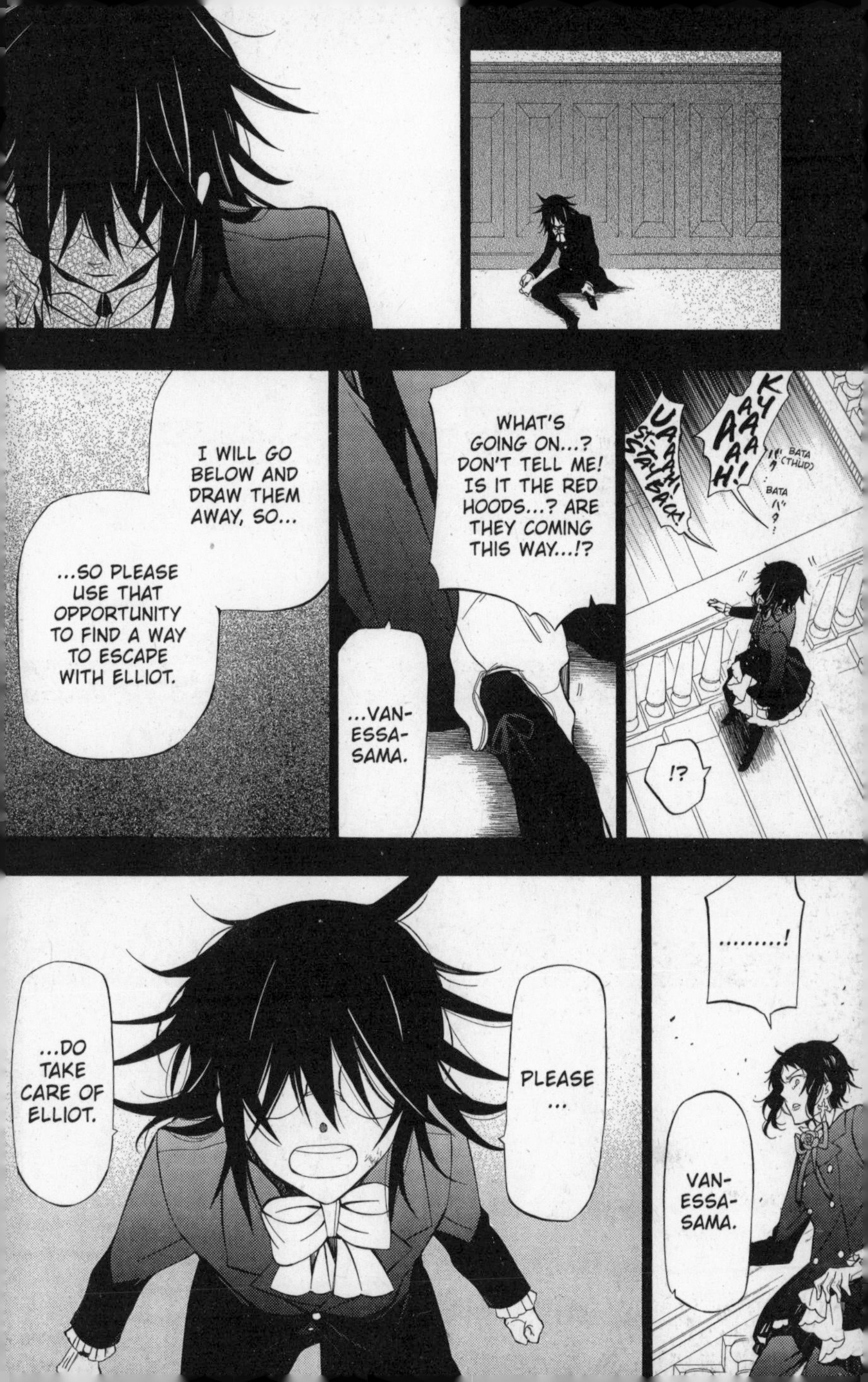
KYAAAAAH!
UAAAAH! ST-STAY BACK!
BATA (THUD)
BATA
!?
WHAT'S GOING ON...? DON'T TELL ME! IS IT THE RED HOODS...? ARE THEY COMING THIS WAY...!?
...VANESSA-SAMA.
I WILL GO BELOW AND DRAW THEM AWAY, SO...
...SO PLEASE USE THAT OPPORTUNITY TO FIND A WAY TO ESCAPE WITH ELLIOT.
.........!
VANESSA-SAMA.
PLEASE...
...DO TAKE CARE OF ELLIOT.

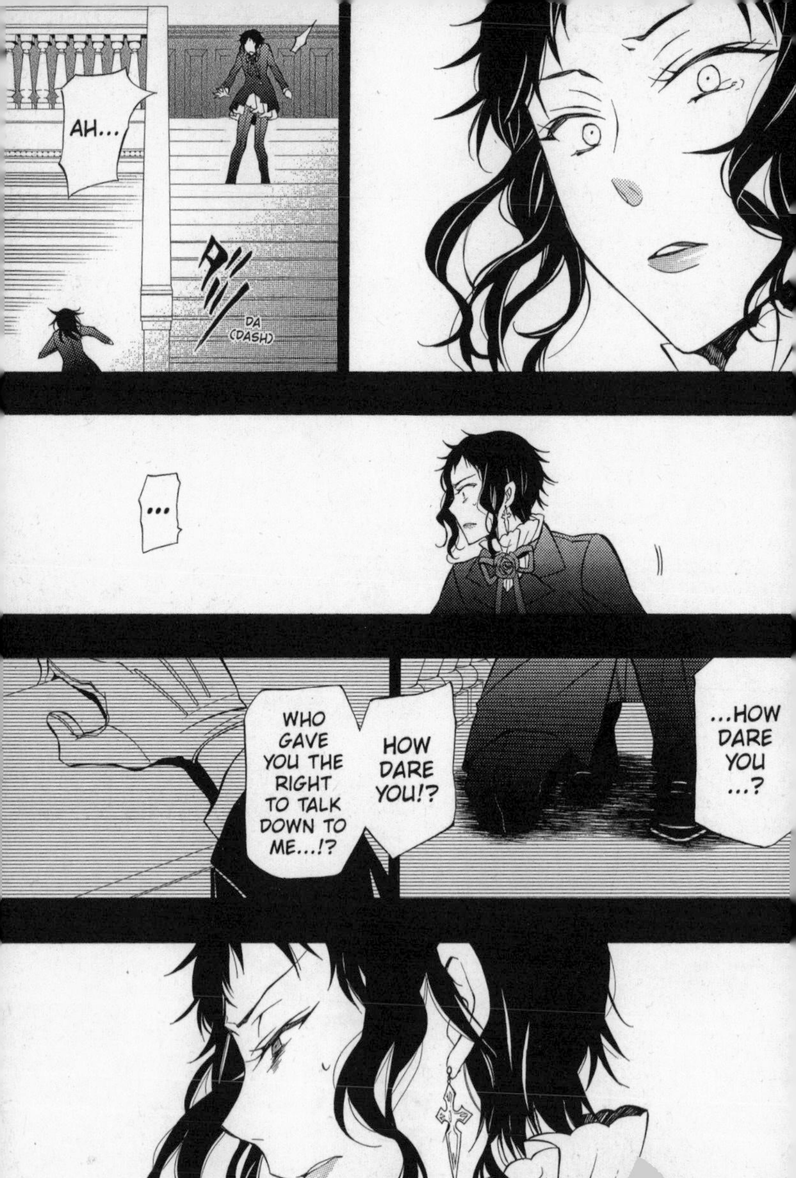
AH...
DA (DASH)
...
...HOW DARE YOU ...?
HOW DARE YOU!?
WHO GAVE YOU THE RIGHT TO TALK DOWN TO ME...!?

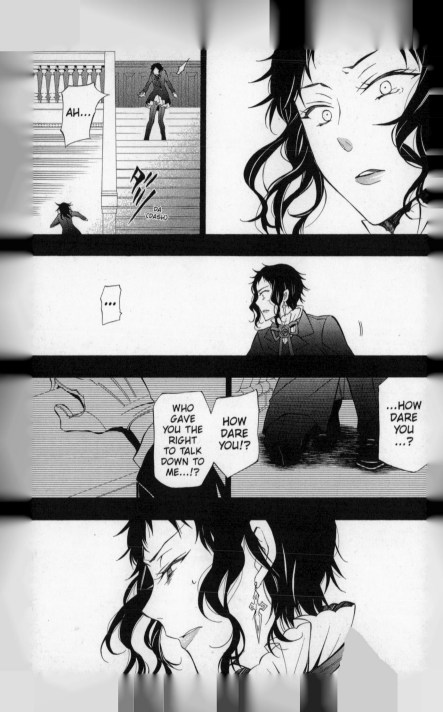

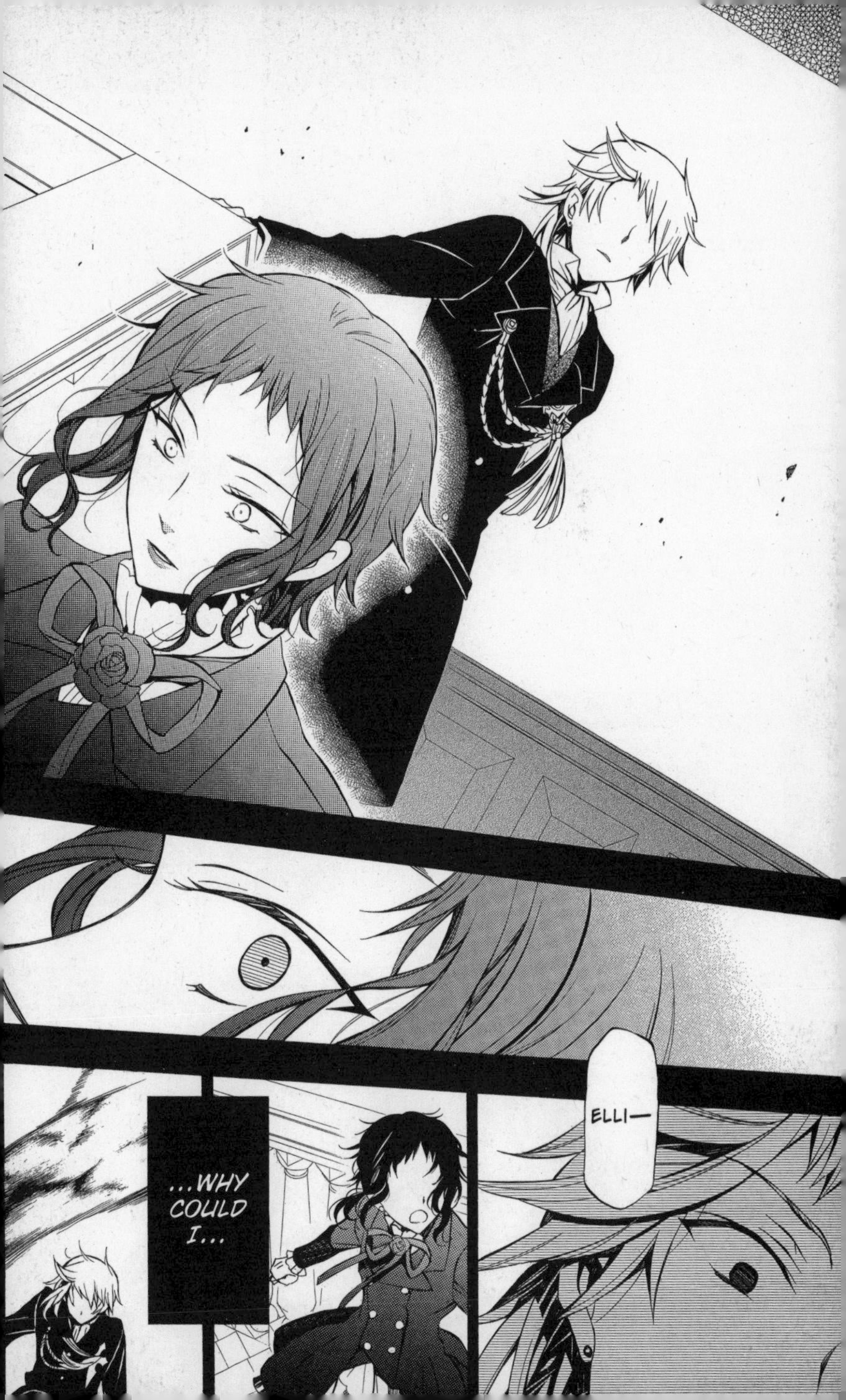
I...
ELLI—
...WHY COULD I...

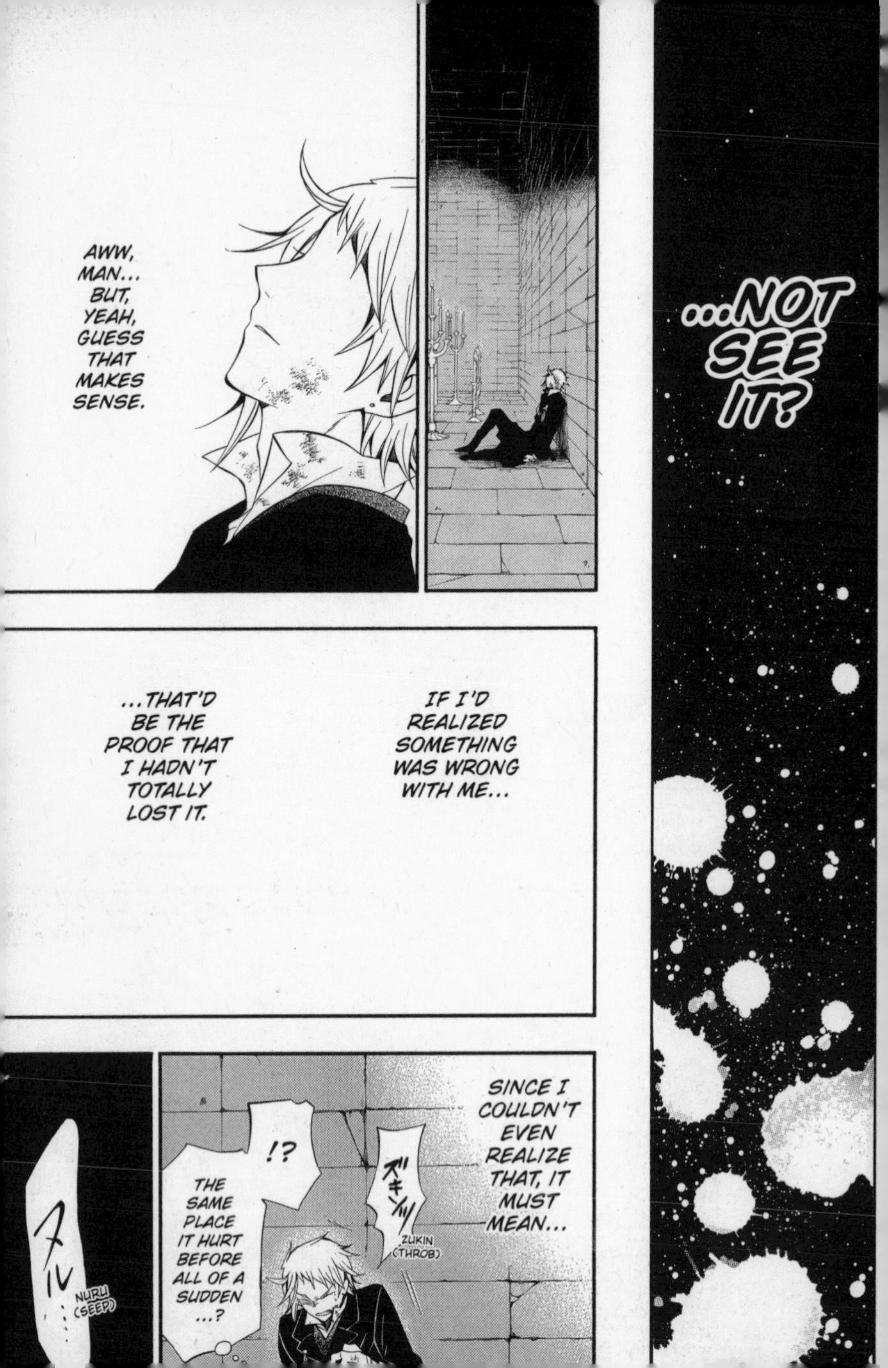
...NOT SEE IT?
AWW, MAN... BUT, YEAH, GUESS THAT MAKES SENSE.
IF I'D REALIZED SOMETHING WAS WRONG WITH ME...
...THAT'D BE THE PROOF THAT I HADN'T TOTALLY LOST IT.
SINCE I COULDN'T EVEN REALIZE THAT, IT MUST MEAN...
ズキン
ZUKIN (THROB)
!?
THE SAME PLACE IT HURT BEFORE ALL OF A SUDDEN ...?
ヌル...
NURU (SEEP)

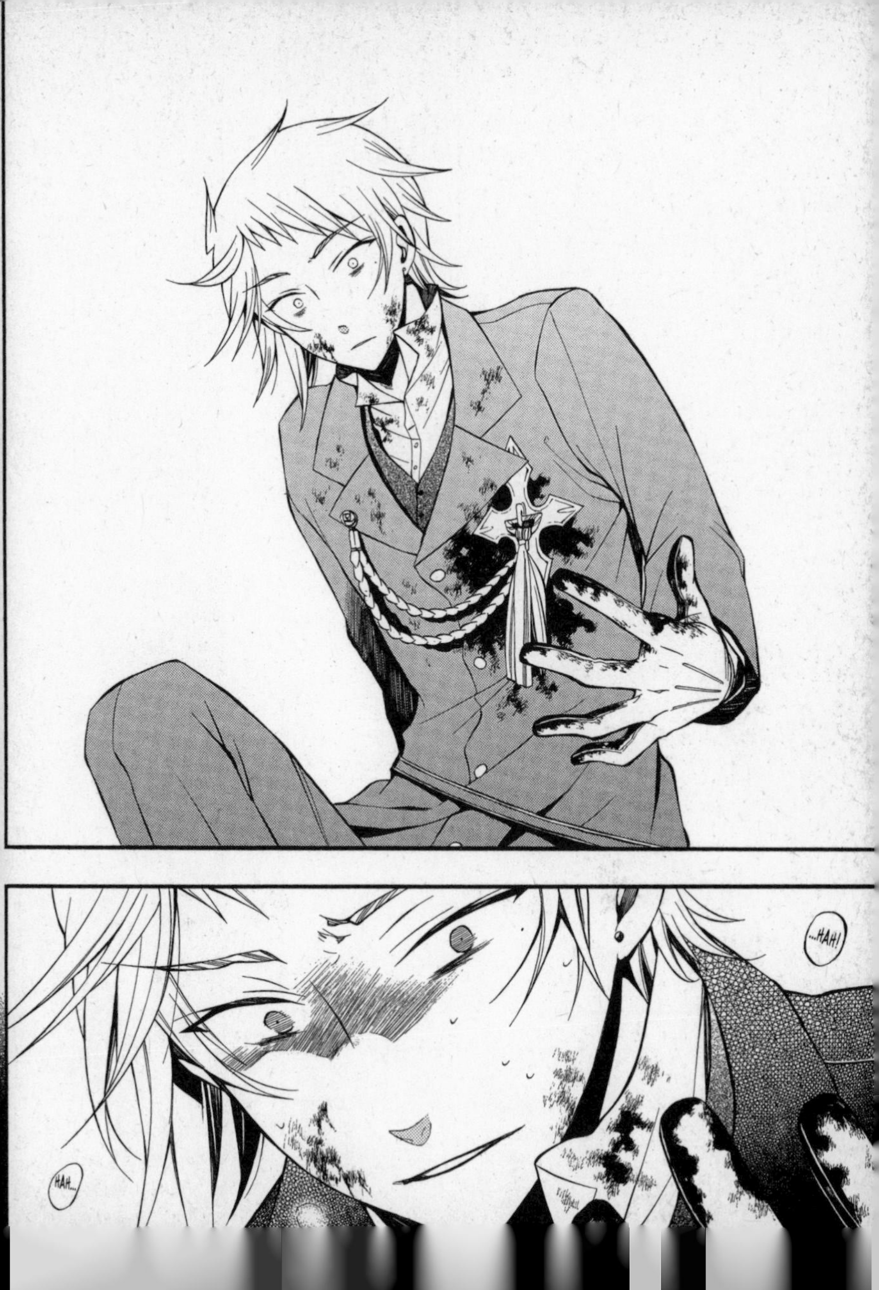
...HAH!
HAH...

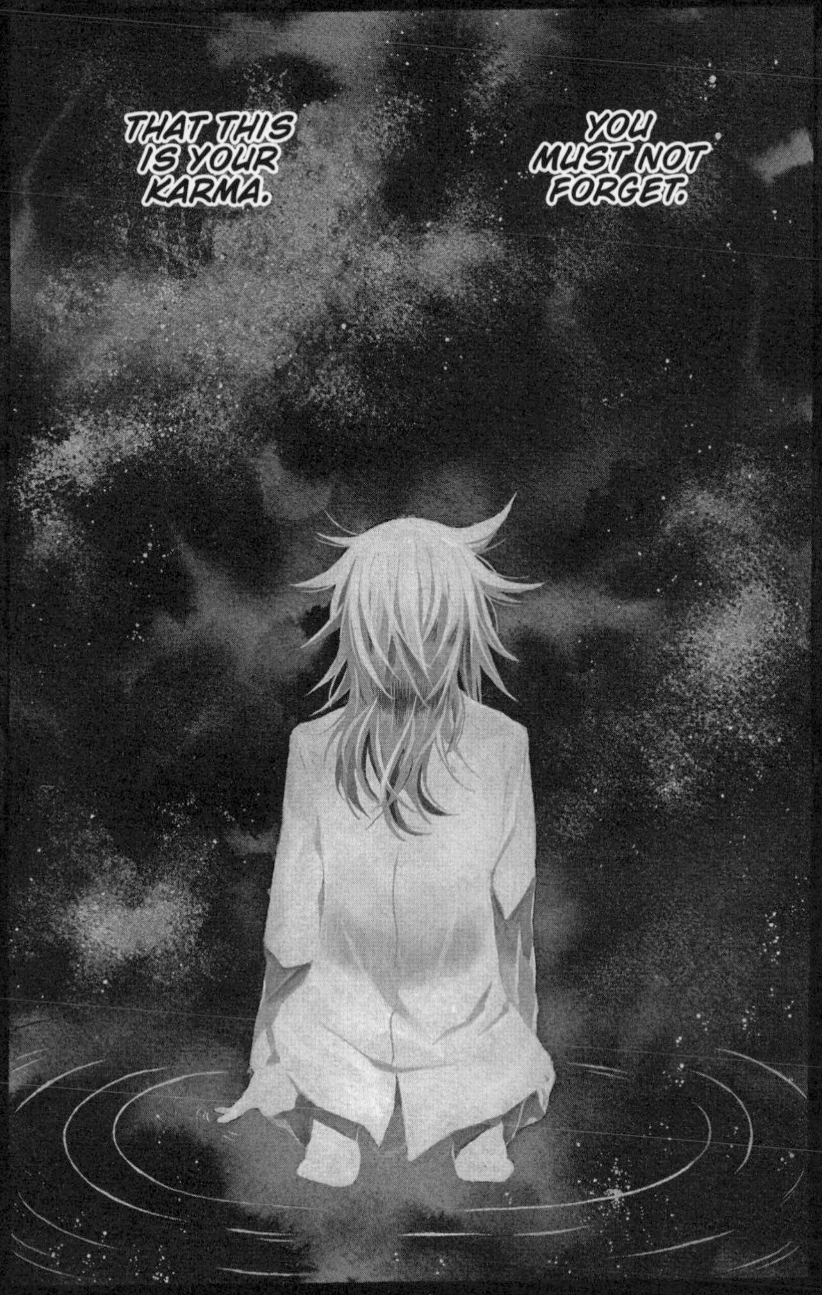
YOU MUST NOT FORGET.
THAT THIS IS YOUR KARMA.

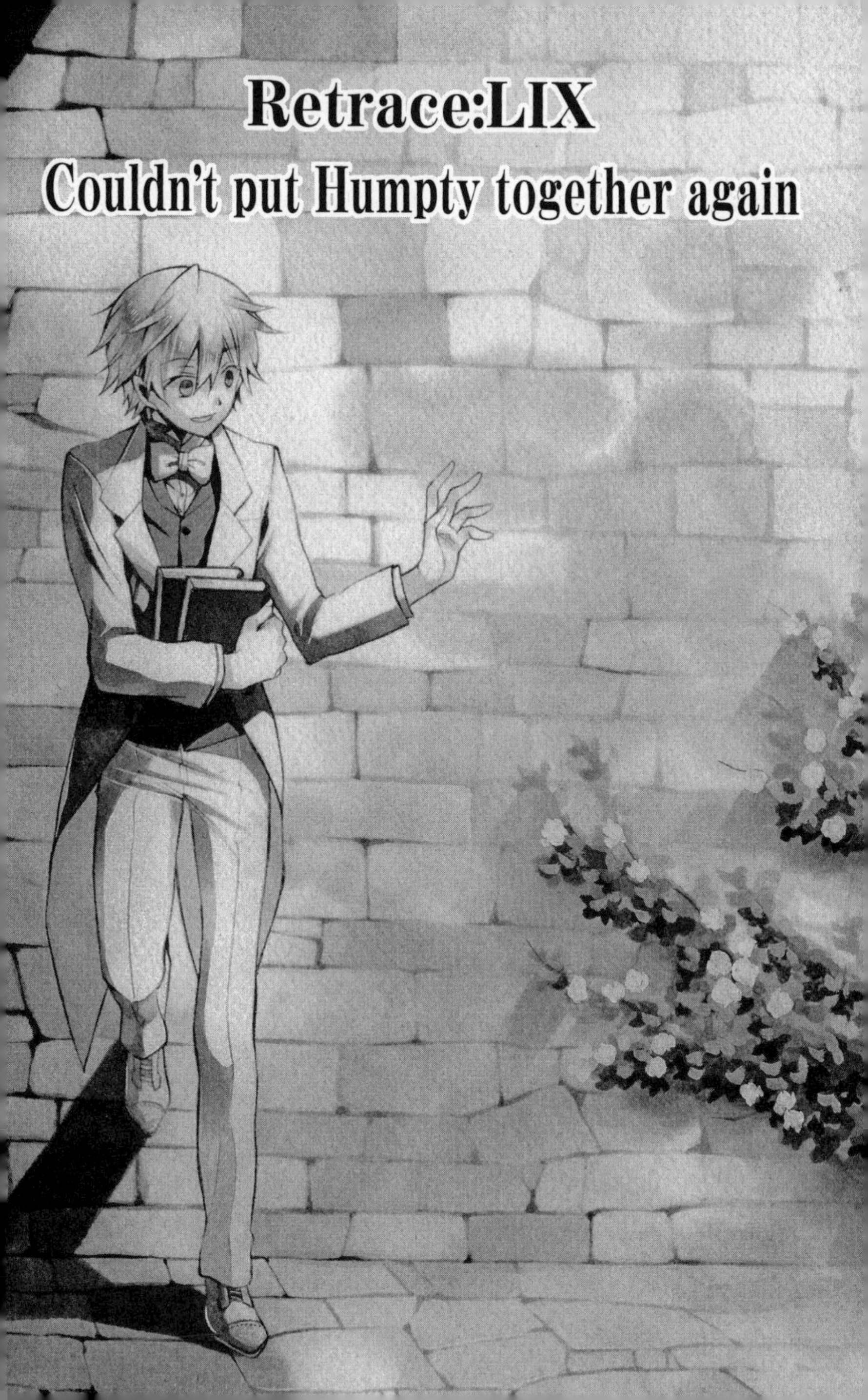
Retrace:LIX
Couldn't put Humpty together again

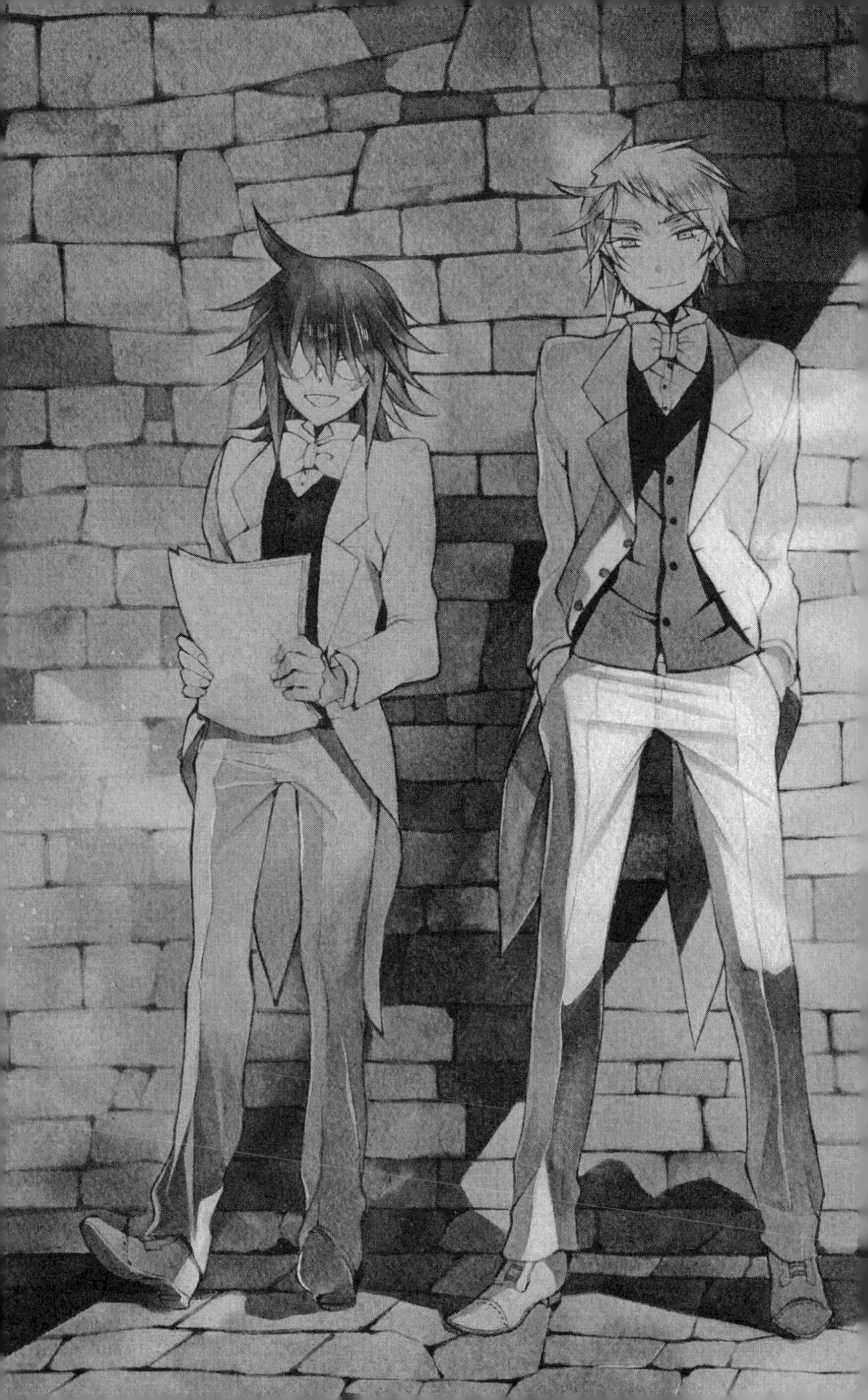

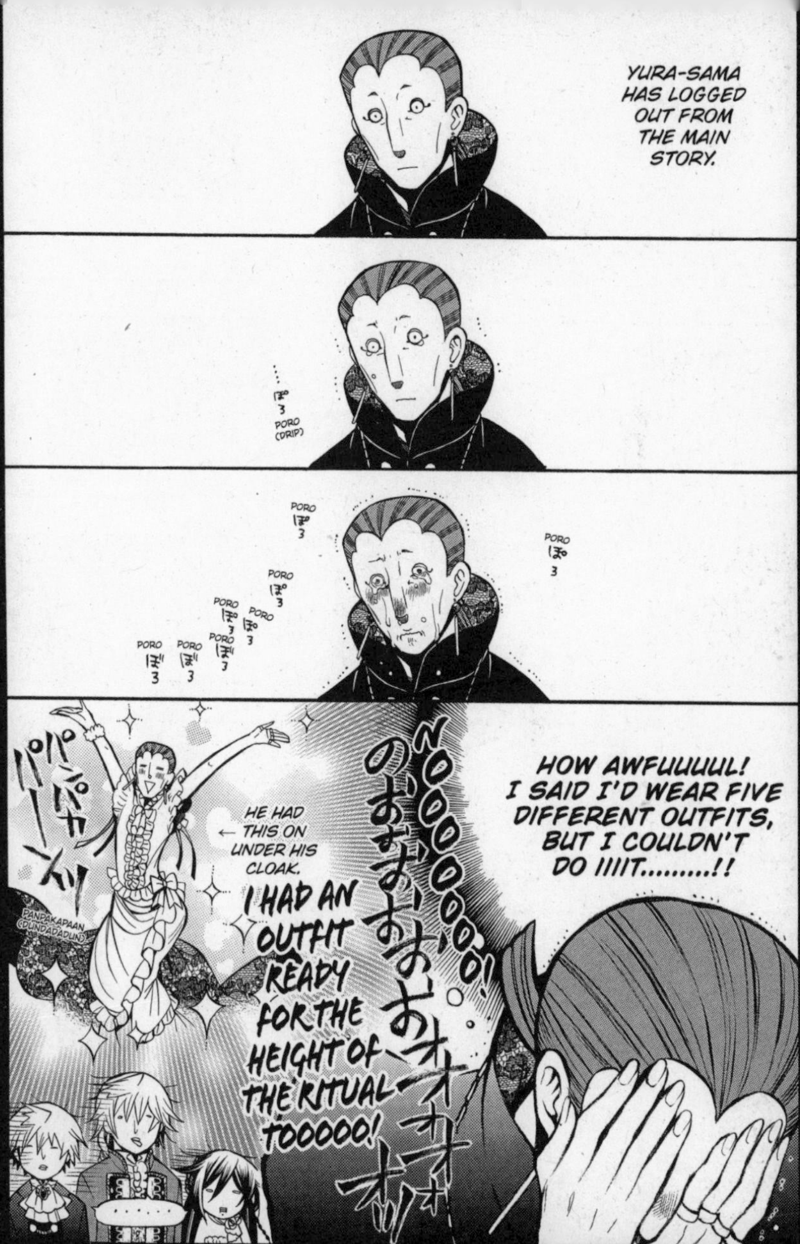
YURA-SAMA HAS LOGGED OUT FROM THE MAIN STORY.
...ぽろ PORO (DRIP)
PORO ぽろ
PORO ぽろ
PORO ぽろ
PORO ぽろ
PORO ぽろ
PORO ぽろ
PORO ぽろ
PORO ぽろ
HOW AWFUUUUL! I SAID I'D WEAR FIVE DIFFERENT OUTFITS, BUT I COULDN'T DO IIIIT.........!!
NOOOOOOOOO!
I HAD AN OUTFIT READY FOR THE HEIGHT OF THE RITUAL TOOOOO!
← HE HAD THIS ON UNDER HIS CLOAK.
PANPAKAPAAN (DUNDADADUN)
....

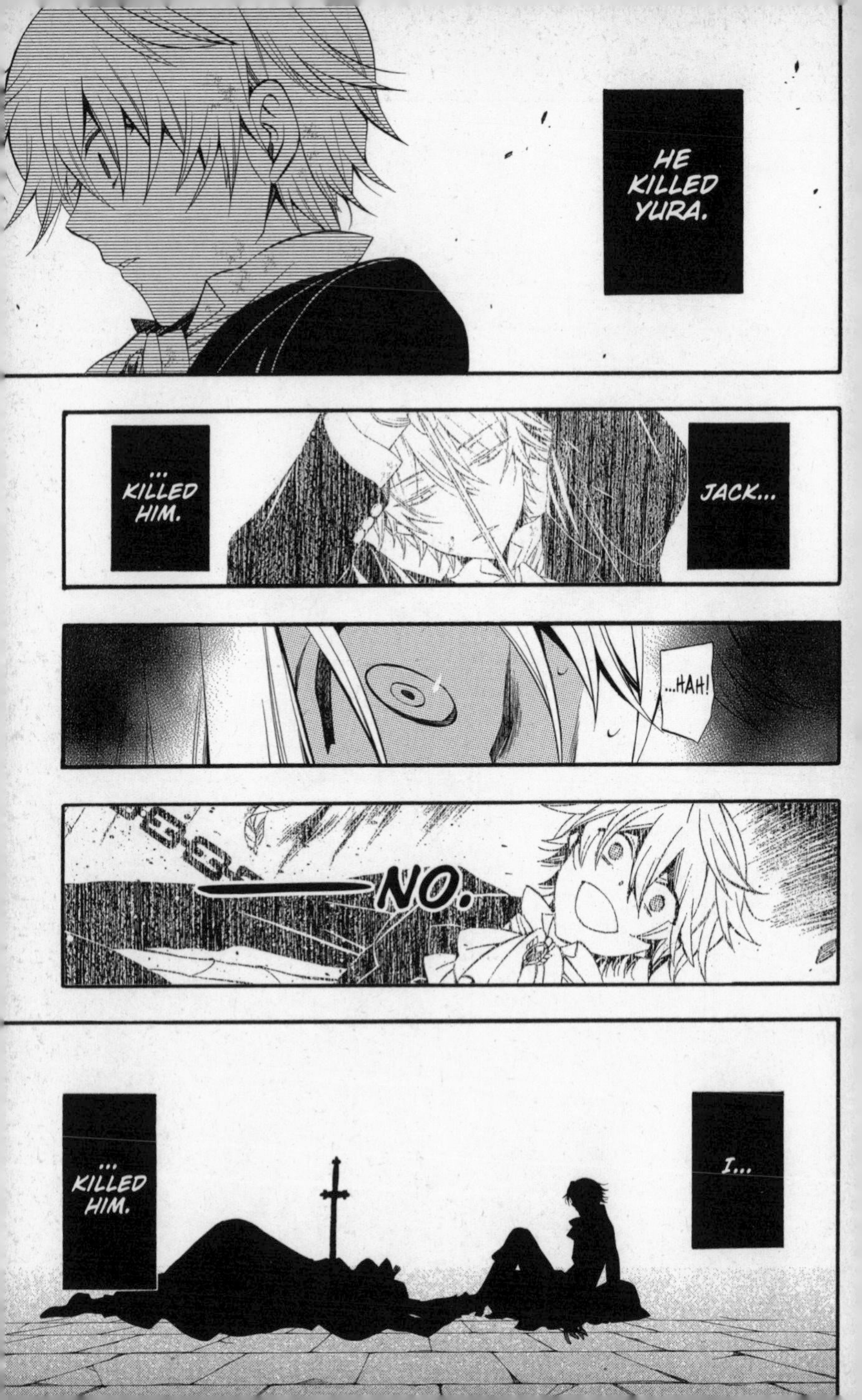
HE KILLED YURA.
JACK...
...KILLED HIM.
...HAH!
———NO.
I...
...KILLED HIM.

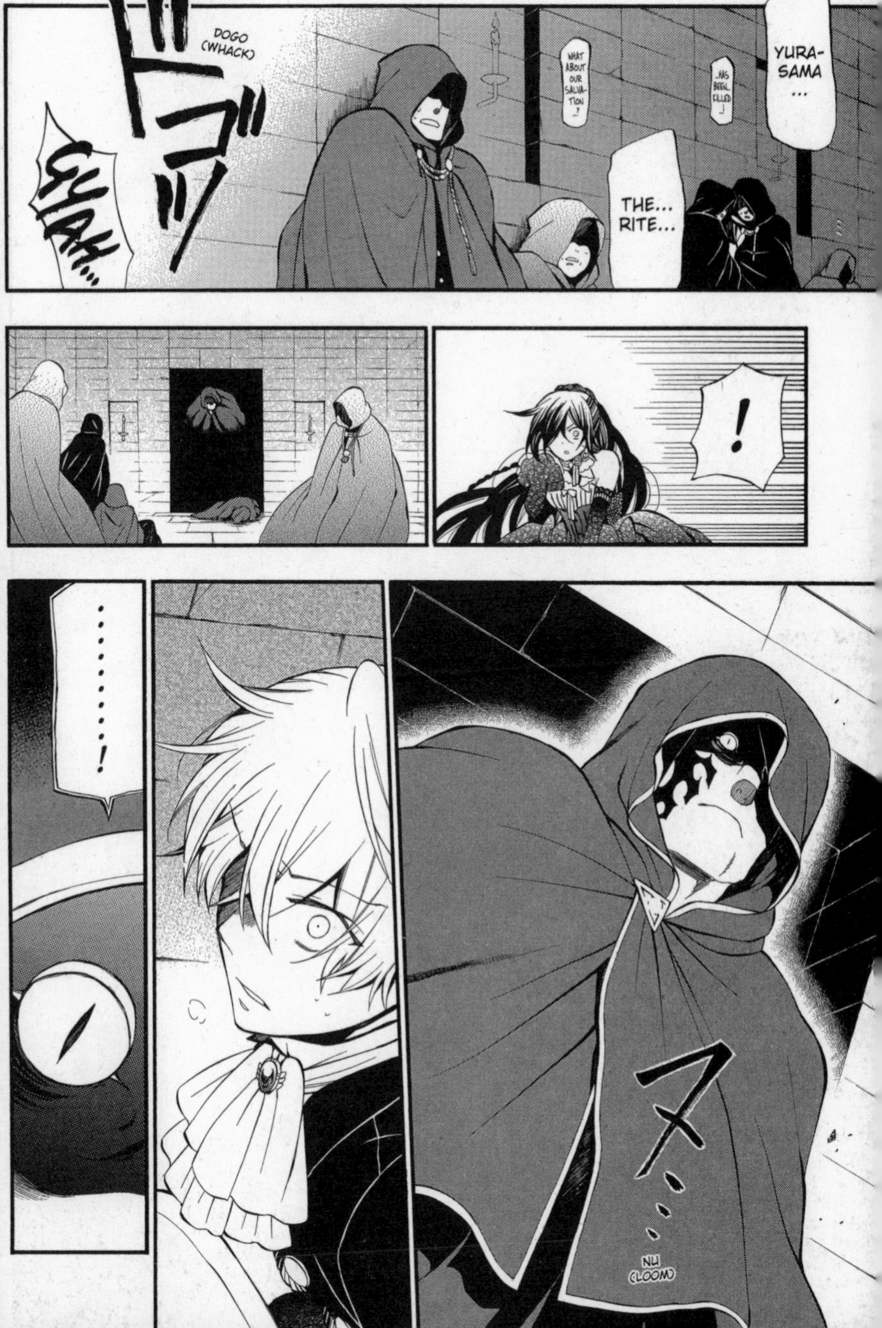
YURA-SAMA ...
...HAS BEEN KILLED ...!
THE... RITE...
WHAT ABOUT OUR SALVATION ...?!
DOGO (WHACK)
GYAAH...
!
NU (LOOM)
..........!

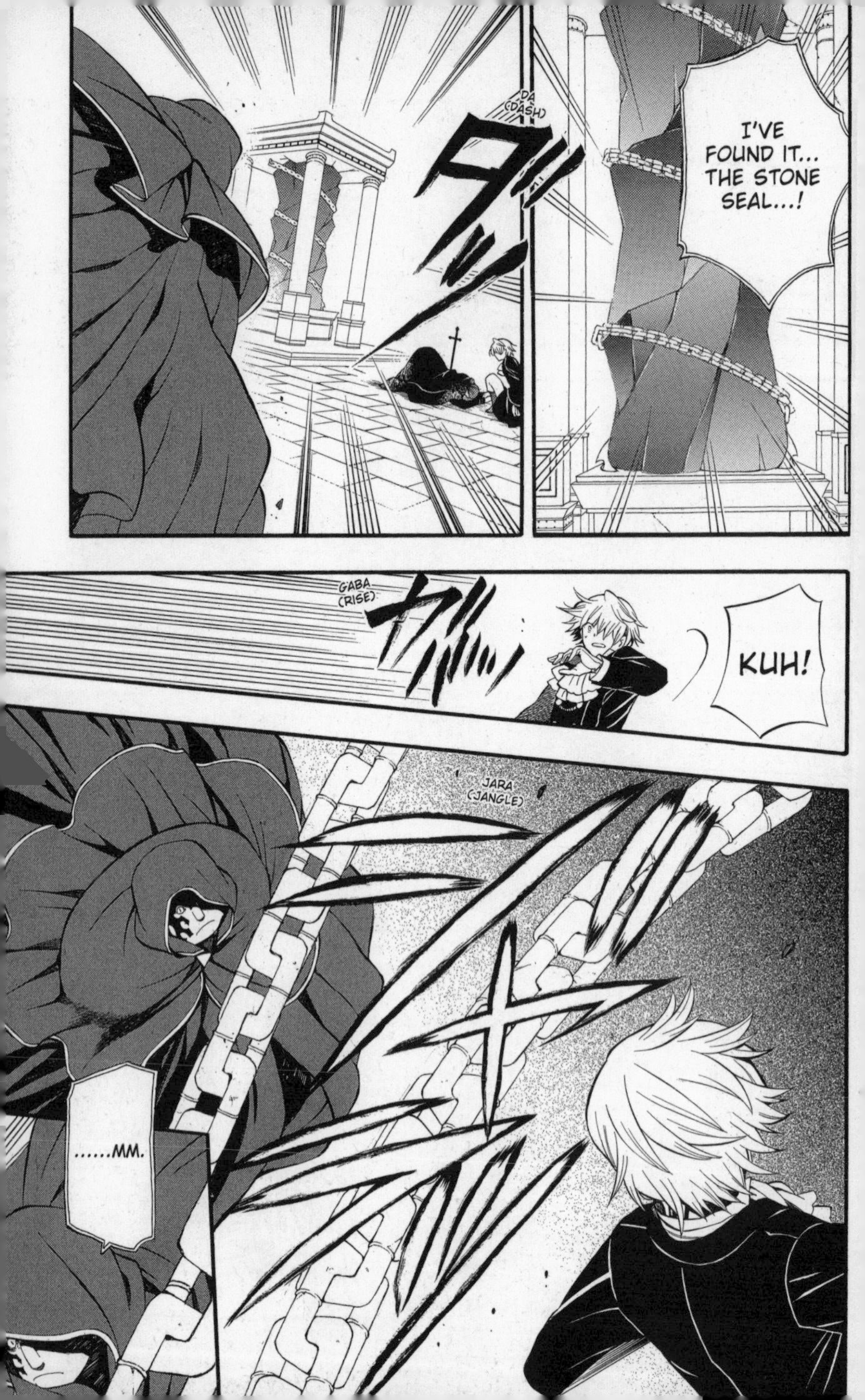
I'VE FOUND IT... THE STONE SEAL...!
DA (DASH)
GABA (RISE)
KUH!
JARA (JANGLE)
......MM.

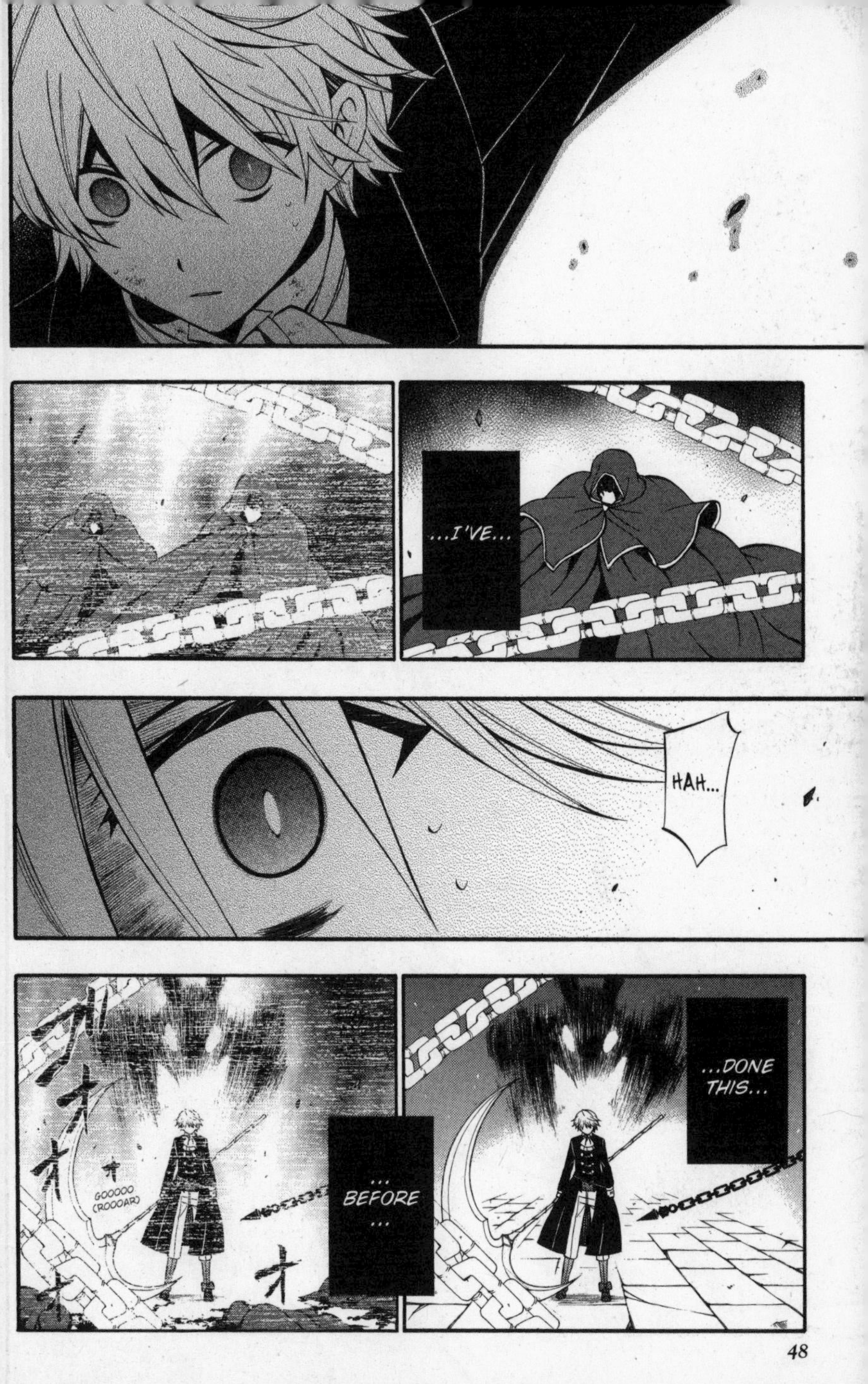
...I'VE...
HAH...
...DONE THIS...
...
BEFORE
...
GOOOOO
(ROOOAR)

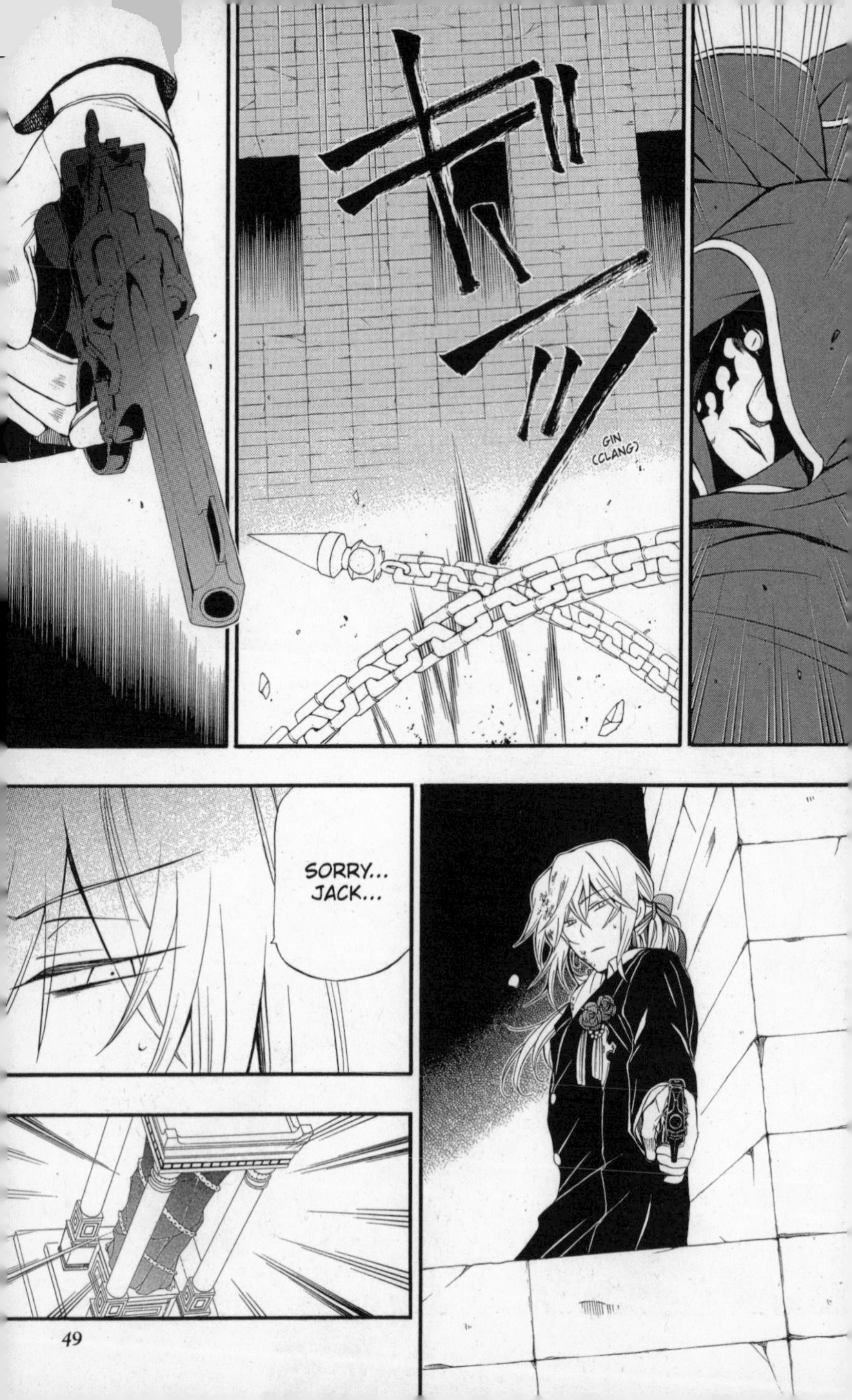
GIN
(CLANG)
SORRY...
JACK...

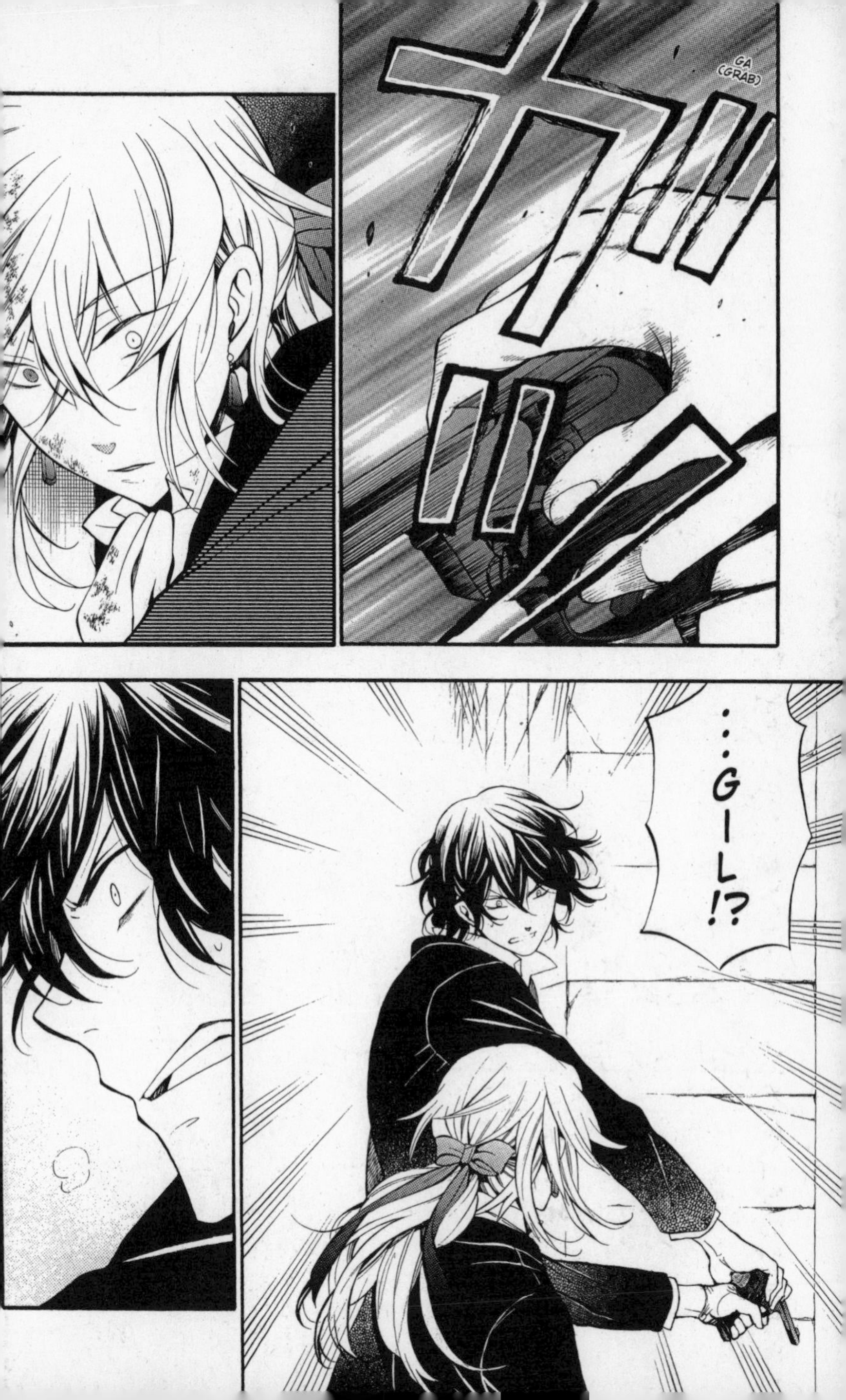
GA (GRAB)
...GIL!?

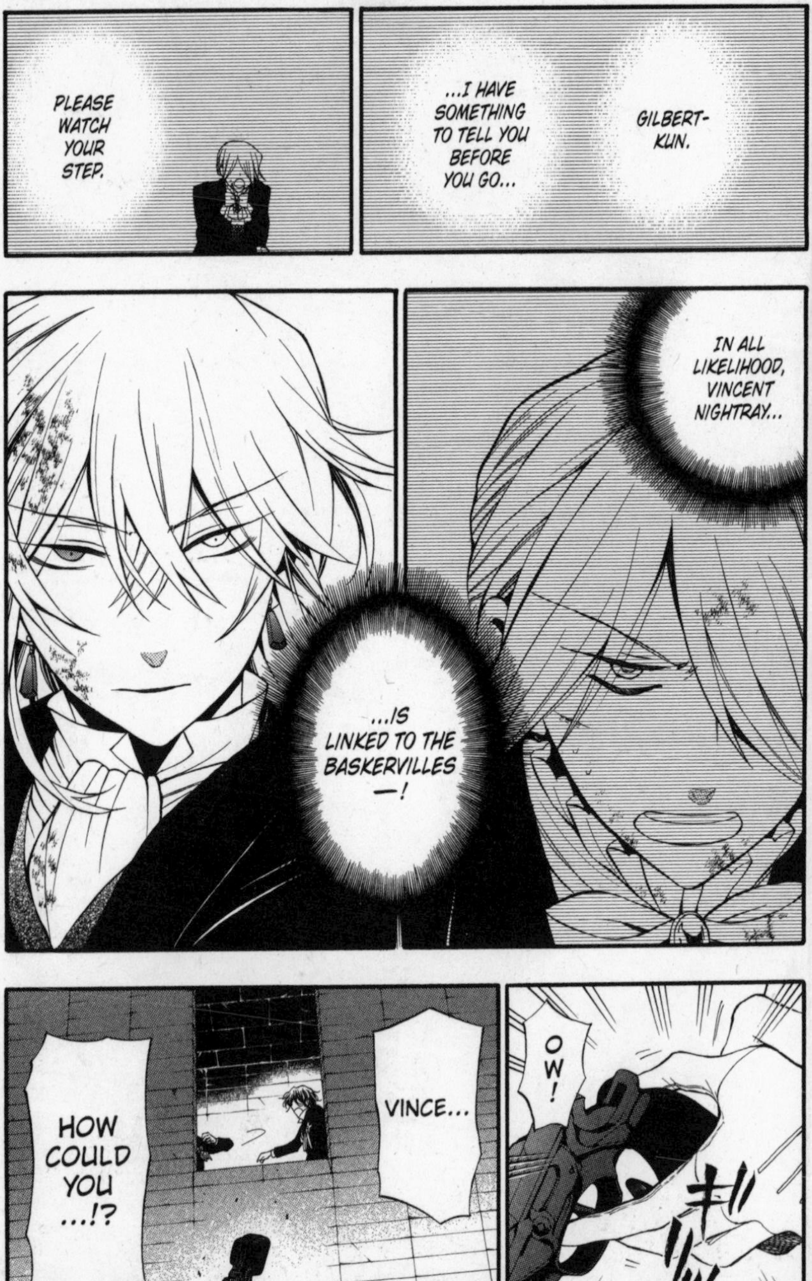
GILBERT-KUN.
...I HAVE SOMETHING TO TELL YOU BEFORE YOU GO...
PLEASE WATCH YOUR STEP.
IN ALL LIKELIHOOD, VINCENT NIGHTRAY...
...IS LINKED TO THE BASKERVILLES—!
OW!
GIRI (TWIST)
VINCE...
HOW COULD YOU ...!?

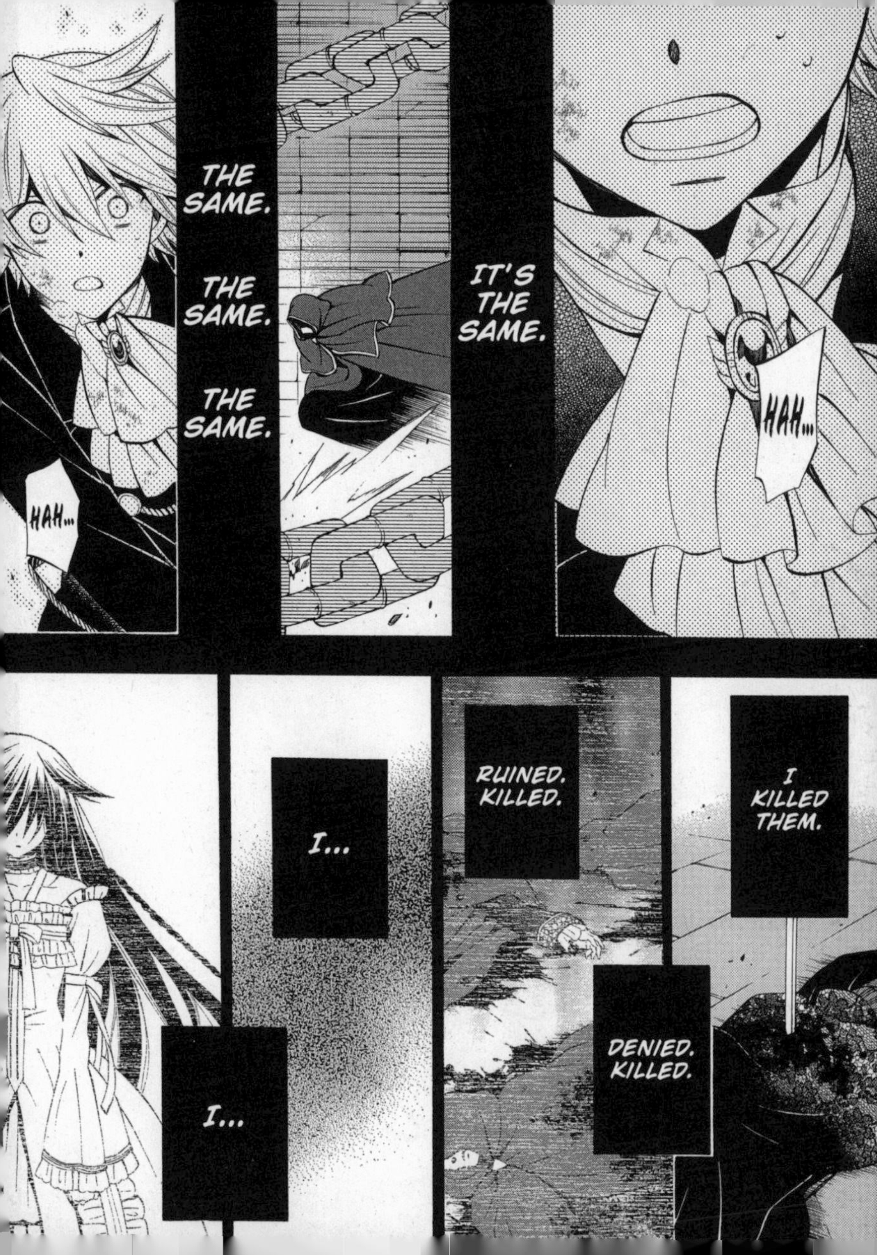
HAH...
IT'S THE SAME.
THE SAME.
THE SAME.
THE SAME.
HAH...
I KILLED THEM.
RUINED. KILLED.
DENIED. KILLED.
I...
I...

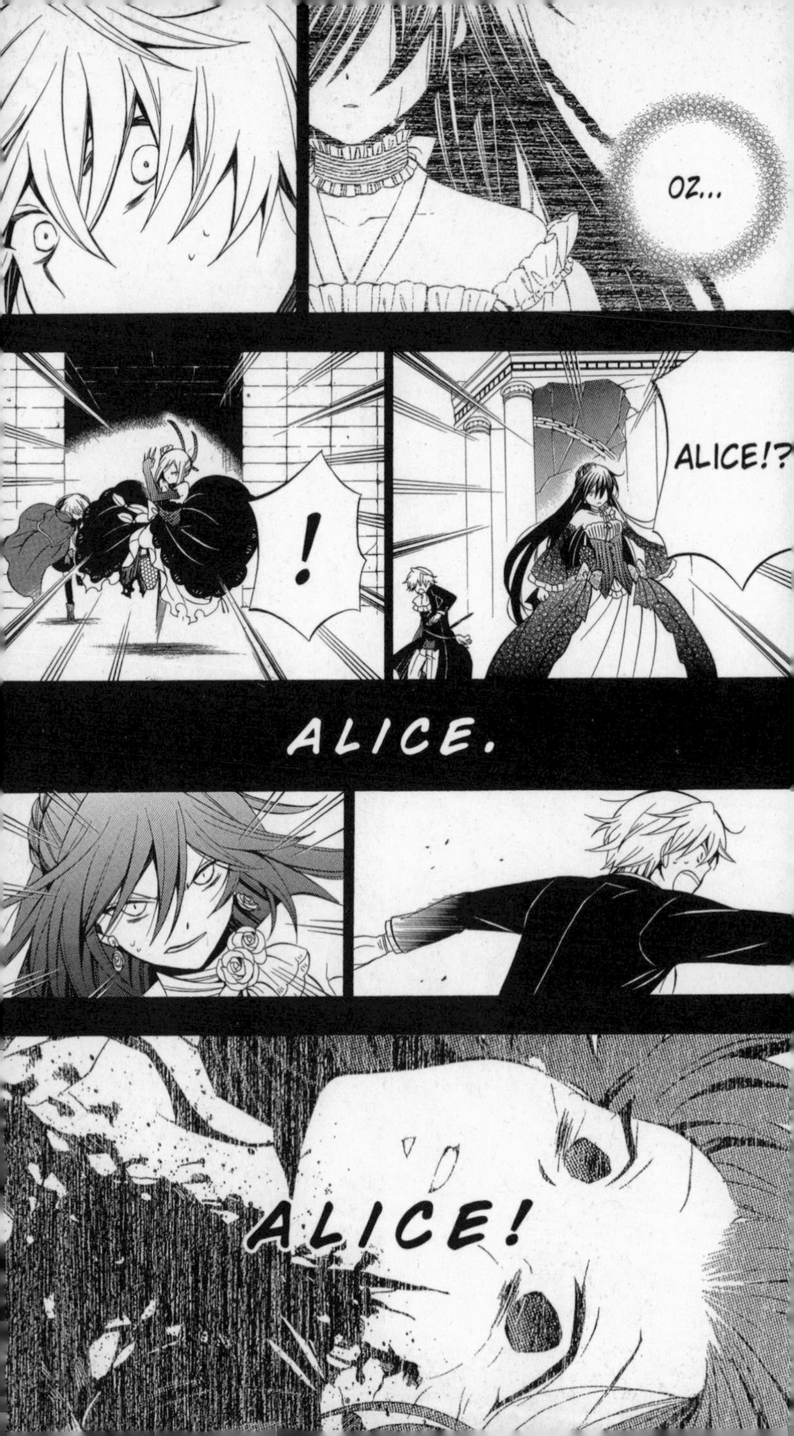
OZ...
ALICE!?
!
ALICE.
ALICE!

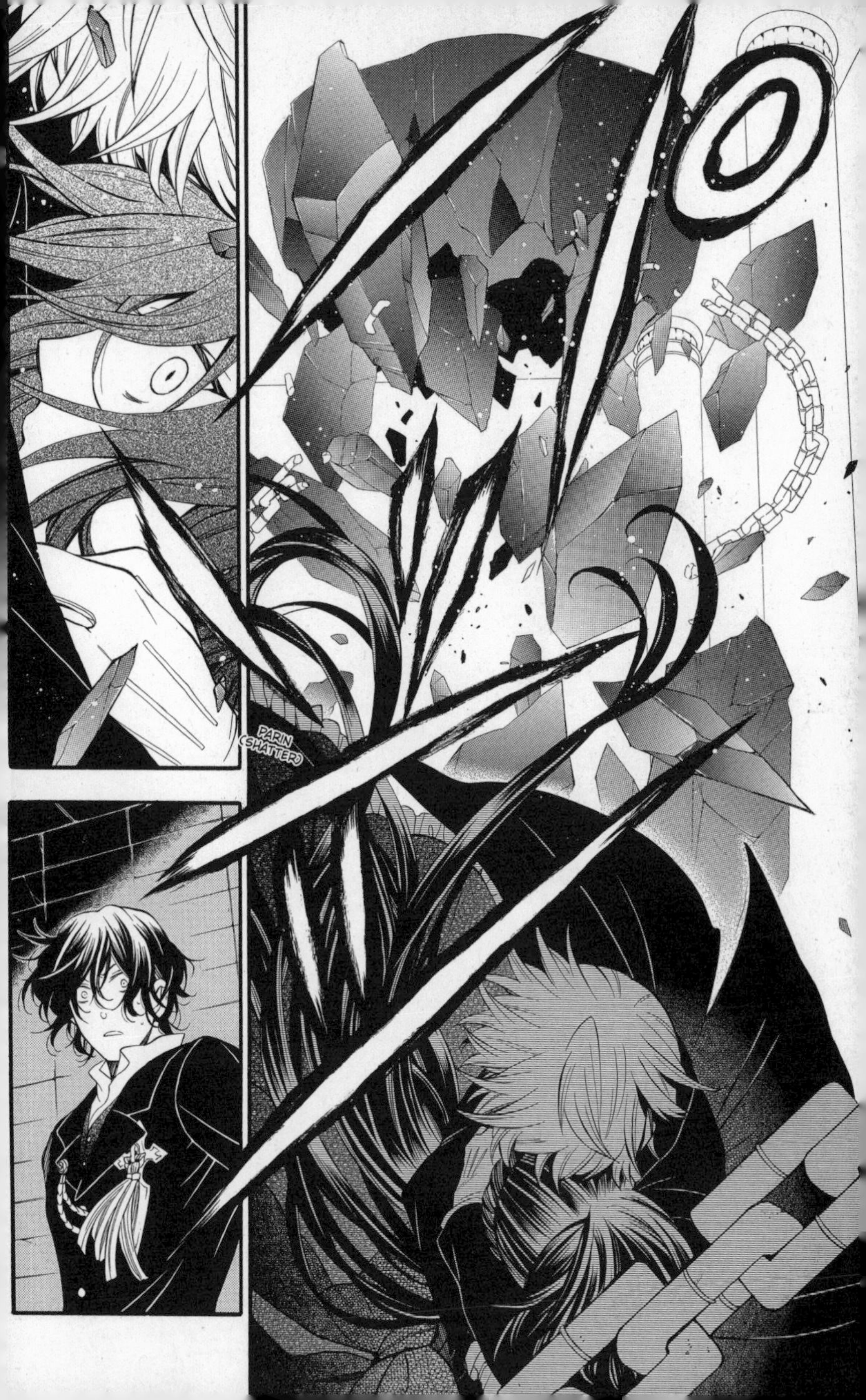
PARIN
(SHATTER)

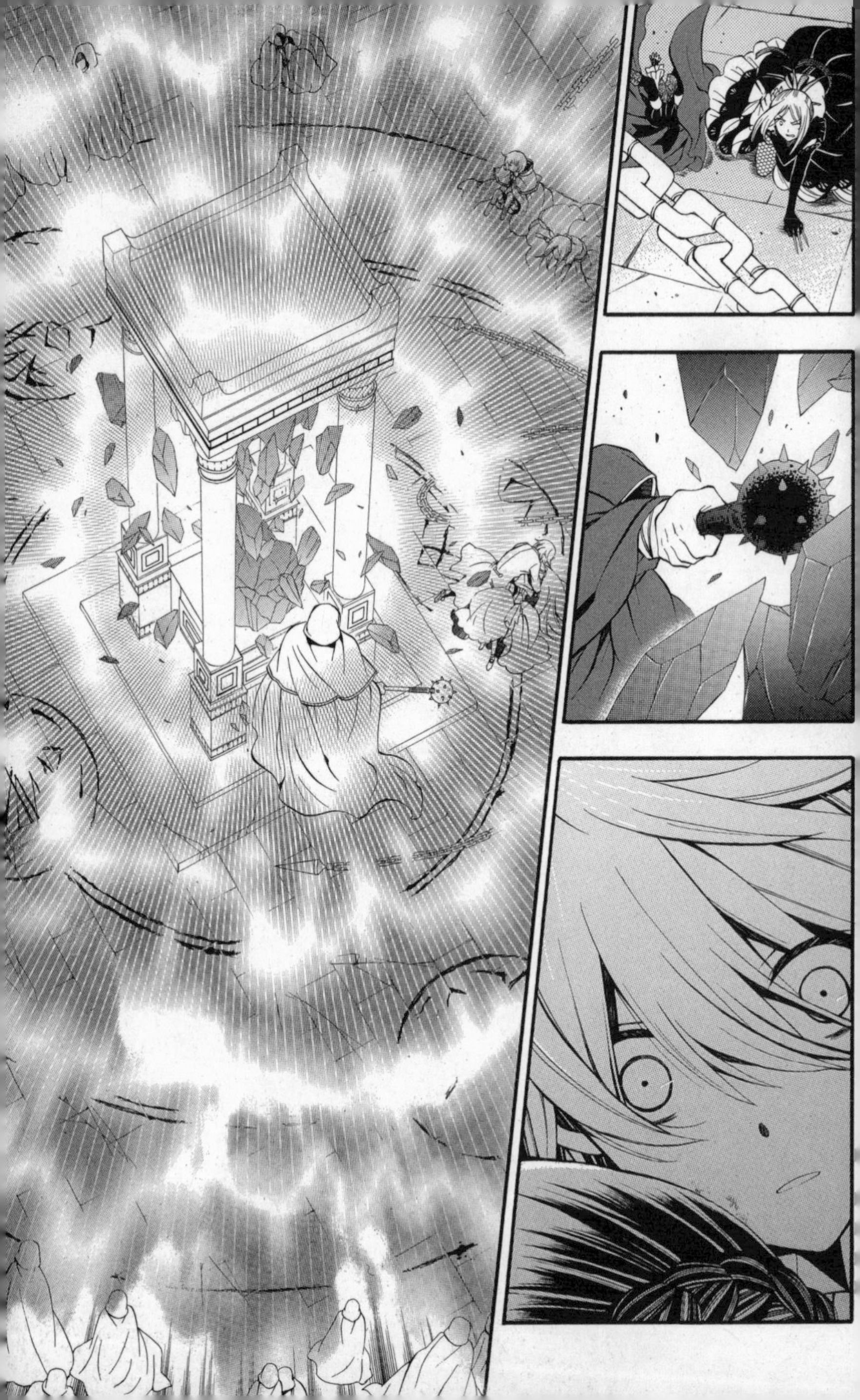

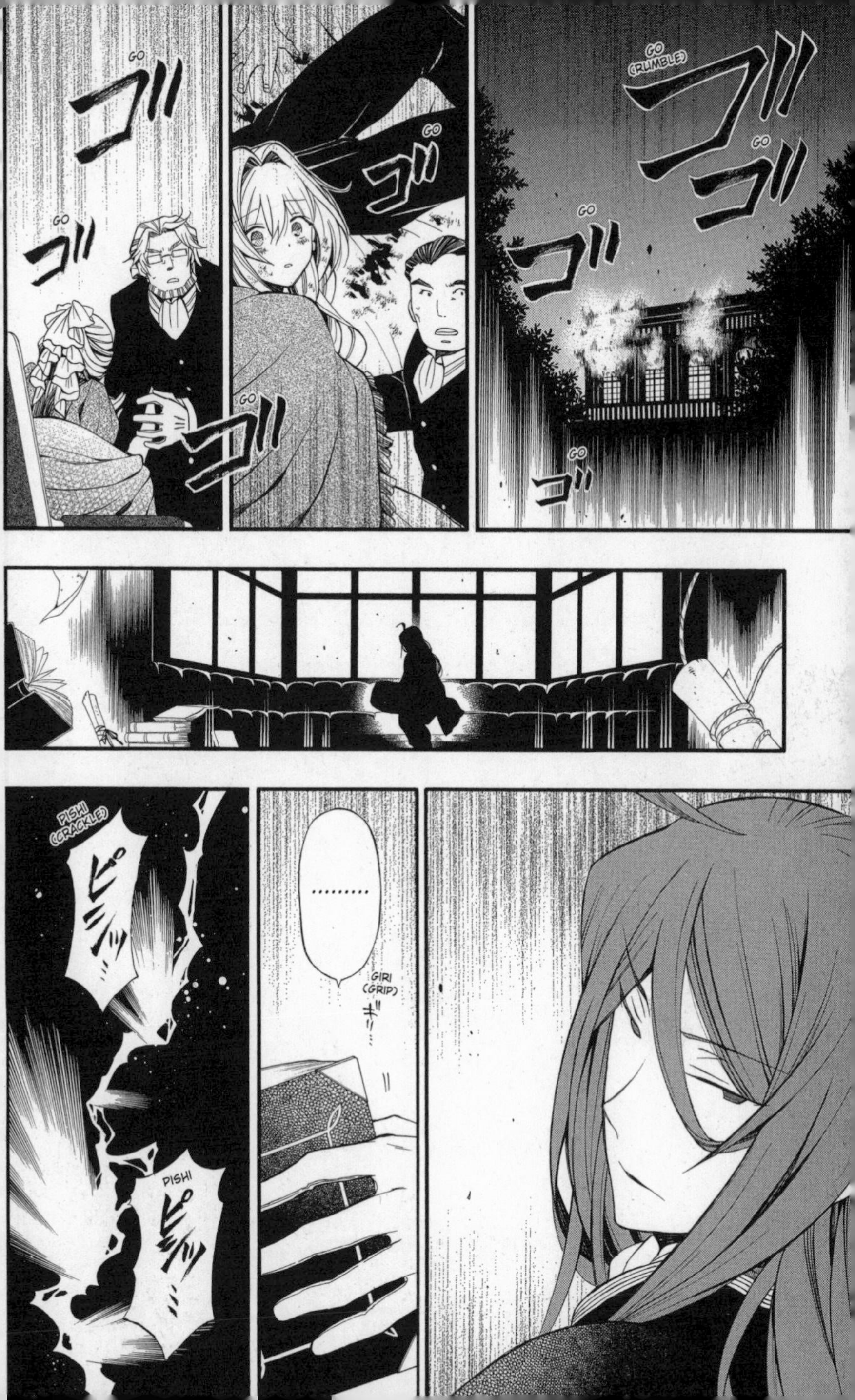
GO (RUMBLE)
GO
GO
GO
GO
GO
GO
GO
....
GIRI (GRIP)
PISHI (CRACKLE)
PISHI

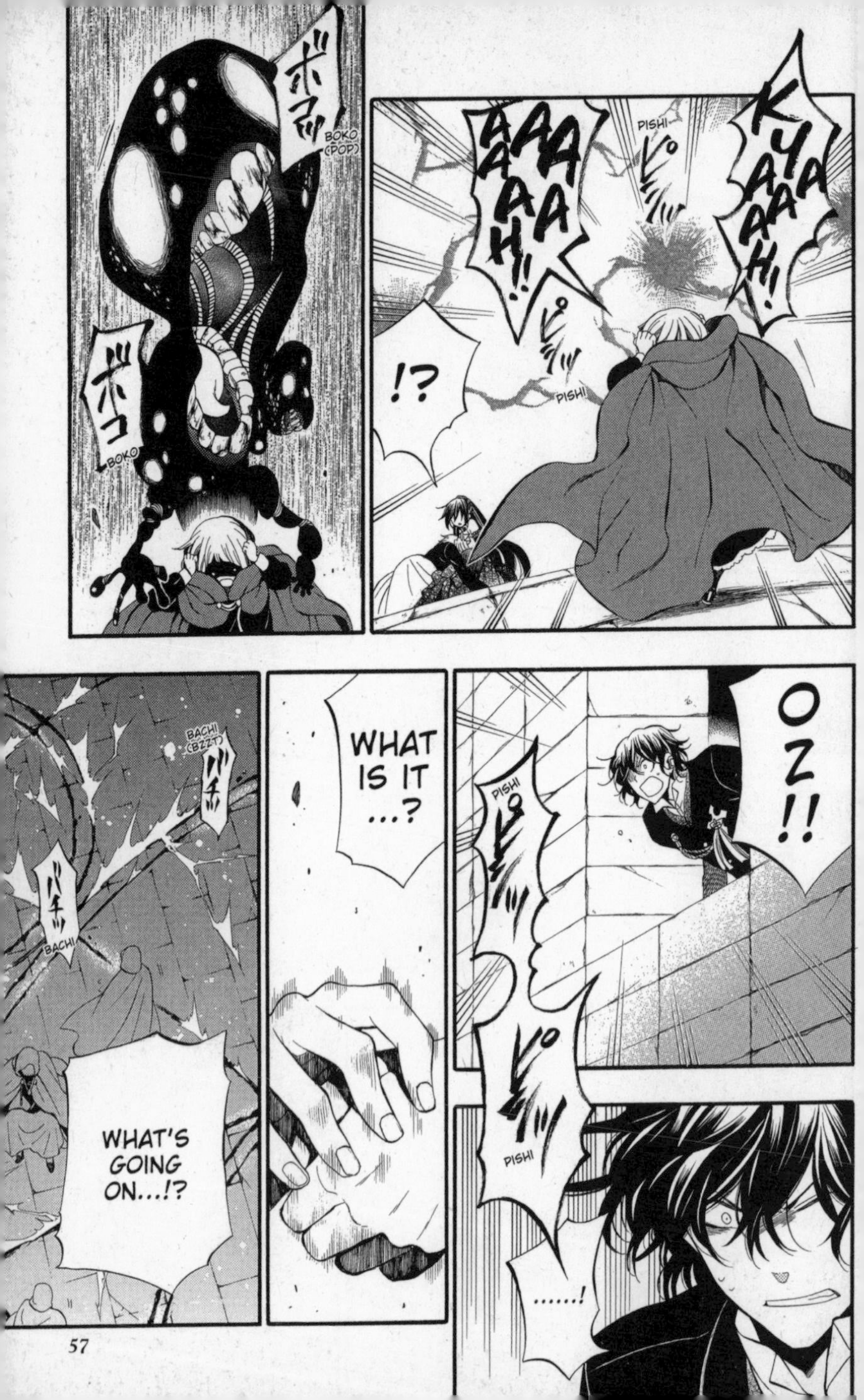
KYAAAAH!!
AAAAAAH!!
PISHI
PISHI
!?
BOKO (POP)
BOKO
OZ!!
PISHI
PISHI
......!
WHAT IS IT ...?
BACHI (BZZT)
BACHI
WHAT'S GOING ON...!?

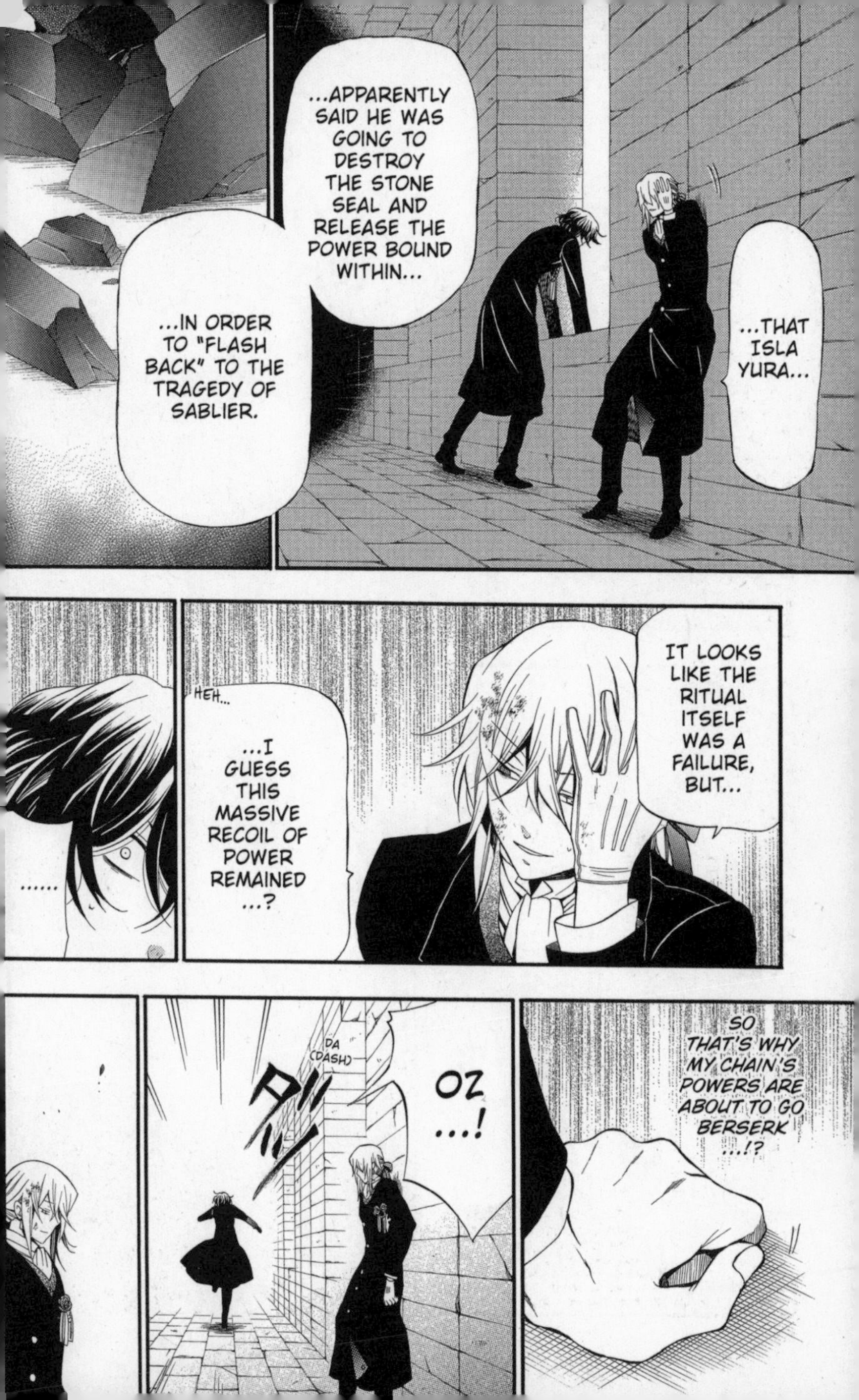
...THAT ISLA YURA...
...APPARENTLY SAID HE WAS GOING TO DESTROY THE STONE SEAL AND RELEASE THE POWER BOUND WITHIN...
...IN ORDER TO "FLASH BACK" TO THE TRAGEDY OF SABLIER.
IT LOOKS LIKE THE RITUAL ITSELF WAS A FAILURE, BUT...
HEH...
...I GUESS THIS MASSIVE RECOIL OF POWER REMAINED ...?
......
SO THAT'S WHY MY CHAIN'S POWERS ARE ABOUT TO GO BERSERK ...!?
OZ ...!
DA (DASH)
!

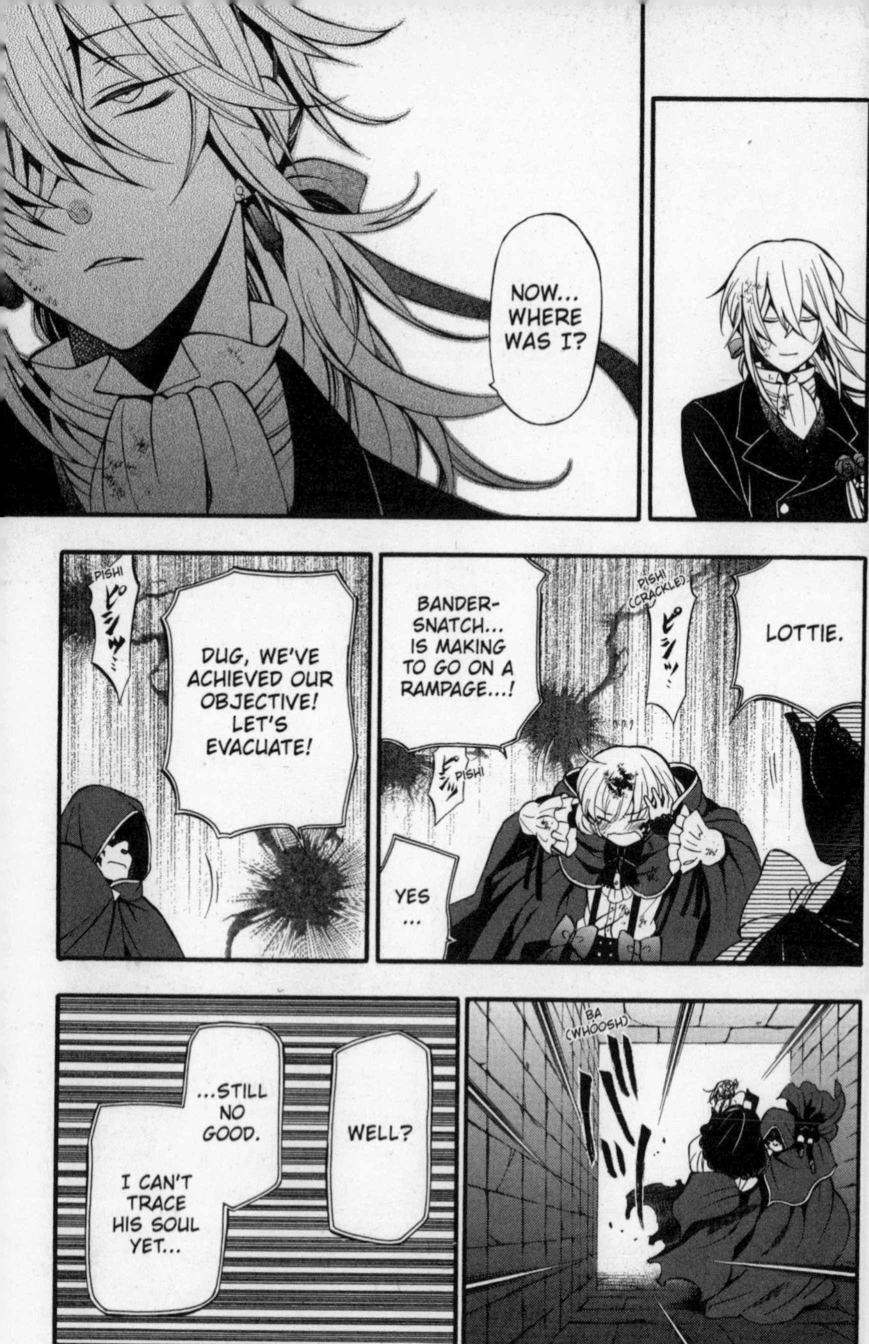
NOW... WHERE WAS I?
LOTTIE.
PISHI (CRACKLE)
ピシッ
BANDER-SNATCH... IS MAKING TO GO ON A RAMPAGE...!
PISHI
YES...
PISHI
ピシッ
DUG, WE'VE ACHIEVED OUR OBJECTIVE! LET'S EVACUATE!
BA (WHOOSH)
WELL?
...STILL NO GOOD.
I CAN'T TRACE HIS SOUL YET...

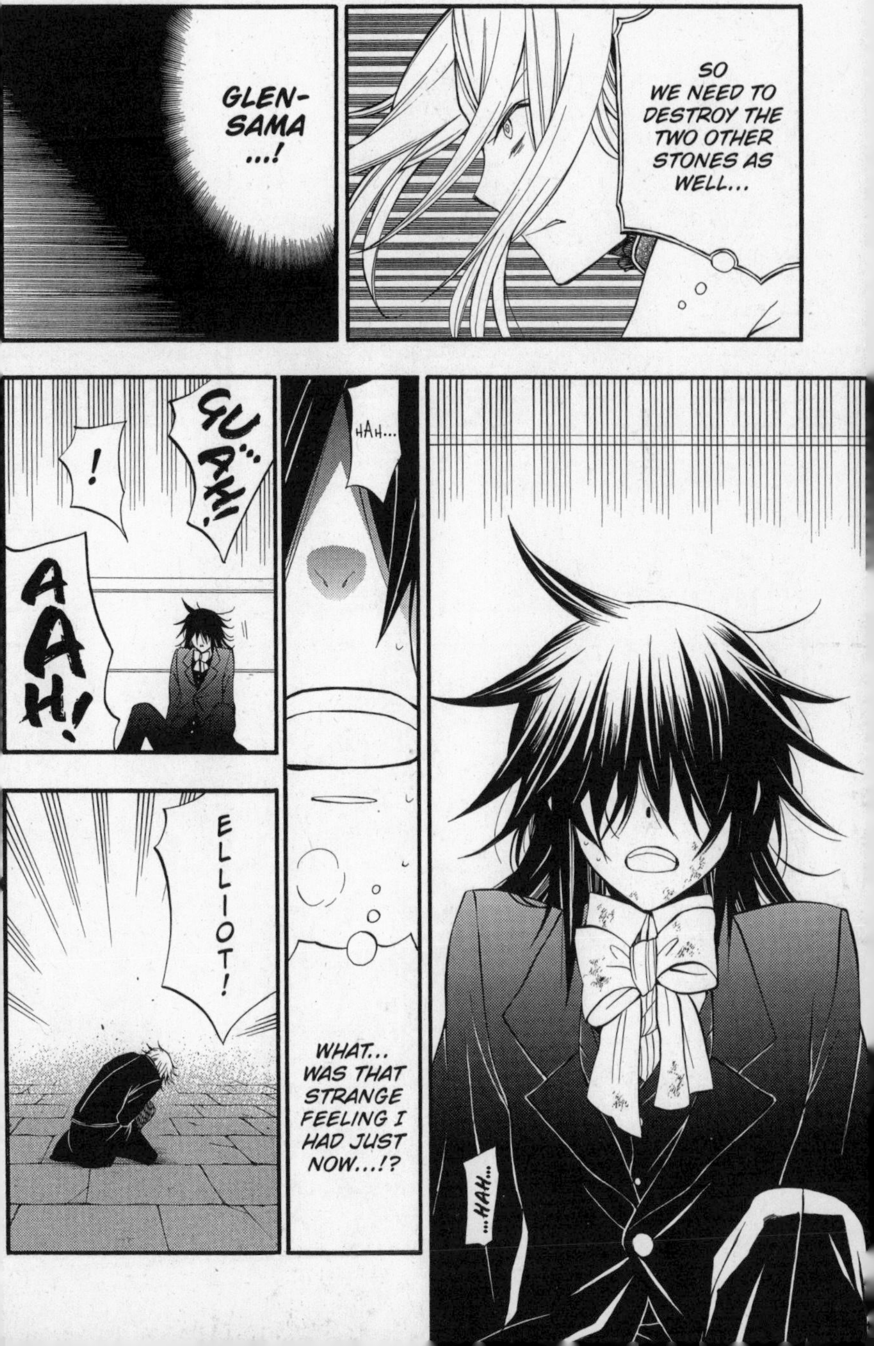
SO WE NEED TO DESTROY THE TWO OTHER STONES AS WELL...
GLEN-SAMA...!
...HAH...
HAH...
WHAT... WAS THAT STRANGE FEELING I HAD JUST NOW...!?
GUAH!
!
AAAH!
ELLIOT!

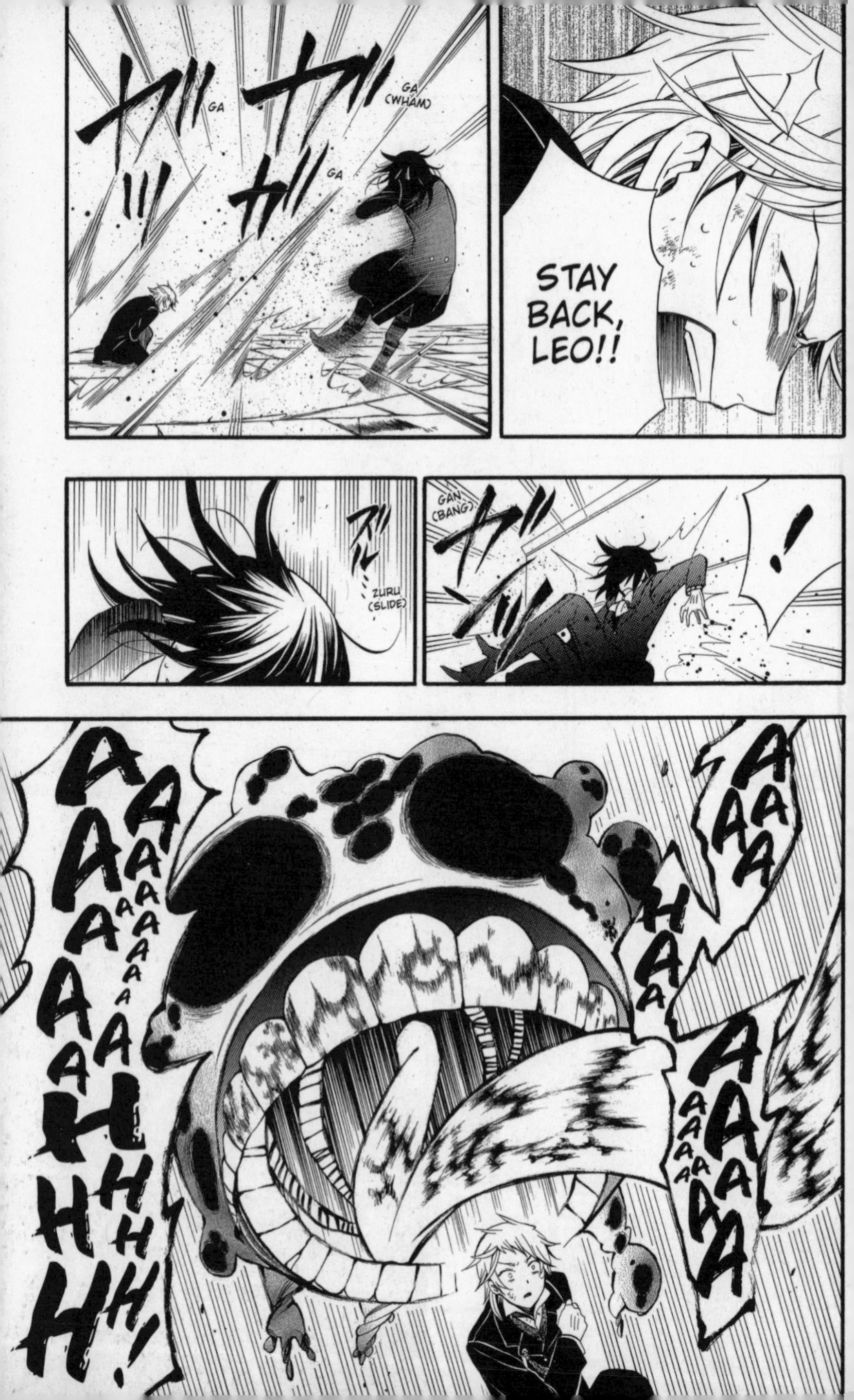

STAY BACK, LEO!!
GA (WHAM)
GA
GA
!
GAN (BANG)
ZURU (SLIDE)
AAAAHAAAAAAAAAAAAAAA
AAAAAAAAAAAAAAAAAAAHHHHHHHH!

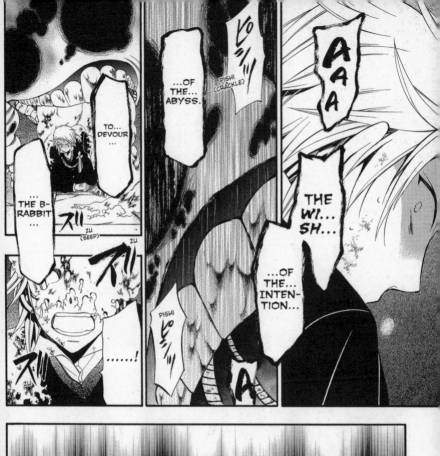

...THE B-RABBIT...

TO... DEVOUR...

...OF THE... ABYSS.

ZU (SEEP)

ZU

ZU

PISHI (CRACKLE)

AAA

THE WI...SH...

...OF THE... INTENTION...

PISHI (CRACKLE)

A

.......!

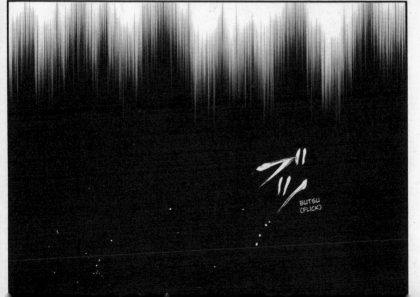

BUTSU (FLICK)

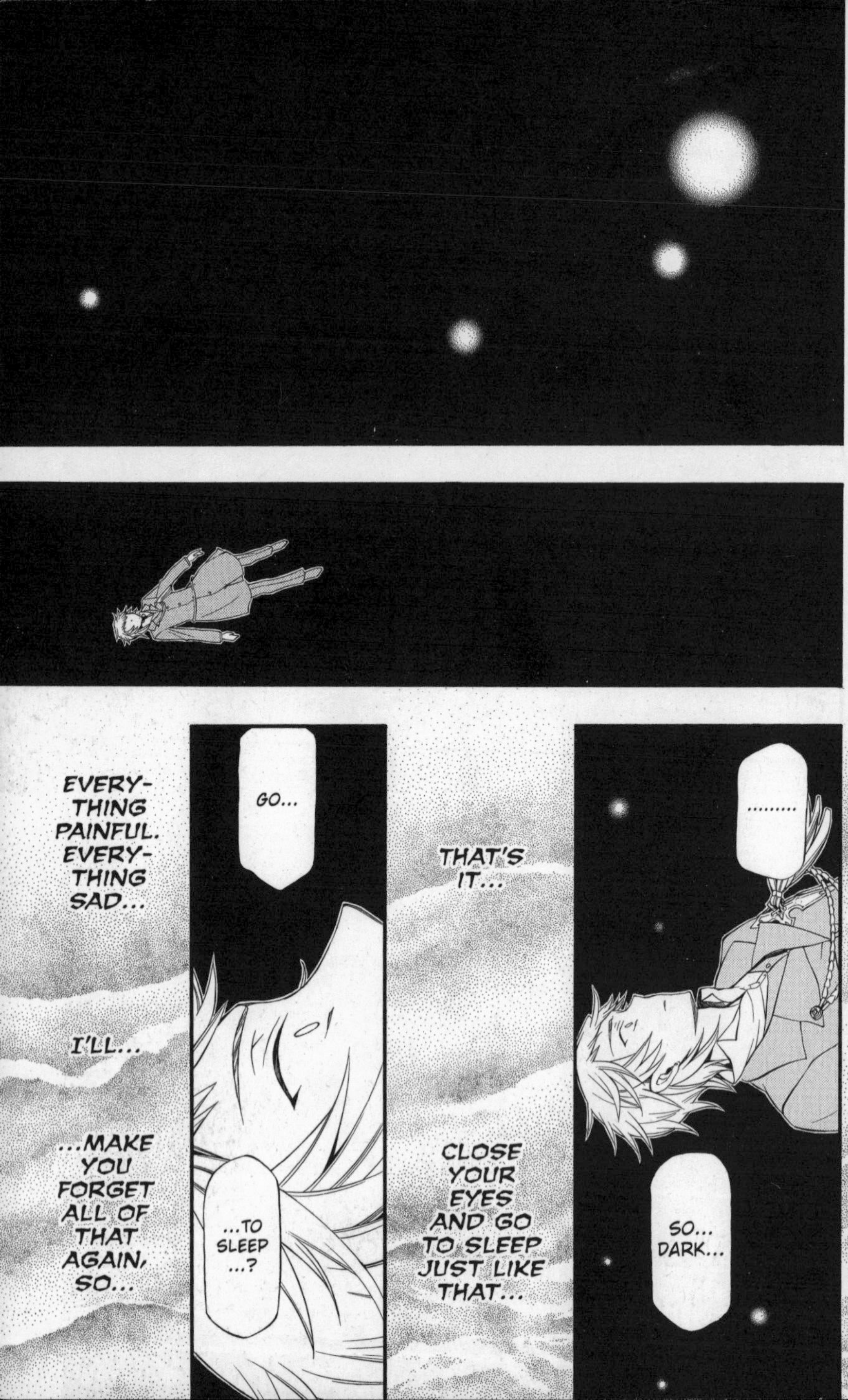
....
SO... DARK...
THAT'S IT...
CLOSE YOUR EYES AND GO TO SLEEP JUST LIKE THAT...
GO...
...TO SLEEP ...?
EVERY-THING PAINFUL. EVERY-THING SAD...
I'LL...
...MAKE YOU FORGET ALL OF THAT AGAIN, SO...

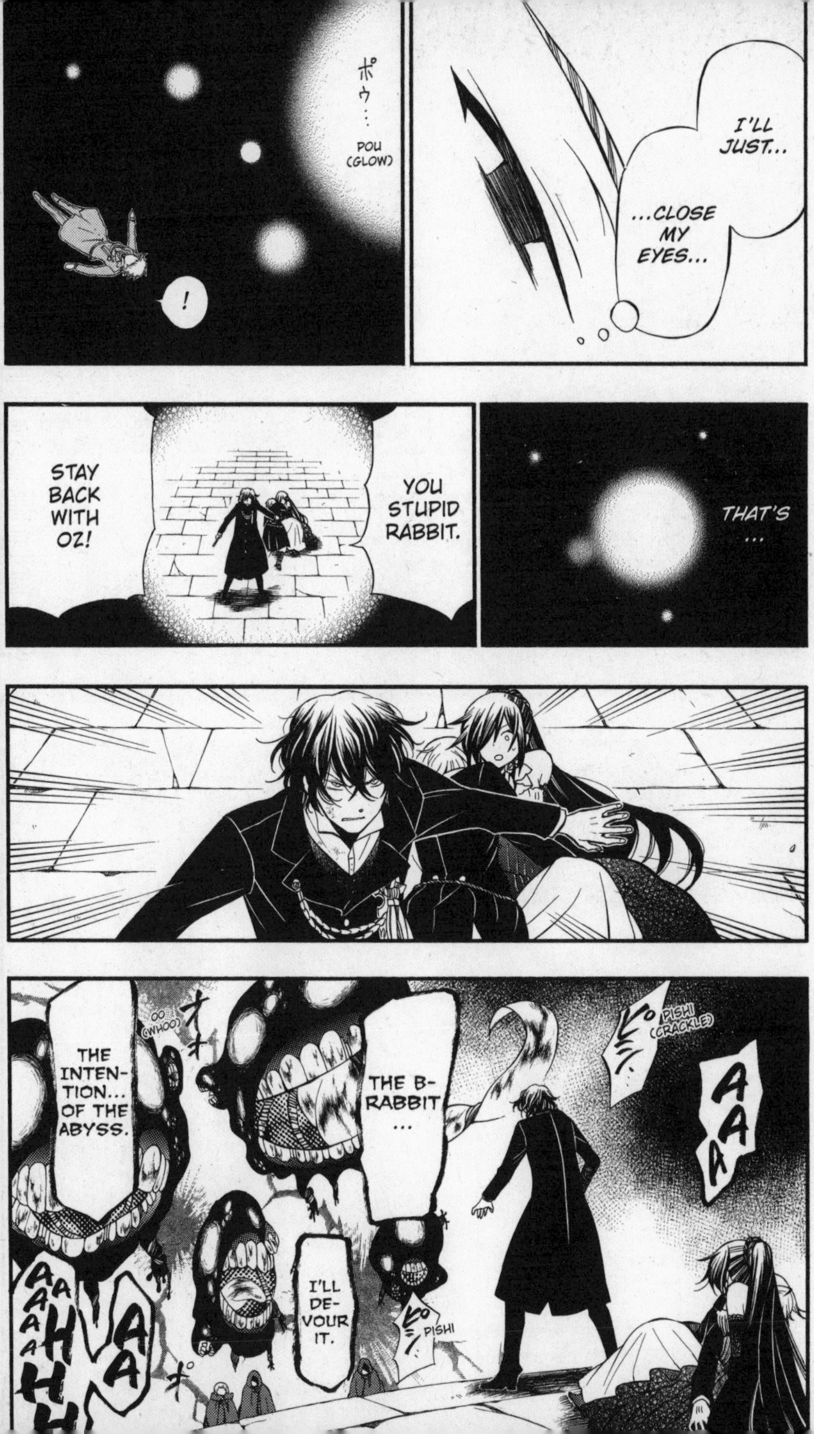
I'LL JUST...
...CLOSE MY EYES...
ポウ…
POU (GLOW)
!
THAT'S ...
YOU STUPID RABBIT.
STAY BACK WITH OZ!
ピシ
PISHI (CRACKLE)
AAAA
THE B-RABBIT ...
オオ
OO (WHOO)
THE INTEN-TION... OF THE ABYSS.
I'LL DE-VOUR IT.
ピシ
PISHI
AA

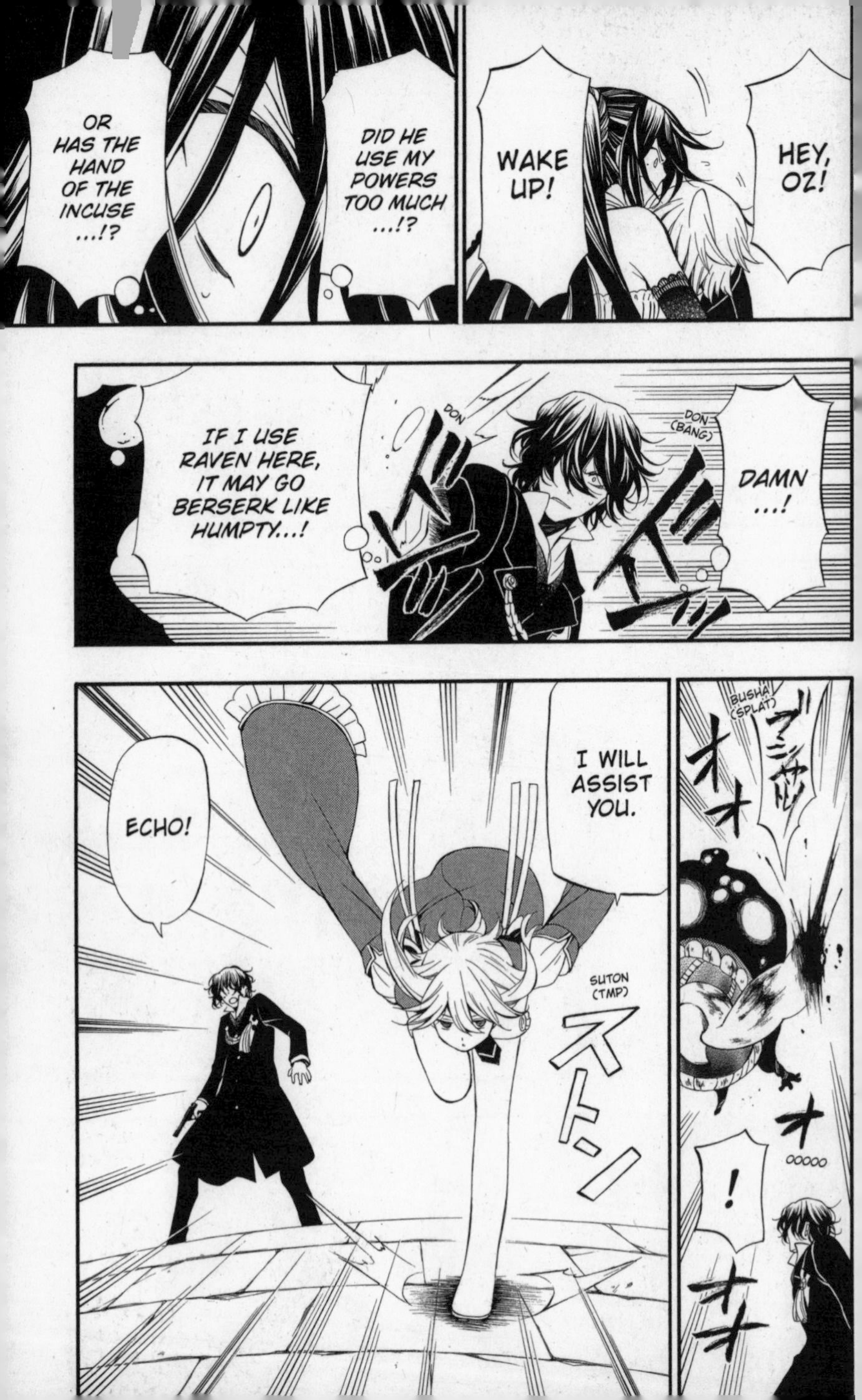
HEY, OZ!
WAKE UP!
DID HE USE MY POWERS TOO MUCH ...!?
OR HAS THE HAND OF THE INCUSE ...!?
DON (BANG)
DAMN ...!
DON
IF I USE RAVEN HERE, IT MAY GO BERSERK LIKE HUMPTY...!
BUSHA (SPLAT)
OOOOO
!
I WILL ASSIST YOU.
ECHO!
SUTON (TMP)

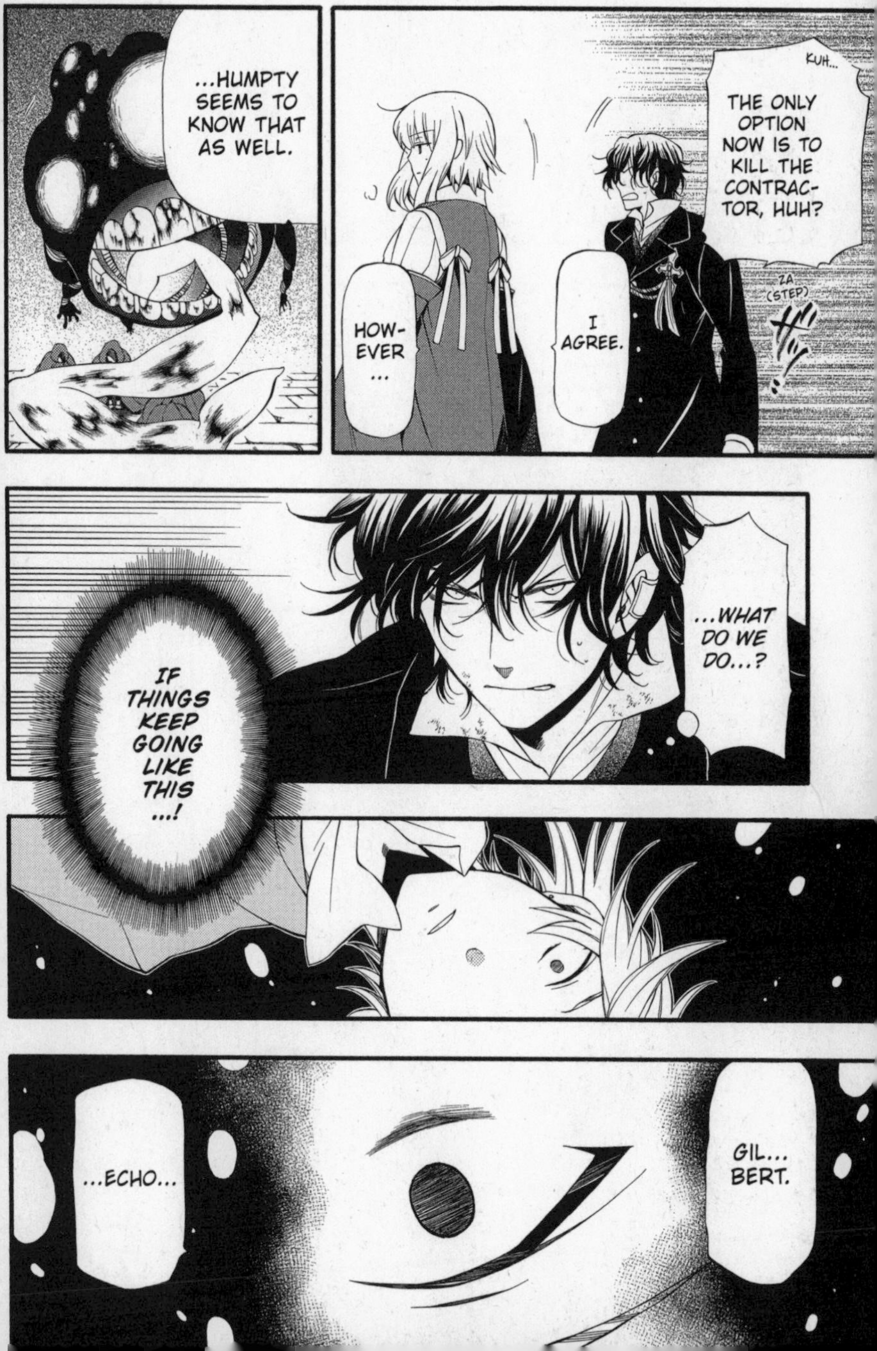
KUH...
THE ONLY OPTION NOW IS TO KILL THE CONTRACTOR, HUH?
ZA (STEP)
I AGREE.
HOWEVER...
...HUMPTY SEEMS TO KNOW THAT AS WELL.
...WHAT DO WE DO...?
IF THINGS KEEP GOING LIKE THIS...!
GIL... BERT.
...ECHO...

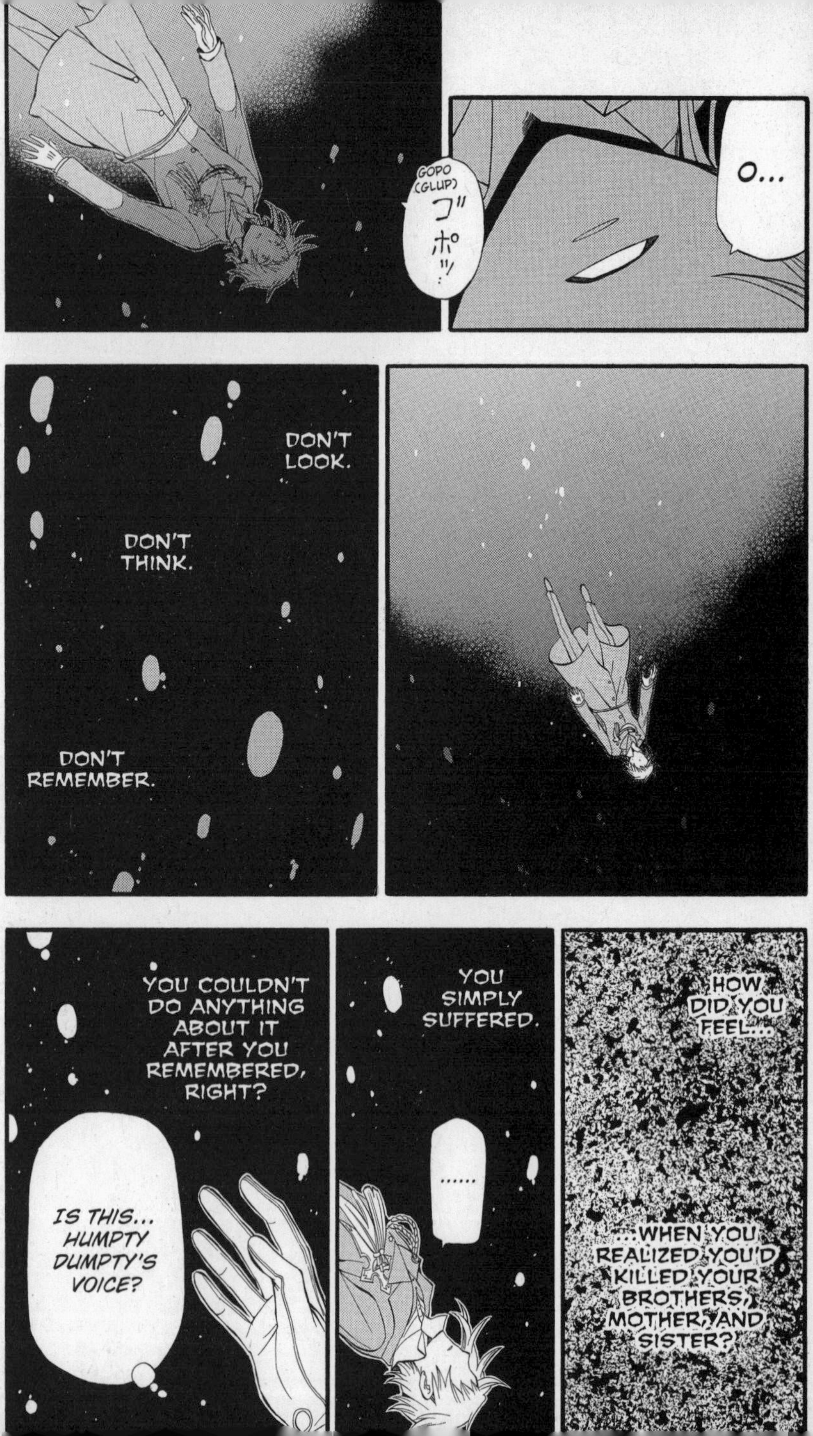
O...
GOPO (GLUP)
ゴポッ
DON'T LOOK.
DON'T THINK.
DON'T REMEMBER.
HOW DID YOU FEEL...
...WHEN YOU REALIZED YOU'D KILLED YOUR BROTHERS, MOTHER, AND SISTER?
YOU SIMPLY SUFFERED.
......
YOU COULDN'T DO ANYTHING ABOUT IT AFTER YOU REMEMBERED, RIGHT?
IS THIS... HUMPTY DUMPTY'S VOICE?

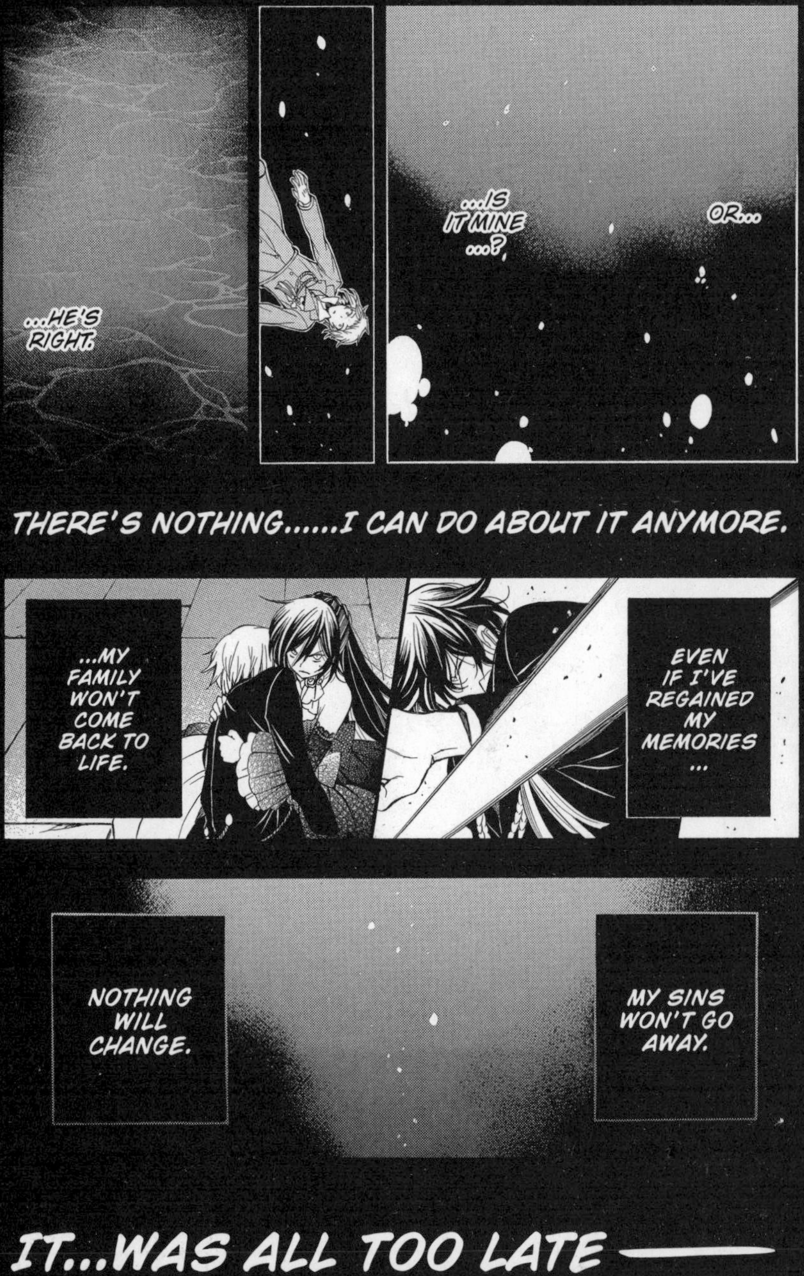
...IS IT MINE ...?
OR...
...HE'S RIGHT.
THERE'S NOTHING......I CAN DO ABOUT IT ANYMORE.
EVEN IF I'VE REGAINED MY MEMORIES ...
...MY FAMILY WON'T COME BACK TO LIFE.
MY SINS WON'T GO AWAY.
NOTHING WILL CHANGE.
IT...WAS ALL TOO LATE —

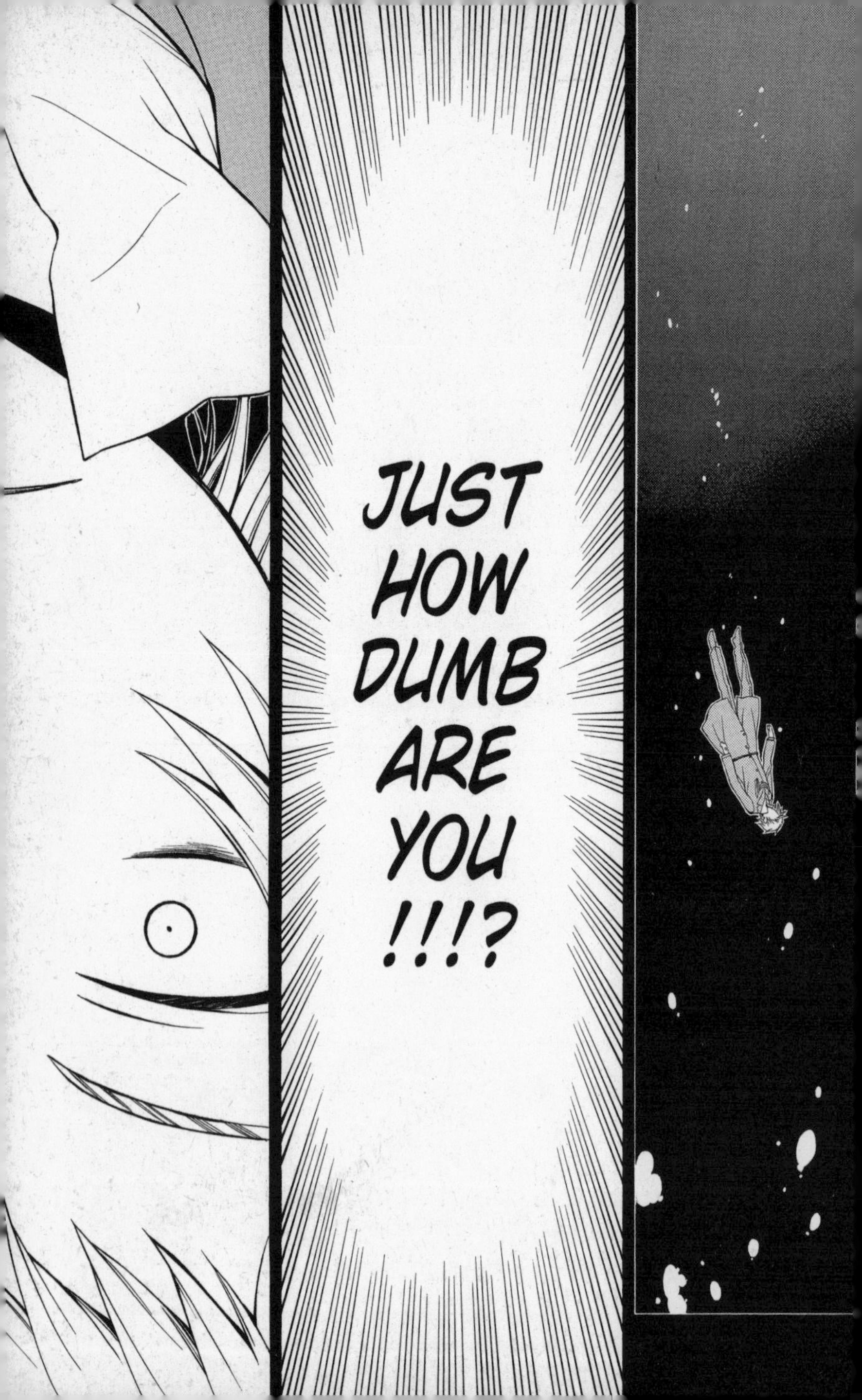
JUST HOW DUMB ARE YOU !!!?

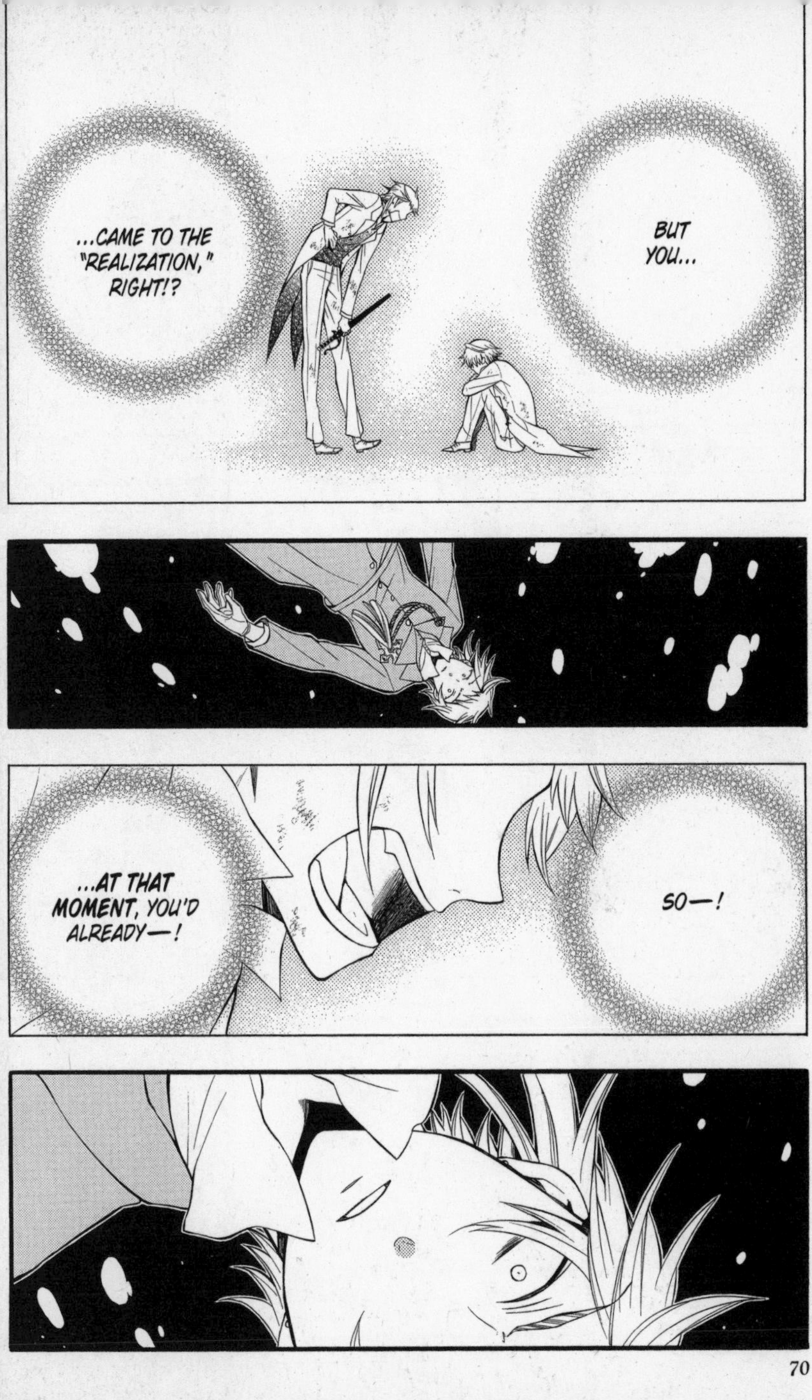
BUT YOU...
...CAME TO THE "REALIZATION," RIGHT!?
SO—!
...AT THAT MOMENT, YOU'D ALREADY—!

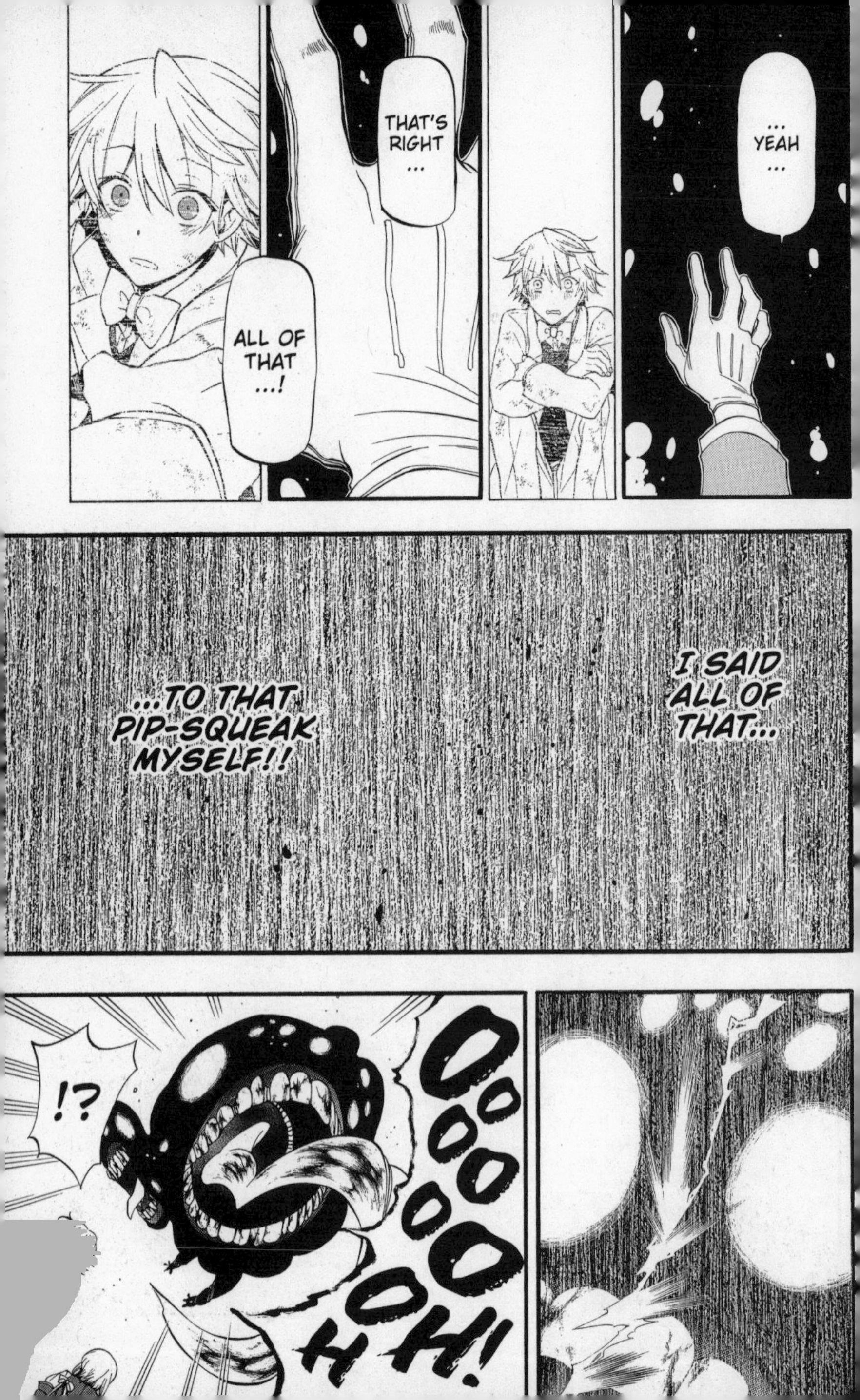

... YEAH ...
THAT'S RIGHT ...
ALL OF THAT ...!
I SAID ALL OF THAT...
...TO THAT PIP-SQUEAK MYSELF!!
OOOOOOOOOH!
!?

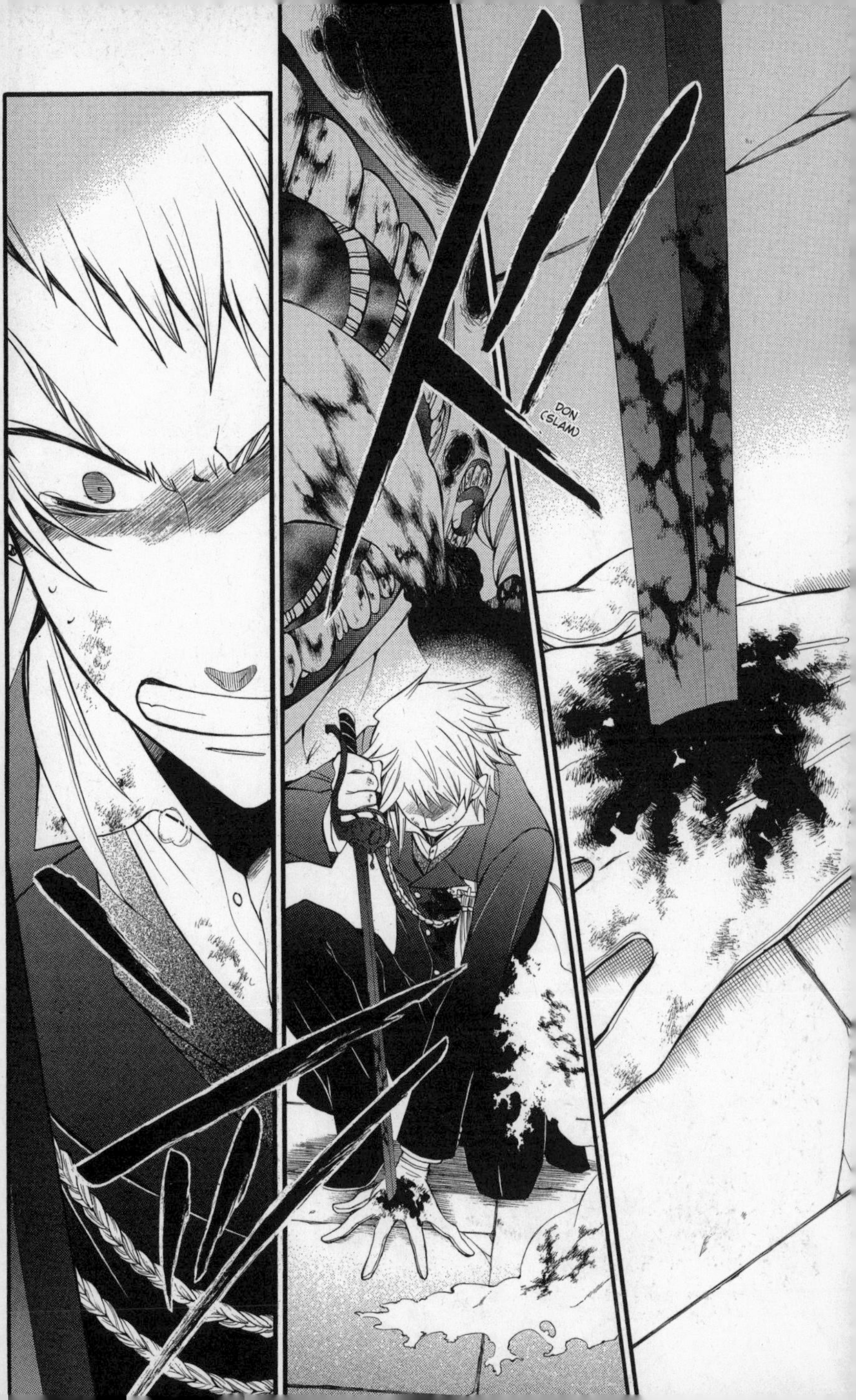
DON
(SLAM)

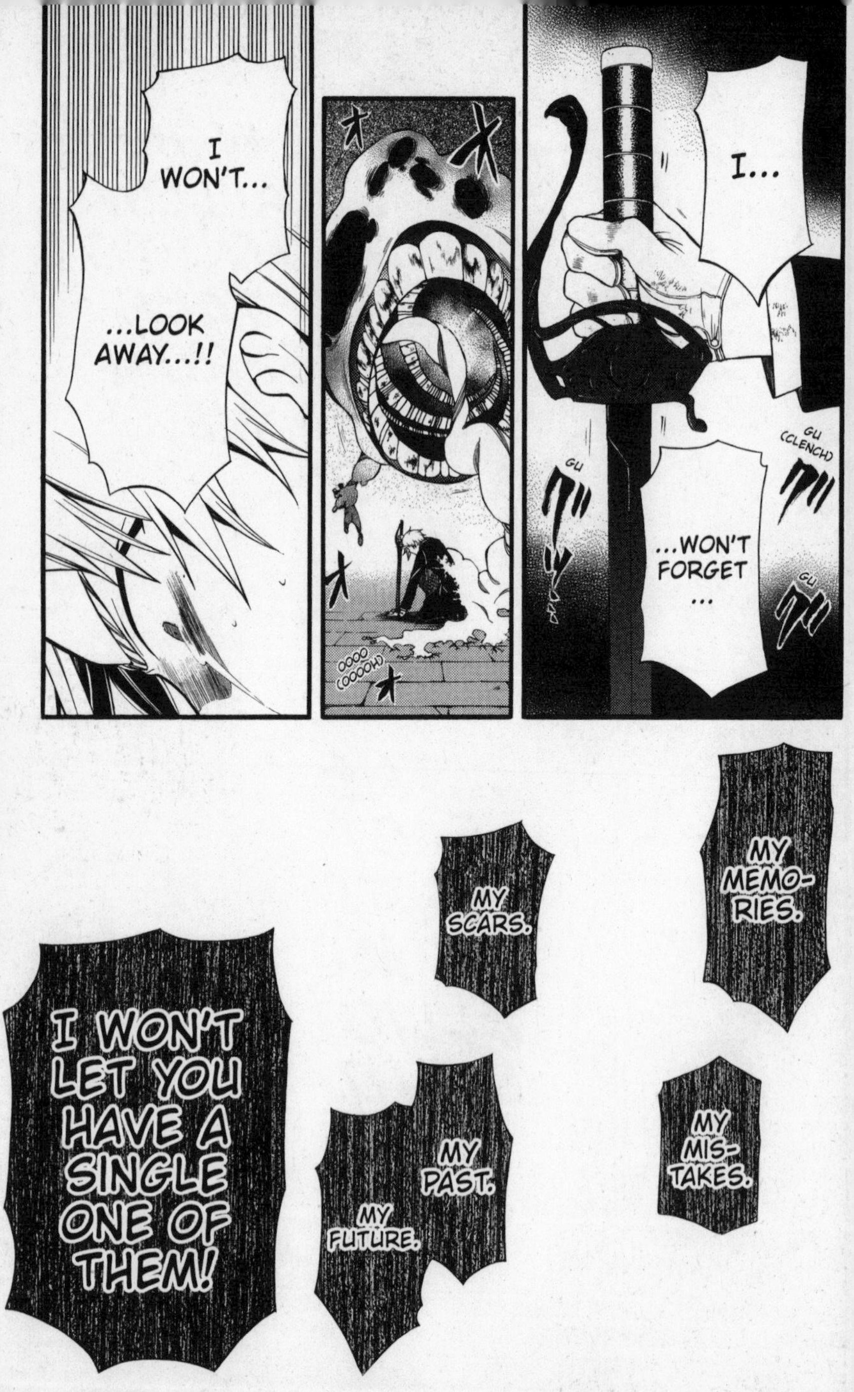
I...
GU (CLENCH)
...WON'T FORGET...
GU
GU
OOOO (OOOOH)
I WON'T...
...LOOK AWAY...!!
MY MEMORIES.
MY SCARS.
MY MISTAKES.
MY PAST.
MY FUTURE.
I WON'T LET YOU HAVE A SINGLE ONE OF THEM!

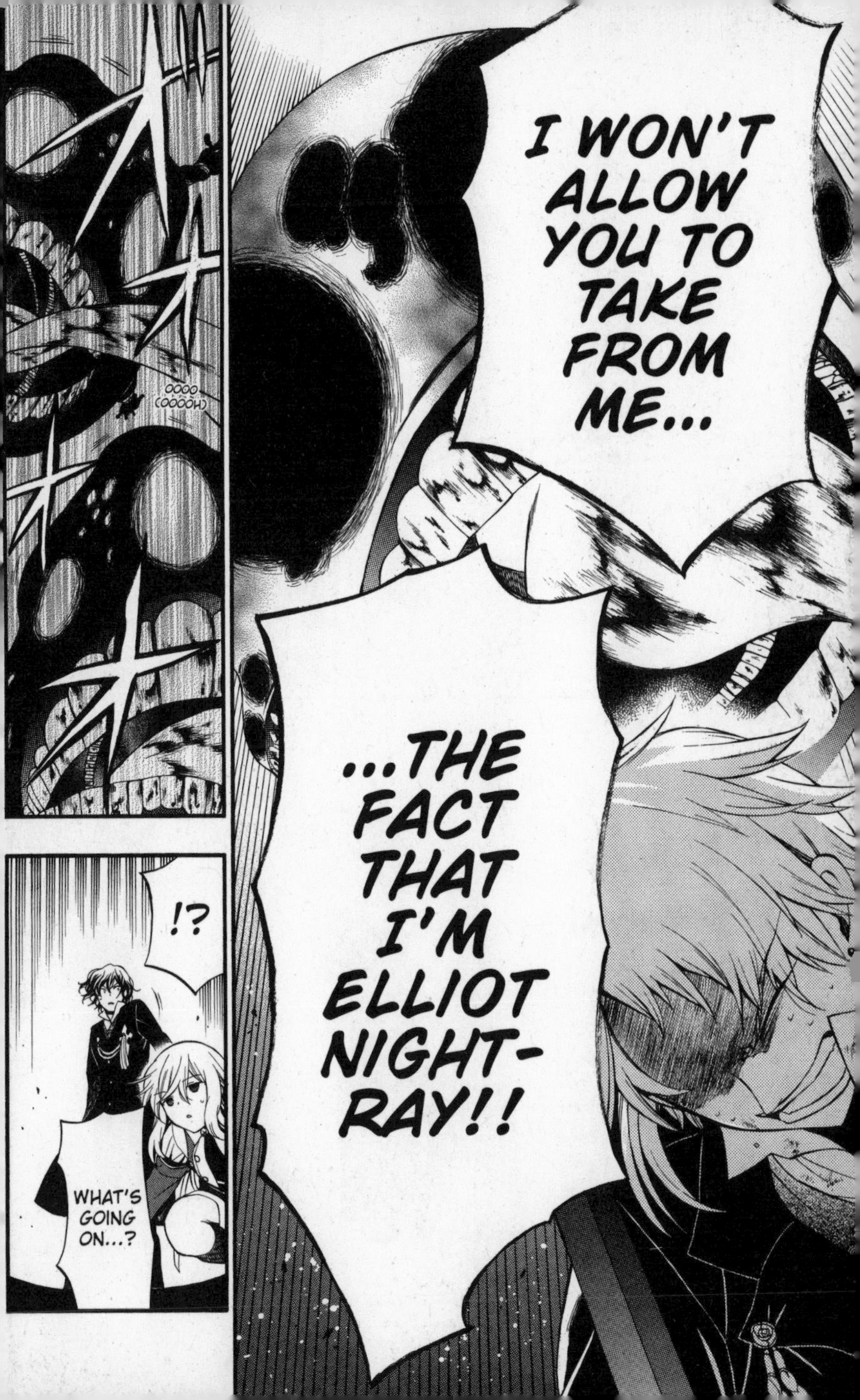
I WON'T ALLOW YOU TO TAKE FROM ME...
...THE FACT THAT I'M ELLIOT NIGHT-RAY!!
OOOO (OOOOH)
!?
WHAT'S GOING ON...?

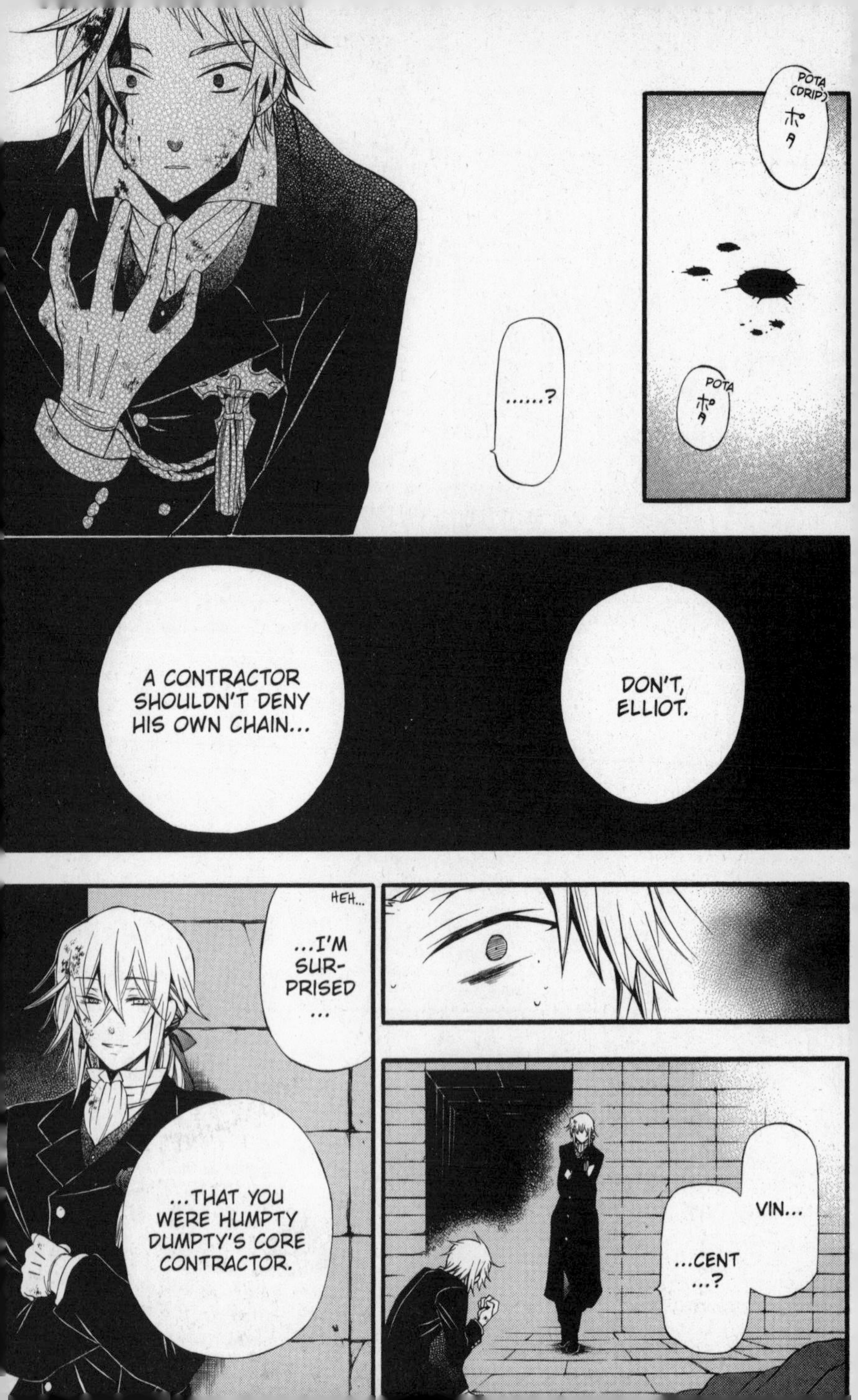
POTA (DRIP) ポタ
POTA ポタ
......?
DON'T, ELLIOT.
A CONTRACTOR SHOULDN'T DENY HIS OWN CHAIN...
VIN...
...CENT ...?
HEH...
...I'M SUR-PRISED ...
...THAT YOU WERE HUMPTY DUMPTY'S CORE CONTRACTOR.

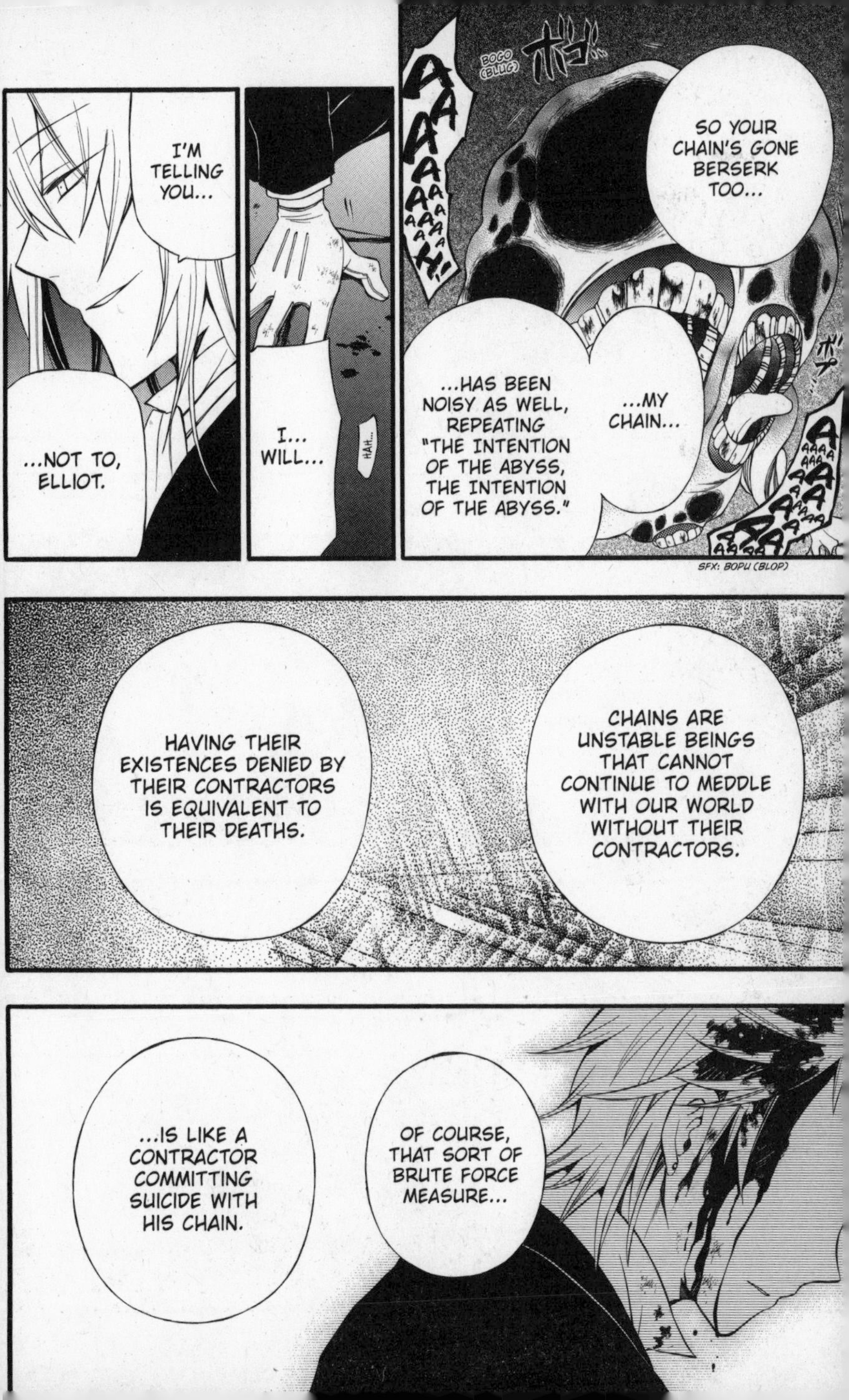
BOGO (BLUG)
SO YOUR CHAIN'S GONE BERSERK TOO...
...MY CHAIN...
...HAS BEEN NOISY AS WELL, REPEATING "THE INTENTION OF THE ABYSS, THE INTENTION OF THE ABYSS."
SFX: BOPU (BLOP)
HAH...
I... WILL...
I'M TELLING YOU...
...NOT TO, ELLIOT.
CHAINS ARE UNSTABLE BEINGS THAT CANNOT CONTINUE TO MEDDLE WITH OUR WORLD WITHOUT THEIR CONTRACTORS.
HAVING THEIR EXISTENCES DENIED BY THEIR CONTRACTORS IS EQUIVALENT TO THEIR DEATHS.
OF COURSE, THAT SORT OF BRUTE FORCE MEASURE...
...IS LIKE A CONTRACTOR COMMITTING SUICIDE WITH HIS CHAIN.

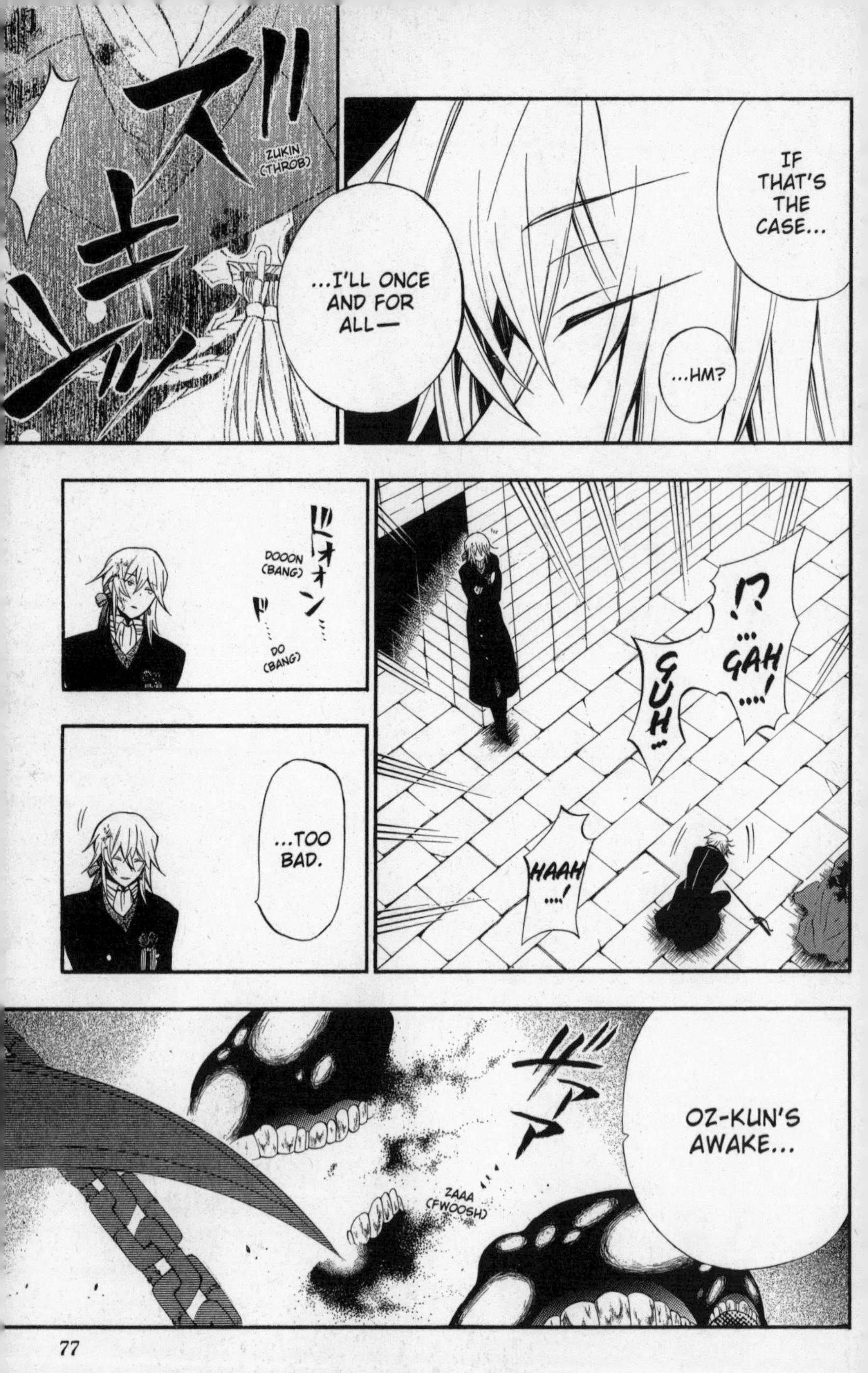
IF THAT'S THE CASE...
...I'LL ONCE AND FOR ALL—
...HM?
ZUKIN (THROB)
!? ...GAH ...!
GUH!!
HAAH ...!
DOOON (BANG)
DO (BANG)
...TOO BAD.
OZ-KUN'S AWAKE...
ZAAA (FWOOSH)

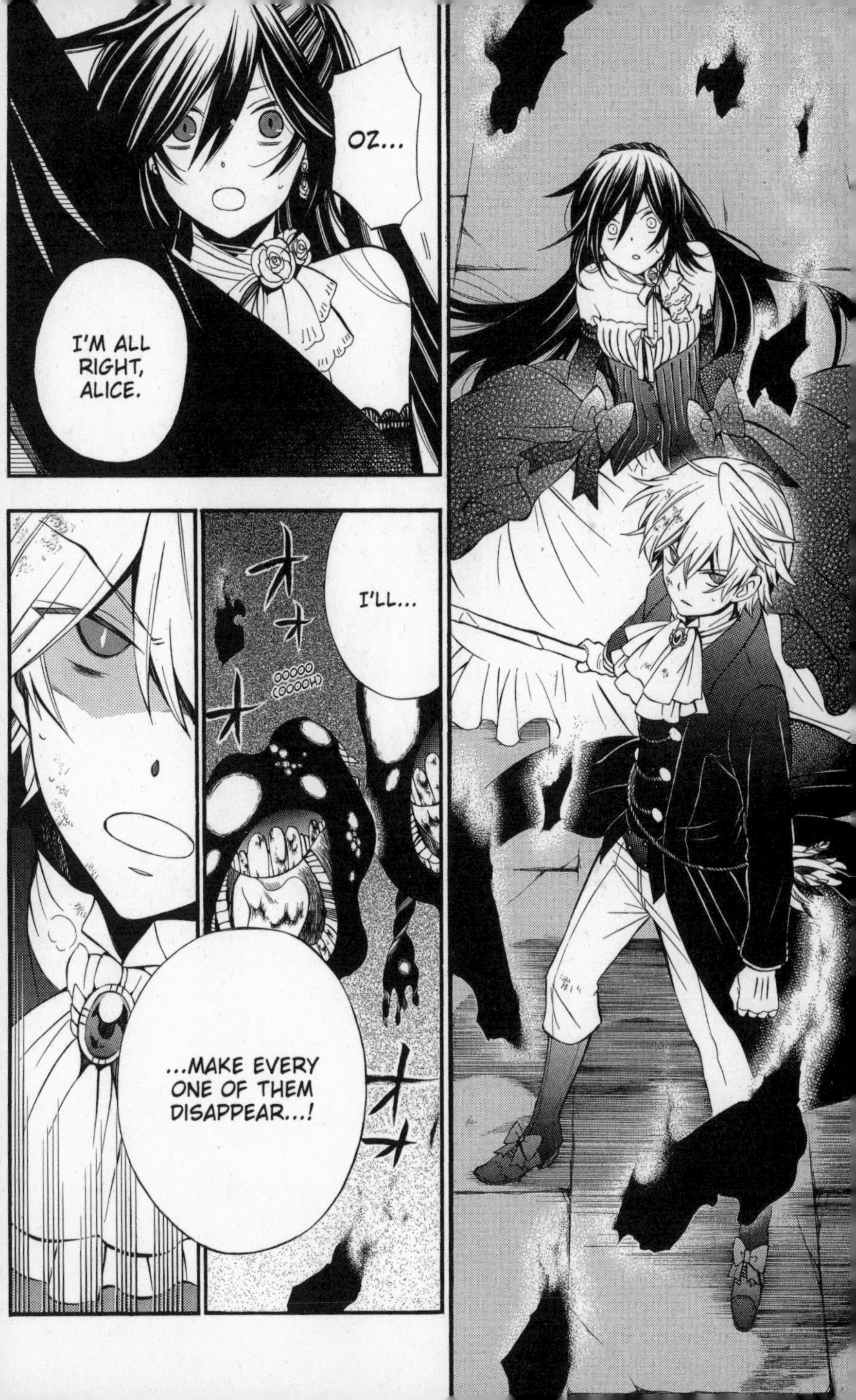
OZ...
I'M ALL RIGHT, ALICE.
I'LL...
OOOOO (OOOOH)
...MAKE EVERY ONE OF THEM DISAPPEAR...!

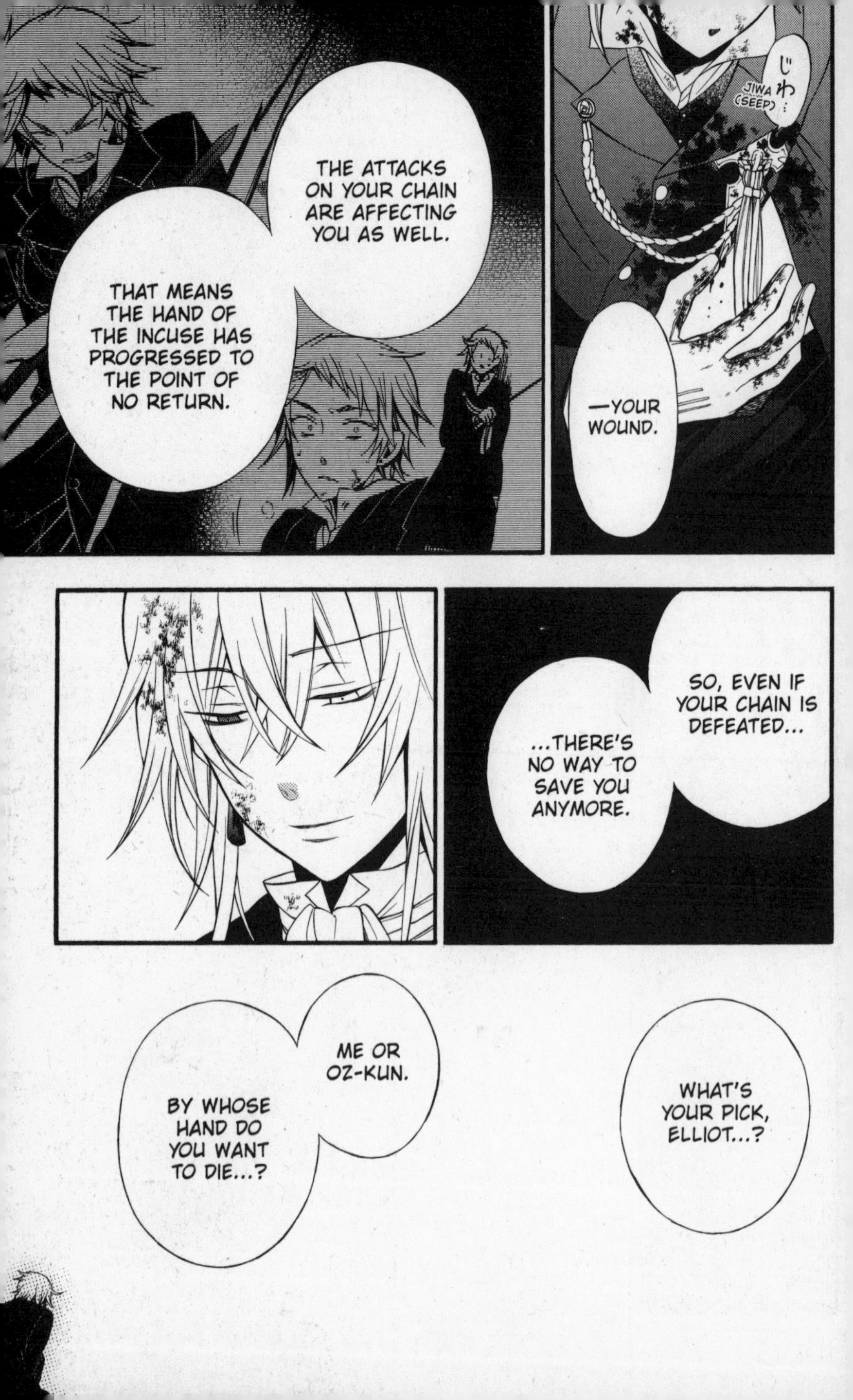
じわ…
JIWA (SEEP)
—YOUR WOUND.
THE ATTACKS ON YOUR CHAIN ARE AFFECTING YOU AS WELL.
THAT MEANS THE HAND OF THE INCUSE HAS PROGRESSED TO THE POINT OF NO RETURN.
SO, EVEN IF YOUR CHAIN IS DEFEATED...
...THERE'S NO WAY TO SAVE YOU ANYMORE.
ME OR OZ-KUN.
BY WHOSE HAND DO YOU WANT TO DIE...?
WHAT'S YOUR PICK, ELLIOT...?

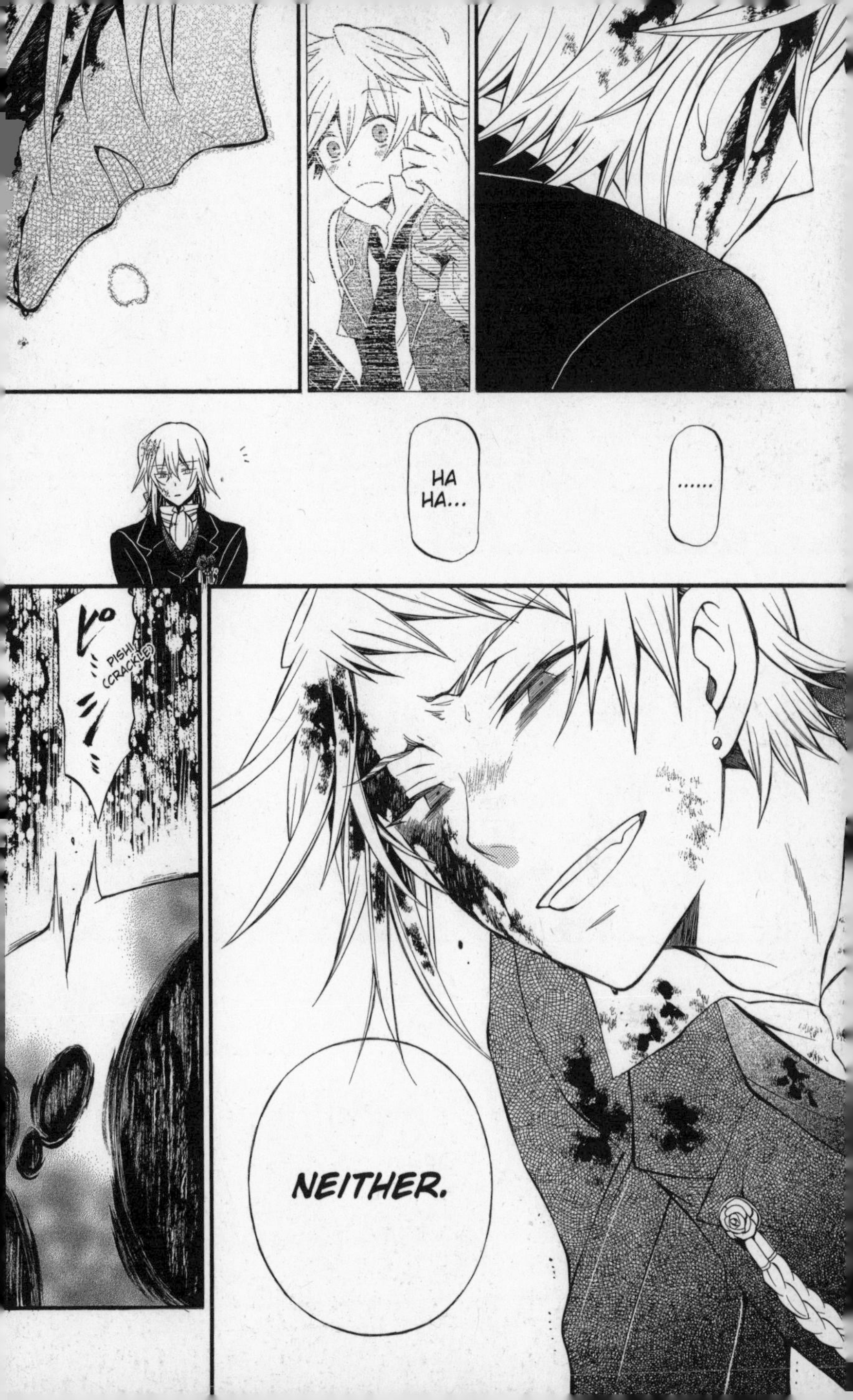
......
HA HA...
NEITHER.
PISHI (CRACKLE)

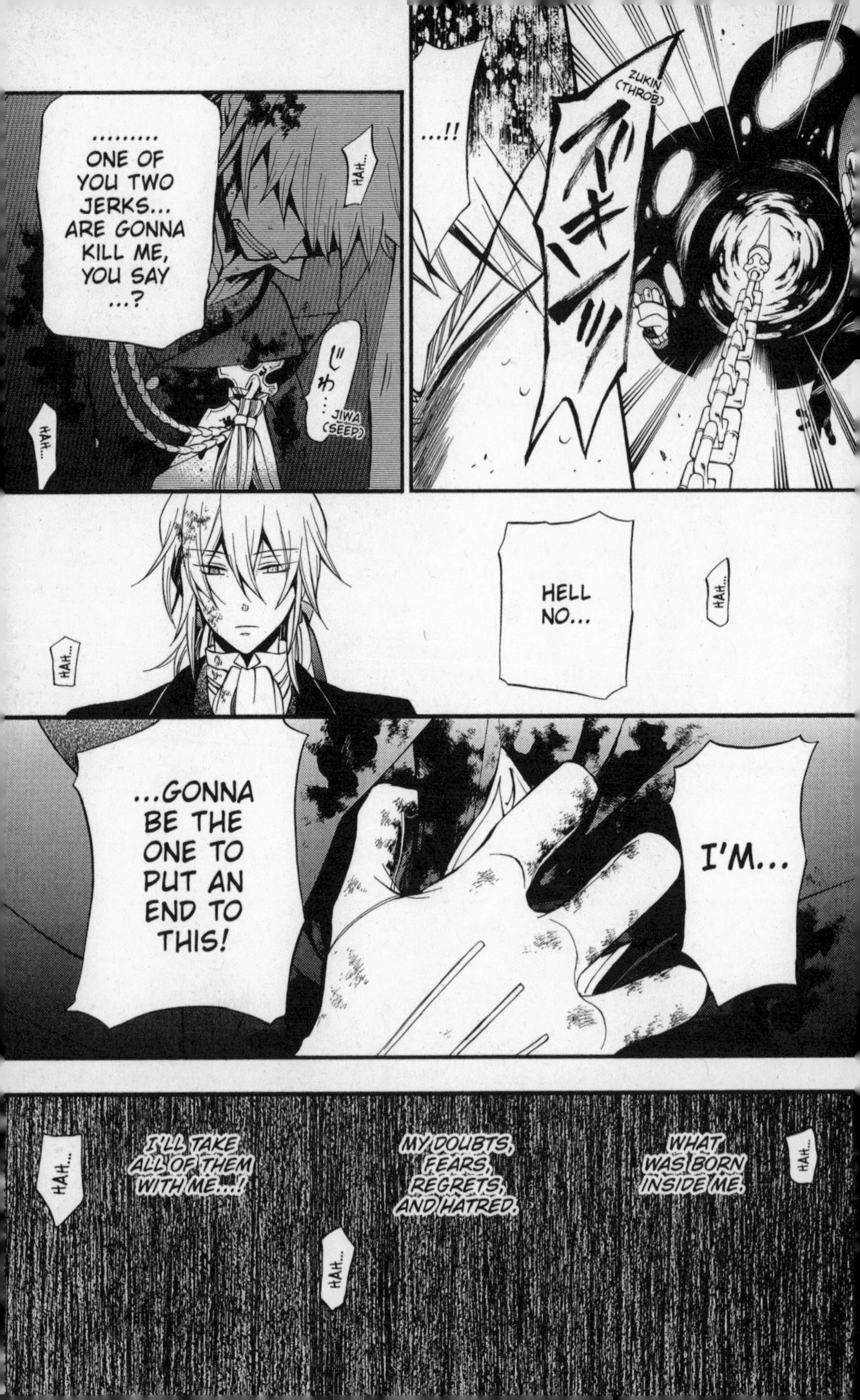
...!!
ZUKIN (THROB)
.... ONE OF YOU TWO JERKS... ARE GONNA KILL ME, YOU SAY ...?
HAH...
じわ...
JIWA (SEEP)
HAH...
HELL NO...
HAH...
HAH...
I'M...
...GONNA BE THE ONE TO PUT AN END TO THIS!
HAH...
WHAT WAS BORN INSIDE ME.
MY DOUBTS, FEARS, REGRETS, AND HATRED.
I'LL TAKE ALL OF THEM WITH ME...!
HAH...
HAH...

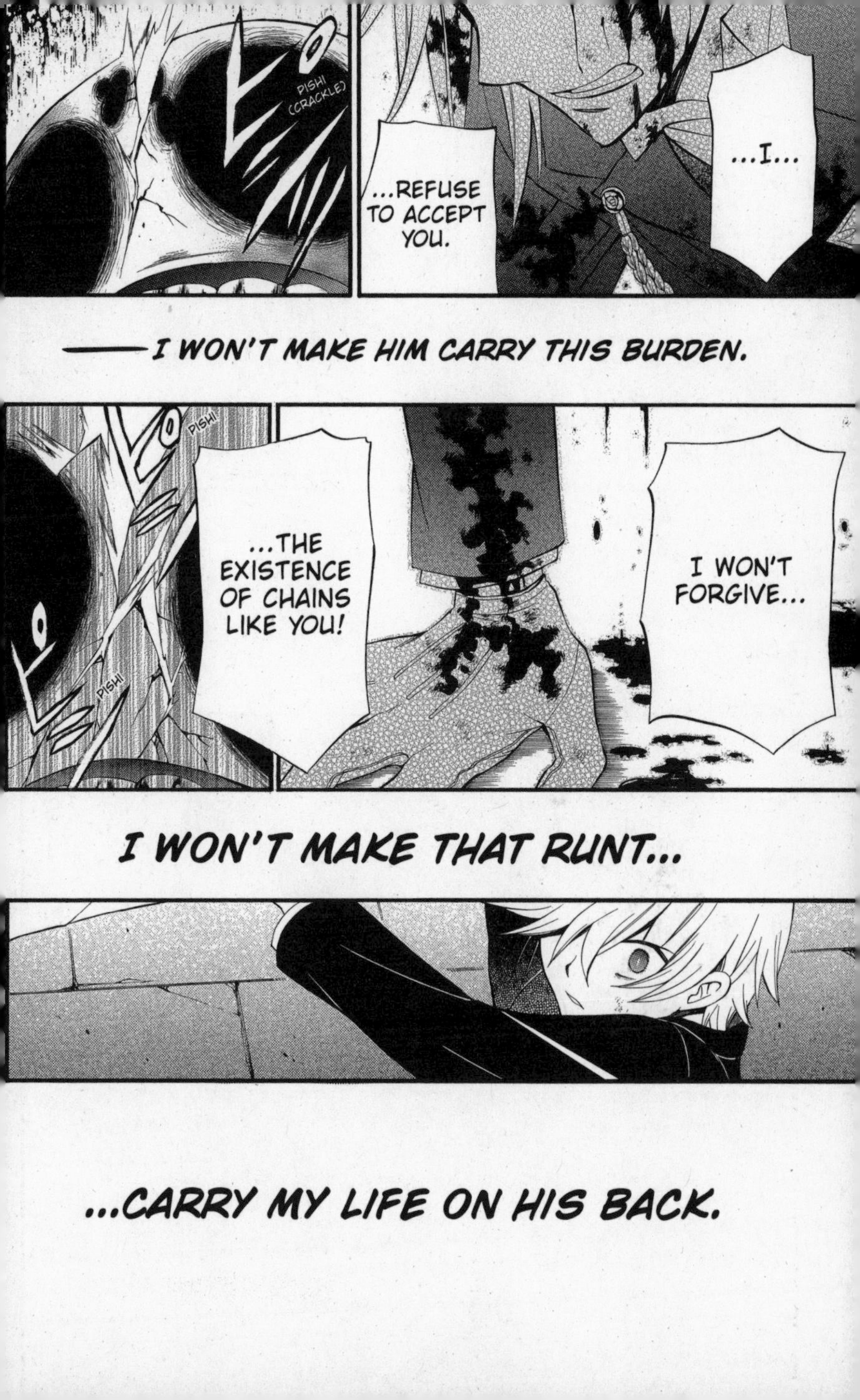
...I...
...REFUSE TO ACCEPT YOU.
PISHI (CRACKLE)
——I WON'T MAKE HIM CARRY THIS BURDEN.
I WON'T FORGIVE...
...THE EXISTENCE OF CHAINS LIKE YOU!
PISHI
PISHI
I WON'T MAKE THAT RUNT...
...CARRY MY LIFE ON HIS BACK.

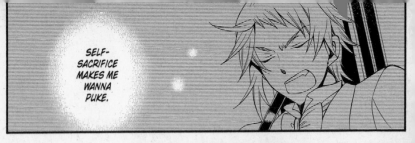

SELF-SACRIFICE MAKES ME WANNA PUKE.

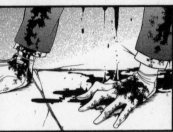

I WONDER WHY THINGS TURNED OUT THIS WAY...

SO TRUE...

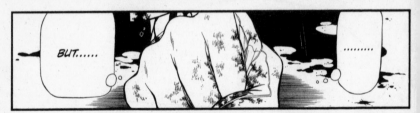

BUT......

....

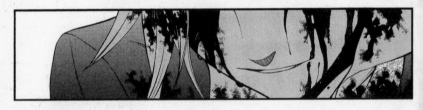

—THAT'S WHY...

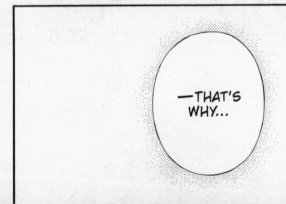

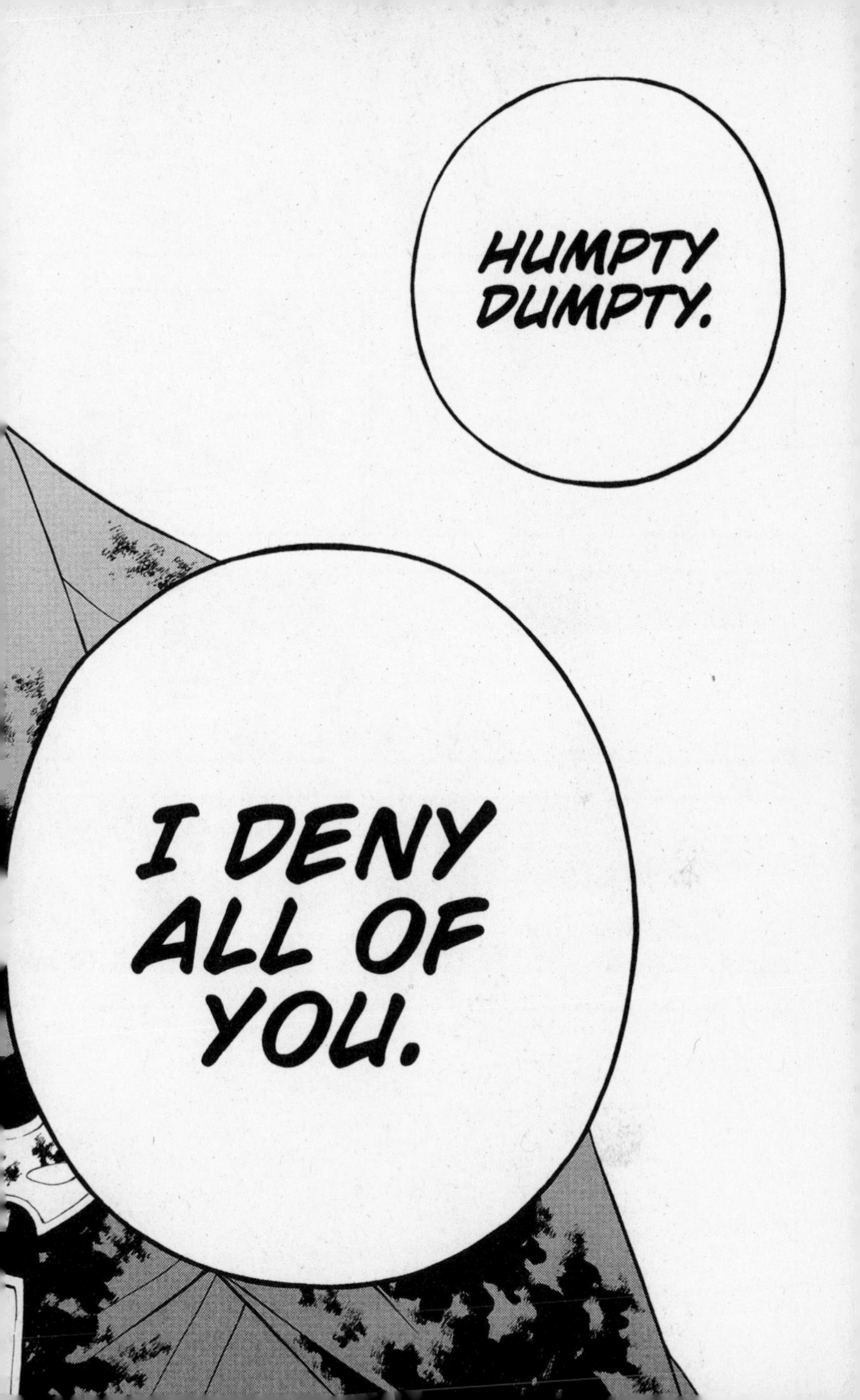
HUMPTY DUMPTY.
I DENY ALL OF YOU.

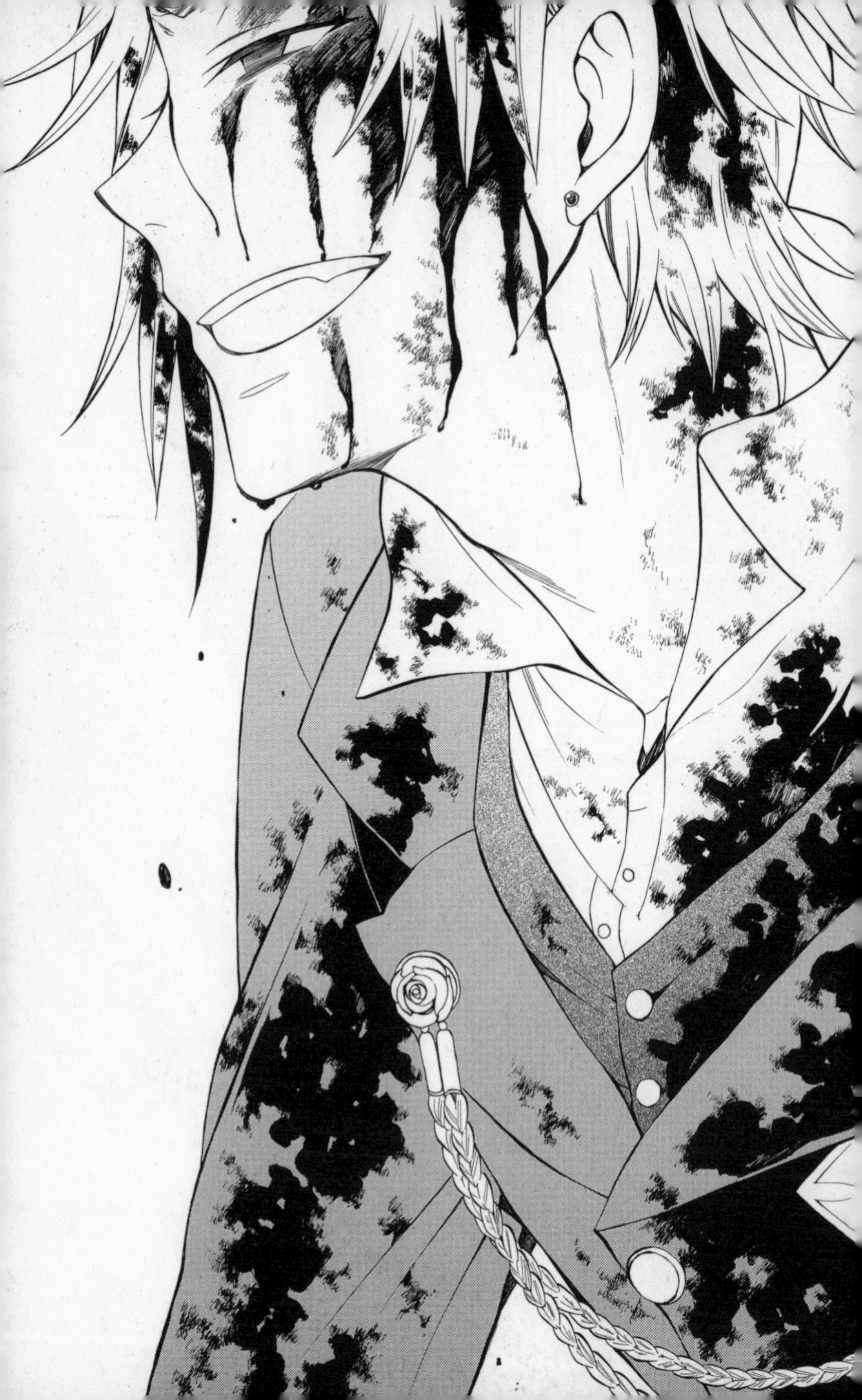

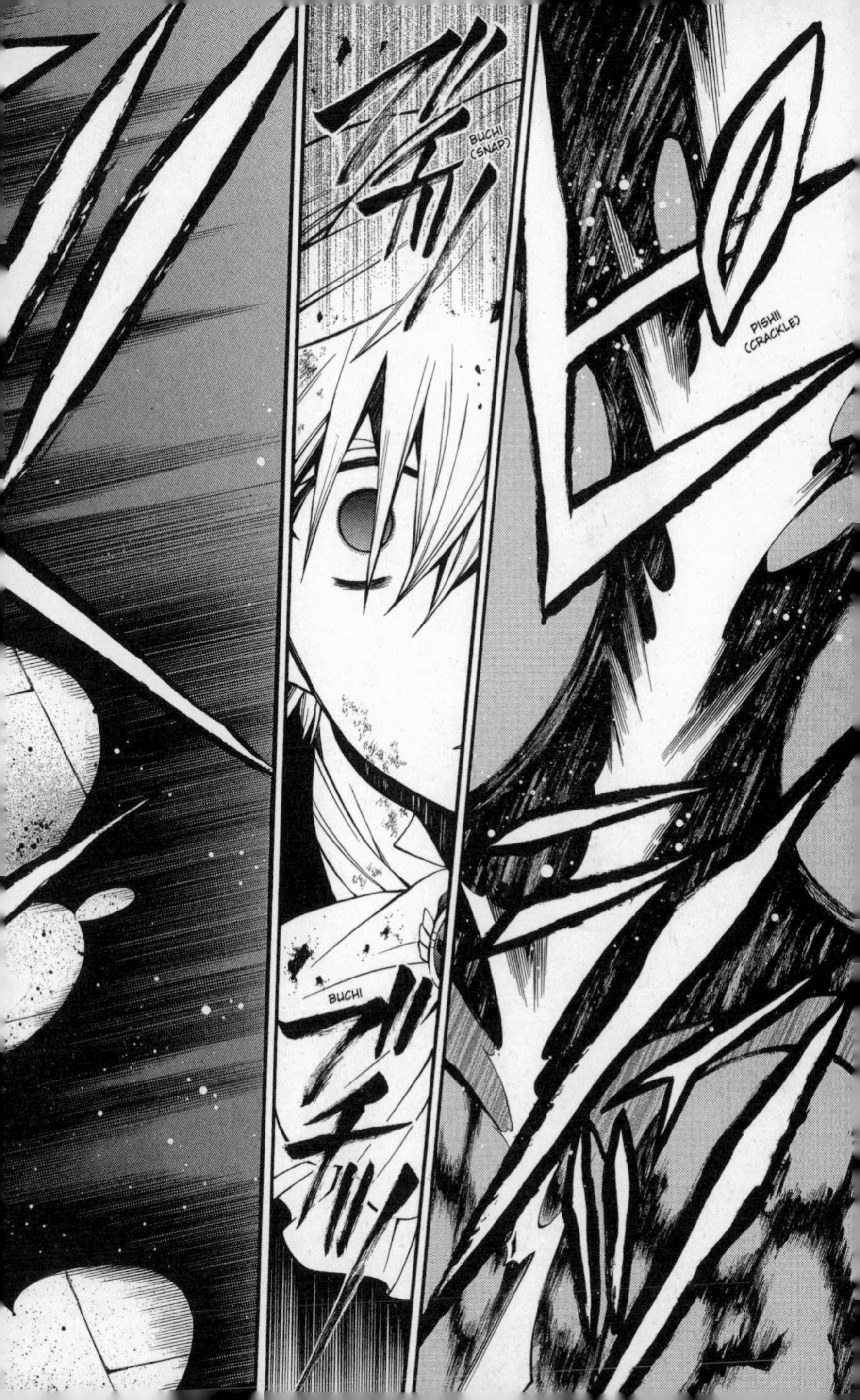
PISHII
(CRACKLE)
BUCHI
(SNAP)
BUCHI

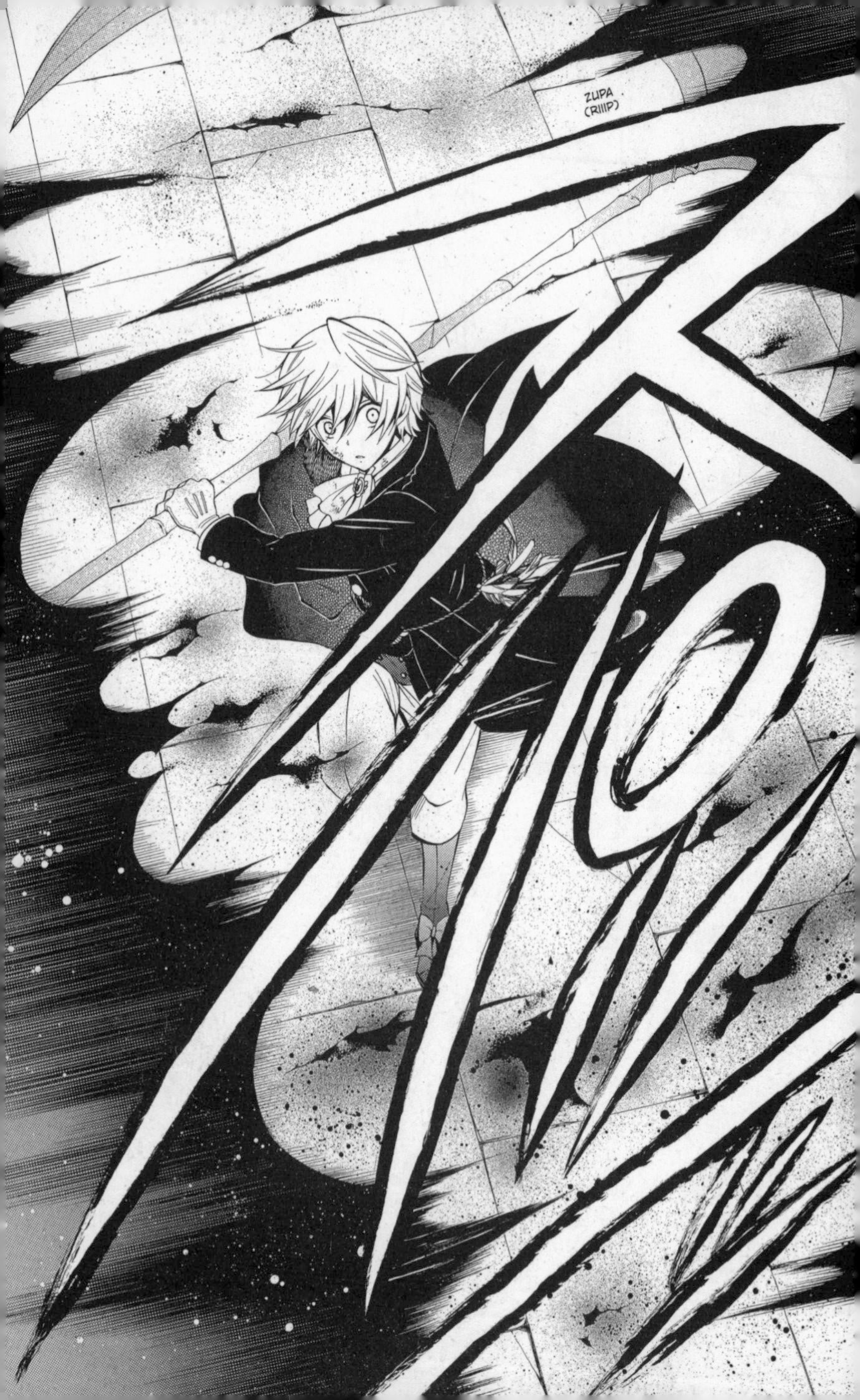
ZUPA
(RIIIP)

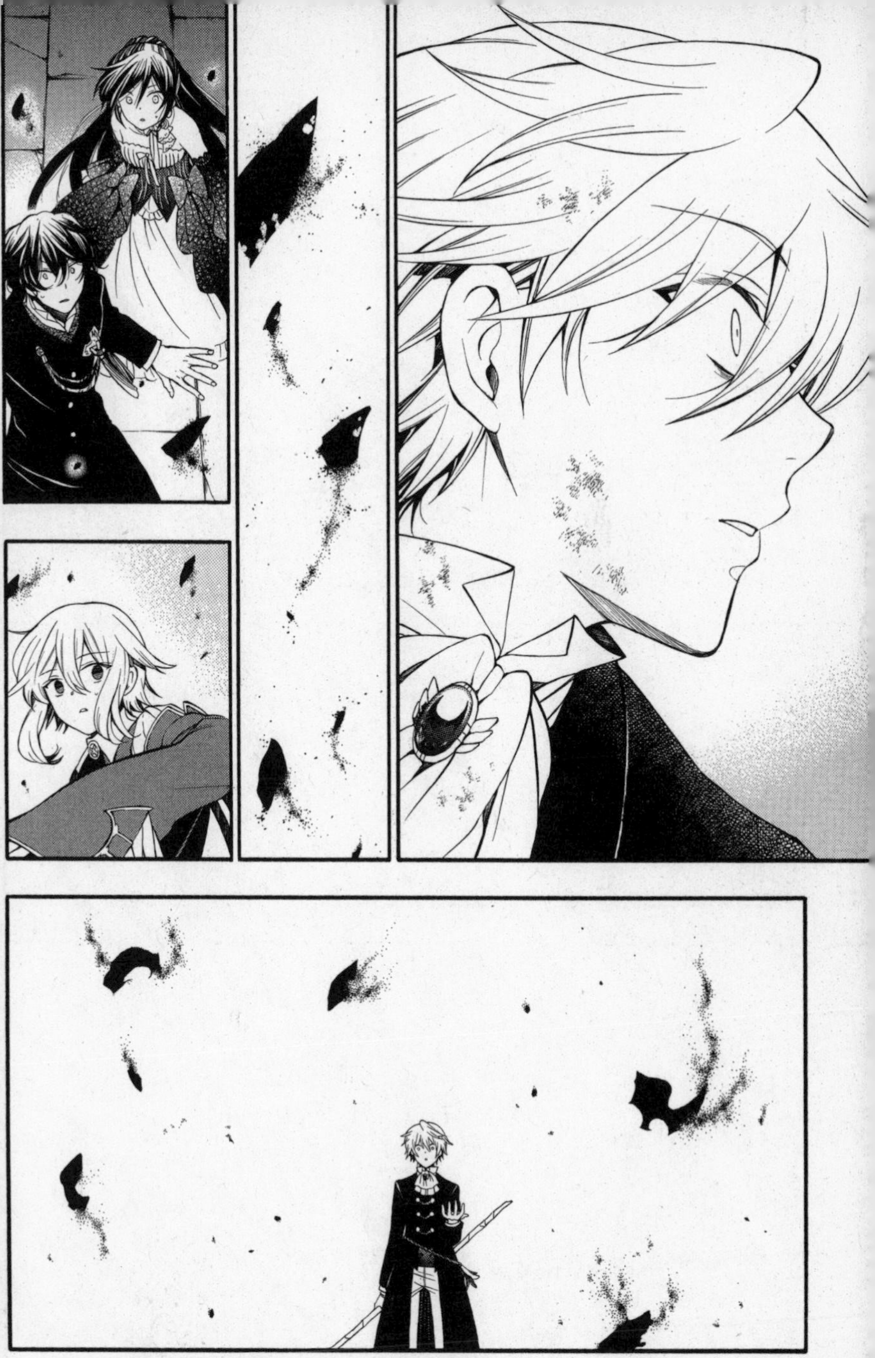

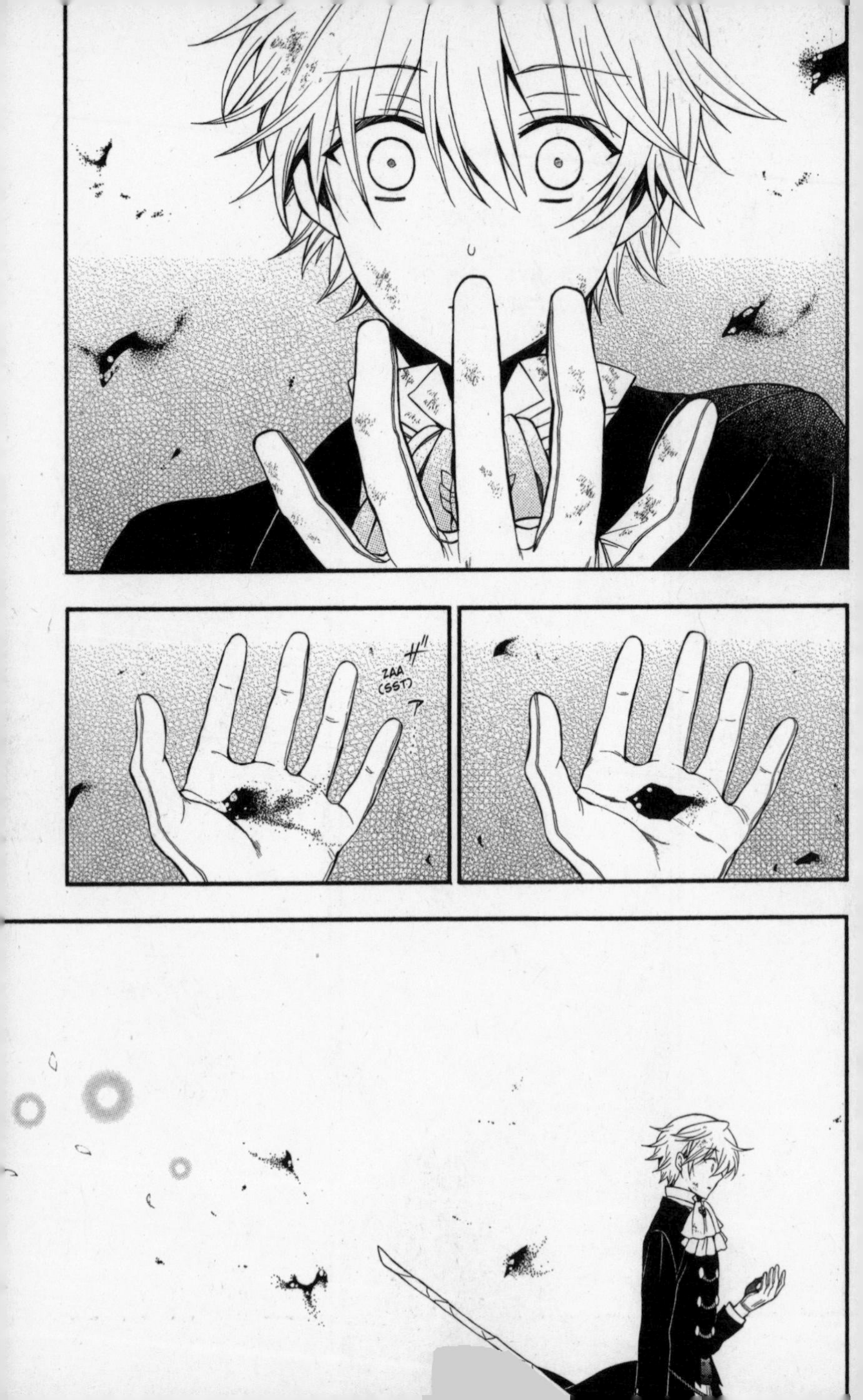
ZAA
(SST)

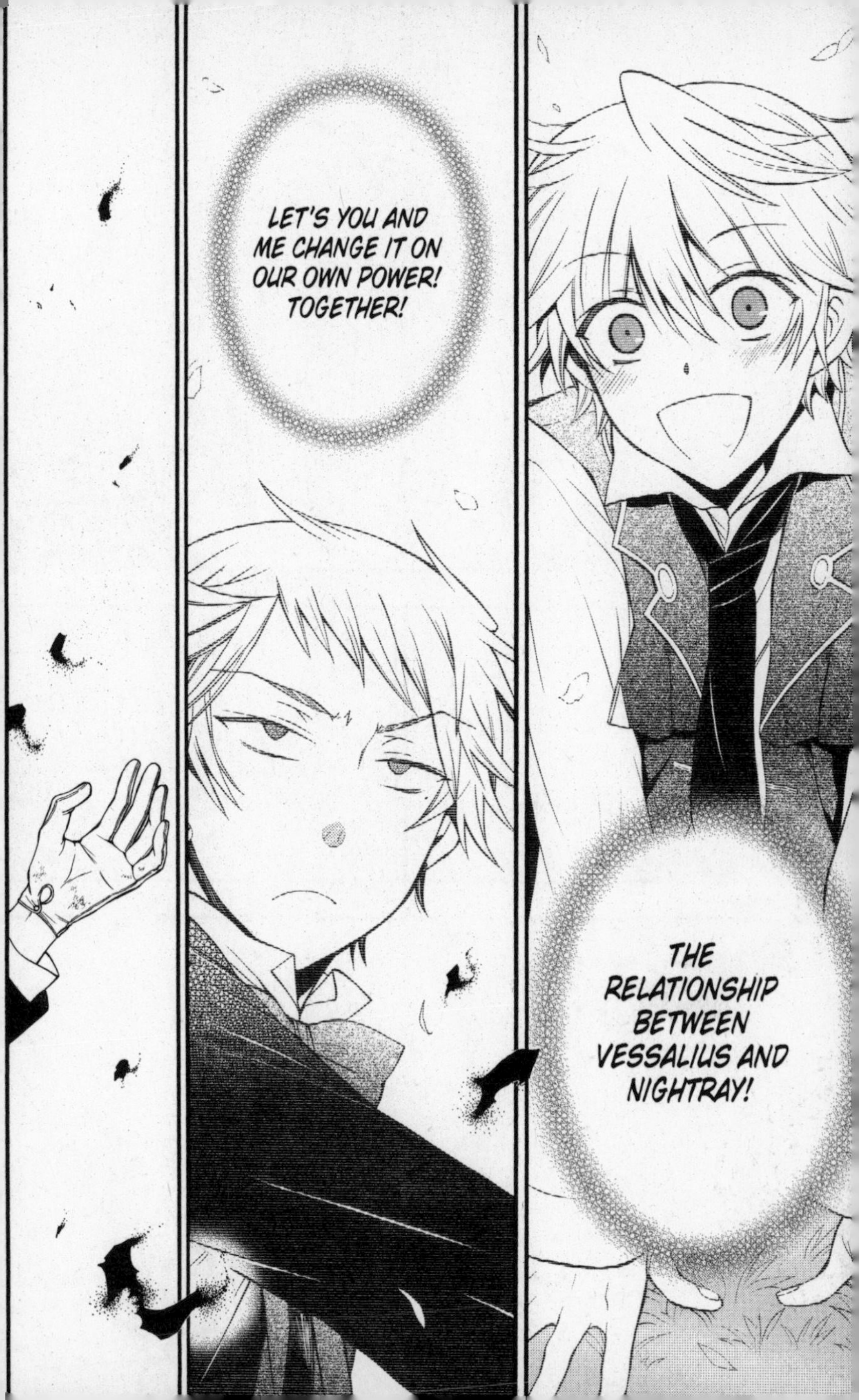
THE RELATIONSHIP BETWEEN VESSALIUS AND NIGHTRAY!
LET'S YOU AND ME CHANGE IT ON OUR OWN POWER! TOGETHER!

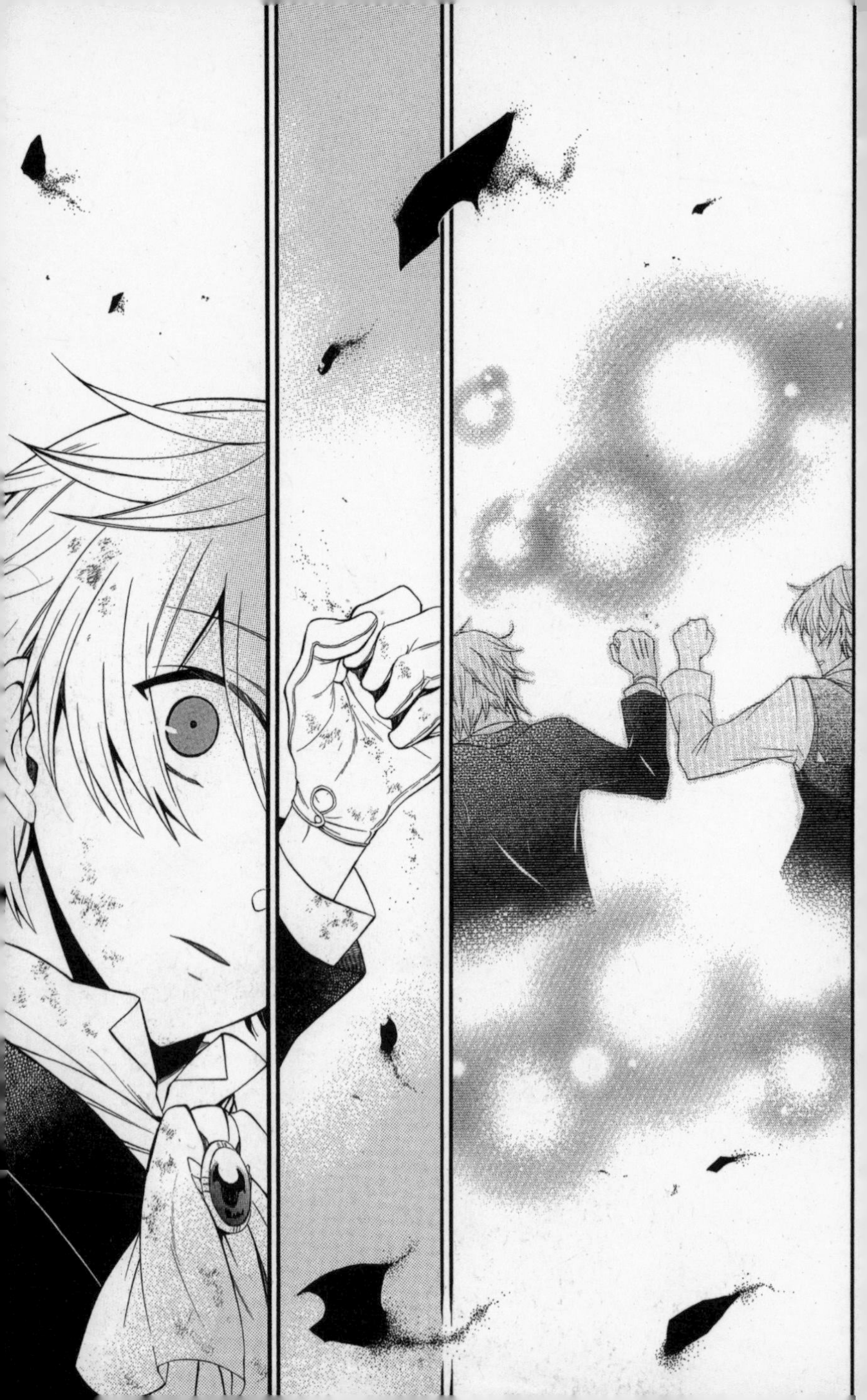

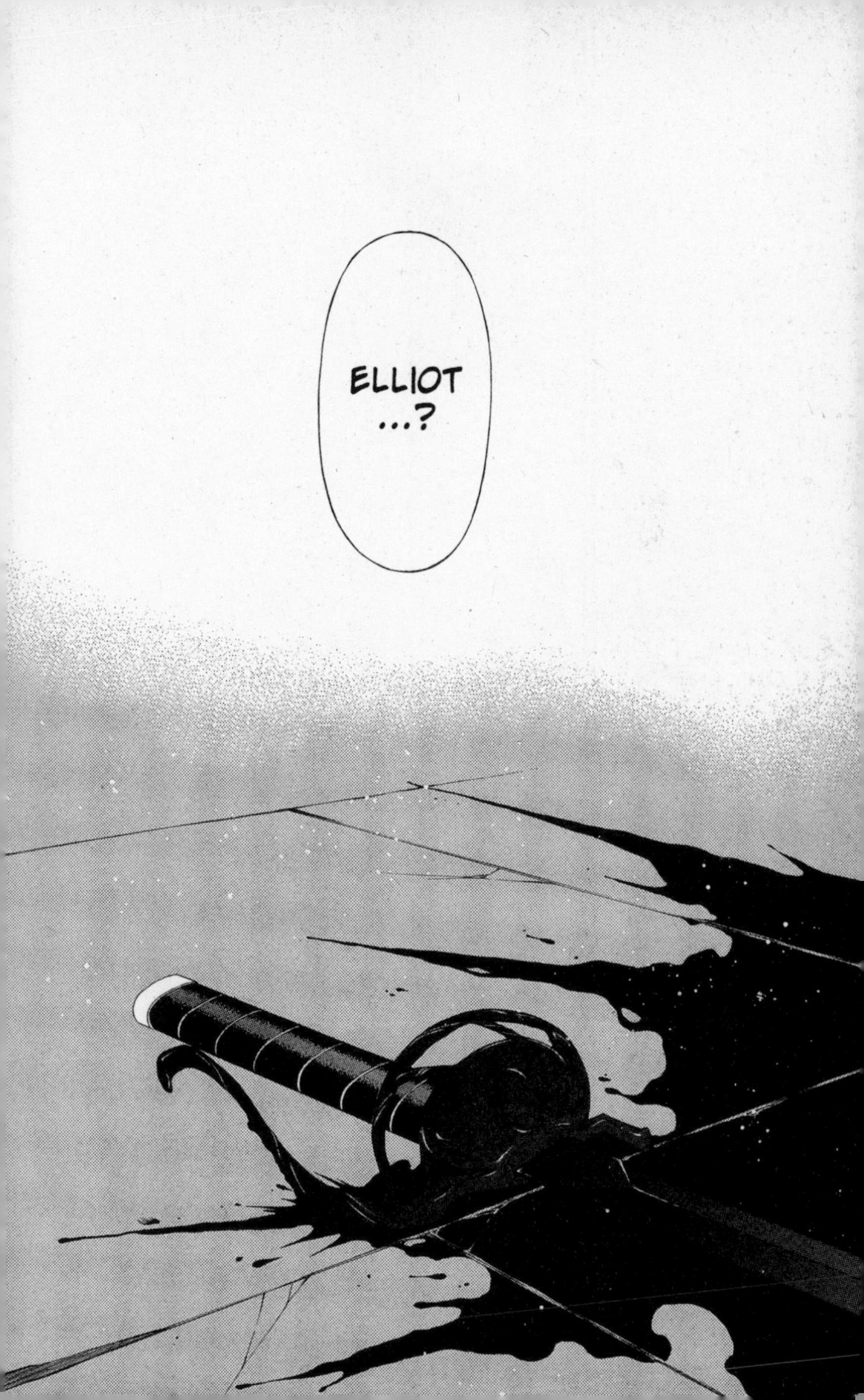
ELLIOT ...?

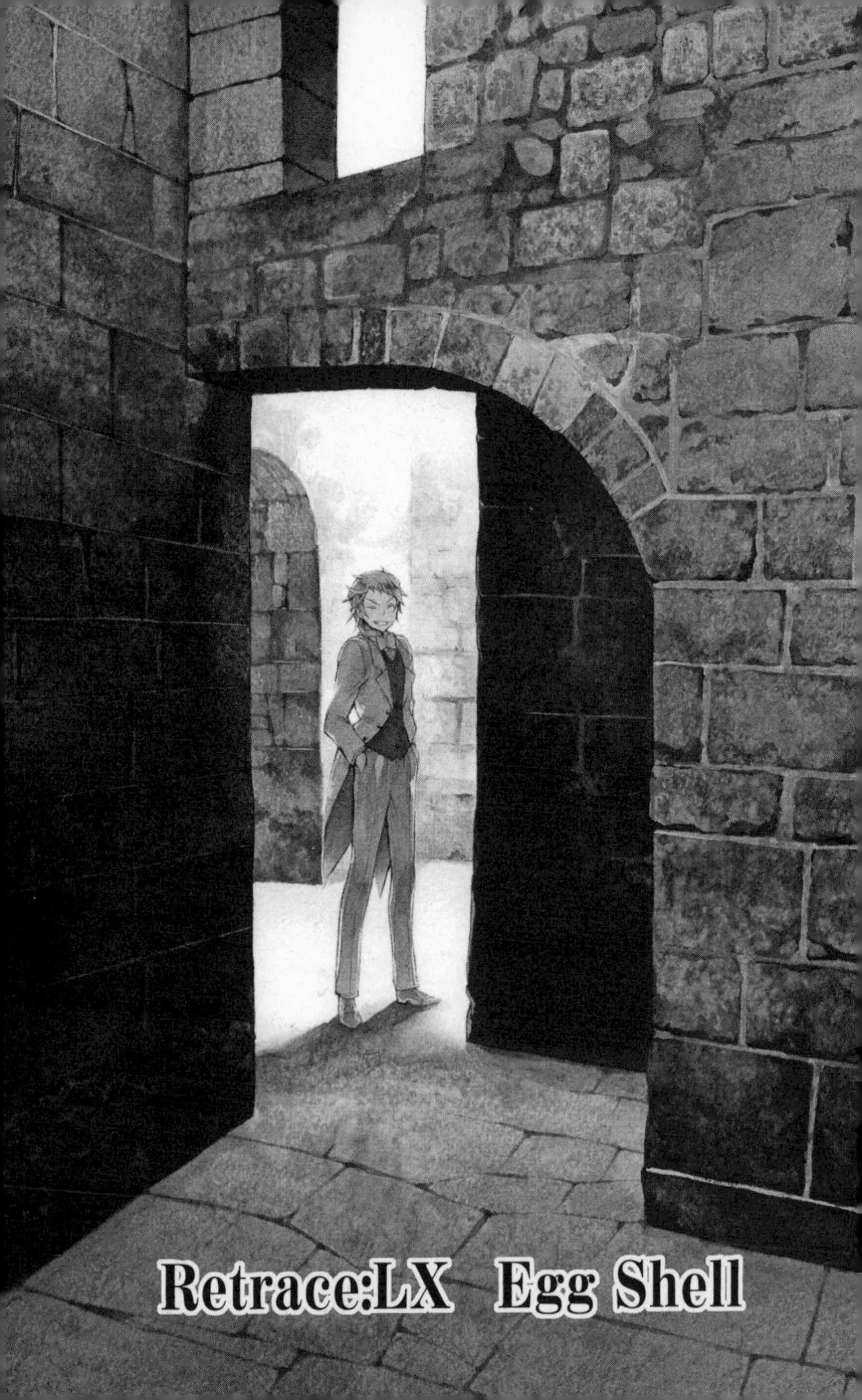

Retrace:LX Egg Shell

—BONUS MANGA UNDER VOLUNTARY RESTRAINT—

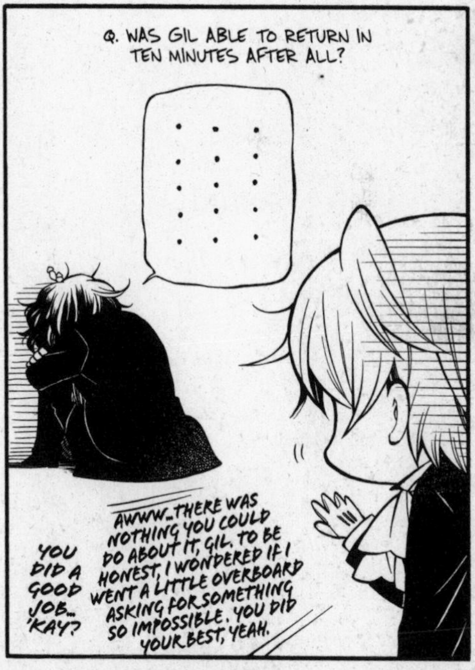
Q. WAS GIL ABLE TO RETURN IN TEN MINUTES AFTER ALL?
AWWW...THERE WAS NOTHING YOU COULD DO ABOUT IT, GIL. TO BE HONEST, I WONDERED IF I WENT A LITTLE OVERBOARD ASKING FOR SOMETHING SO IMPOSSIBLE. YOU DID YOUR BEST, YEAH.
YOU DID A GOOD JOB... 'KAY?

ELLIOT...

...IS DEAD——

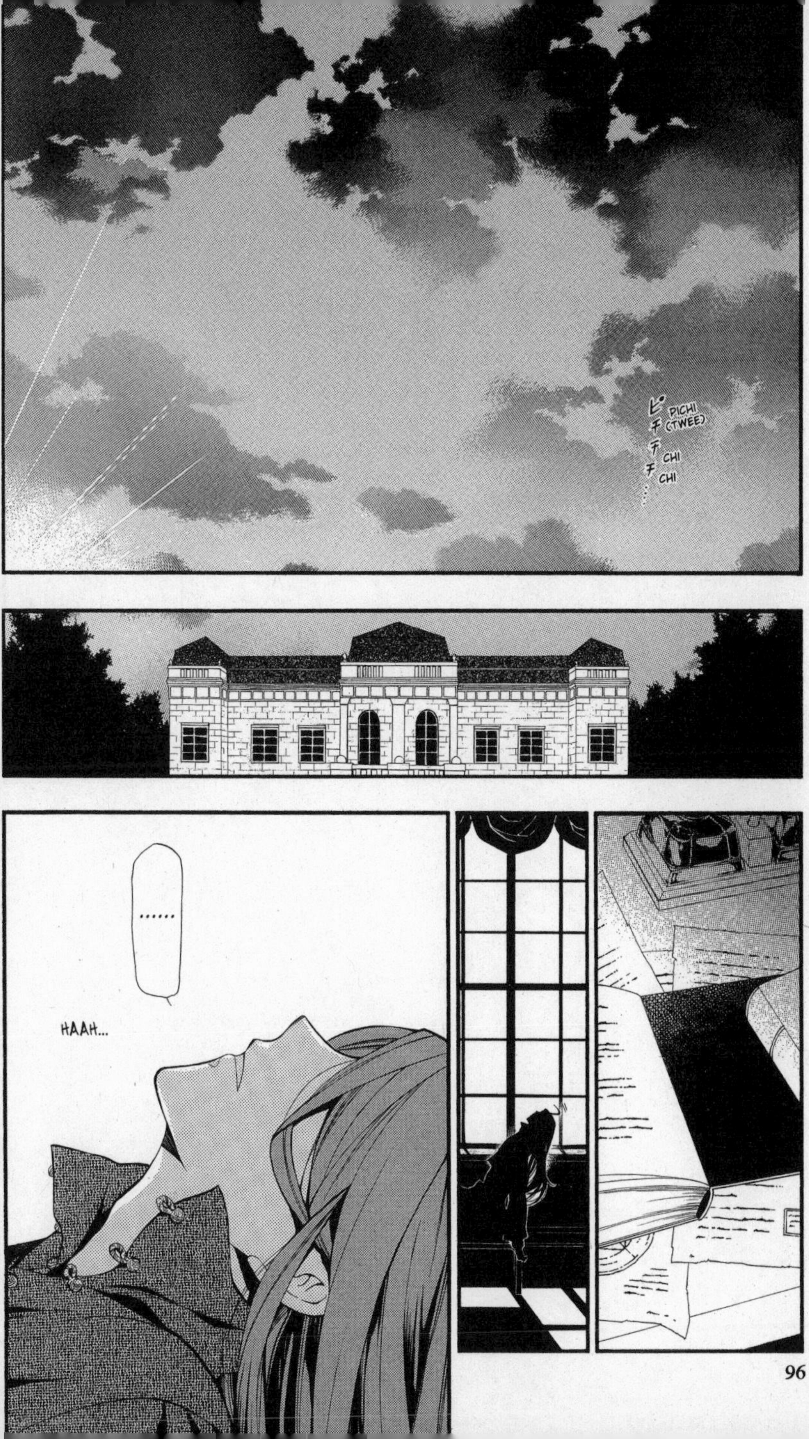
ピ PICHI (TWEE)
チ
チ CHI
チ CHI
…
......
HAAH...

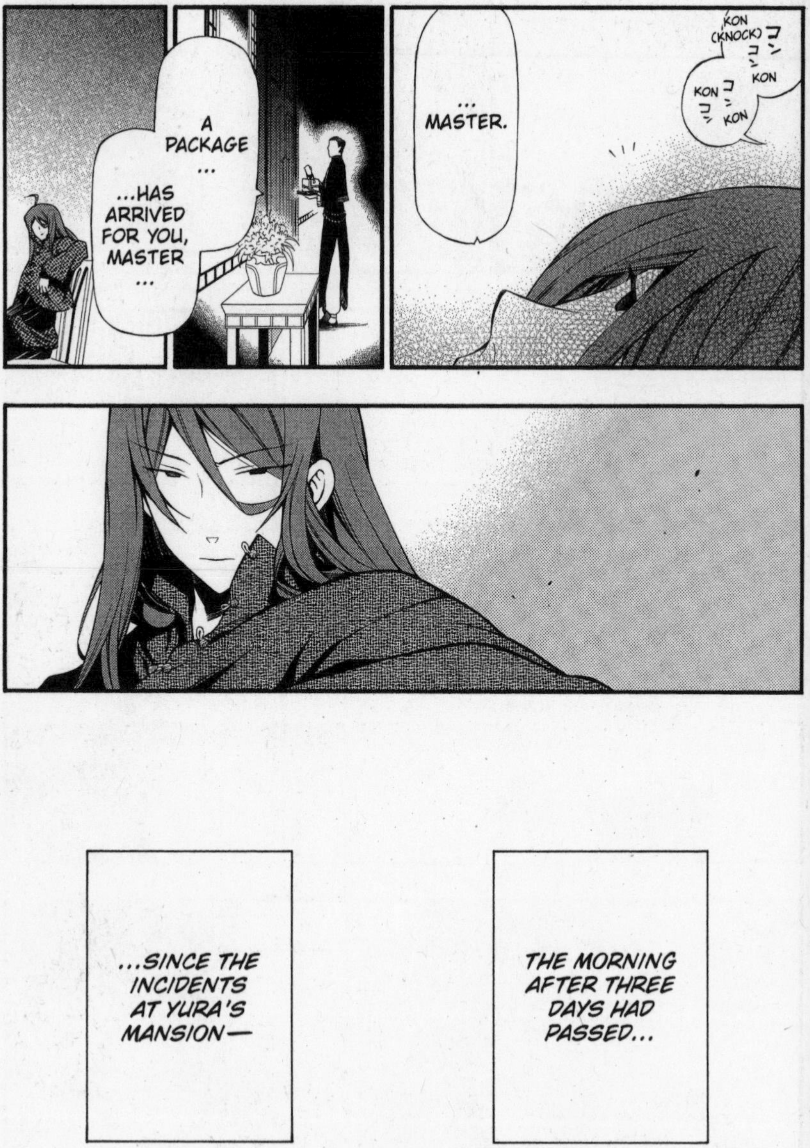
KON (KNOCK) コン
コン KON
KON コン
コン KON
... MASTER.
A PACKAGE ...
...HAS ARRIVED FOR YOU, MASTER ...
THE MORNING AFTER THREE DAYS HAD PASSED...
...SINCE THE INCIDENTS AT YURA'S MANSION—

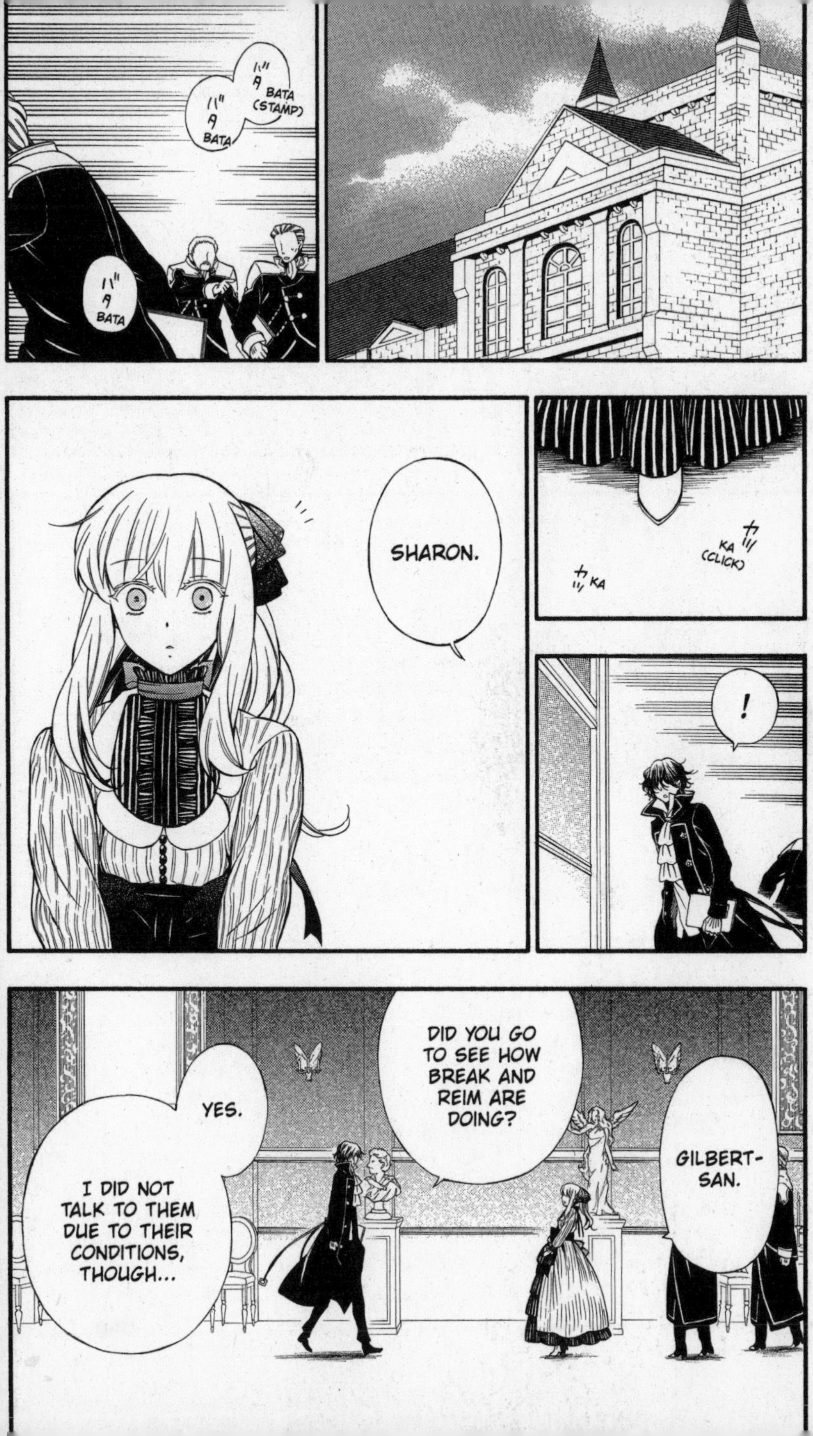
バタ
BATA (STAMP)
バタ
BATA
バタ
BATA
カッ
KA (CLICK)
カッ
KA
!
SHARON.
GILBERT-SAN.
DID YOU GO TO SEE HOW BREAK AND REIM ARE DOING?
YES.
I DID NOT TALK TO THEM DUE TO THEIR CONDITIONS, THOUGH...

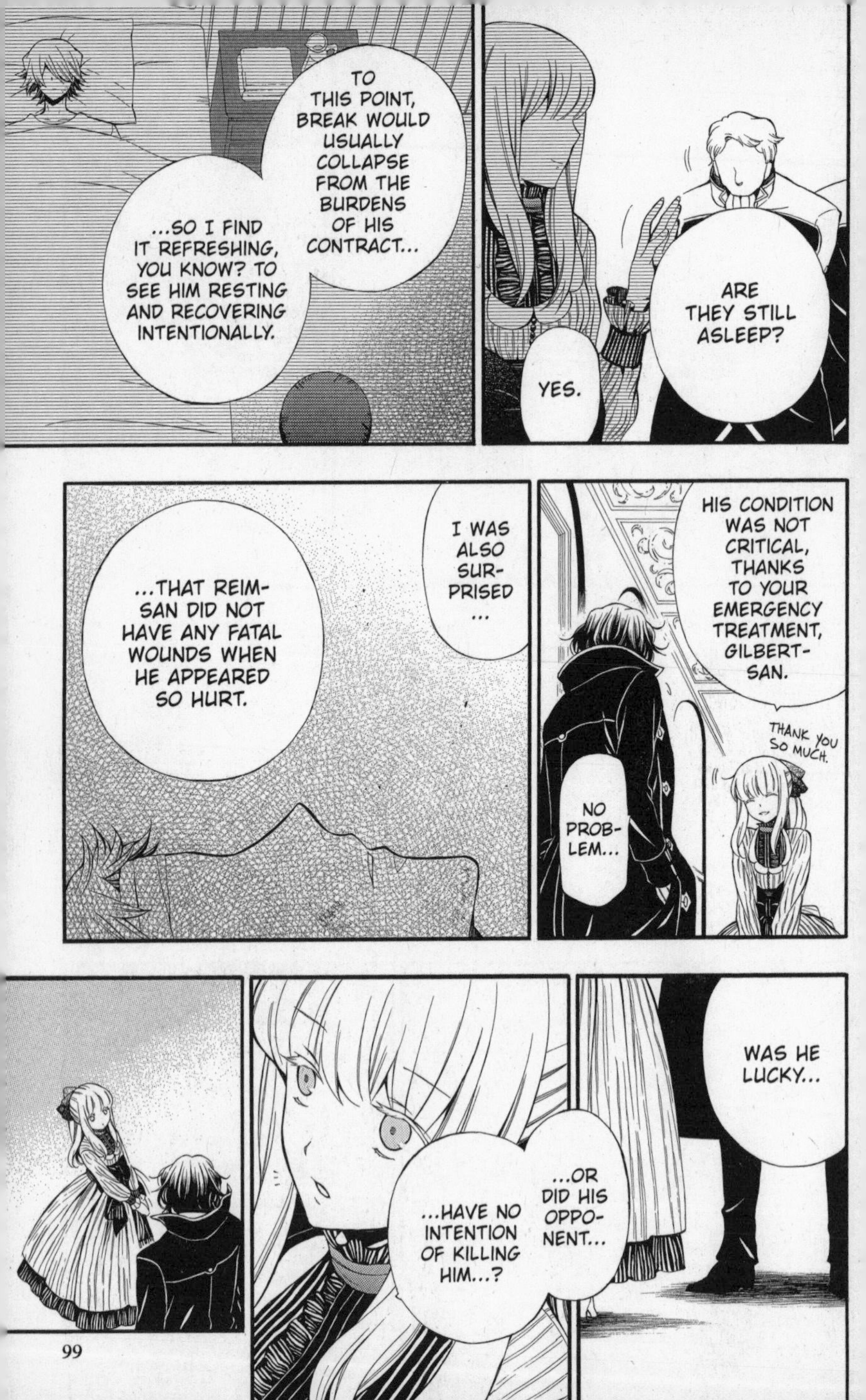
ARE THEY STILL ASLEEP?
YES.
TO THIS POINT, BREAK WOULD USUALLY COLLAPSE FROM THE BURDENS OF HIS CONTRACT...
...SO I FIND IT REFRESHING, YOU KNOW? TO SEE HIM RESTING AND RECOVERING INTENTIONALLY.
HIS CONDITION WAS NOT CRITICAL, THANKS TO YOUR EMERGENCY TREATMENT, GILBERT-SAN.
THANK YOU SO MUCH.
NO PROB-LEM...
I WAS ALSO SUR-PRISED ...
...THAT REIM-SAN DID NOT HAVE ANY FATAL WOUNDS WHEN HE APPEARED SO HURT.
WAS HE LUCKY...
...OR DID HIS OPPO-NENT...
...HAVE NO INTENTION OF KILLING HIM...?

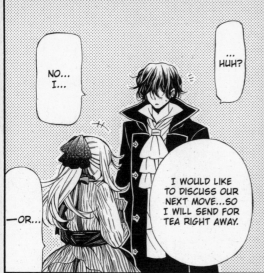

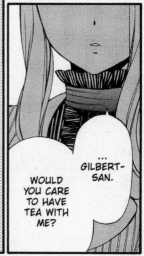

...
GILBERT-SAN.
WOULD YOU CARE TO HAVE TEA WITH ME?
...
HUH?
NO...
I...
I WOULD LIKE TO DISCUSS OUR NEXT MOVE...SO I WILL SEND FOR TEA RIGHT AWAY.
—OR...
...ARE YOU IMPLYING YOU CANNOT DRINK A TEA OF MY RECOMMENDATION...?
ZAWA (MURMUR)
...I'LL HAVE SOME.
.....
SHARON... SORRY, BUT I'M GOING BACK TO OZ—
!
HOW IS OZ-SAMA DOING?

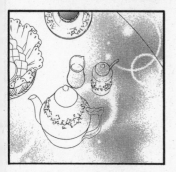

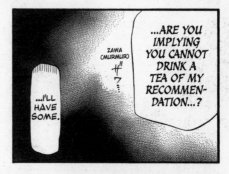

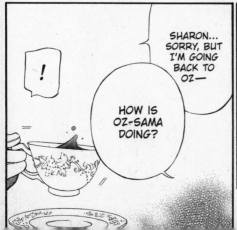

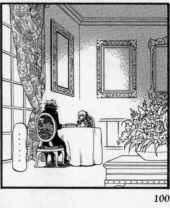

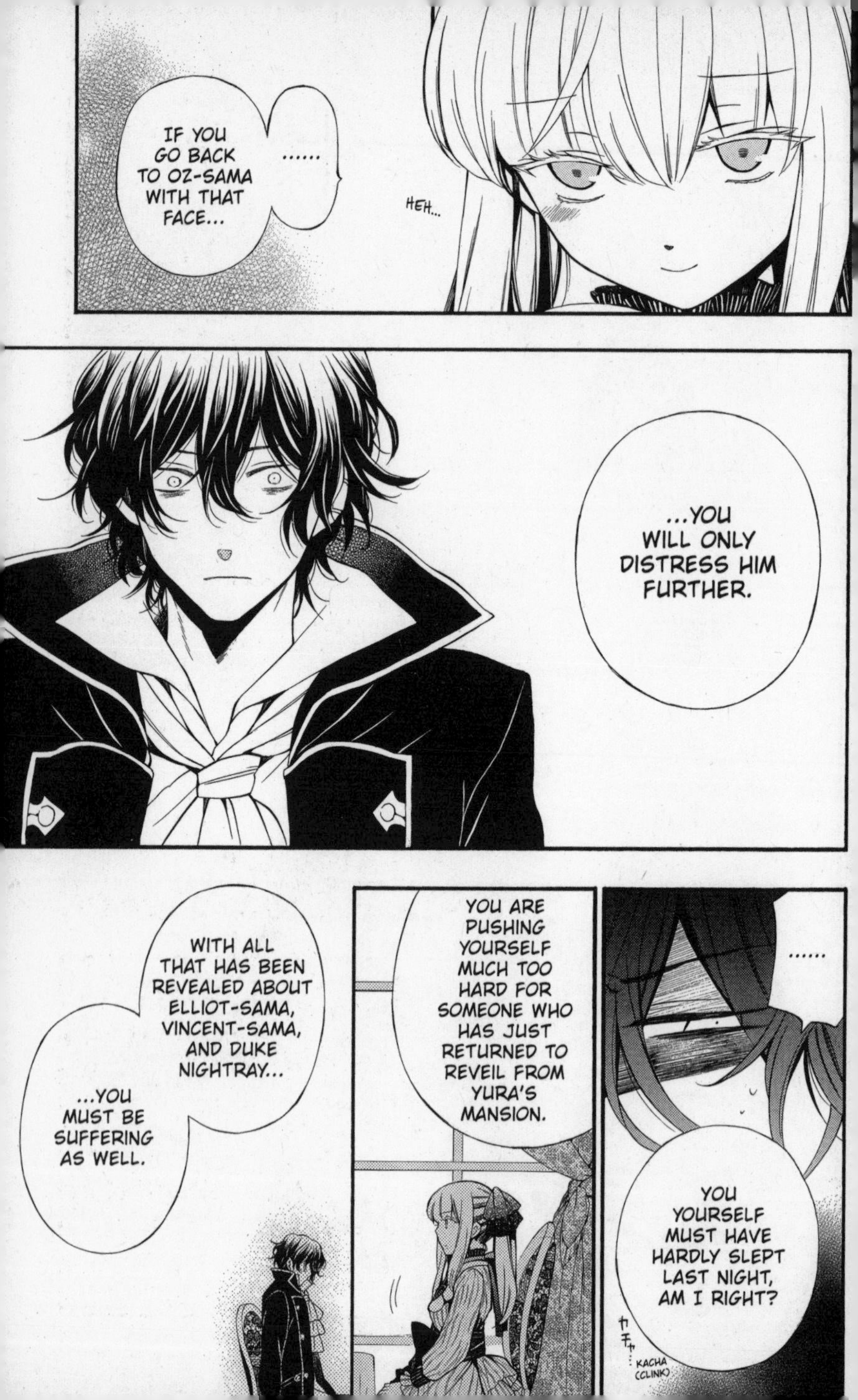
HEH...
......
IF YOU GO BACK TO OZ-SAMA WITH THAT FACE...
...YOU WILL ONLY DISTRESS HIM FURTHER.
......
YOU YOURSELF MUST HAVE HARDLY SLEPT LAST NIGHT, AM I RIGHT?
KACHA (CLINK)
YOU ARE PUSHING YOURSELF MUCH TOO HARD FOR SOMEONE WHO HAS JUST RETURNED TO REVEIL FROM YURA'S MANSION.
WITH ALL THAT HAS BEEN REVEALED ABOUT ELLIOT-SAMA, VINCENT-SAMA, AND DUKE NIGHTRAY...
...YOU MUST BE SUFFERING AS WELL.

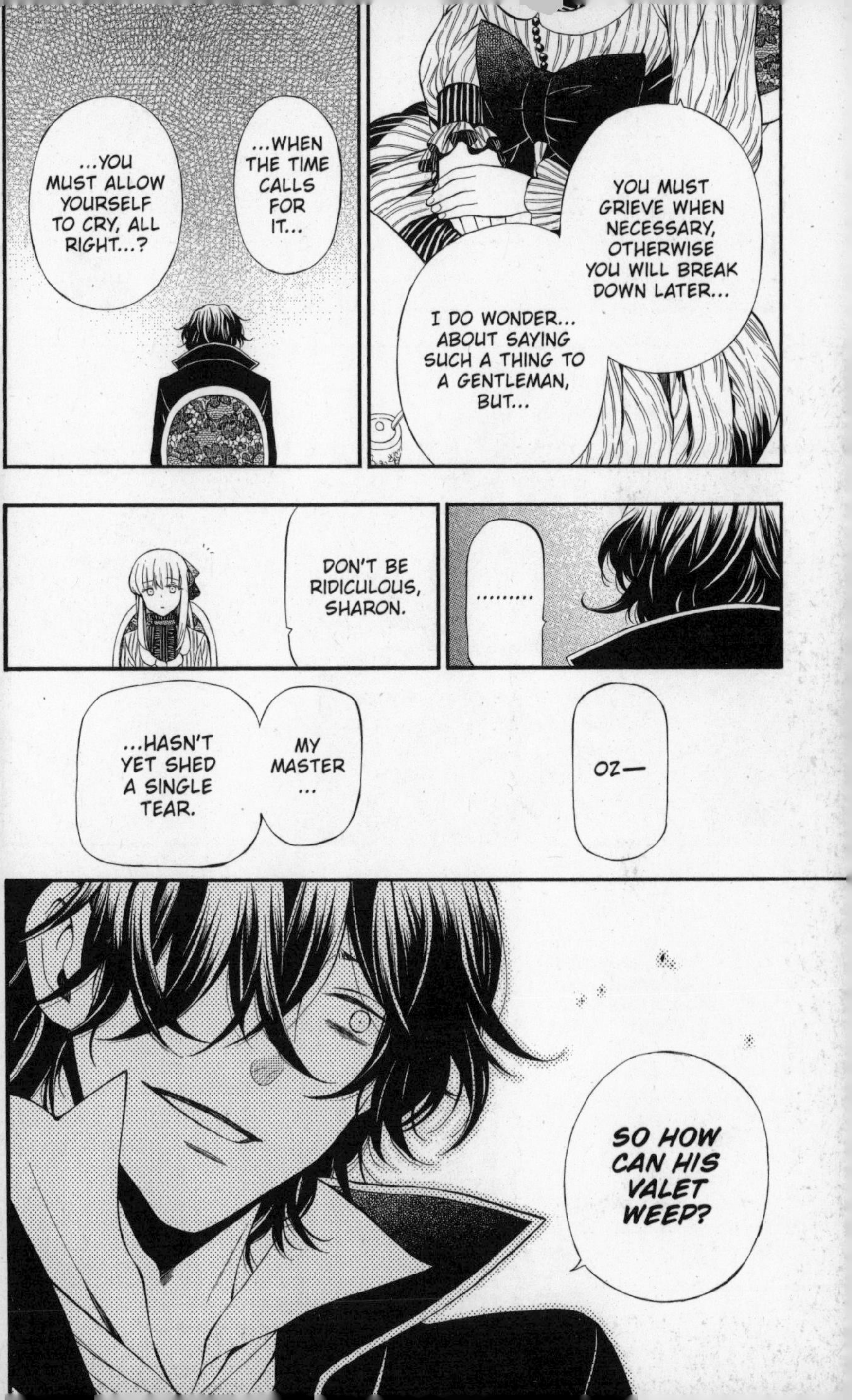
YOU MUST GRIEVE WHEN NECESSARY, OTHERWISE YOU WILL BREAK DOWN LATER...
I DO WONDER... ABOUT SAYING SUCH A THING TO A GENTLEMAN, BUT...
...WHEN THE TIME CALLS FOR IT...
...YOU MUST ALLOW YOURSELF TO CRY, ALL RIGHT...?
....
DON'T BE RIDICULOUS, SHARON.
OZ—
MY MASTER ...
...HASN'T YET SHED A SINGLE TEAR.
SO HOW CAN HIS VALET WEEP?

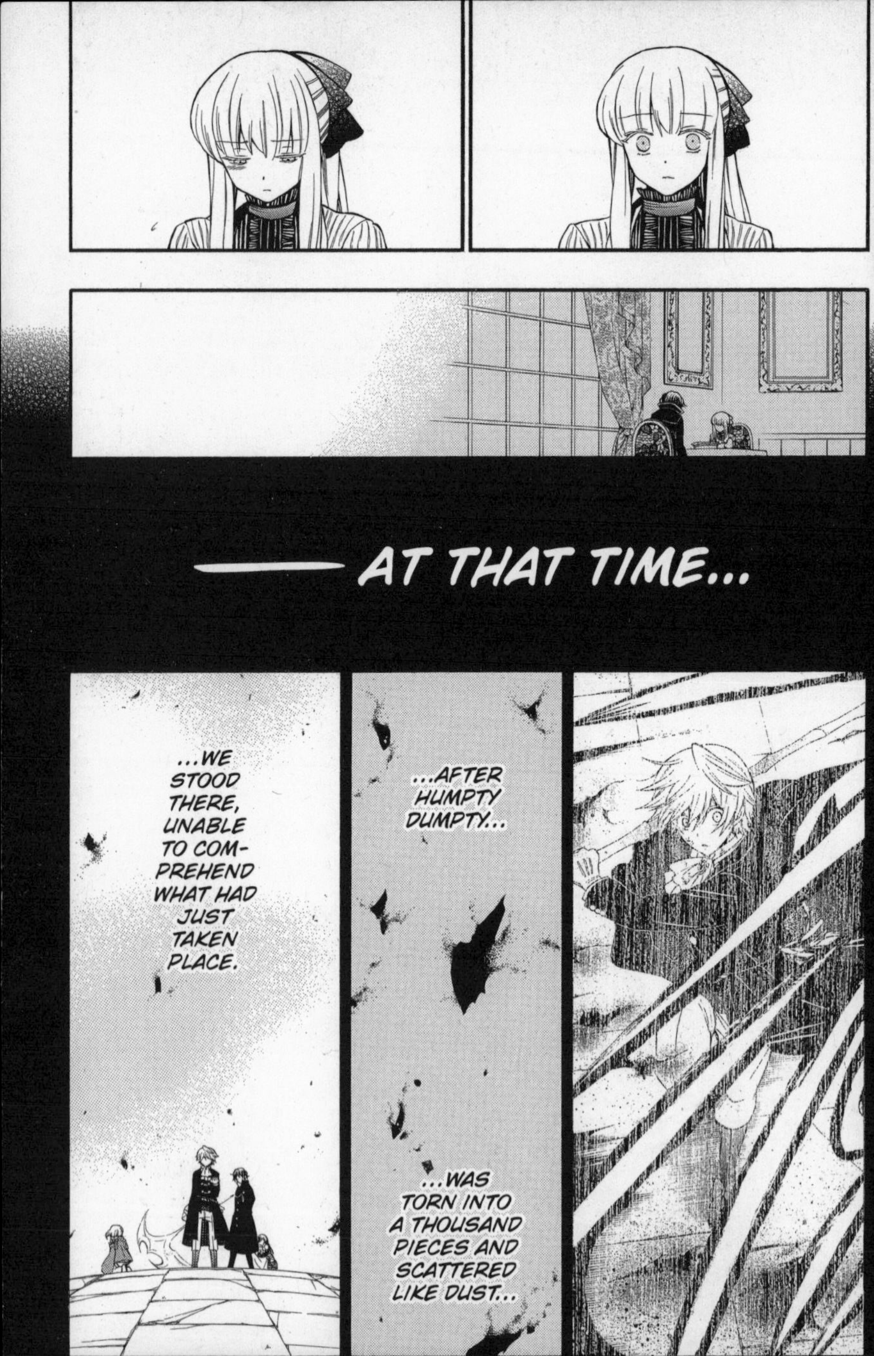
——AT THAT TIME...
...AFTER HUMPTY DUMPTY...
...WAS TORN INTO A THOUSAND PIECES AND SCATTERED LIKE DUST...
...WE STOOD THERE, UNABLE TO COMPREHEND WHAT HAD JUST TAKEN PLACE.

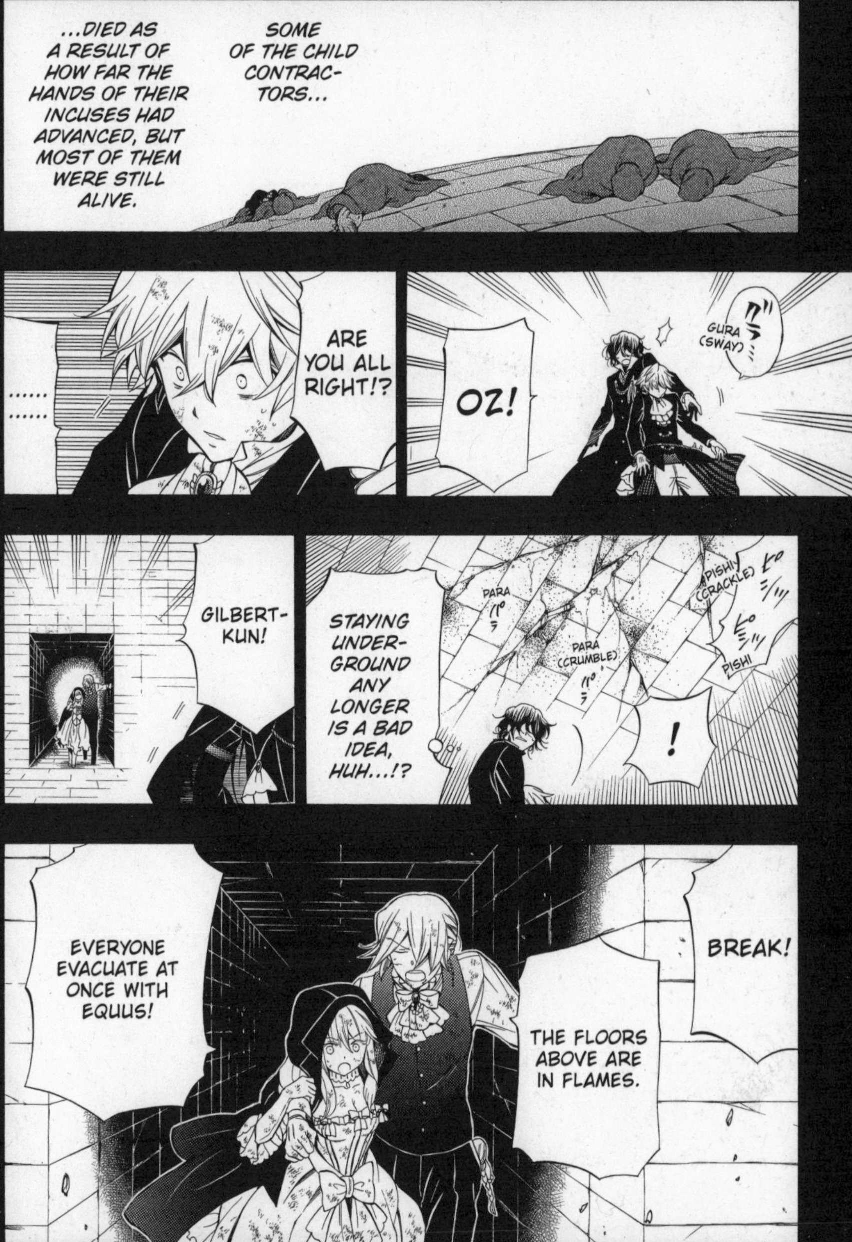
SOME OF THE CHILD CONTRAC-TORS...
...DIED AS A RESULT OF HOW FAR THE HANDS OF THEIR INCUSES HAD ADVANCED, BUT MOST OF THEM WERE STILL ALIVE.
GURA (SWAY)
OZ!
ARE YOU ALL RIGHT!?
......
......
PISHI (CRACKLE)
PISHI
PARA
PARA (CRUMBLE)
!
STAYING UNDER-GROUND ANY LONGER IS A BAD IDEA, HUH...!?
GILBERT-KUN!
BREAK!
THE FLOORS ABOVE ARE IN FLAMES.
EVERYONE EVACUATE AT ONCE WITH EQUUS!

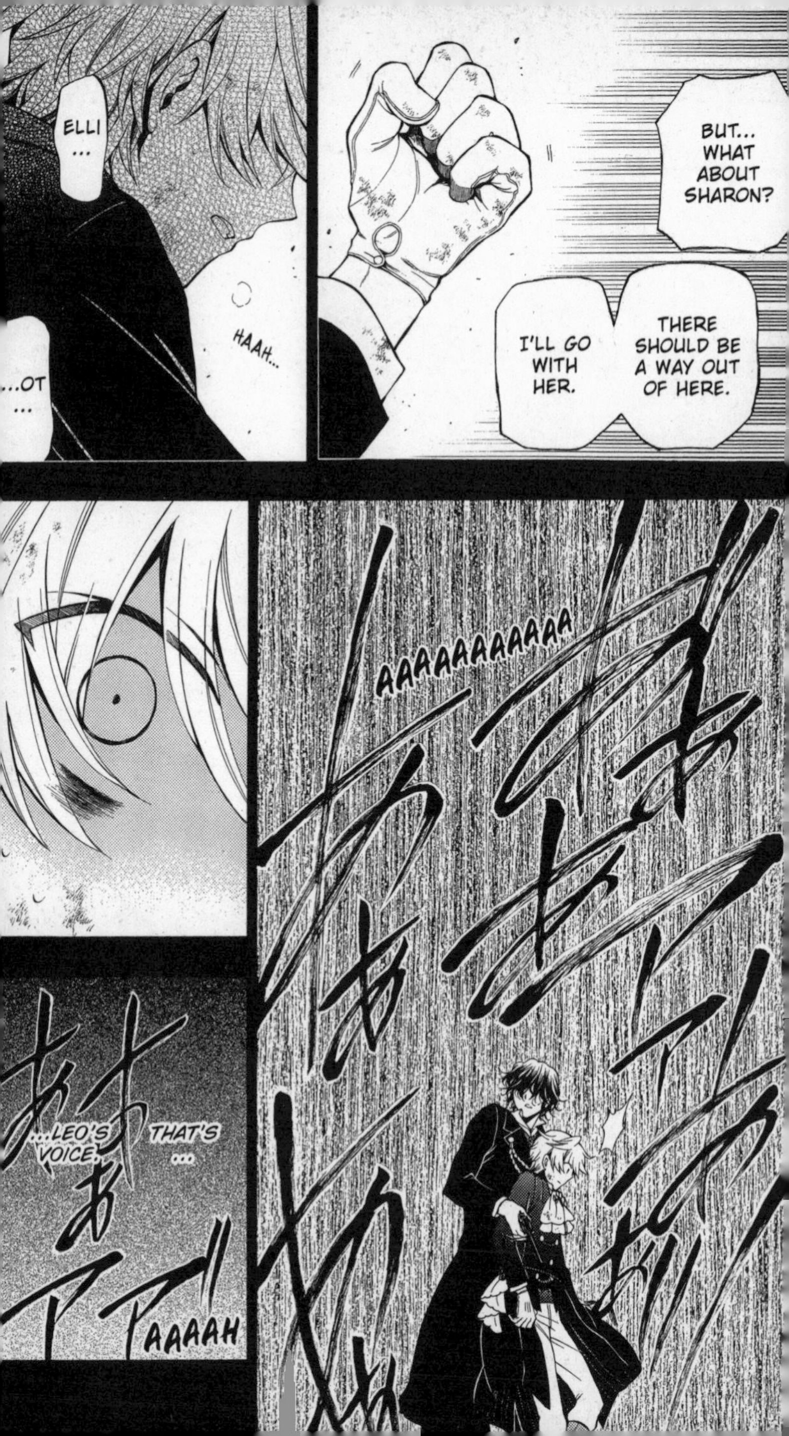
BUT... WHAT ABOUT SHARON?
THERE SHOULD BE A WAY OUT OF HERE.
I'LL GO WITH HER.
ELLI ...
HAAH...
...OT ...
AAAAAAAAAA
THAT'S ...
...LEO'S VOICE.
AAAAH

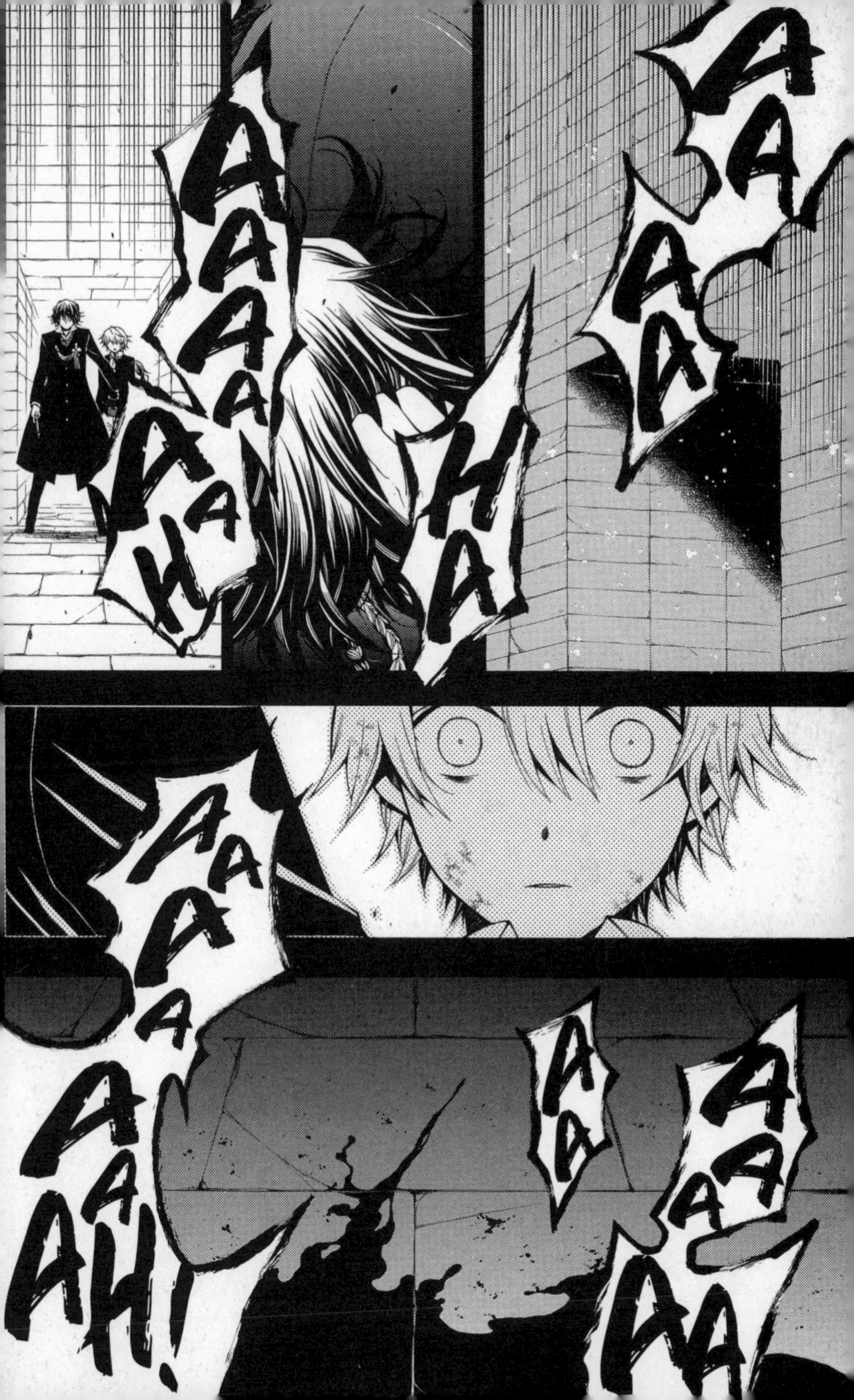
AAAAAA
HAHA
AAAAAAAHAH
AAAAAAA
AAA
AAAAAAAAAAH!

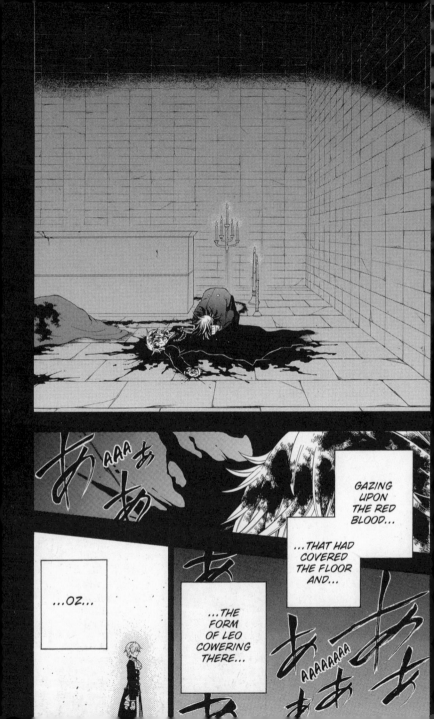

ＡＡＡ

GAZING
UPON
THE RED
BLOOD...

...THAT HAD
COVERED
THE FLOOR
AND...

...THE
FORM
OF LEO
COWERING
THERE...

...OZ...

AAAAAAAA

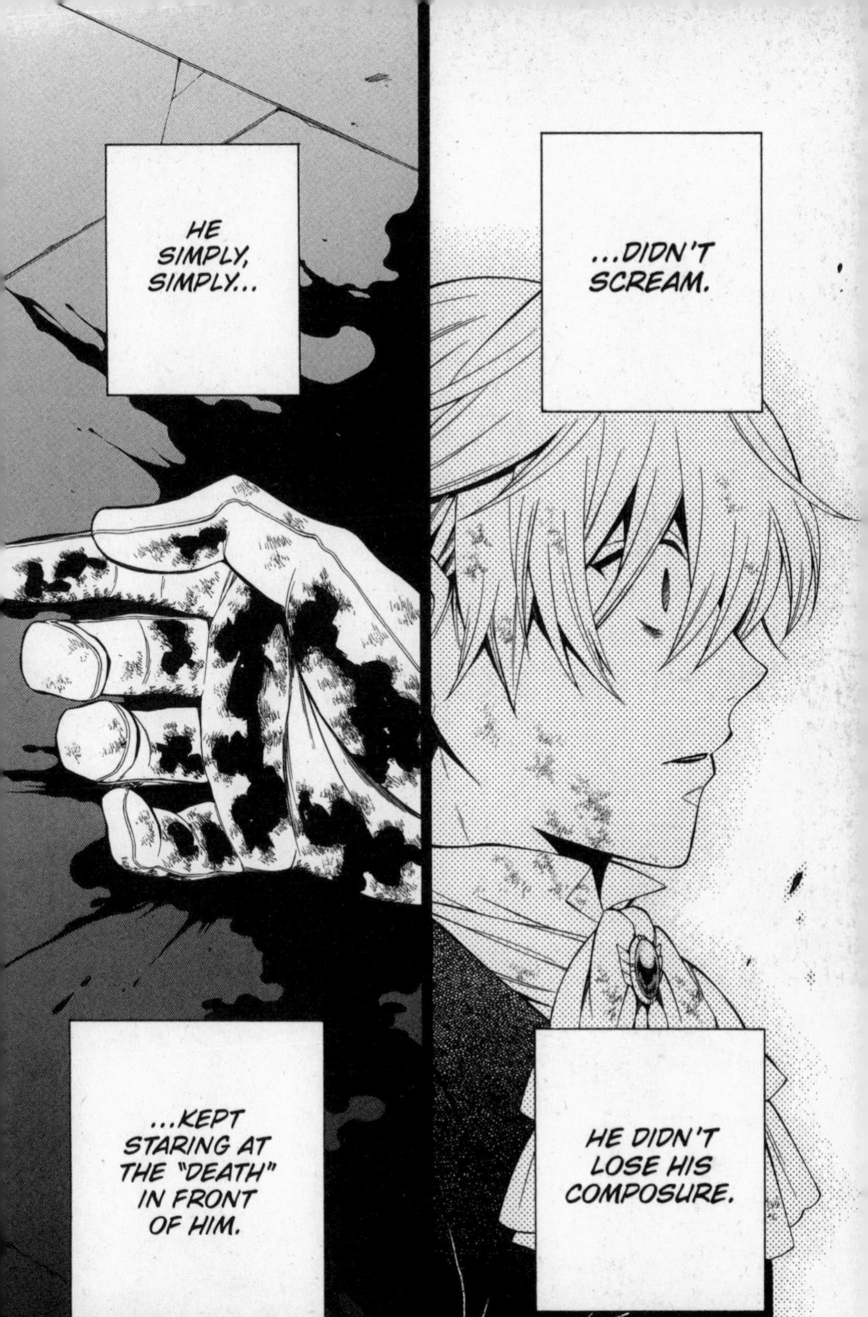
...DIDN'T SCREAM.
HE DIDN'T LOSE HIS COMPOSURE.
HE SIMPLY, SIMPLY...
...KEPT STARING AT THE "DEATH" IN FRONT OF HIM.

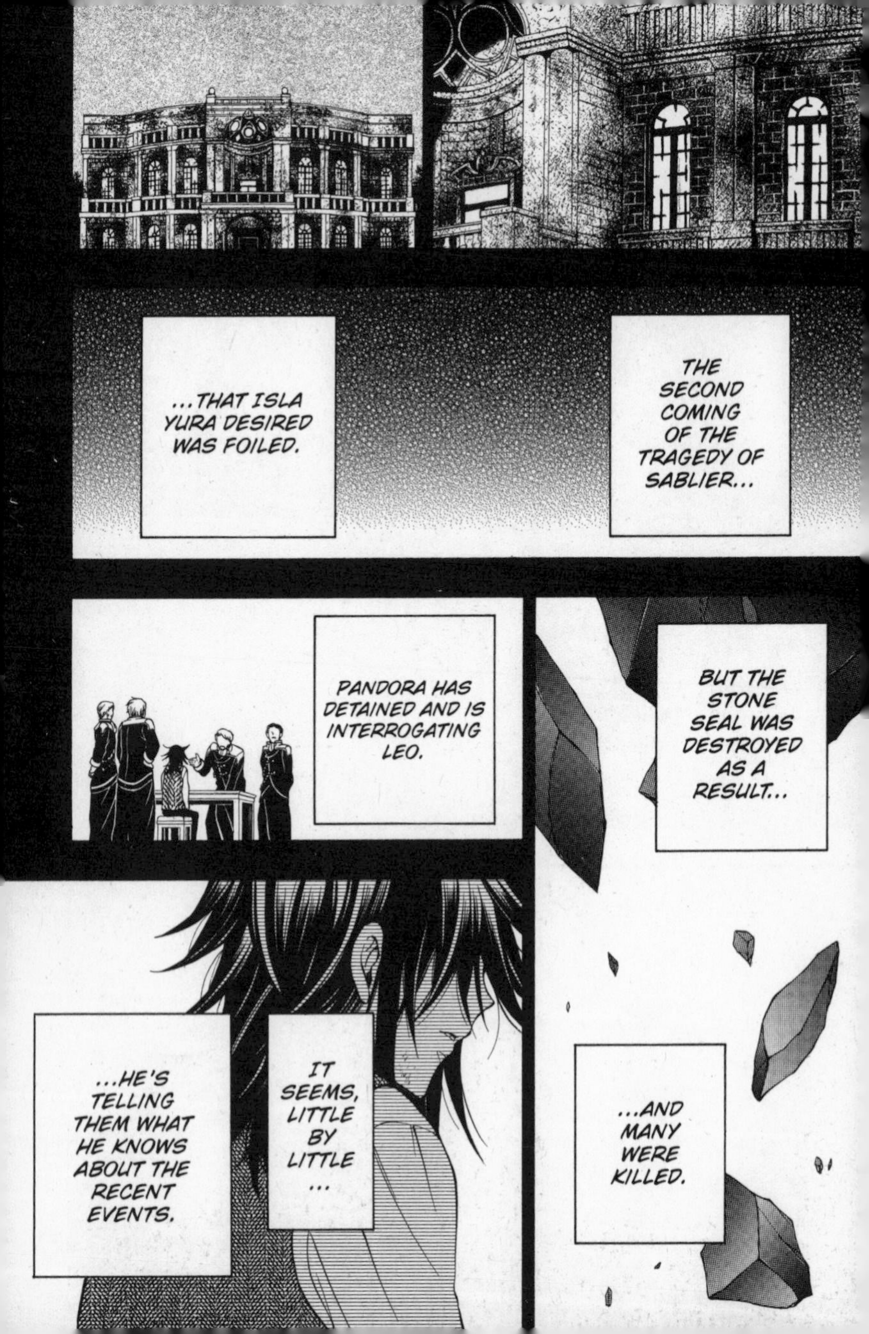
THE SECOND COMING OF THE TRAGEDY OF SABLIER...
...THAT ISLA YURA DESIRED WAS FOILED.
BUT THE STONE SEAL WAS DESTROYED AS A RESULT...
...AND MANY WERE KILLED.
PANDORA HAS DETAINED AND IS INTERROGATING LEO.
IT SEEMS, LITTLE BY LITTLE...
...HE'S TELLING THEM WHAT HE KNOWS ABOUT THE RECENT EVENTS.

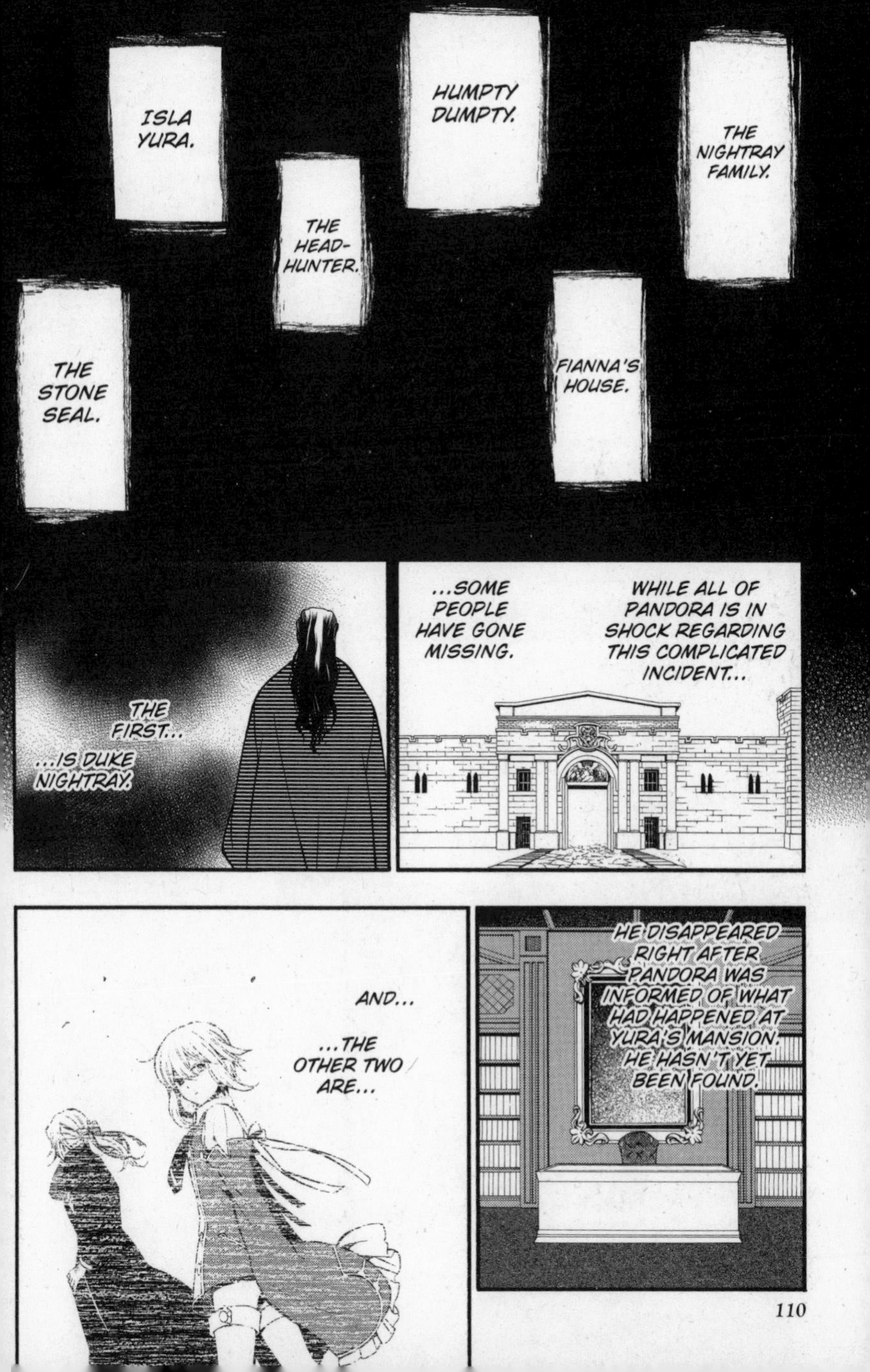
THE NIGHTRAY FAMILY.
HUMPTY DUMPTY.
FIANNA'S HOUSE.
THE HEAD-HUNTER.
ISLA YURA.
THE STONE SEAL.
WHILE ALL OF PANDORA IS IN SHOCK REGARDING THIS COMPLICATED INCIDENT...
...SOME PEOPLE HAVE GONE MISSING.
THE FIRST...
...IS DUKE NIGHTRAY.
HE DISAPPEARED RIGHT AFTER PANDORA WAS INFORMED OF WHAT HAD HAPPENED AT YURA'S MANSION. HE HASN'T YET BEEN FOUND.
AND...
...THE OTHER TWO ARE...

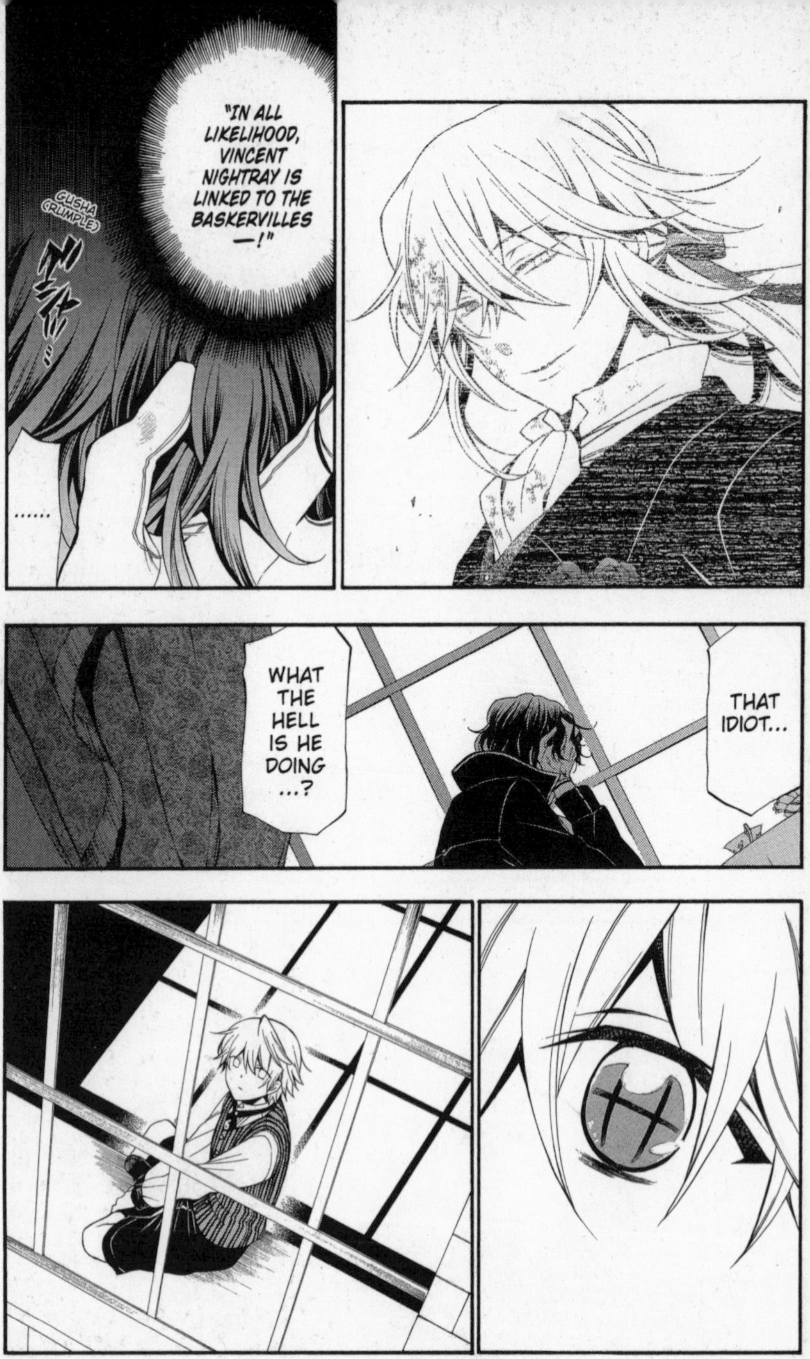
"IN ALL LIKELIHOOD, VINCENT NIGHTRAY IS LINKED TO THE BASKERVILLES—!"
GUSHA (RUMPLE)
......
THAT IDIOT...
WHAT THE HELL IS HE DOING ...?

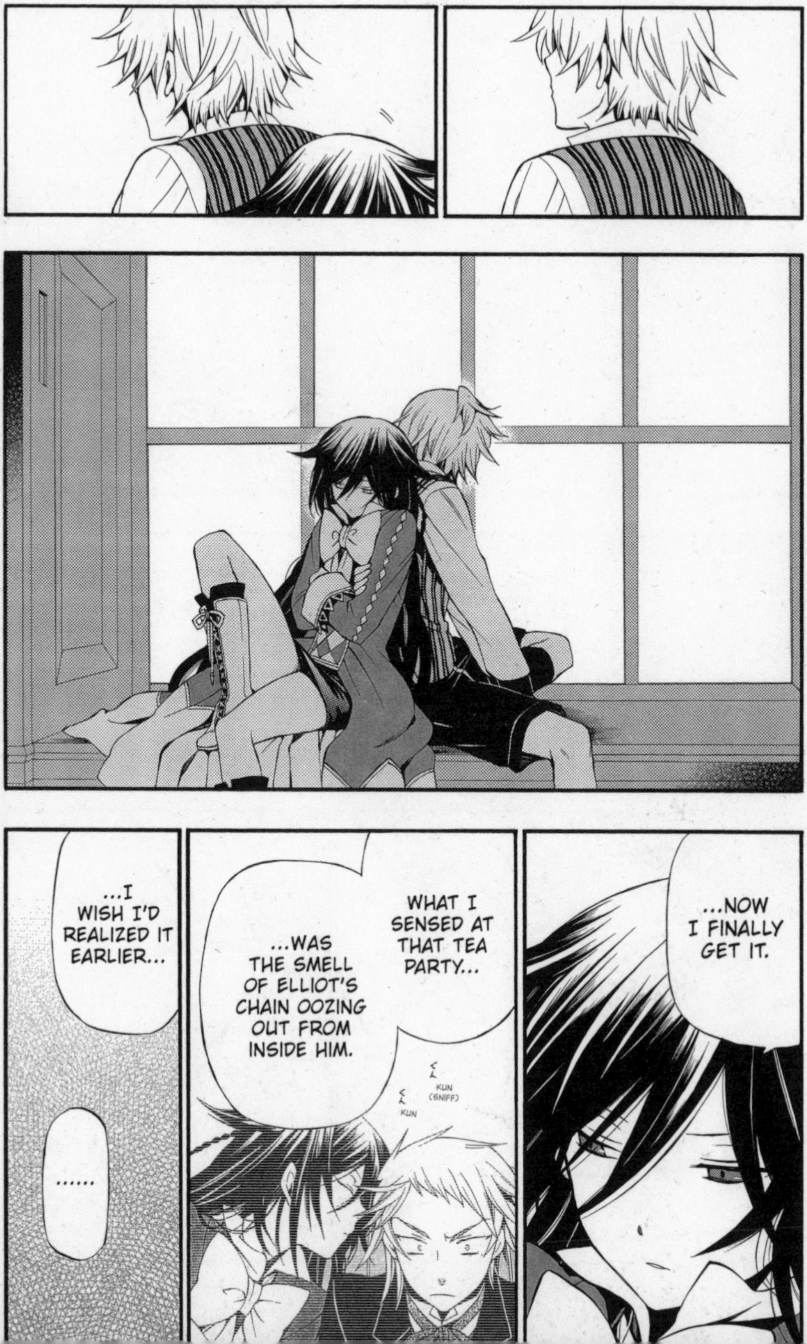
...NOW I FINALLY GET IT.
WHAT I SENSED AT THAT TEA PARTY...
...WAS THE SMELL OF ELLIOT'S CHAIN OOZING OUT FROM INSIDE HIM.
くん KUN (SNIFF)
くん KUN
...I WISH I'D REALIZED IT EARLIER...
......

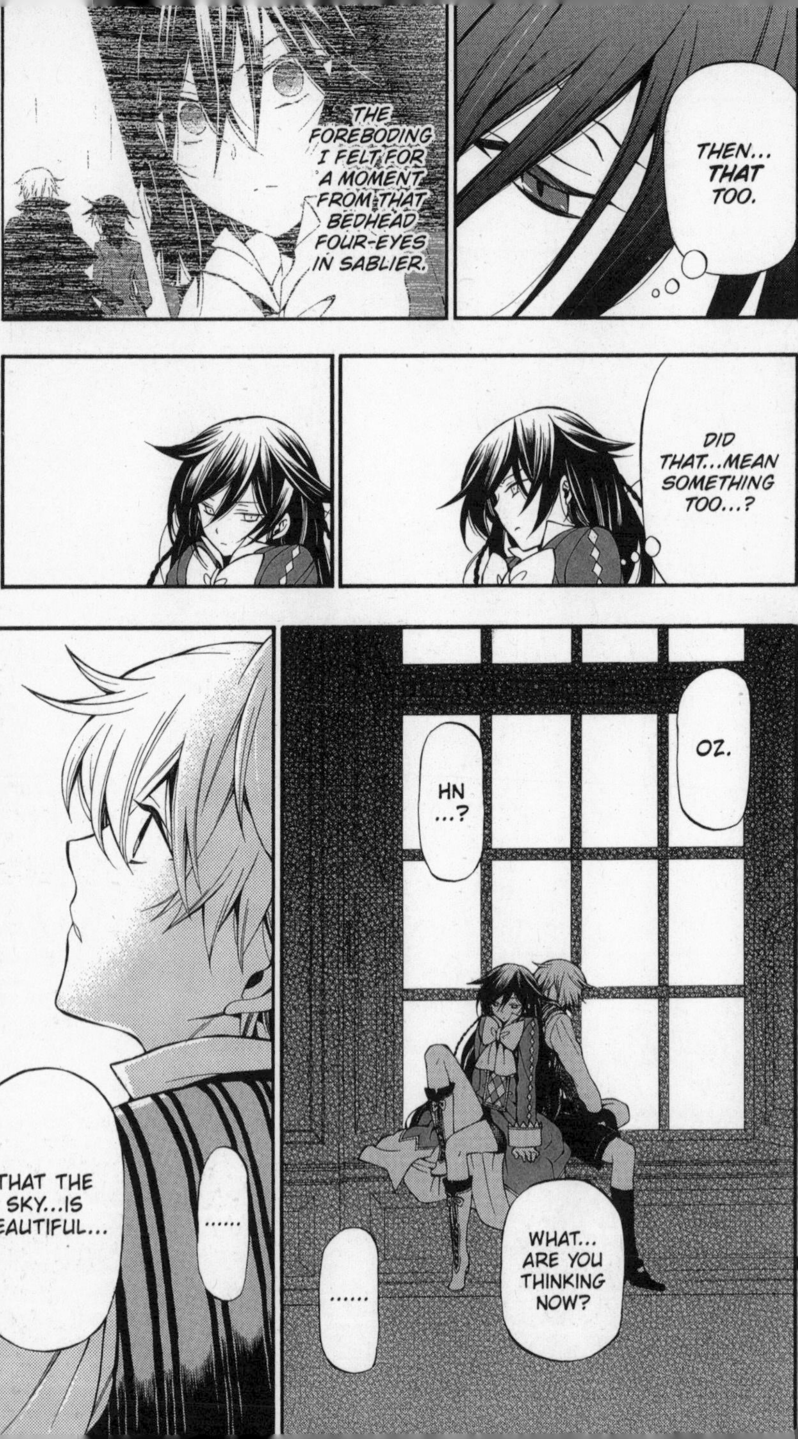
THEN... THAT TOO.
THE FOREBODING I FELT FOR A MOMENT FROM THAT BEDHEAD FOUR-EYES IN SABLIER.
DID THAT...MEAN SOMETHING TOO...?
OZ.
HN ...?
WHAT... ARE YOU THINKING NOW?
......
......
THAT THE SKY...IS BEAUTIFUL...

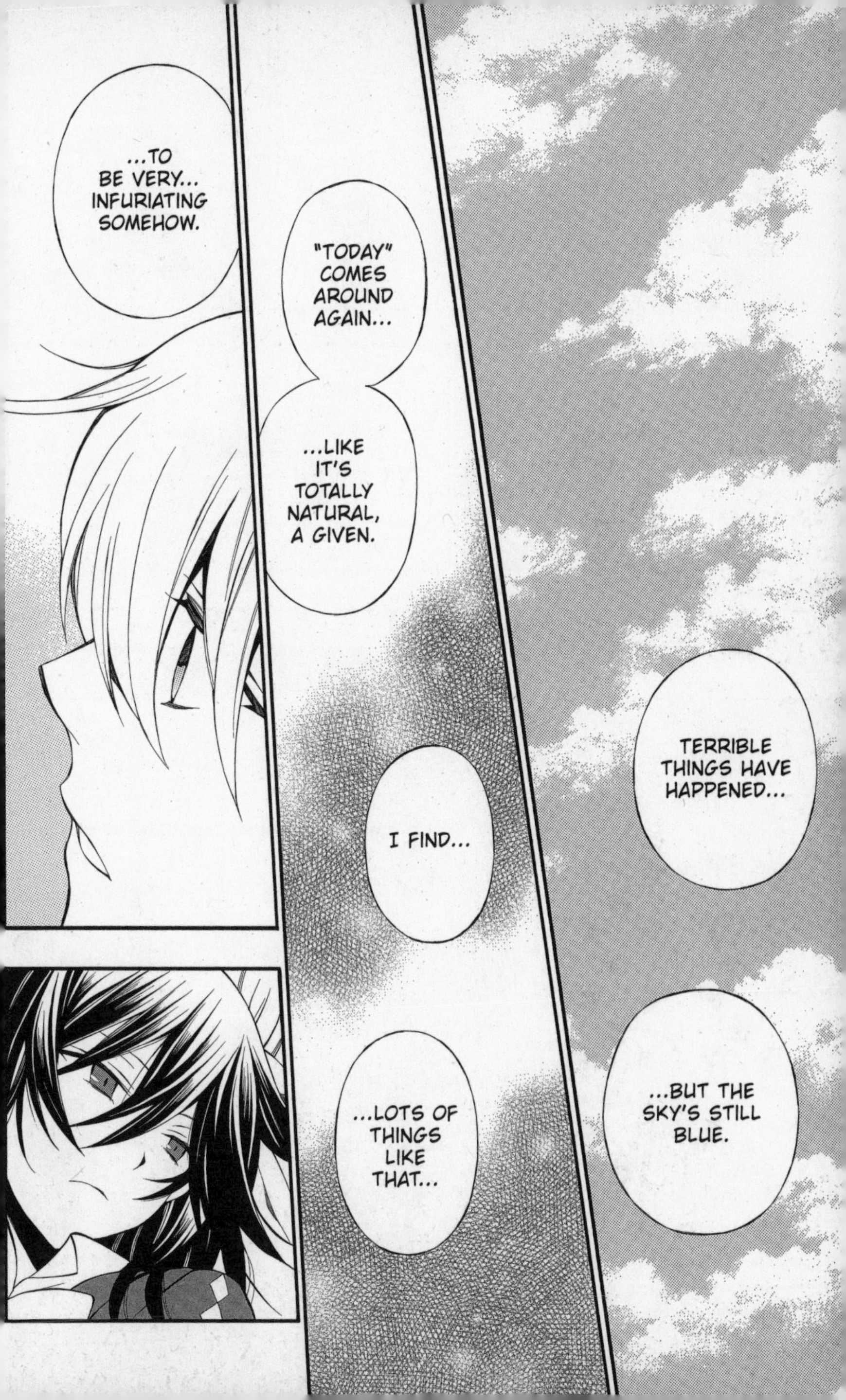
TERRIBLE THINGS HAVE HAPPENED...
...BUT THE SKY'S STILL BLUE.
"TODAY" COMES AROUND AGAIN...
...LIKE IT'S TOTALLY NATURAL, A GIVEN.
I FIND...
...LOTS OF THINGS LIKE THAT...
...TO BE VERY... INFURIATING SOMEHOW.

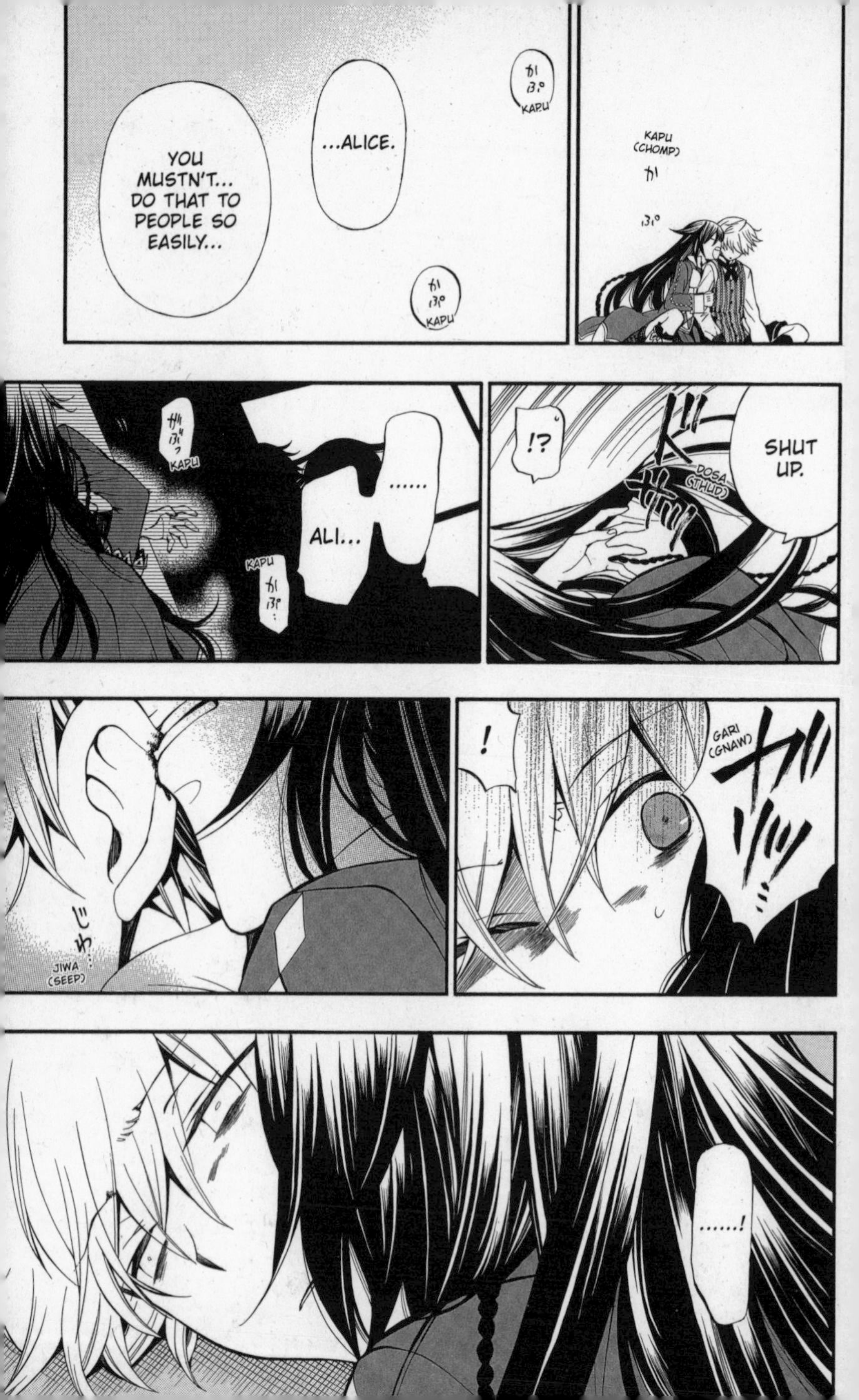
KAPU (CHOMP)
かぷ
かぷ
KAPU
...ALICE.
YOU MUSTN'T... DO THAT TO PEOPLE SO EASILY...
かぷ
KAPU
SHUT UP.
!?
DOSA (THUD)
ドサッ
......
ALI...
かぷ
KAPU
がぶっ
KAPU
GARI (GNAW)
ガリッ
!
じわ…
JIWA (SEEP)
......!

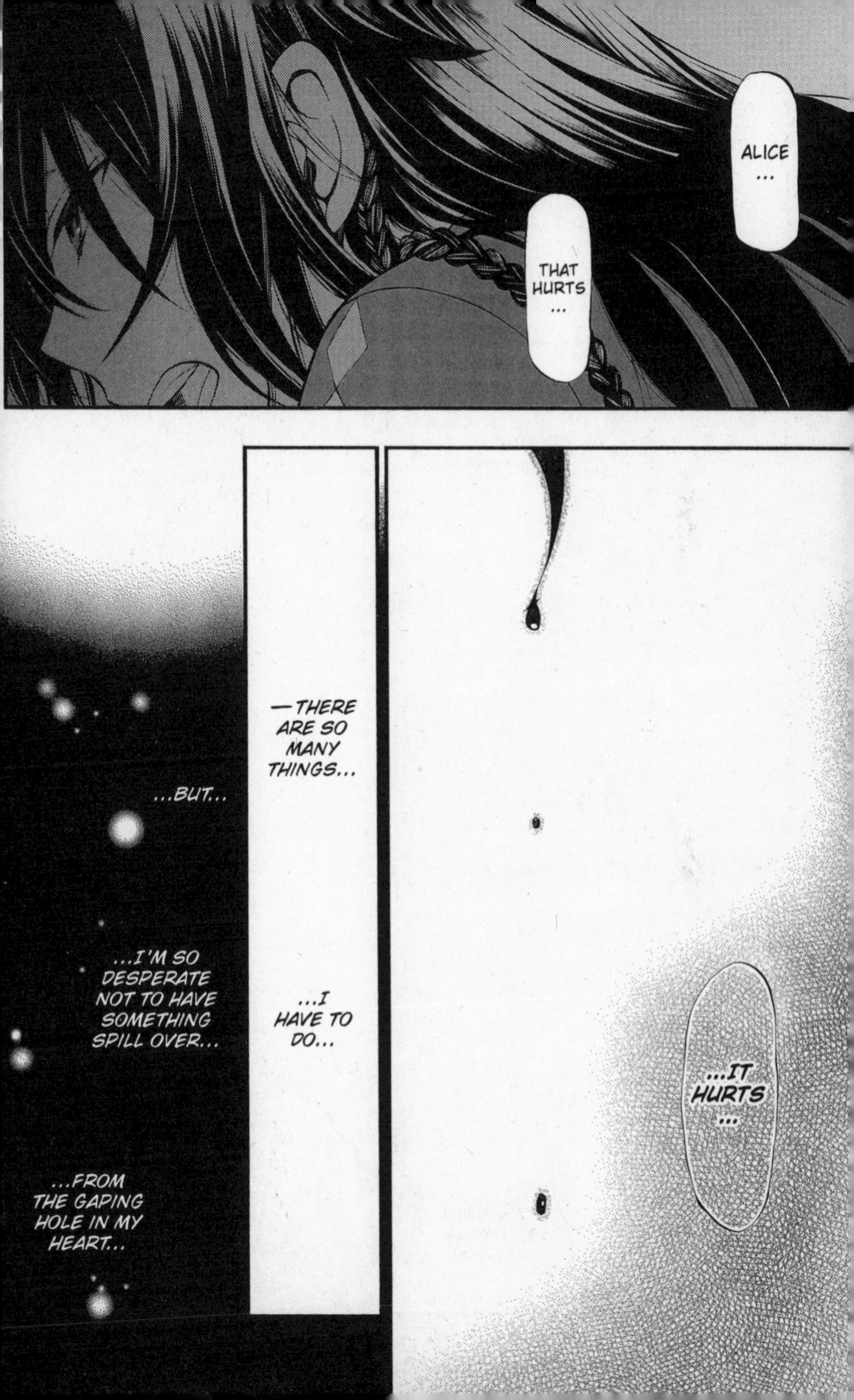
ALICE ...
THAT HURTS ...
...IT HURTS ...
—THERE ARE SO MANY THINGS...
...I HAVE TO DO...
...BUT...
...I'M SO DESPERATE NOT TO HAVE SOMETHING SPILL OVER...
...FROM THE GAPING HOLE IN MY HEART...

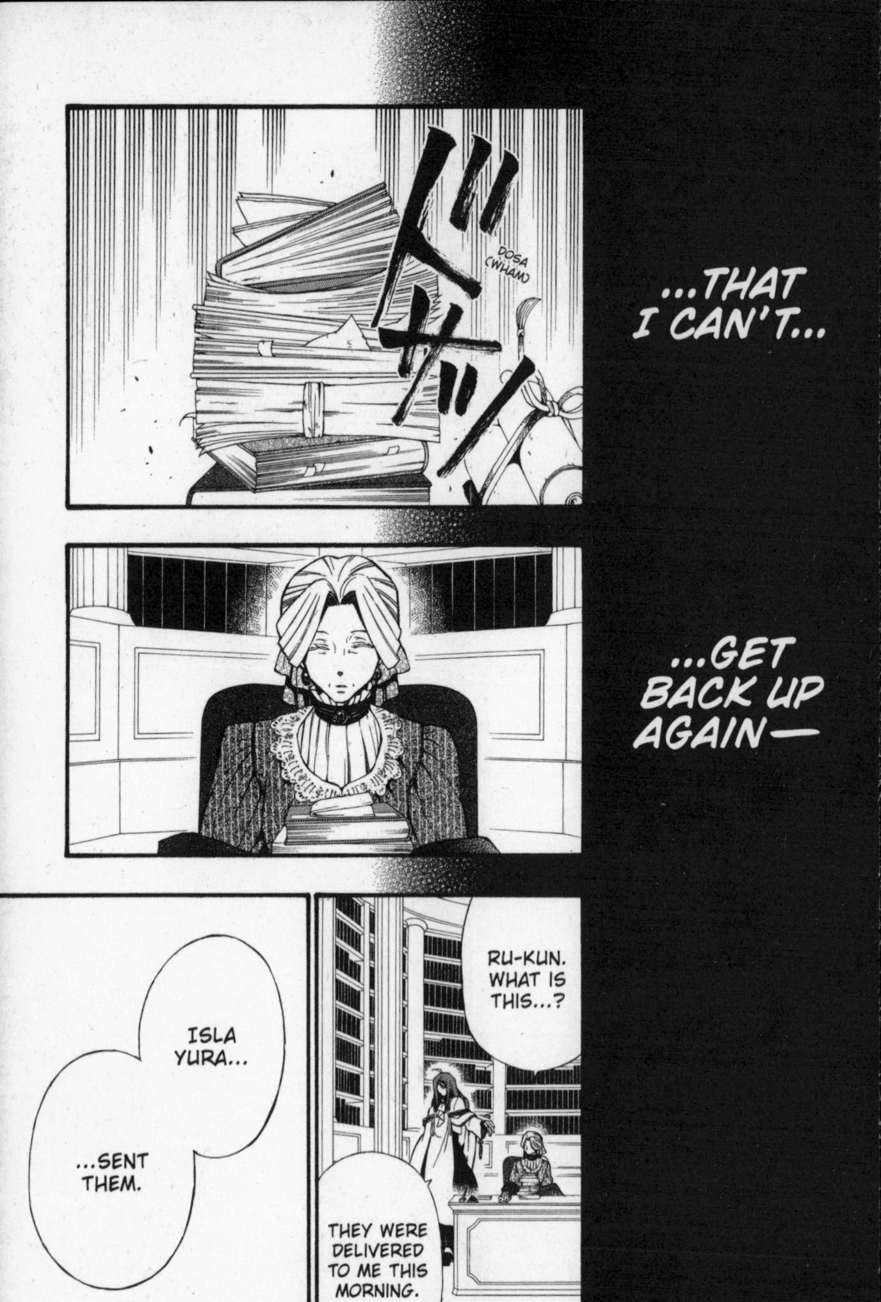
...THAT I CAN'T...
DOSA (WHAM)
...GET BACK UP AGAIN—
RU-KUN. WHAT IS THIS...?
THEY WERE DELIVERED TO ME THIS MORNING.
ISLA YURA...
...SENT THEM.

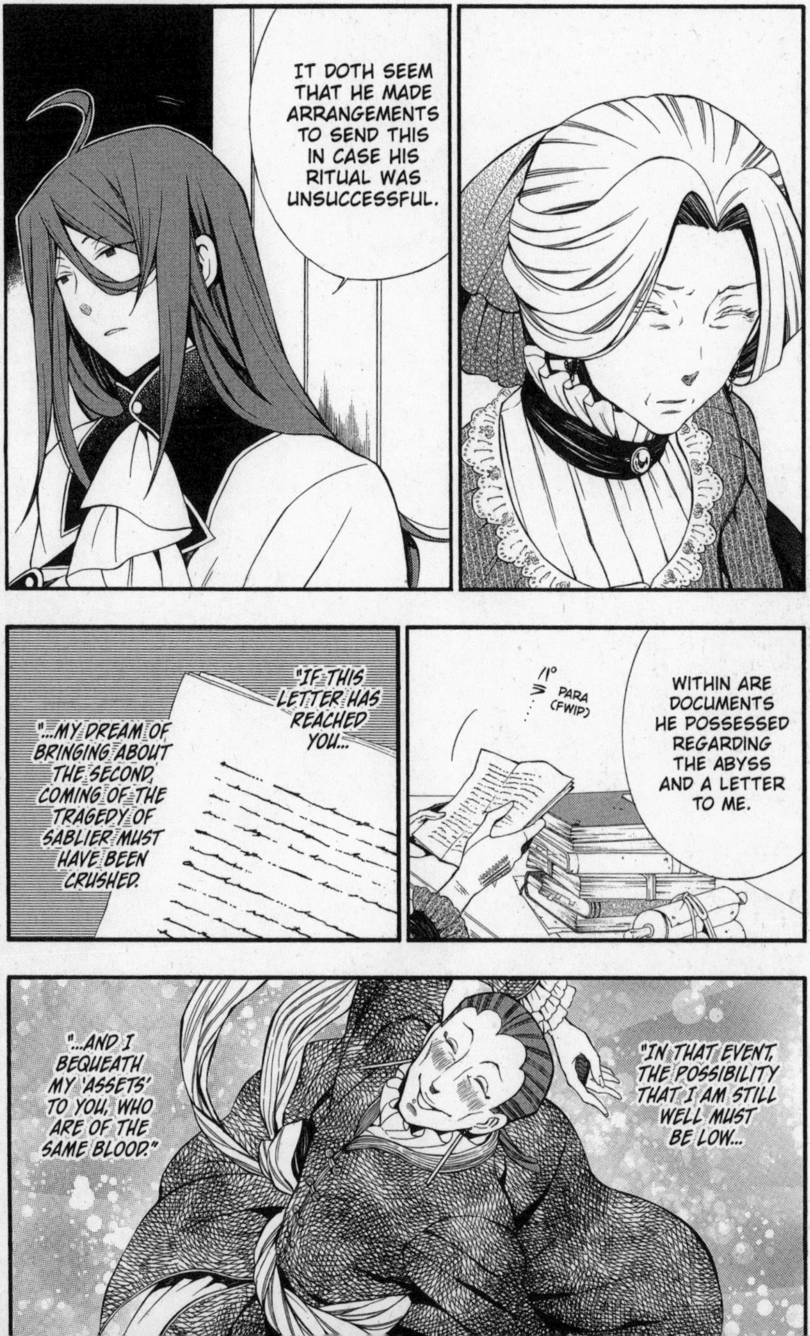
IT DOTH SEEM THAT HE MADE ARRANGEMENTS TO SEND THIS IN CASE HIS RITUAL WAS UNSUCCESSFUL.
WITHIN ARE DOCUMENTS HE POSSESSED REGARDING THE ABYSS AND A LETTER TO ME.
PARA (FWIP)
"IF THIS LETTER HAS REACHED YOU...
"...MY DREAM OF BRINGING ABOUT THE SECOND COMING OF THE TRAGEDY OF SABLIER MUST HAVE BEEN CRUSHED.
"IN THAT EVENT, THE POSSIBILITY THAT I AM STILL WELL MUST BE LOW...
"...AND I BEQUEATH MY 'ASSETS' TO YOU, WHO ARE OF THE SAME BLOOD."

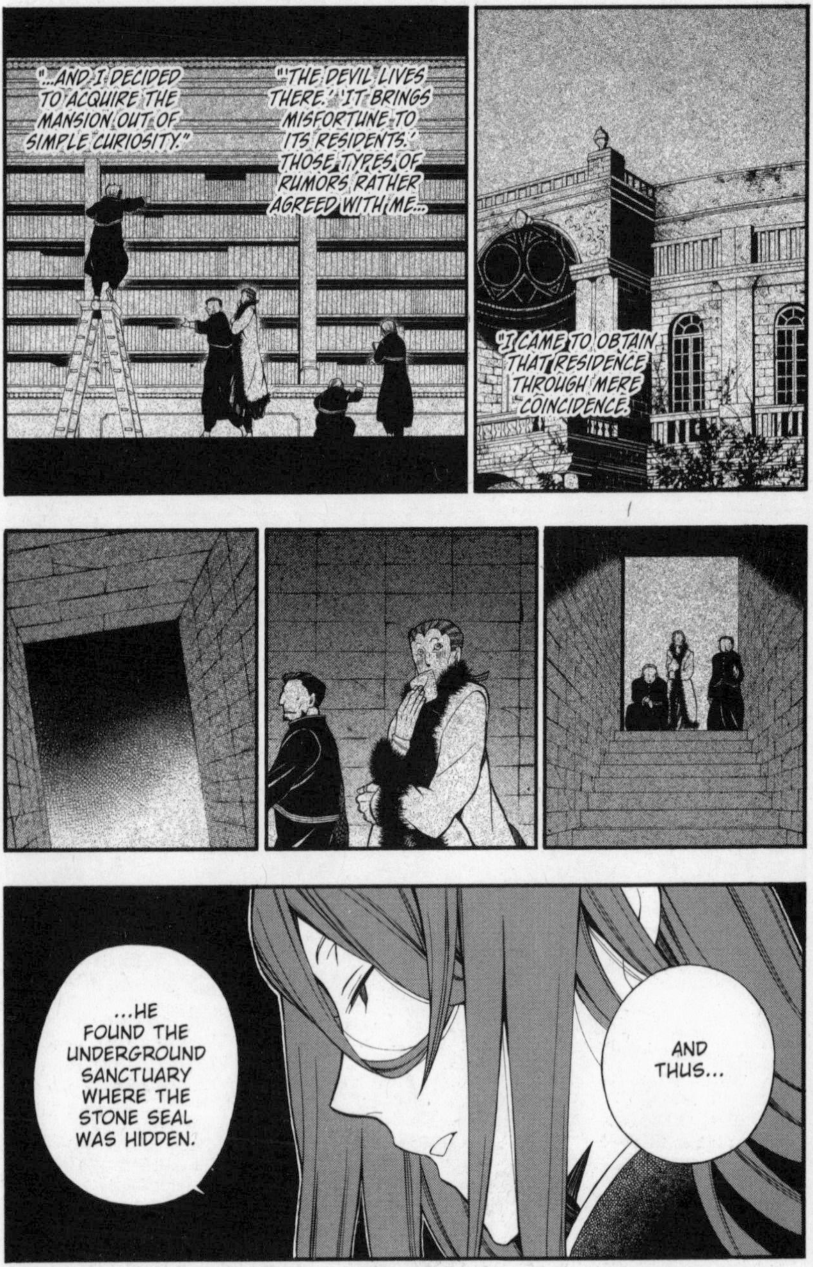
"I CAME TO OBTAIN THAT RESIDENCE THROUGH MERE COINCIDENCE.
"'THE DEVIL LIVES THERE.' 'IT BRINGS MISFORTUNE TO ITS RESIDENTS.' THOSE TYPES OF RUMORS RATHER AGREED WITH ME...
"...AND I DECIDED TO ACQUIRE THE MANSION OUT OF SIMPLE CURIOSITY."
AND THUS...
...HE FOUND THE UNDERGROUND SANCTUARY WHERE THE STONE SEAL WAS HIDDEN.

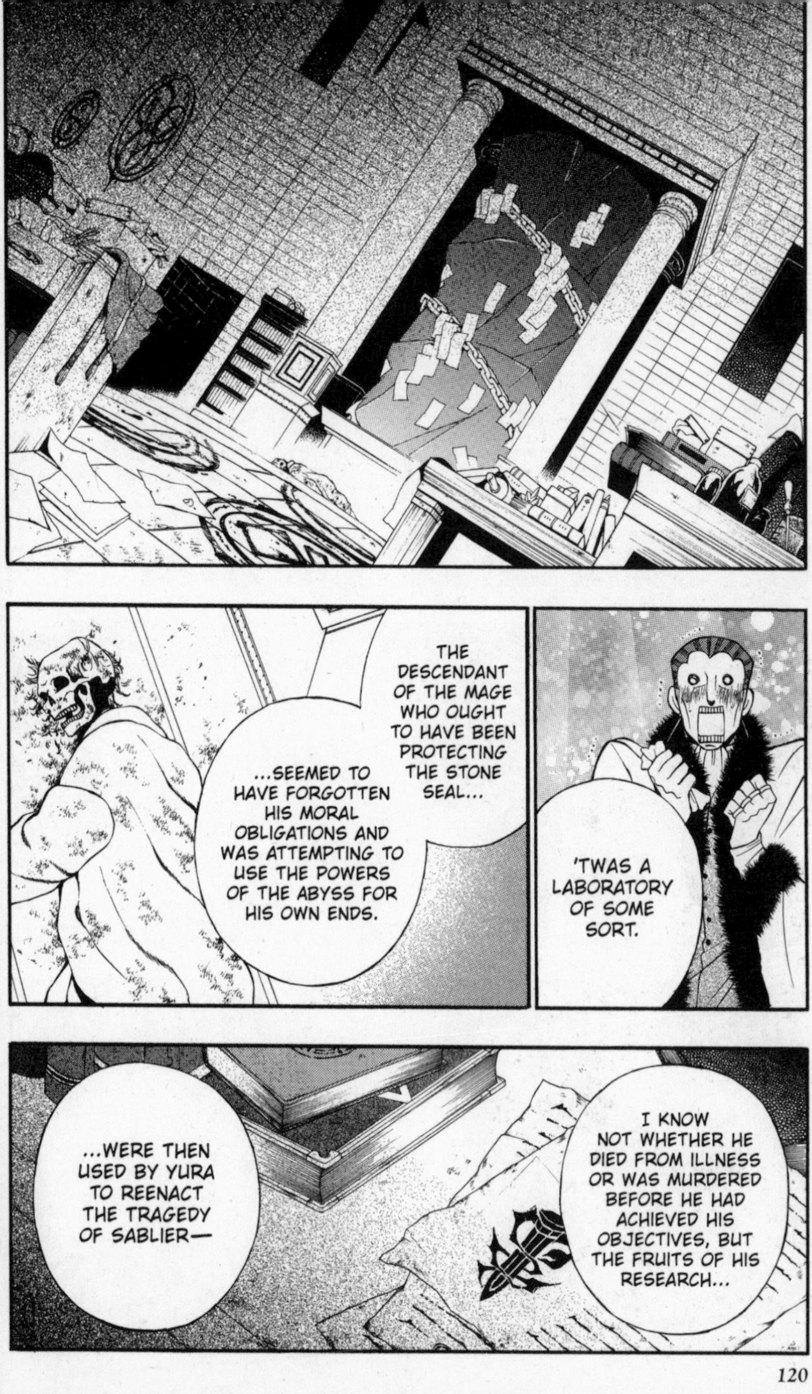
'TWAS A LABORATORY OF SOME SORT.
THE DESCENDANT OF THE MAGE WHO OUGHT TO HAVE BEEN PROTECTING THE STONE SEAL...
...SEEMED TO HAVE FORGOTTEN HIS MORAL OBLIGATIONS AND WAS ATTEMPTING TO USE THE POWERS OF THE ABYSS FOR HIS OWN ENDS.
I KNOW NOT WHETHER HE DIED FROM ILLNESS OR WAS MURDERED BEFORE HE HAD ACHIEVED HIS OBJECTIVES, BUT THE FRUITS OF HIS RESEARCH...
...WERE THEN USED BY YURA TO REENACT THE TRAGEDY OF SABLIER—

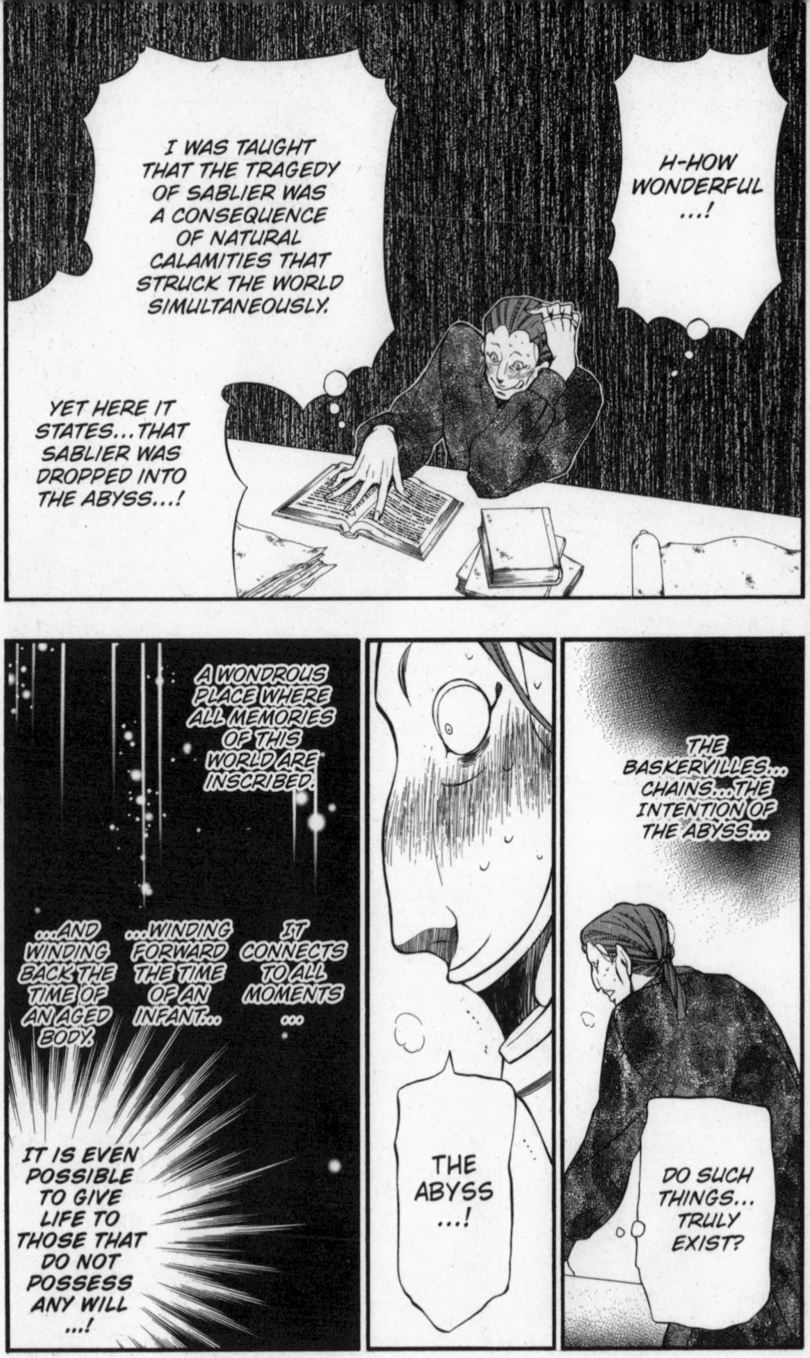
H-HOW WONDERFUL ...!
I WAS TAUGHT THAT THE TRAGEDY OF SABLIER WAS A CONSEQUENCE OF NATURAL CALAMITIES THAT STRUCK THE WORLD SIMULTANEOUSLY.
YET HERE IT STATES...THAT SABLIER WAS DROPPED INTO THE ABYSS...!
THE BASKERVILLES... CHAINS...THE INTENTION OF THE ABYSS...
DO SUCH THINGS... TRULY EXIST?
THE ABYSS ...!
A WONDROUS PLACE WHERE ALL MEMORIES OF THIS WORLD ARE INSCRIBED.
IT CONNECTS TO ALL MOMENTS ...
...WINDING FORWARD THE TIME OF AN INFANT...
...AND WINDING BACK THE TIME OF AN AGED BODY.
IT IS EVEN POSSIBLE TO GIVE LIFE TO THOSE THAT DO NOT POSSESS ANY WILL ...!

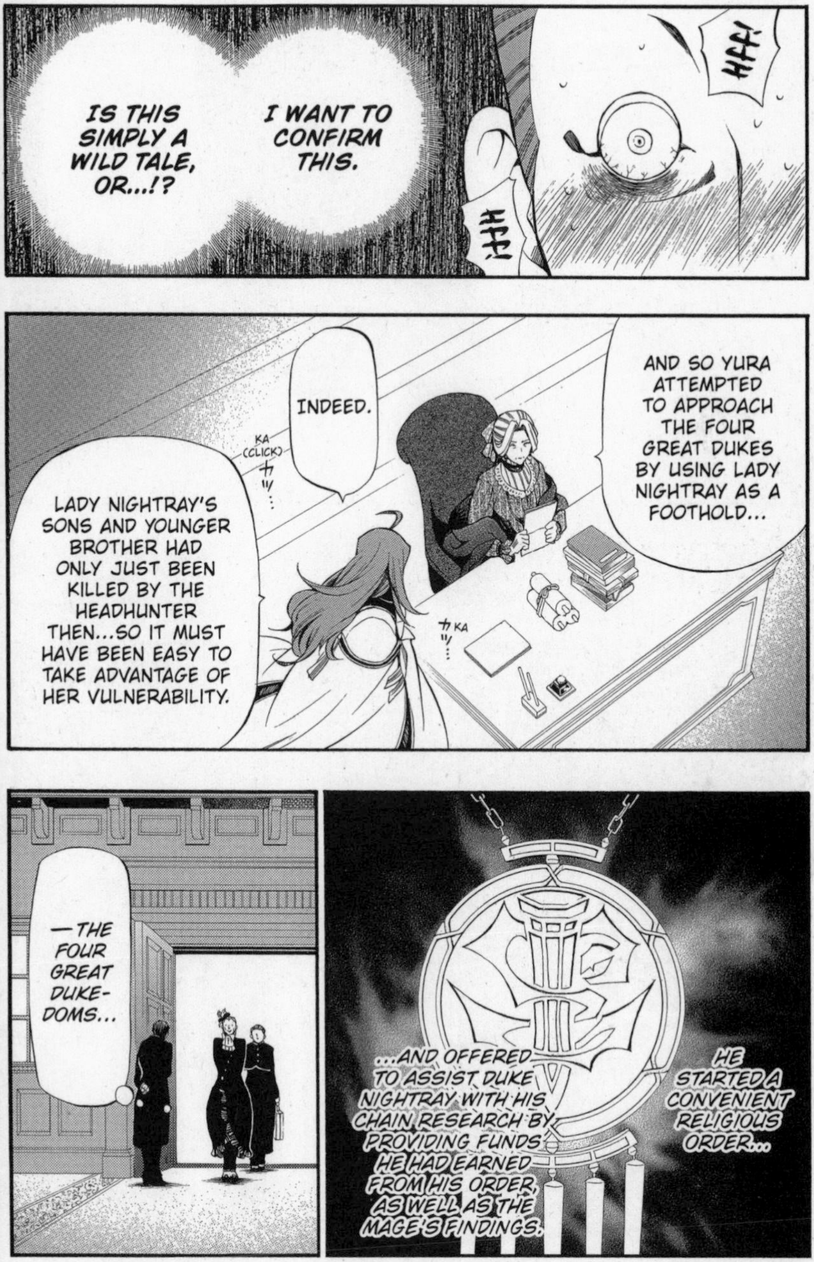
HFF!
I WANT TO CONFIRM THIS.
IS THIS SIMPLY A WILD TALE, OR...!?
HFF!
AND SO YURA ATTEMPTED TO APPROACH THE FOUR GREAT DUKES BY USING LADY NIGHTRAY AS A FOOTHOLD...
INDEED.
KA (CLICK)
LADY NIGHTRAY'S SONS AND YOUNGER BROTHER HAD ONLY JUST BEEN KILLED BY THE HEADHUNTER THEN...SO IT MUST HAVE BEEN EASY TO TAKE ADVANTAGE OF HER VULNERABILITY.
KA
HE STARTED A CONVENIENT RELIGIOUS ORDER...
...AND OFFERED TO ASSIST DUKE NIGHTRAY WITH HIS CHAIN RESEARCH BY PROVIDING FUNDS HE HAD EARNED FROM HIS ORDER, AS WELL AS THE MAGE'S FINDINGS.
—THE FOUR GREAT DUKE-DOMS...

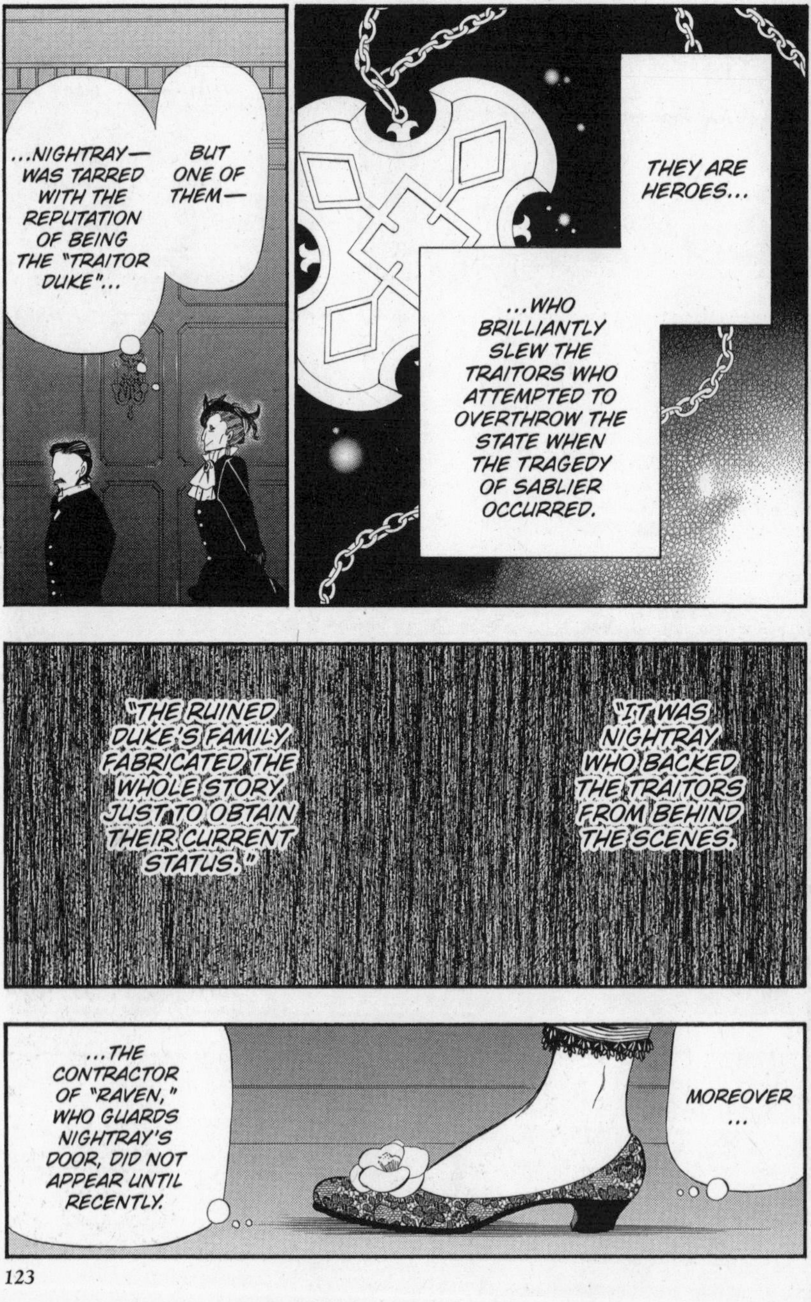
THEY ARE HEROES...
...WHO BRILLIANTLY SLEW THE TRAITORS WHO ATTEMPTED TO OVERTHROW THE STATE WHEN THE TRAGEDY OF SABLIER OCCURRED.
BUT ONE OF THEM—
...NIGHTRAY—WAS TARRED WITH THE REPUTATION OF BEING THE "TRAITOR DUKE"...
"IT WAS NIGHTRAY WHO BACKED THE TRAITORS FROM BEHIND THE SCENES.
"THE RUINED DUKE'S FAMILY FABRICATED THE WHOLE STORY JUST TO OBTAIN THEIR CURRENT STATUS."
MOREOVER...
...THE CONTRACTOR OF "RAVEN," WHO GUARDS NIGHTRAY'S DOOR, DID NOT APPEAR UNTIL RECENTLY.

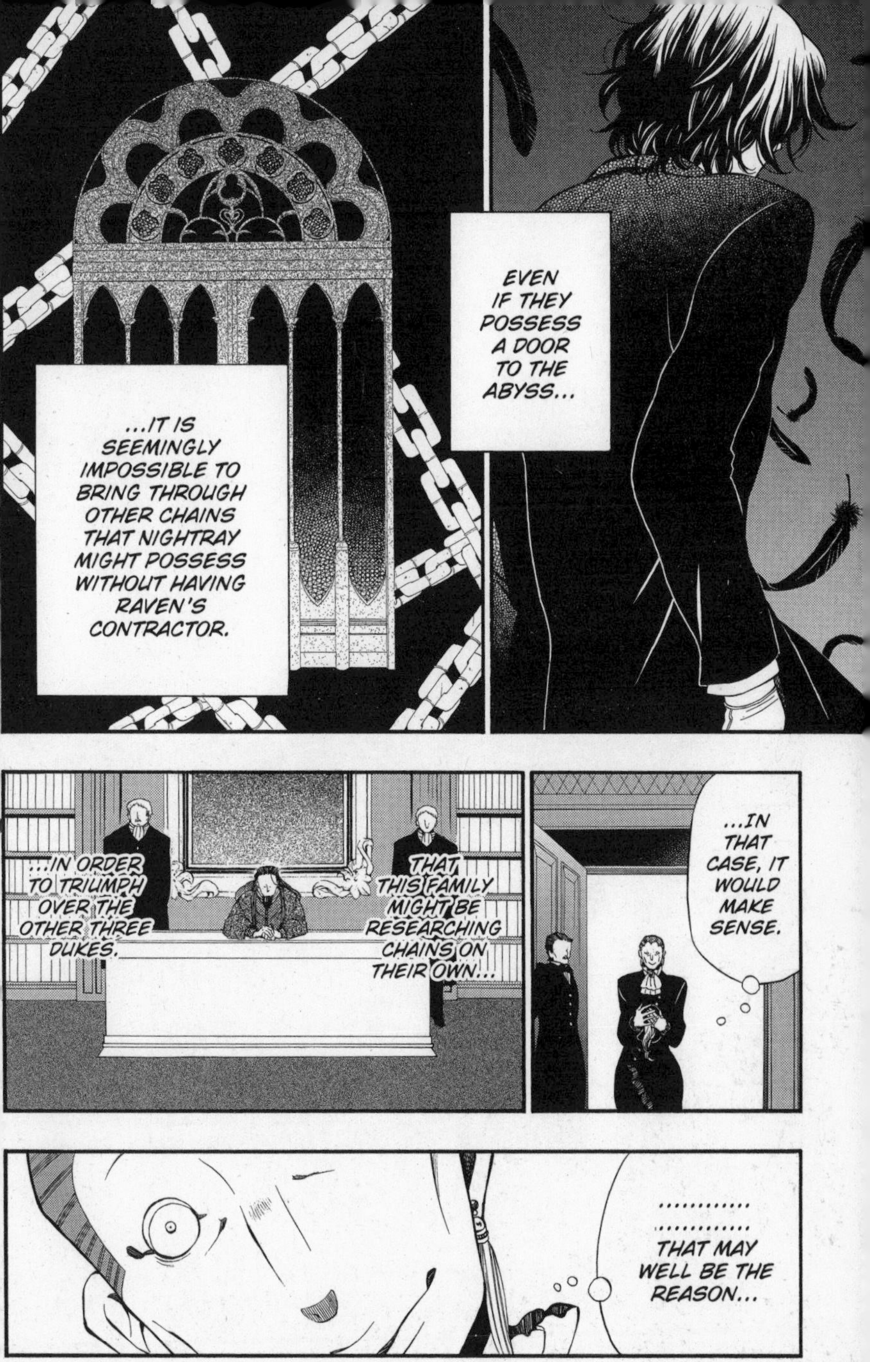
EVEN IF THEY POSSESS A DOOR TO THE ABYSS...
...IT IS SEEMINGLY IMPOSSIBLE TO BRING THROUGH OTHER CHAINS THAT NIGHTRAY MIGHT POSSESS WITHOUT HAVING RAVEN'S CONTRACTOR.
...IN THAT CASE, IT WOULD MAKE SENSE.
THAT THIS FAMILY MIGHT BE RESEARCHING CHAINS ON THEIR OWN...
...IN ORDER TO TRIUMPH OVER THE OTHER THREE DUKES.
....
....
THAT MAY WELL BE THE REASON...

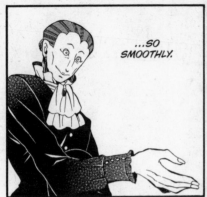

...SO SMOOTHLY.

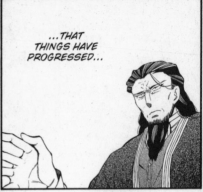

...THAT THINGS HAVE PROGRESSED...

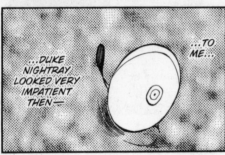

...DUKE NIGHTRAY LOOKED VERY IMPATIENT THEN—

....TO ME...

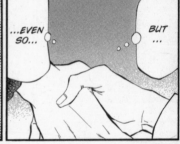

...EVEN SO...

BUT...

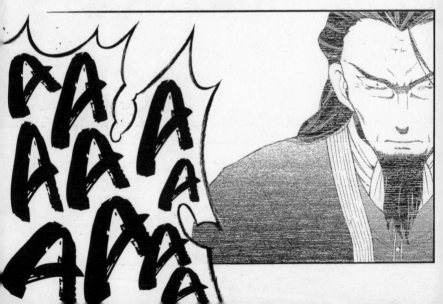

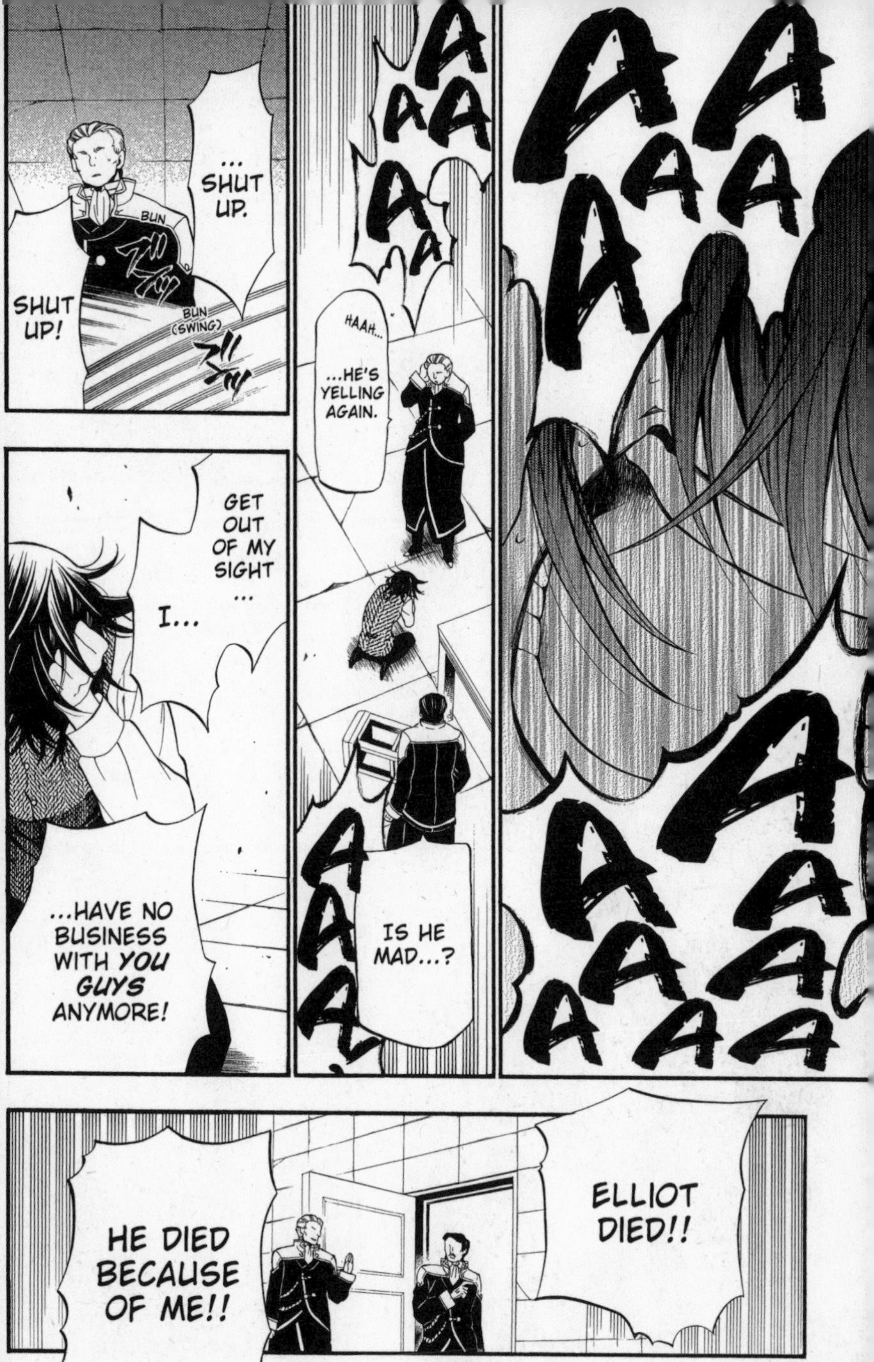
AAAAAA
AAAAAAAAAAAA
AAAAAA
HAAH...
...HE'S YELLING AGAIN.
AAAAA
IS HE MAD...?
... SHUT UP.
BUN
BUN (SWING)
SHUT UP!
GET OUT OF MY SIGHT ...
I...
...HAVE NO BUSINESS WITH *YOU GUYS* ANYMORE!
ELLIOT DIED!!
HE DIED BECAUSE OF ME!!

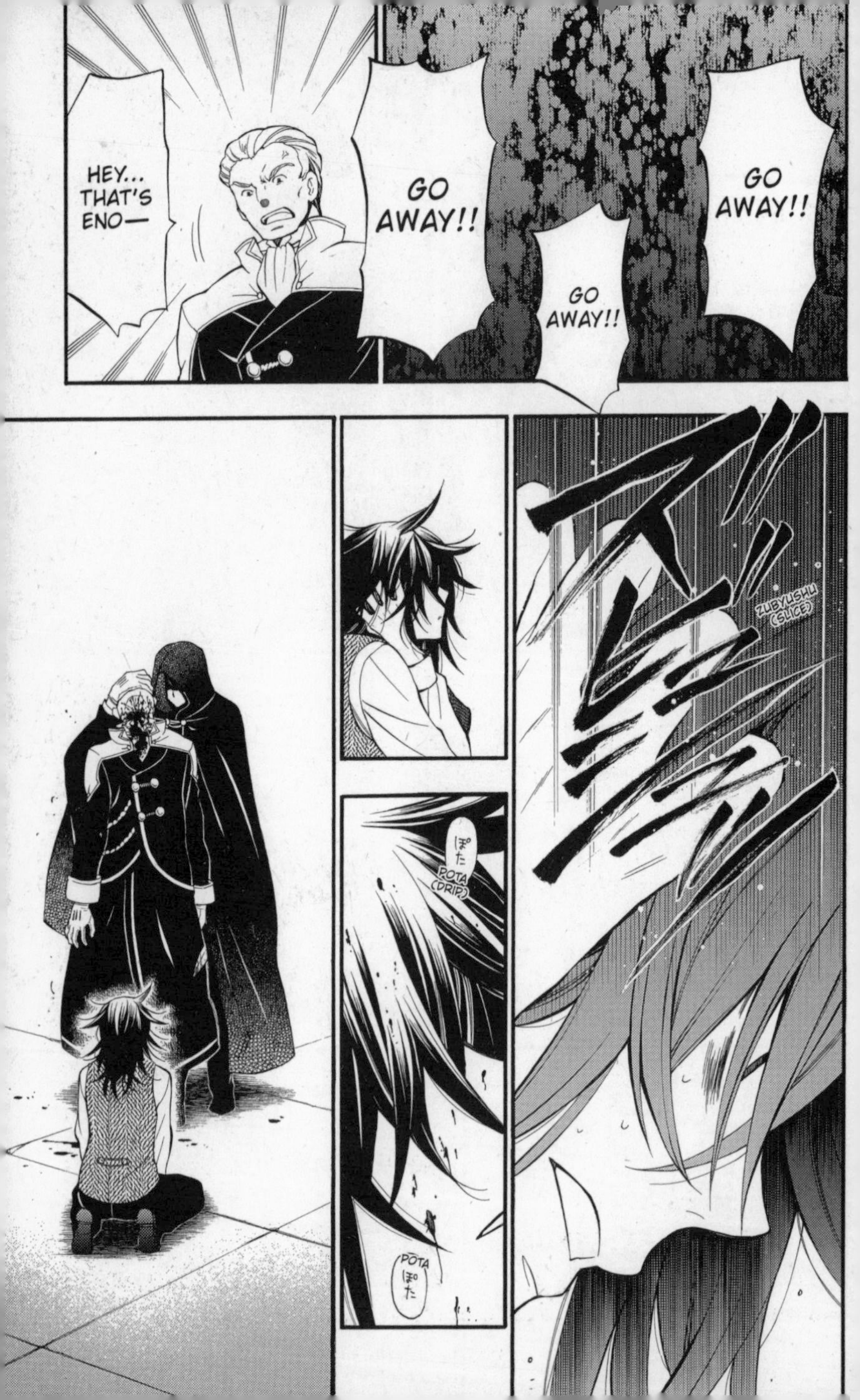
GO AWAY!!
GO AWAY!!
GO AWAY!!
HEY... THAT'S ENO—
ZUBYUSHU (SLICE)
ぽた POTA (DRIP)
POTA ぽた

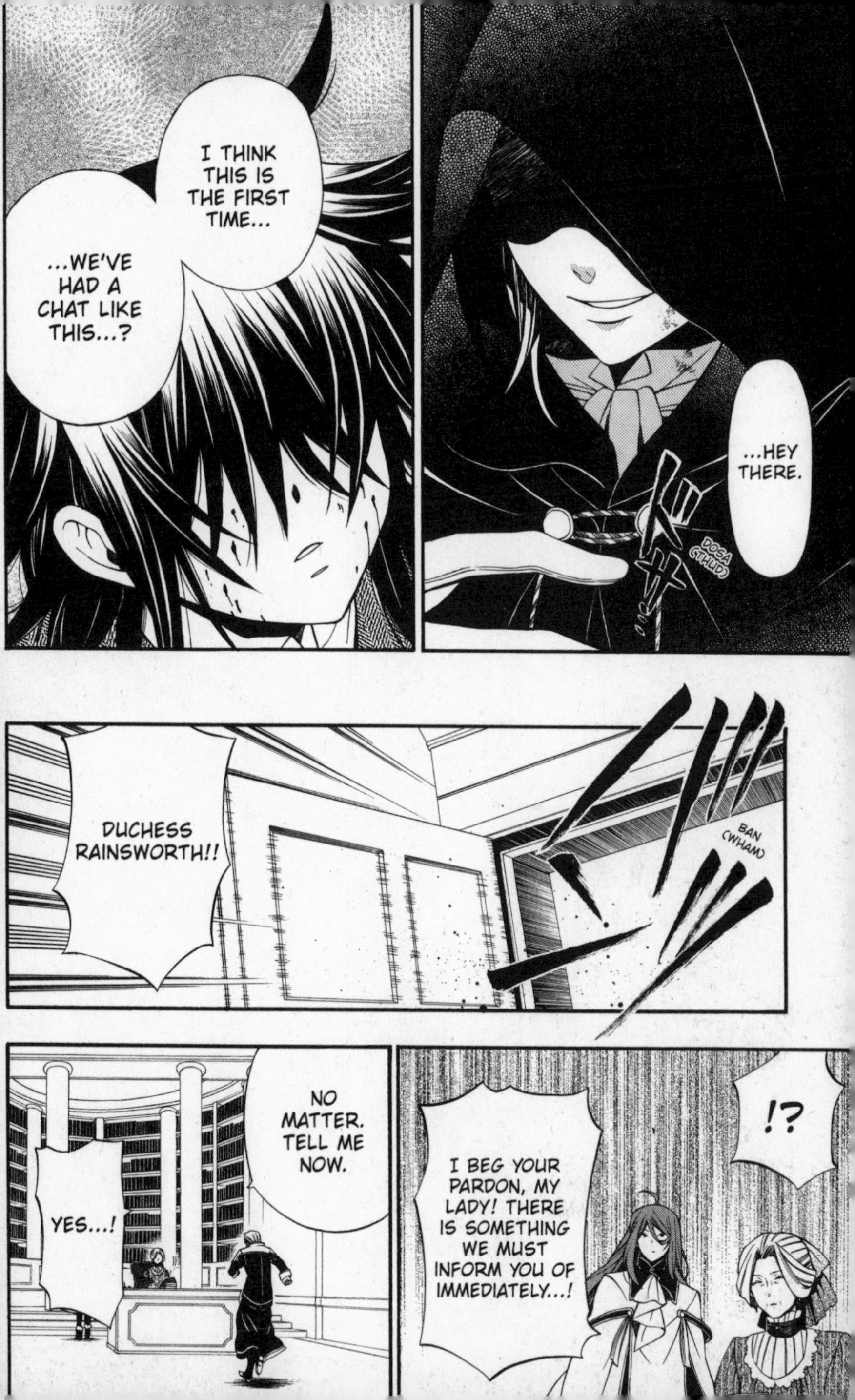
...HEY THERE.
DOSA (THUD)
I THINK THIS IS THE FIRST TIME...
...WE'VE HAD A CHAT LIKE THIS...?
BAN (WHAM)
DUCHESS RAINSWORTH!!
!?
I BEG YOUR PARDON, MY LADY! THERE IS SOMETHING WE MUST INFORM YOU OF IMMEDIATELY...!
NO MATTER. TELL ME NOW.
YES...!

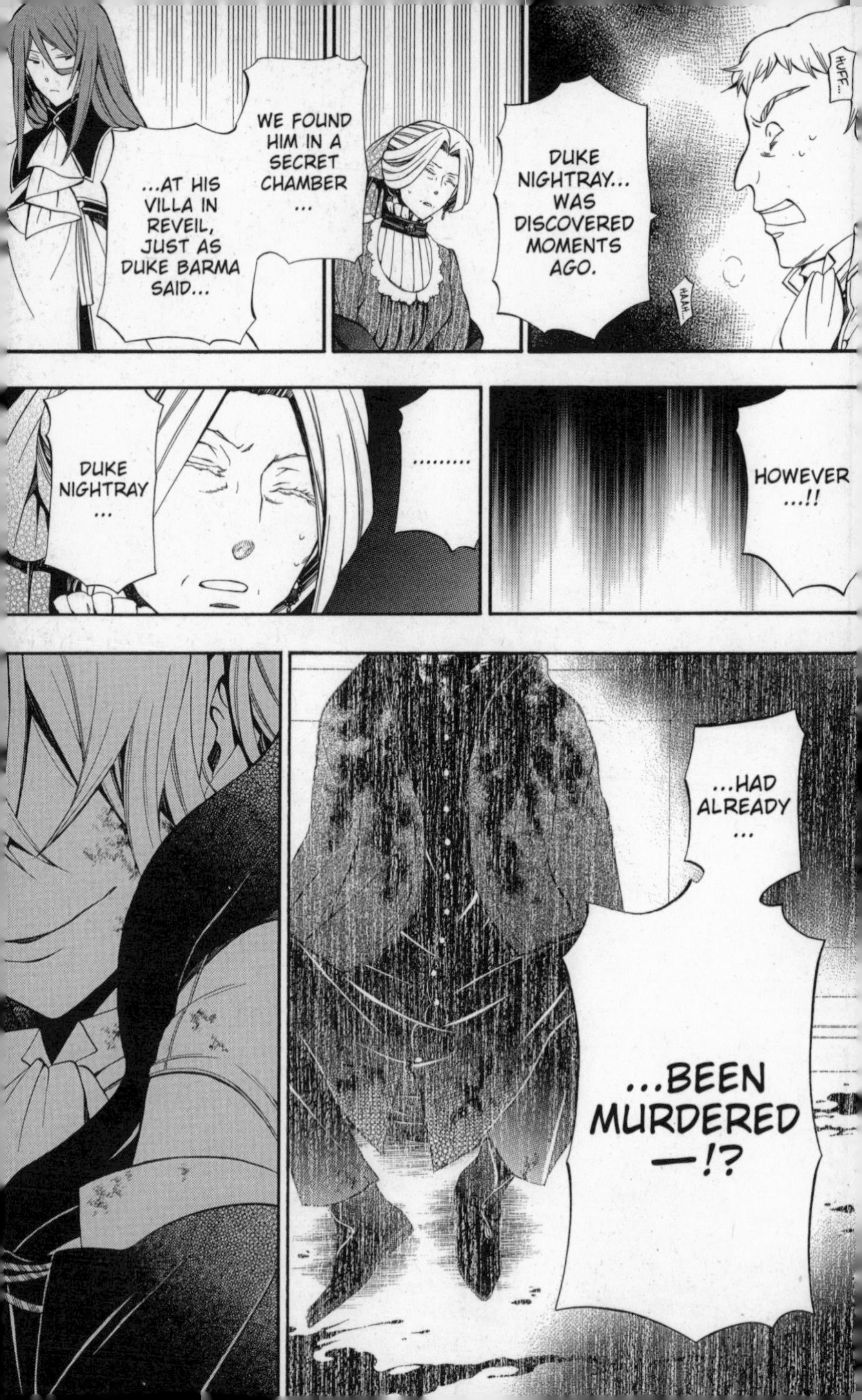
HUFF...
DUKE NIGHTRAY... WAS DISCOVERED MOMENTS AGO.
HAAH...
WE FOUND HIM IN A SECRET CHAMBER ...
...AT HIS VILLA IN REVEIL, JUST AS DUKE BARMA SAID...
HOWEVER ...!!
....
DUKE NIGHTRAY ...
...HAD ALREADY ...
...BEEN MURDERED —!?

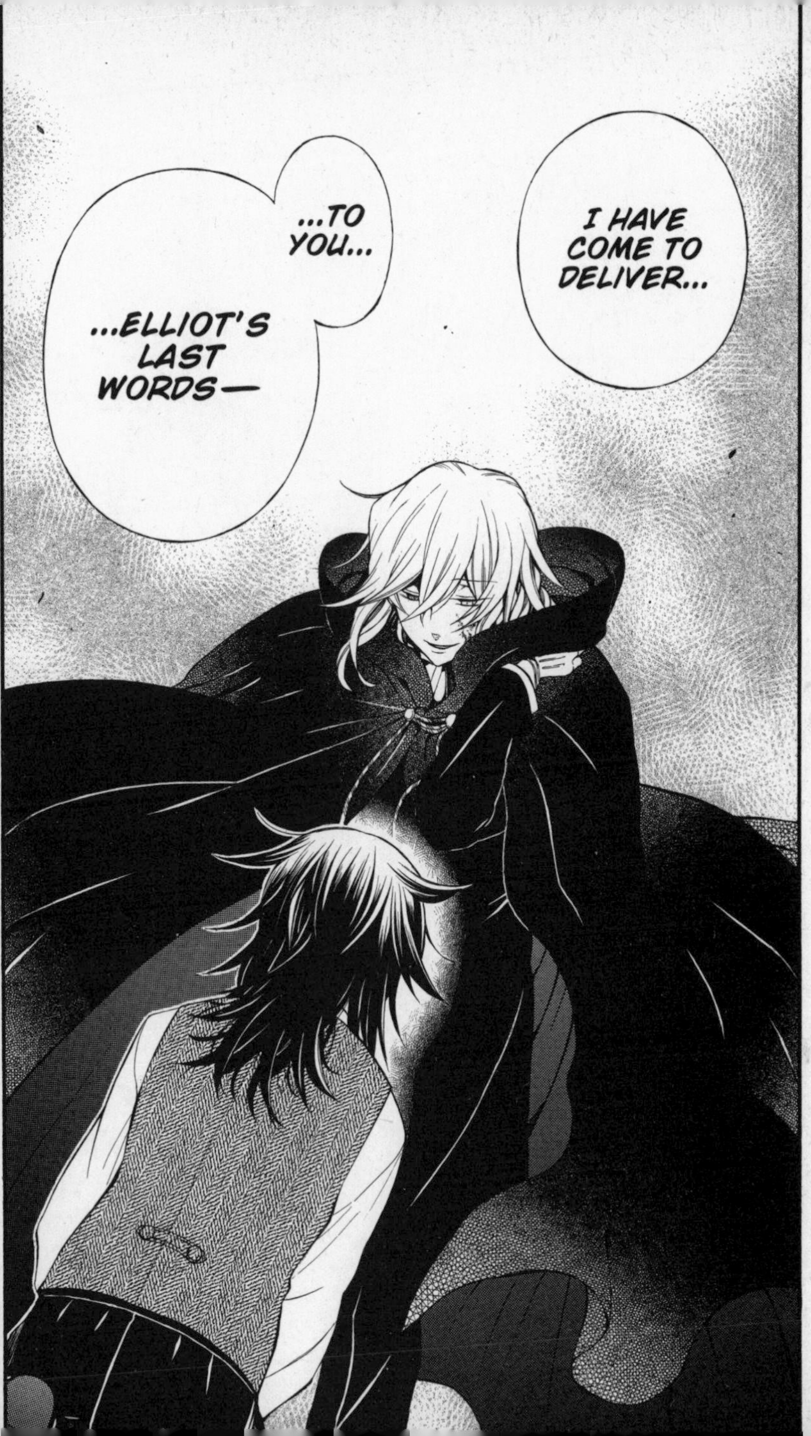
I HAVE COME TO DELIVER...
...TO YOU...
...ELLIOT'S LAST WORDS—

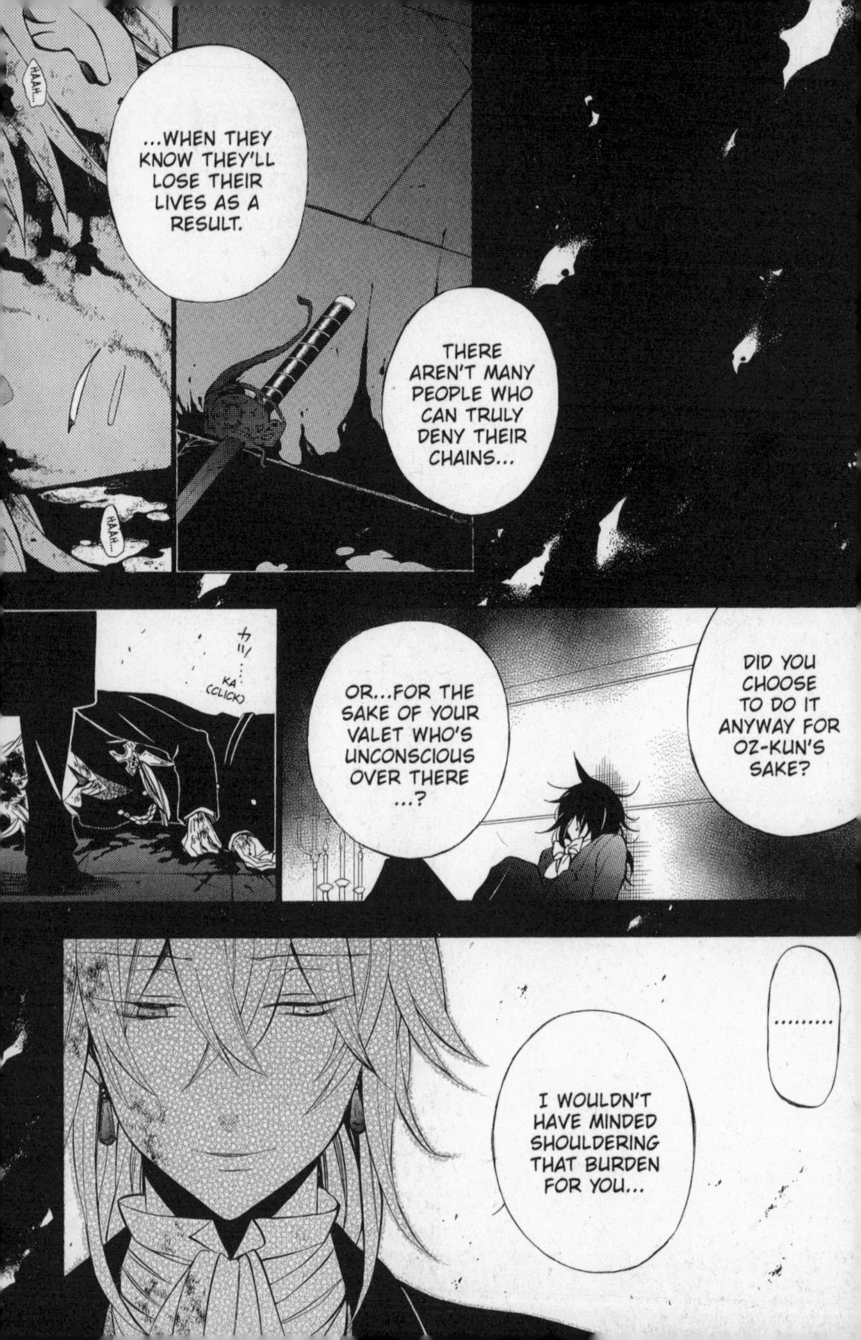
THERE AREN'T MANY PEOPLE WHO CAN TRULY DENY THEIR CHAINS...
...WHEN THEY KNOW THEY'LL LOSE THEIR LIVES AS A RESULT.
HAAH...
HAAH...
DID YOU CHOOSE TO DO IT ANYWAY FOR OZ-KUN'S SAKE?
OR...FOR THE SAKE OF YOUR VALET WHO'S UNCONSCIOUS OVER THERE ...?
KA (CLICK)
....
I WOULDN'T HAVE MINDED SHOULDERING THAT BURDEN FOR YOU...

Retrace:LXI Demios

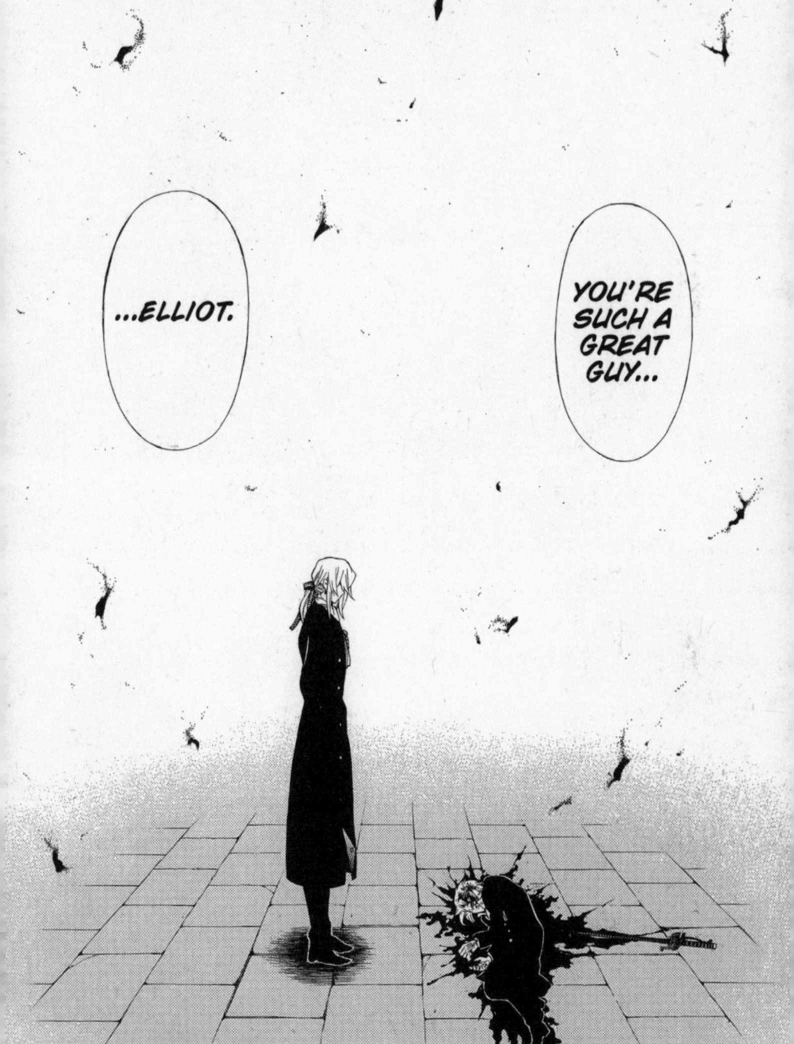
YOU'RE SUCH A GREAT GUY...
...ELLIOT.

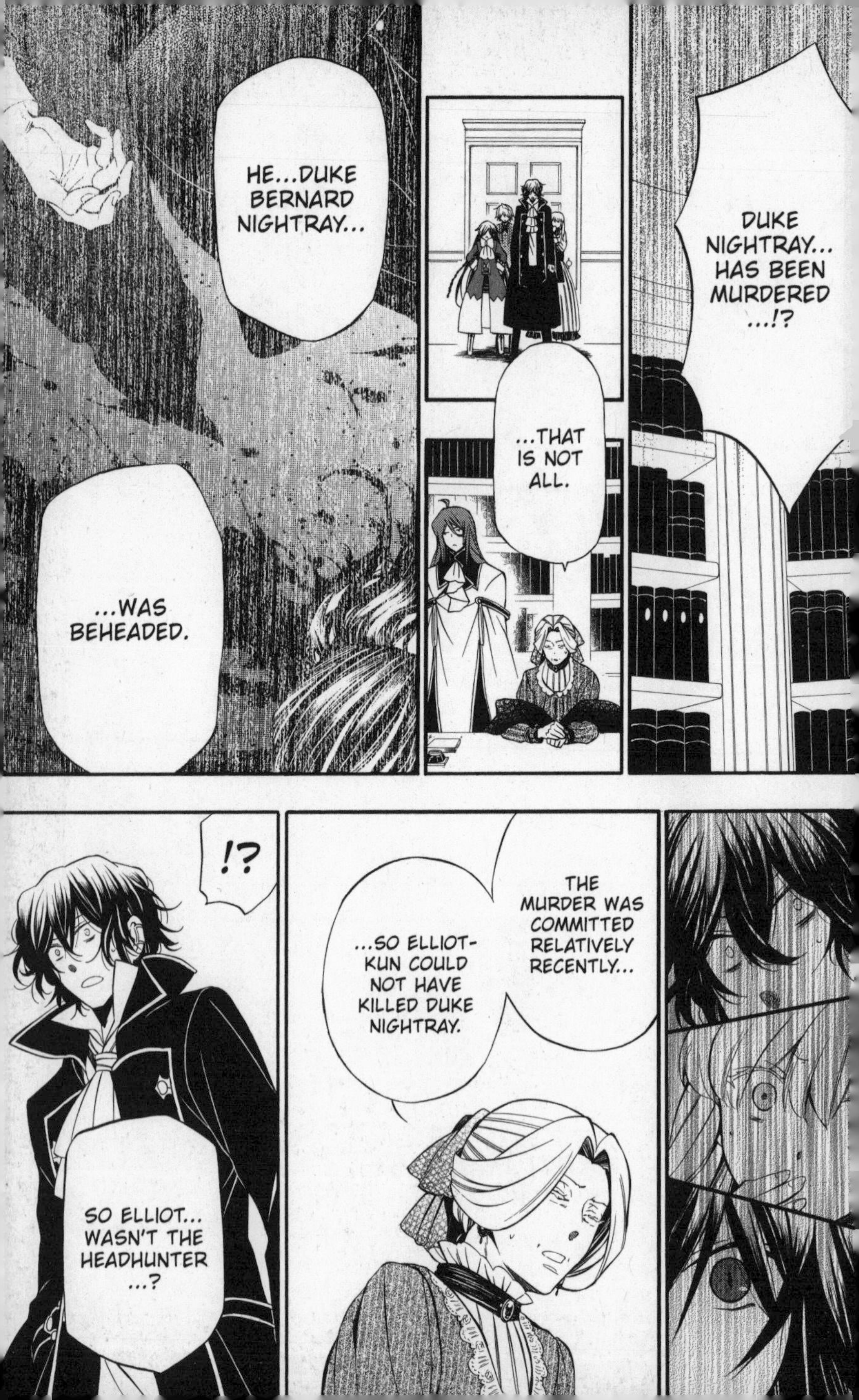
DUKE NIGHTRAY... HAS BEEN MURDERED ...!?
...THAT IS NOT ALL.
HE...DUKE BERNARD NIGHTRAY...
...WAS BEHEADED.
THE MURDER WAS COMMITTED RELATIVELY RECENTLY...
...SO ELLIOT-KUN COULD NOT HAVE KILLED DUKE NIGHTRAY.
!?
SO ELLIOT... WASN'T THE HEADHUNTER ...?

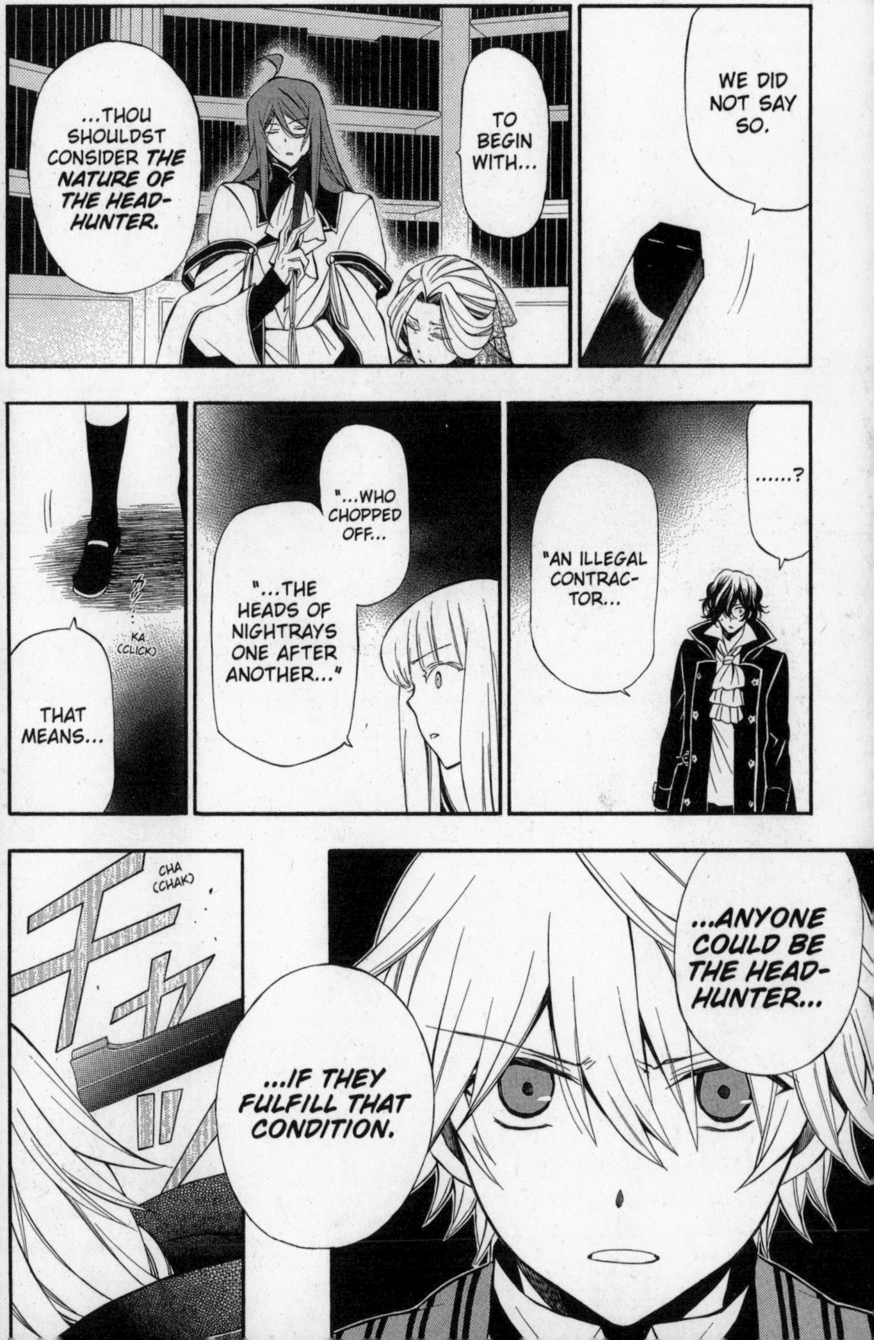
WE DID NOT SAY SO.
TO BEGIN WITH...
...THOU SHOULDST CONSIDER THE NATURE OF THE HEAD-HUNTER.
......?
"AN ILLEGAL CONTRACTOR...
"...WHO CHOPPED OFF...
"...THE HEADS OF NIGHTRAYS ONE AFTER ANOTHER..."
KA (CLICK)
THAT MEANS...
...ANYONE COULD BE THE HEAD-HUNTER...
...IF THEY FULFILL THAT CONDITION.
CHA (CHAK)

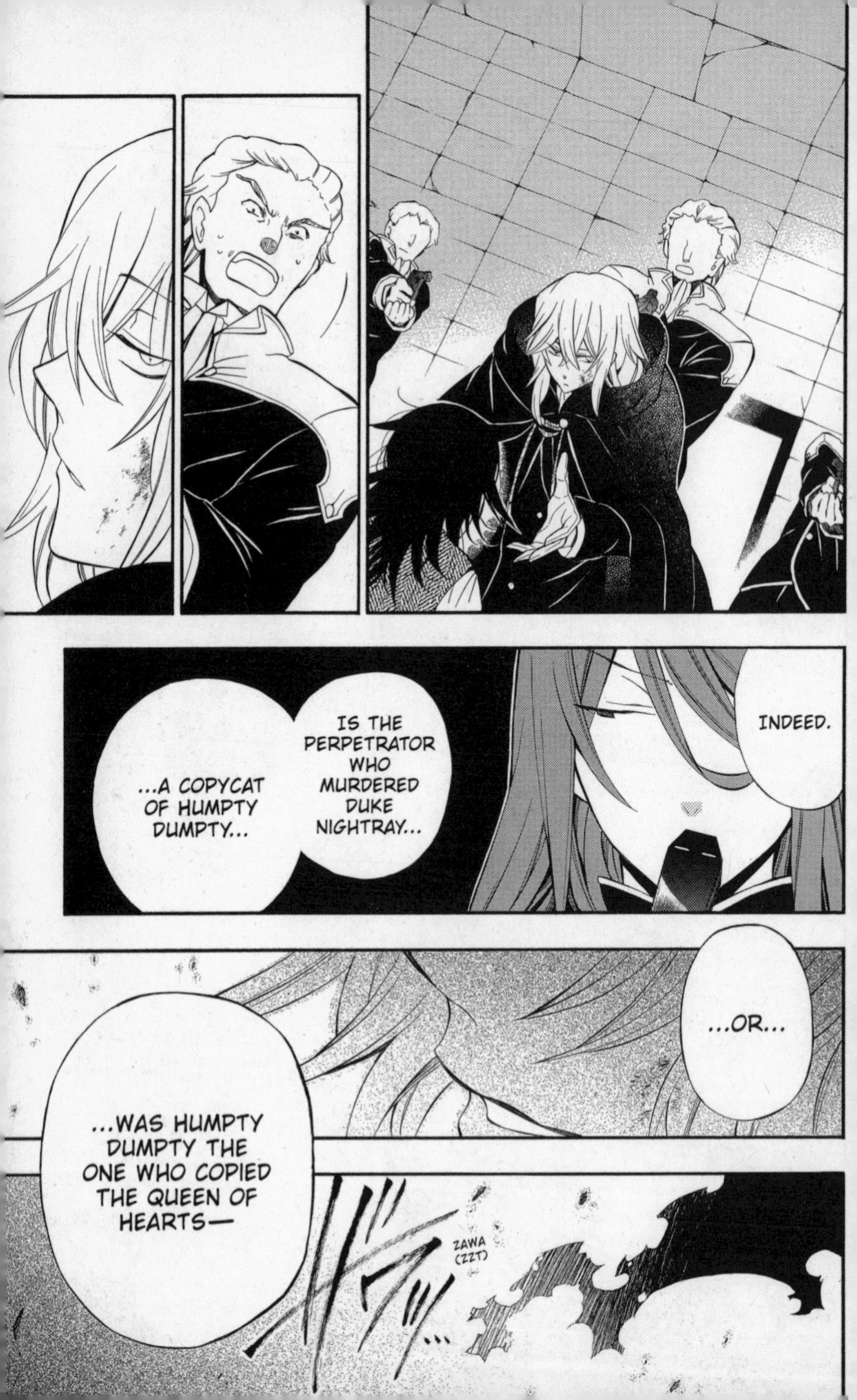
INDEED.
IS THE PERPETRATOR WHO MURDERED DUKE NIGHTRAY...
...A COPYCAT OF HUMPTY DUMPTY...
...OR...
...WAS HUMPTY DUMPTY THE ONE WHO COPIED THE QUEEN OF HEARTS—
ZAWA (ZZT)

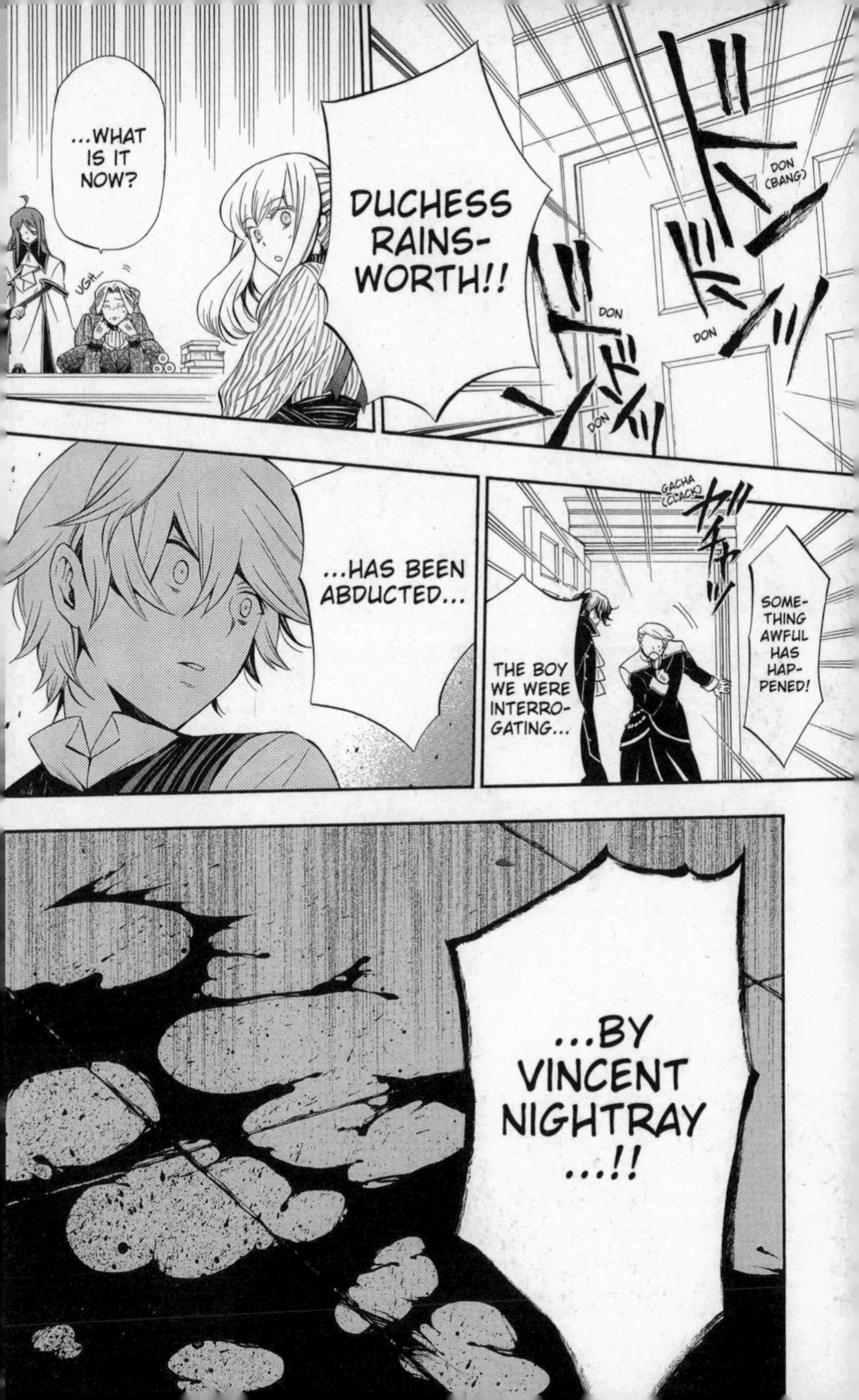
DON (BANG)
DON
DON
DON
DUCHESS RAINS-WORTH!!
...WHAT IS IT NOW?
UGH...
GACHA (CLACK)
SOME-THING AWFUL HAS HAP-PENED!
THE BOY WE WERE INTERRO-GATING...
...HAS BEEN ABDUCTED...
...BY VINCENT NIGHTRAY ...!!

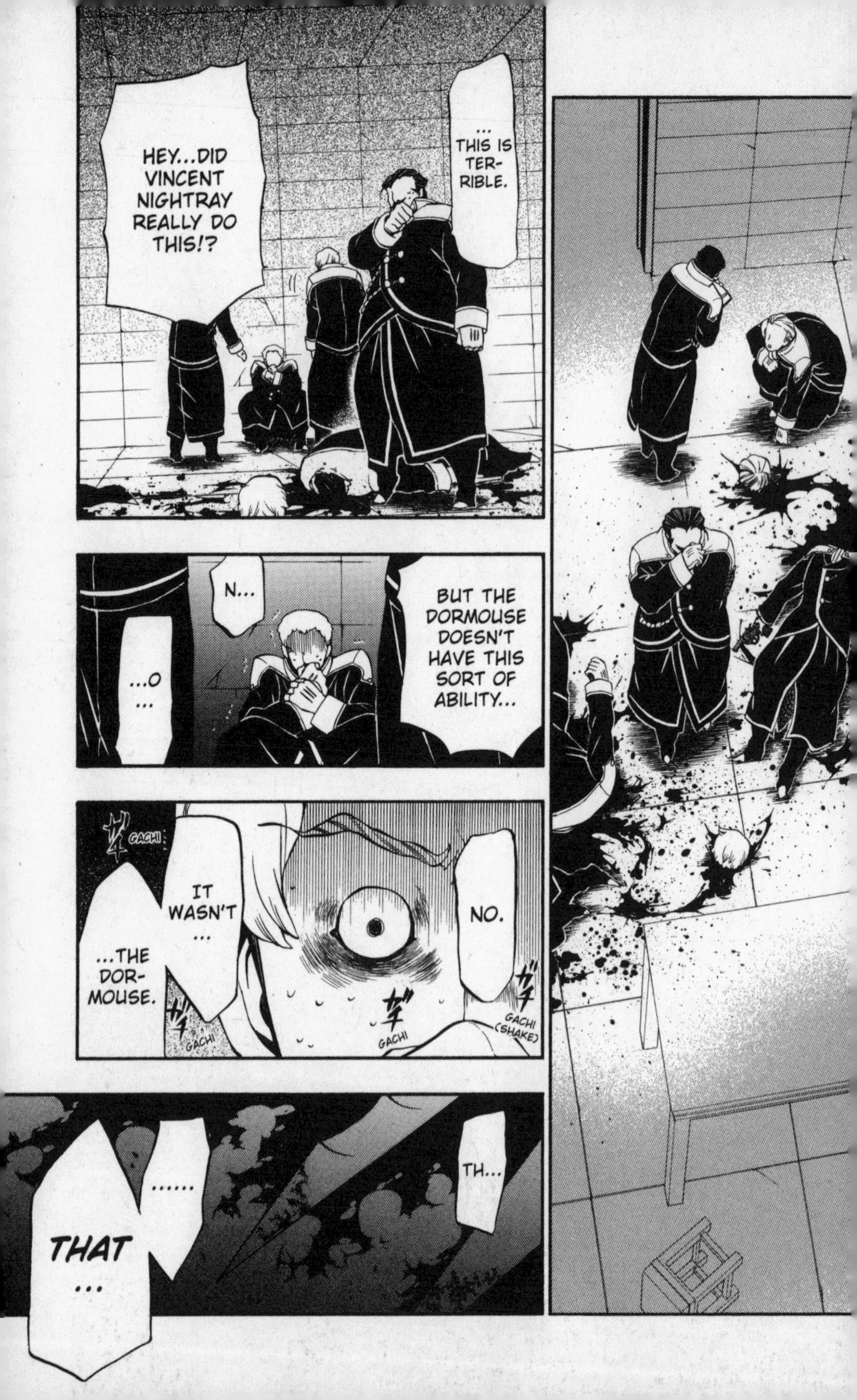
...THIS IS TERRIBLE.
HEY...DID VINCENT NIGHTRAY REALLY DO THIS!?
BUT THE DORMOUSE DOESN'T HAVE THIS SORT OF ABILITY...
N...
...O ...
GACHI (SHAKE)
GACHI
NO.
IT WASN'T ...
...THE DORMOUSE.
GACHI
GACHI
TH...
......
THAT ...

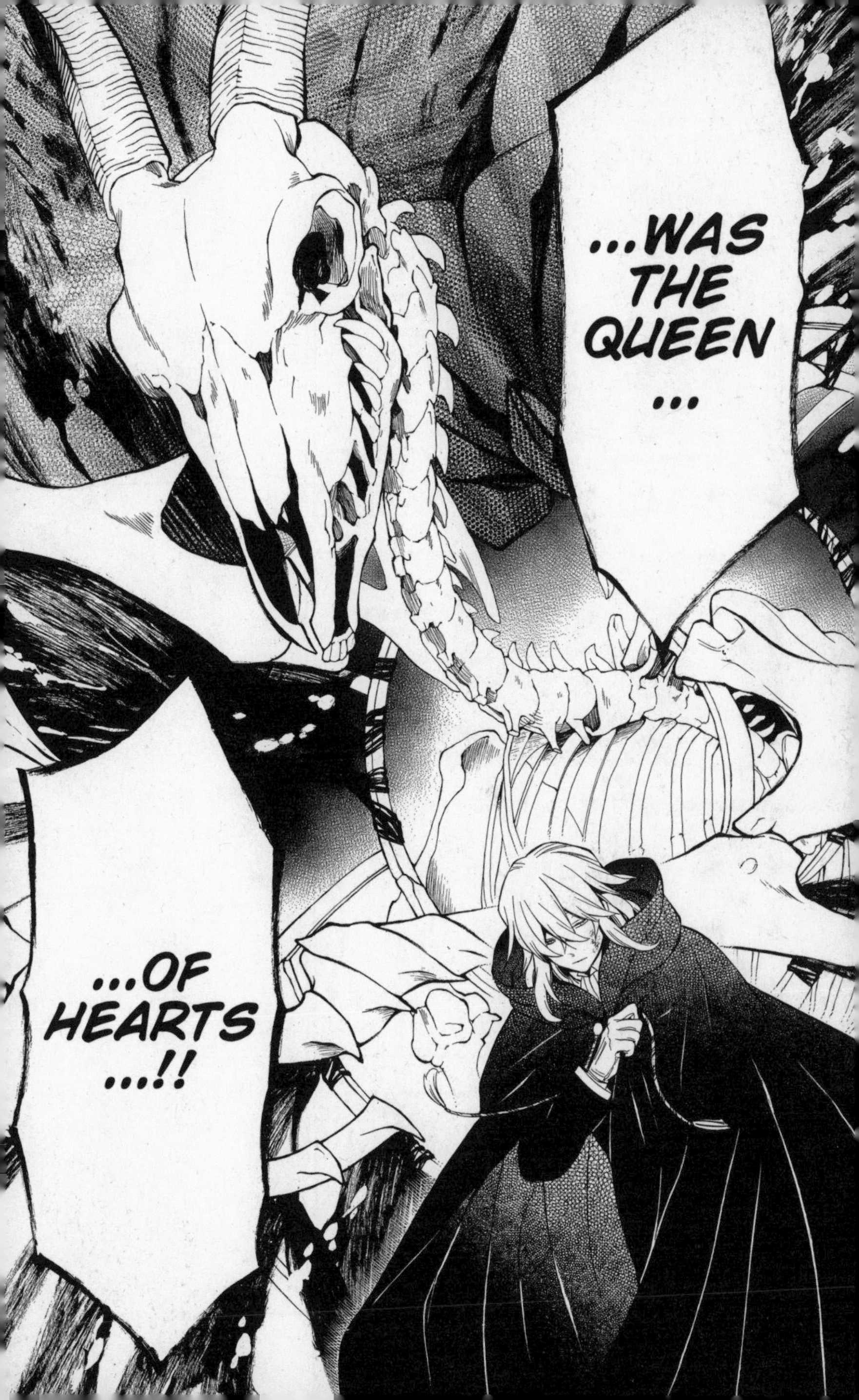
...WAS THE QUEEN ...
...OF HEARTS ...!!

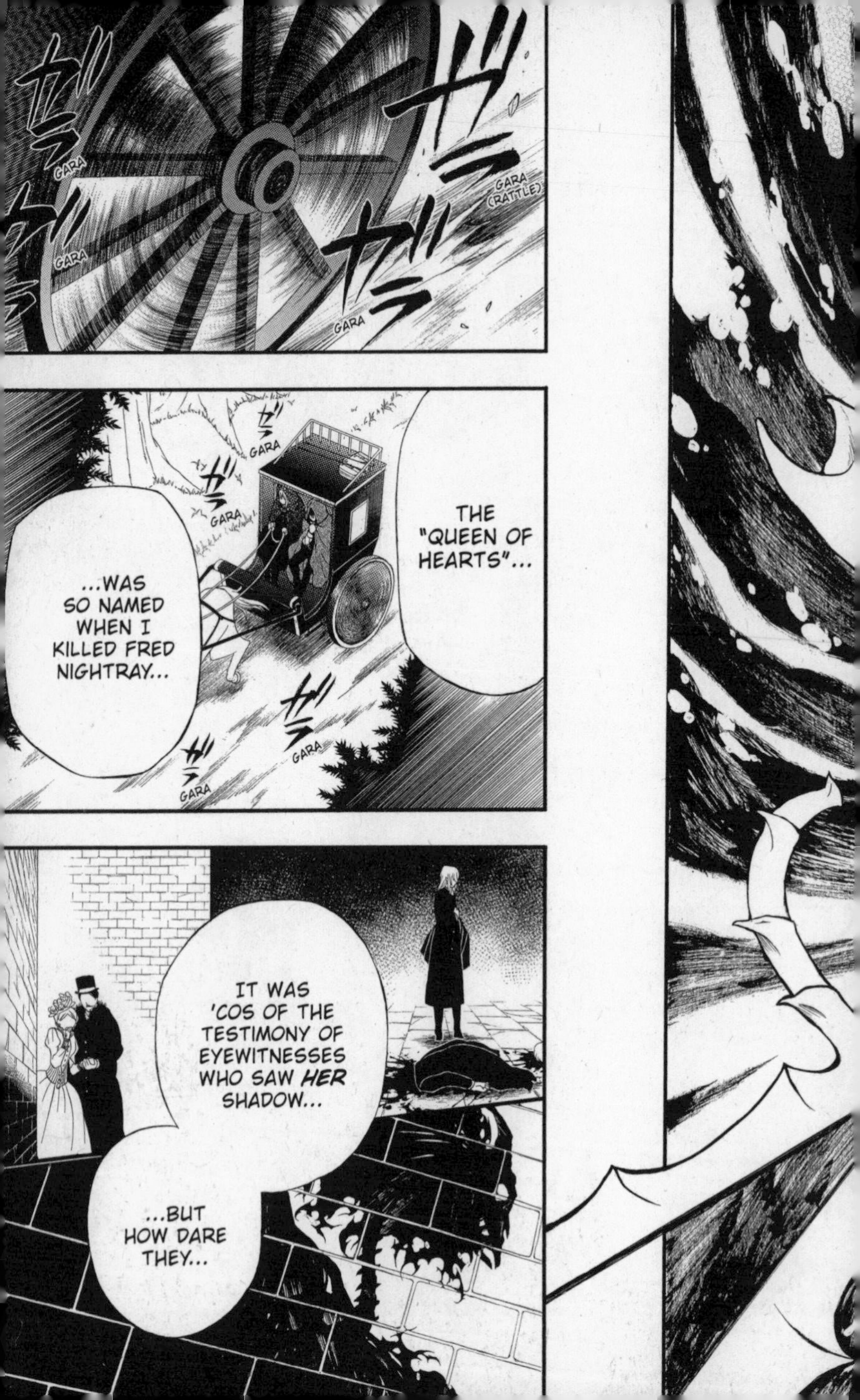
GARA (RATTLE)
GARA
GARA
GARA
THE "QUEEN OF HEARTS"...
GARA
GARA
...WAS SO NAMED WHEN I KILLED FRED NIGHTRAY...
GARA
GARA
IT WAS 'COS OF THE TESTIMONY OF EYEWITNESSES WHO SAW *HER* SHADOW...
...BUT HOW DARE THEY...

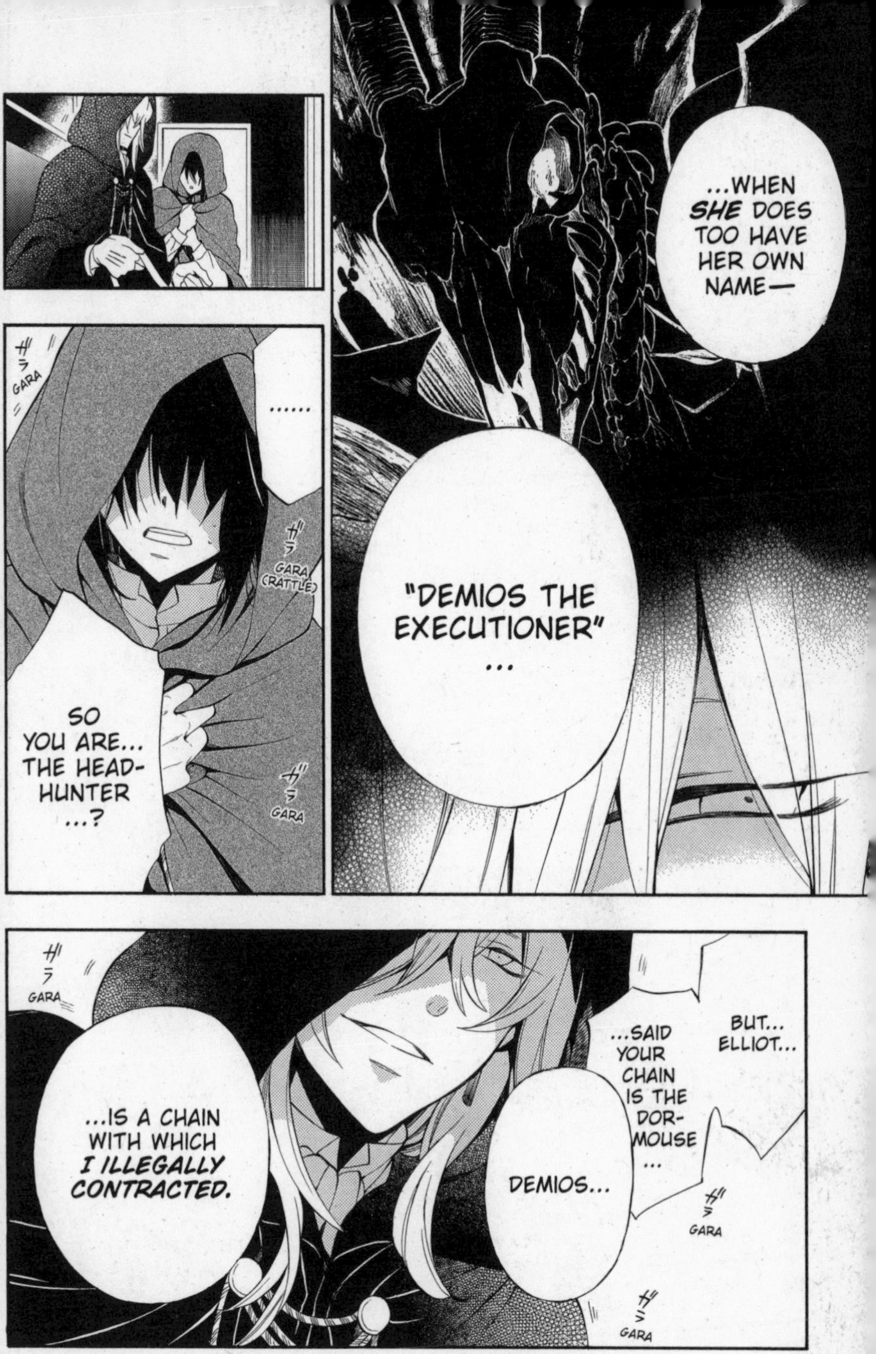
...WHEN SHE DOES TOO HAVE HER OWN NAME—
"DEMIOS THE EXECUTIONER" ...
ガラ GARA
......
ガラ GARA (RATTLE)
SO YOU ARE... THE HEAD-HUNTER ...?
ガラ GARA
BUT... ELLIOT...
...SAID YOUR CHAIN IS THE DOR-MOUSE ...
ガラ GARA
DEMIOS...
ガラ GARA
...IS A CHAIN WITH WHICH I ILLEGALLY CONTRACTED.
ガラ GARA

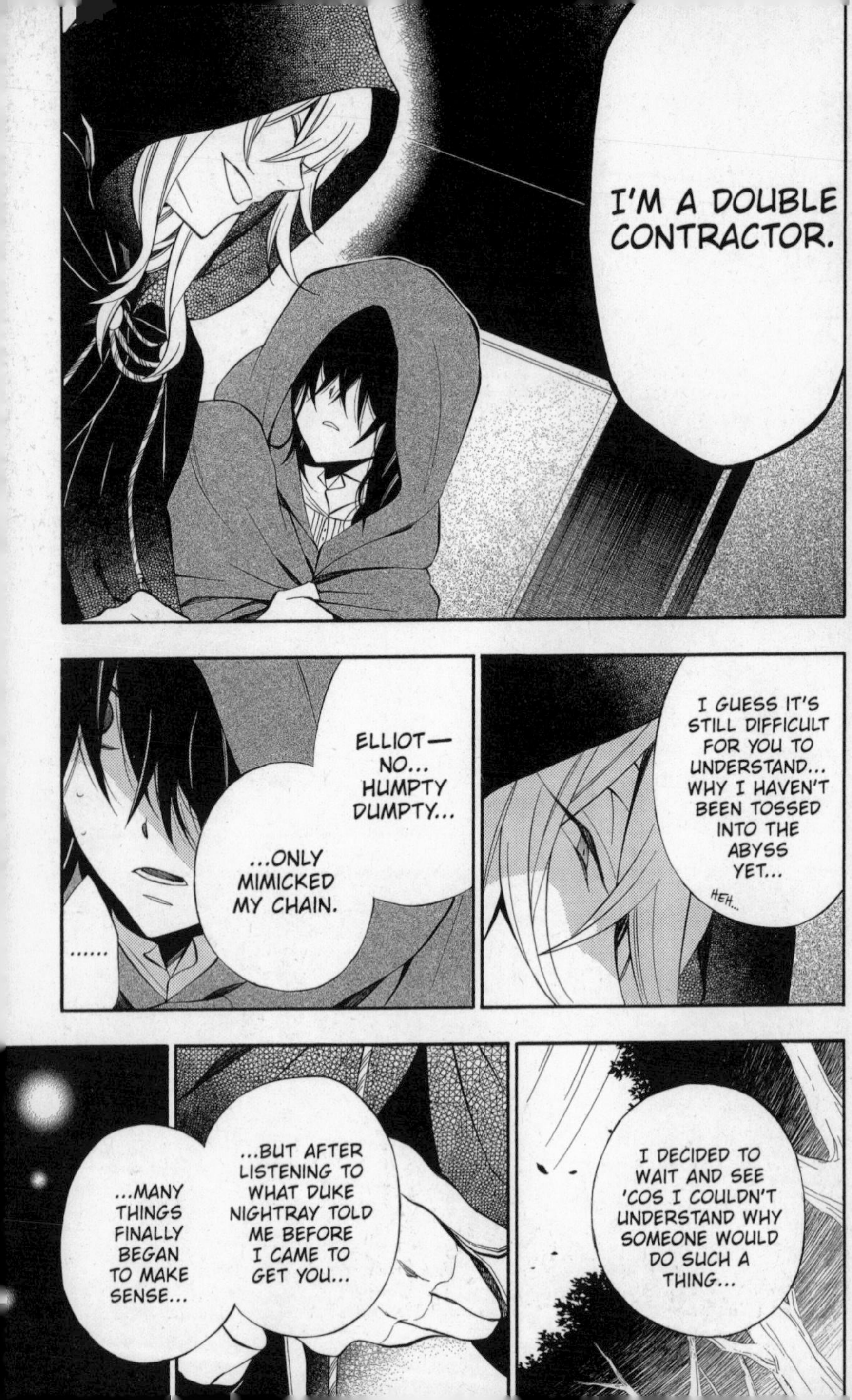
I'M A DOUBLE CONTRACTOR.
I GUESS IT'S STILL DIFFICULT FOR YOU TO UNDERSTAND... WHY I HAVEN'T BEEN TOSSED INTO THE ABYSS YET...
HEH...
ELLIOT— NO... HUMPTY DUMPTY...
...ONLY MIMICKED MY CHAIN.
......
I DECIDED TO WAIT AND SEE 'COS I COULDN'T UNDERSTAND WHY SOMEONE WOULD DO SUCH A THING...
...BUT AFTER LISTENING TO WHAT DUKE NIGHTRAY TOLD ME BEFORE I CAME TO GET YOU...
...MANY THINGS FINALLY BEGAN TO MAKE SENSE...

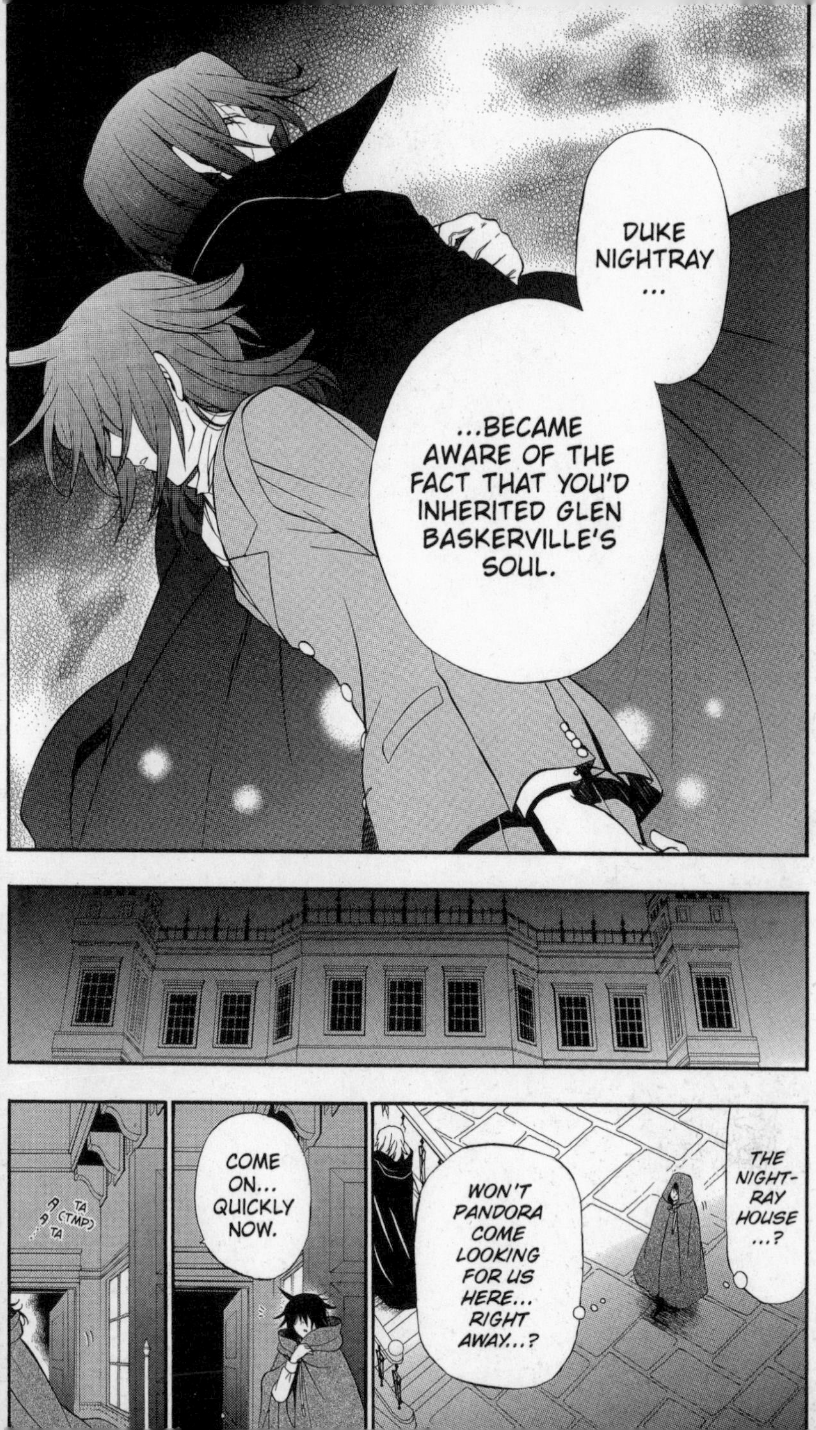
DUKE NIGHTRAY ...
...BECAME AWARE OF THE FACT THAT YOU'D INHERITED GLEN BASKERVILLE'S SOUL.
THE NIGHT-RAY HOUSE ...?
WON'T PANDORA COME LOOKING FOR US HERE... RIGHT AWAY...?
COME ON... QUICKLY NOW.

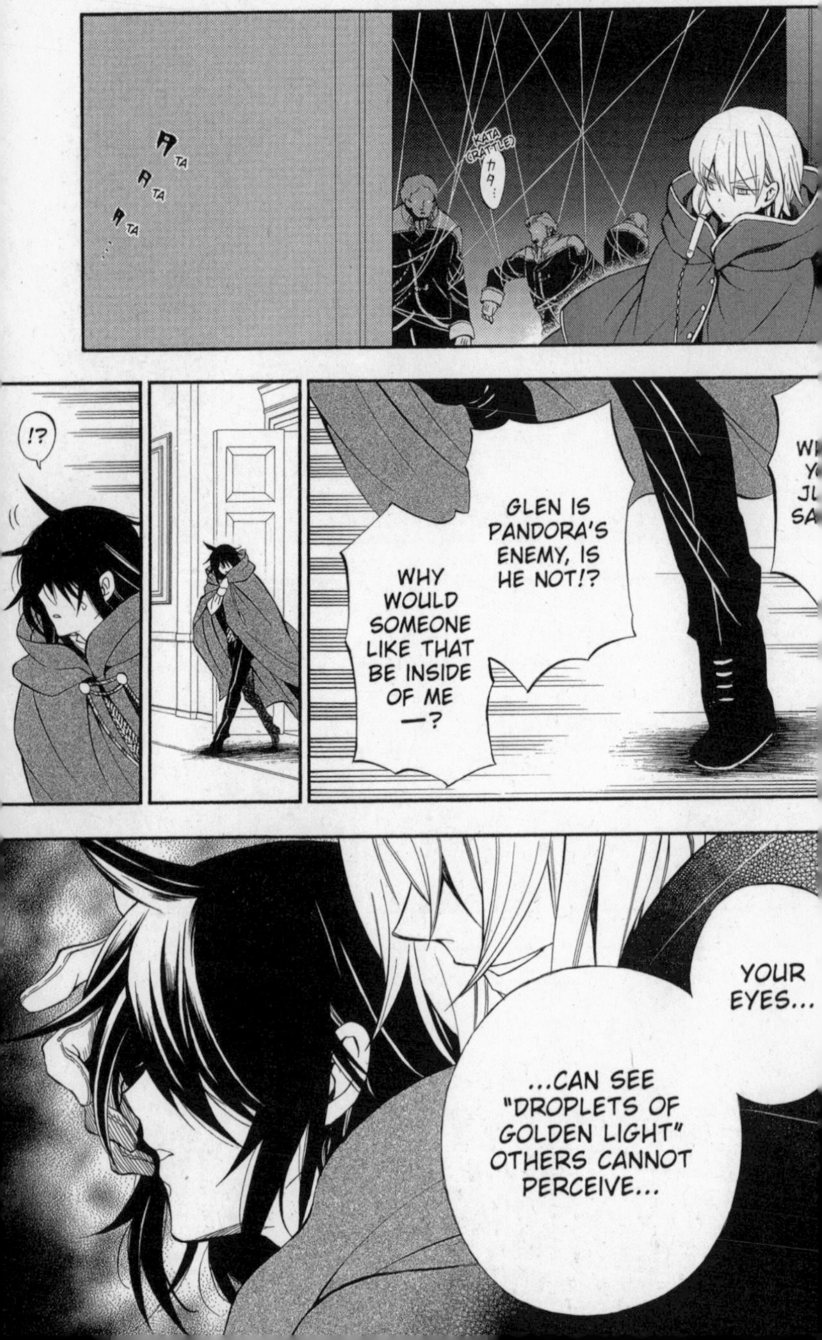
KATA (RATTLE)
カタ…
TA TA TA…
GLEN IS PANDORA'S ENEMY, IS HE NOT!?
WHY WOULD SOMEONE LIKE THAT BE INSIDE OF ME —?
!?
YOUR EYES…
…CAN SEE "DROPLETS OF GOLDEN LIGHT" OTHERS CANNOT PERCEIVE…

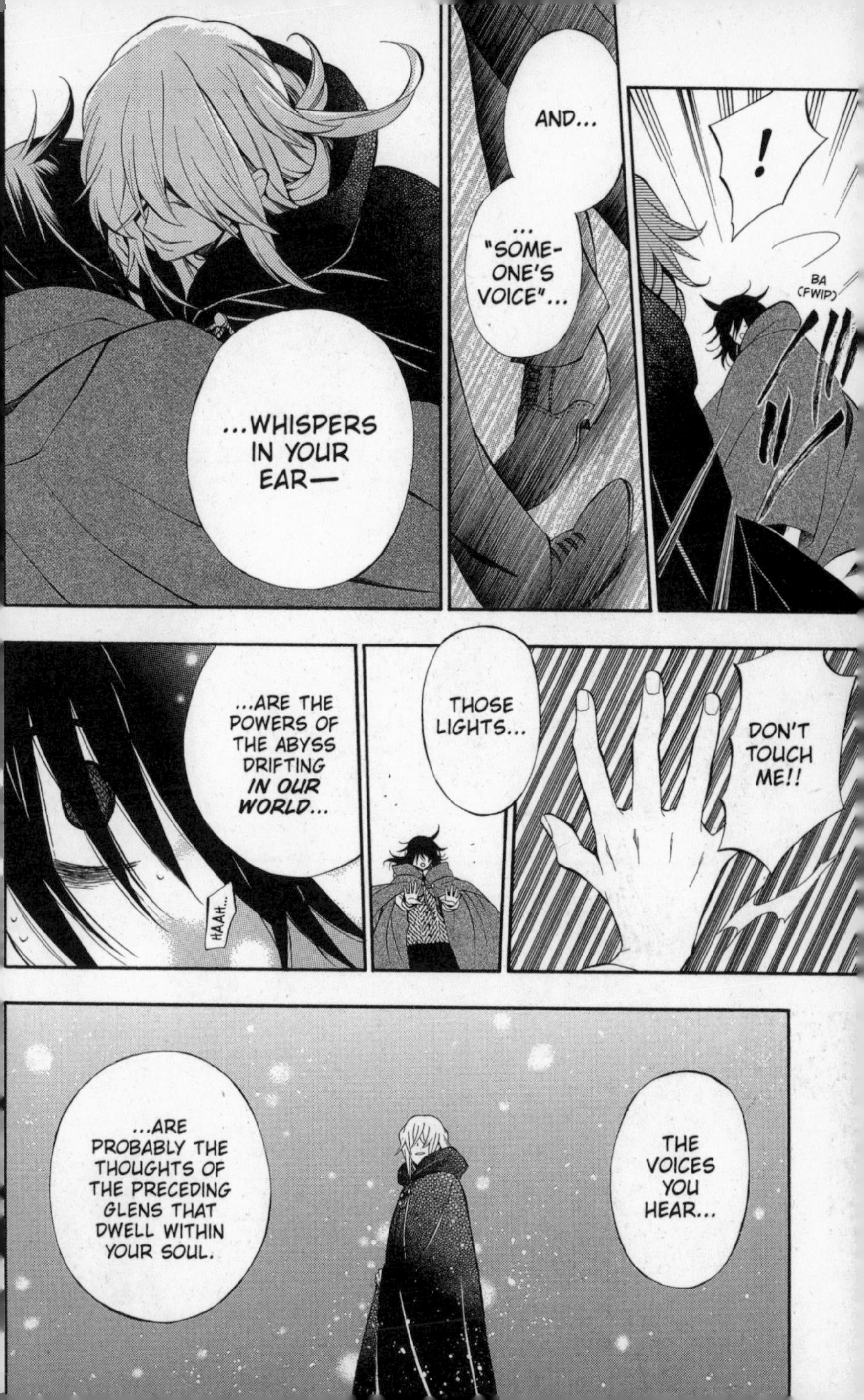
!
BA (FWIP)
AND...
... "SOME-ONE'S VOICE"...
...WHISPERS IN YOUR EAR—
DON'T TOUCH ME!!
THOSE LIGHTS...
...ARE THE POWERS OF THE ABYSS DRIFTING *IN OUR WORLD*...
HAAH...
THE VOICES YOU HEAR...
...ARE PROBABLY THE THOUGHTS OF THE PRECEDING GLENS THAT DWELL WITHIN YOUR SOUL.

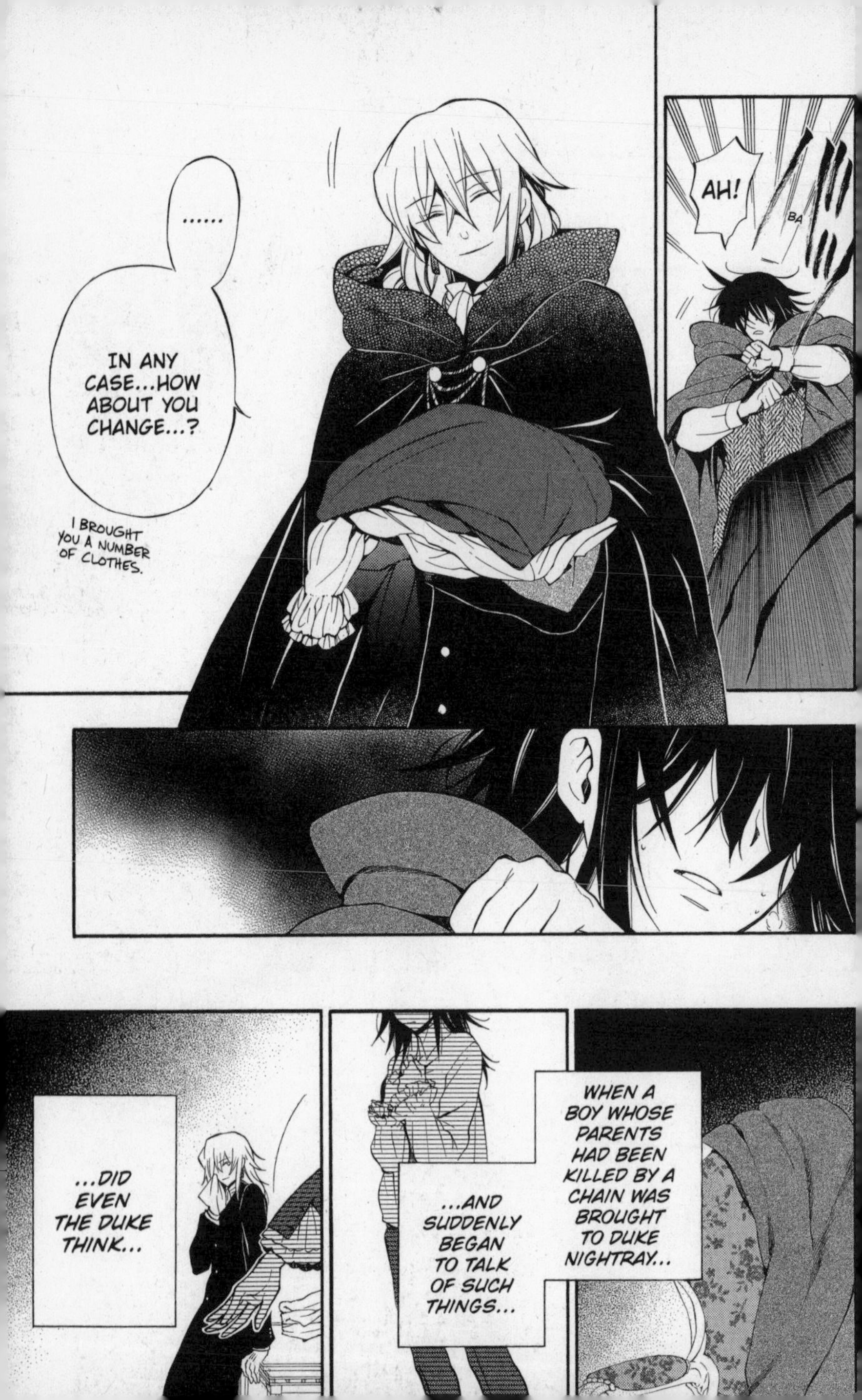
AH!
BA
......
IN ANY CASE...HOW ABOUT YOU CHANGE...?
I BROUGHT YOU A NUMBER OF CLOTHES.
WHEN A BOY WHOSE PARENTS HAD BEEN KILLED BY A CHAIN WAS BROUGHT TO DUKE NIGHTRAY...
...AND SUDDENLY BEGAN TO TALK OF SUCH THINGS...
...DID EVEN THE DUKE THINK...

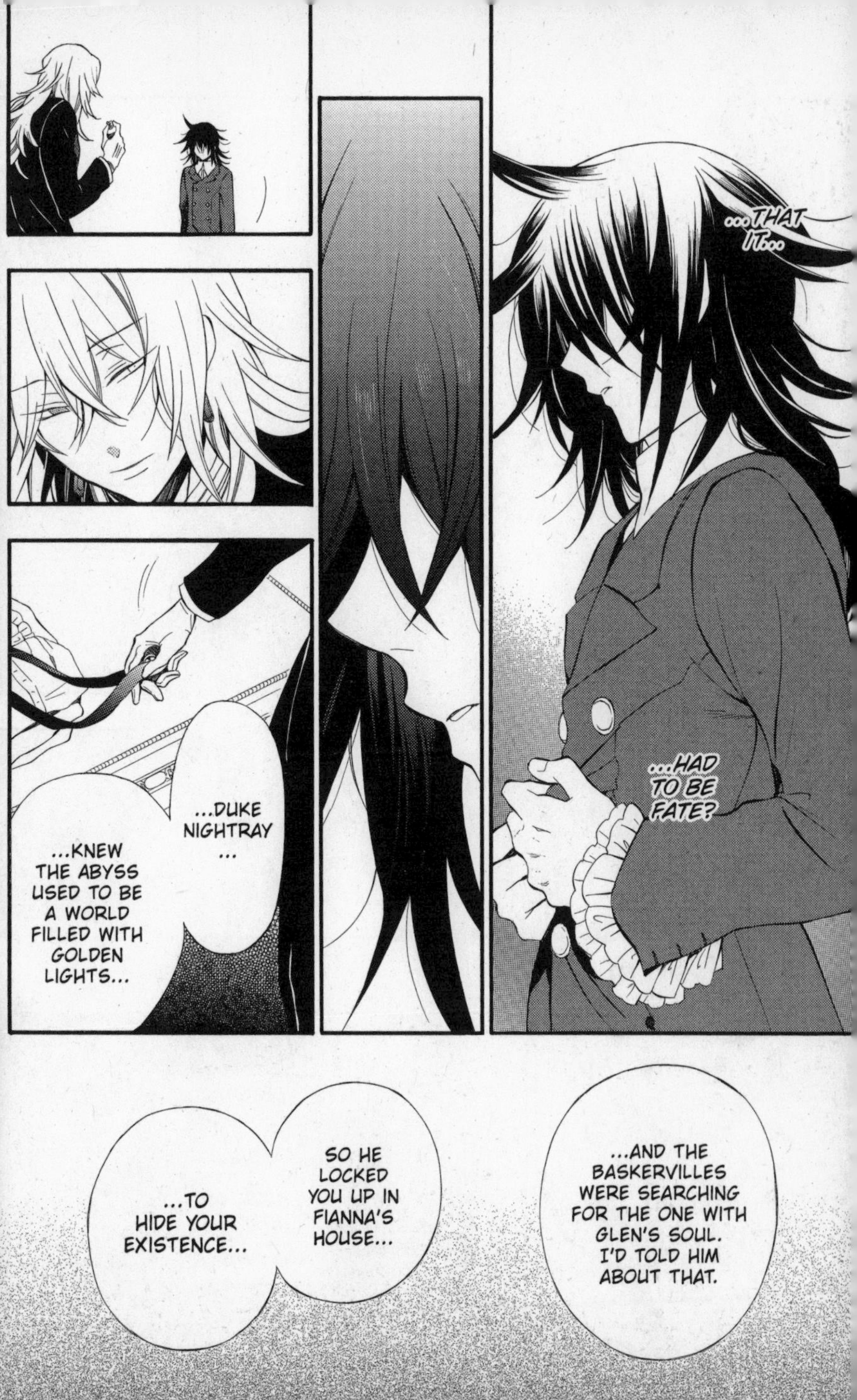
...THAT IT...
...HAD TO BE FATE?
...DUKE NIGHTRAY ...
...KNEW THE ABYSS USED TO BE A WORLD FILLED WITH GOLDEN LIGHTS...
...AND THE BASKERVILLES WERE SEARCHING FOR THE ONE WITH GLEN'S SOUL. I'D TOLD HIM ABOUT THAT.
SO HE LOCKED YOU UP IN FIANNA'S HOUSE...
...TO HIDE YOUR EXISTENCE...

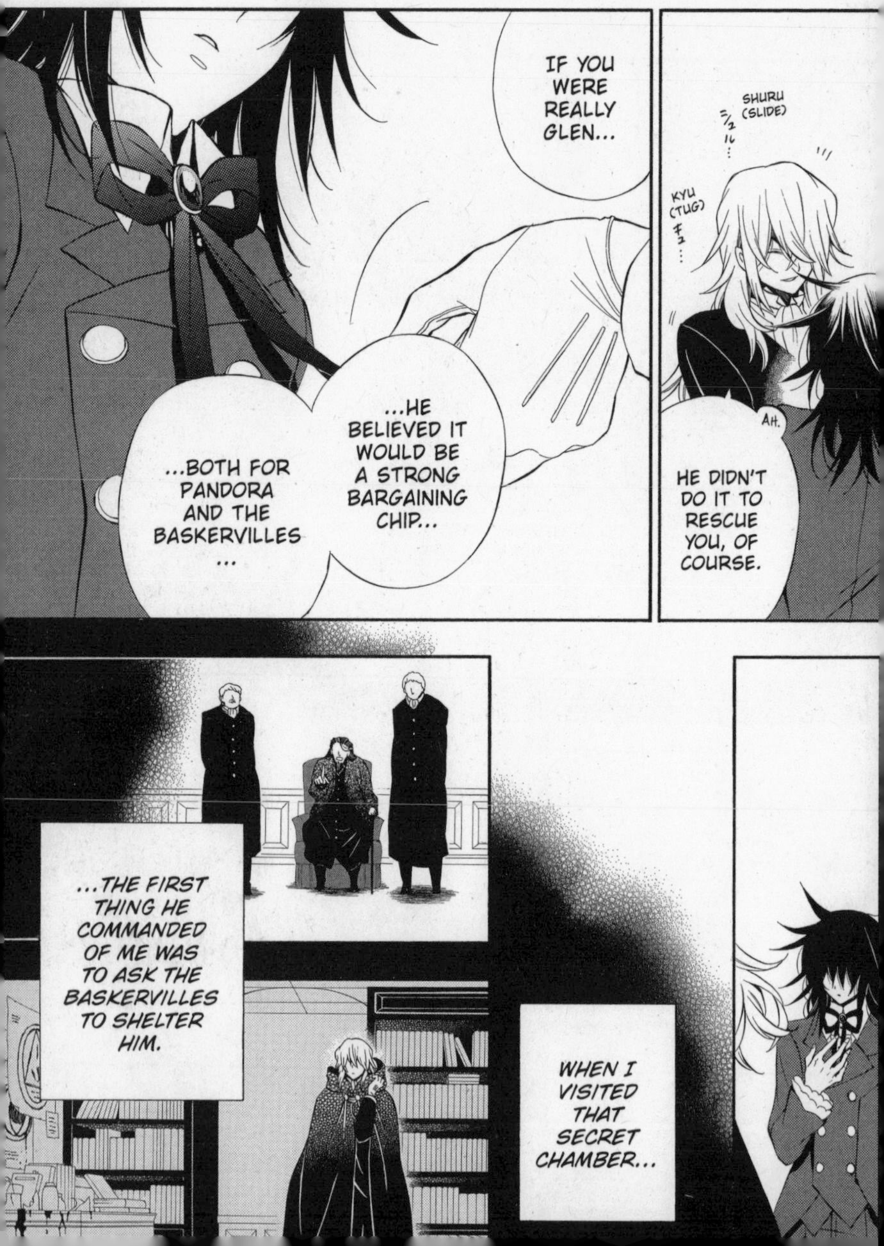

SHURU (SLIDE)
KYU (TUG)
AH.
HE DIDN'T DO IT TO RESCUE YOU, OF COURSE.
IF YOU WERE REALLY GLEN...
...HE BELIEVED IT WOULD BE A STRONG BARGAINING CHIP...
...BOTH FOR PANDORA AND THE BASKERVILLES...
WHEN I VISITED THAT SECRET CHAMBER...
...THE FIRST THING HE COMMANDED OF ME WAS TO ASK THE BASKERVILLES TO SHELTER HIM.

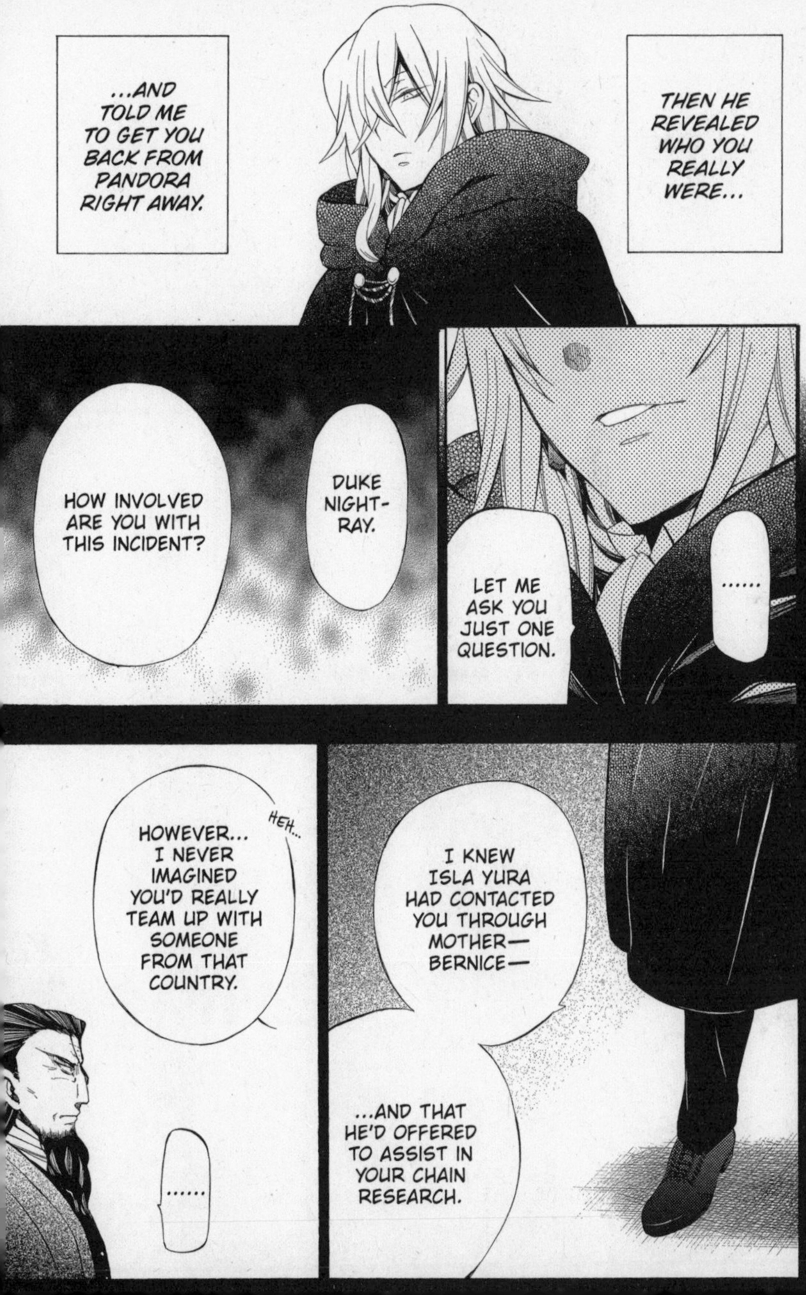
THEN HE REVEALED WHO YOU REALLY WERE...
...AND TOLD ME TO GET YOU BACK FROM PANDORA RIGHT AWAY.
......
LET ME ASK YOU JUST ONE QUESTION.
DUKE NIGHT-RAY.
HOW INVOLVED ARE YOU WITH THIS INCIDENT?
I KNEW ISLA YURA HAD CONTACTED YOU THROUGH MOTHER—BERNICE—
...AND THAT HE'D OFFERED TO ASSIST IN YOUR CHAIN RESEARCH.
HEH...
HOWEVER... I NEVER IMAGINED YOU'D REALLY TEAM UP WITH SOMEONE FROM THAT COUNTRY.
......

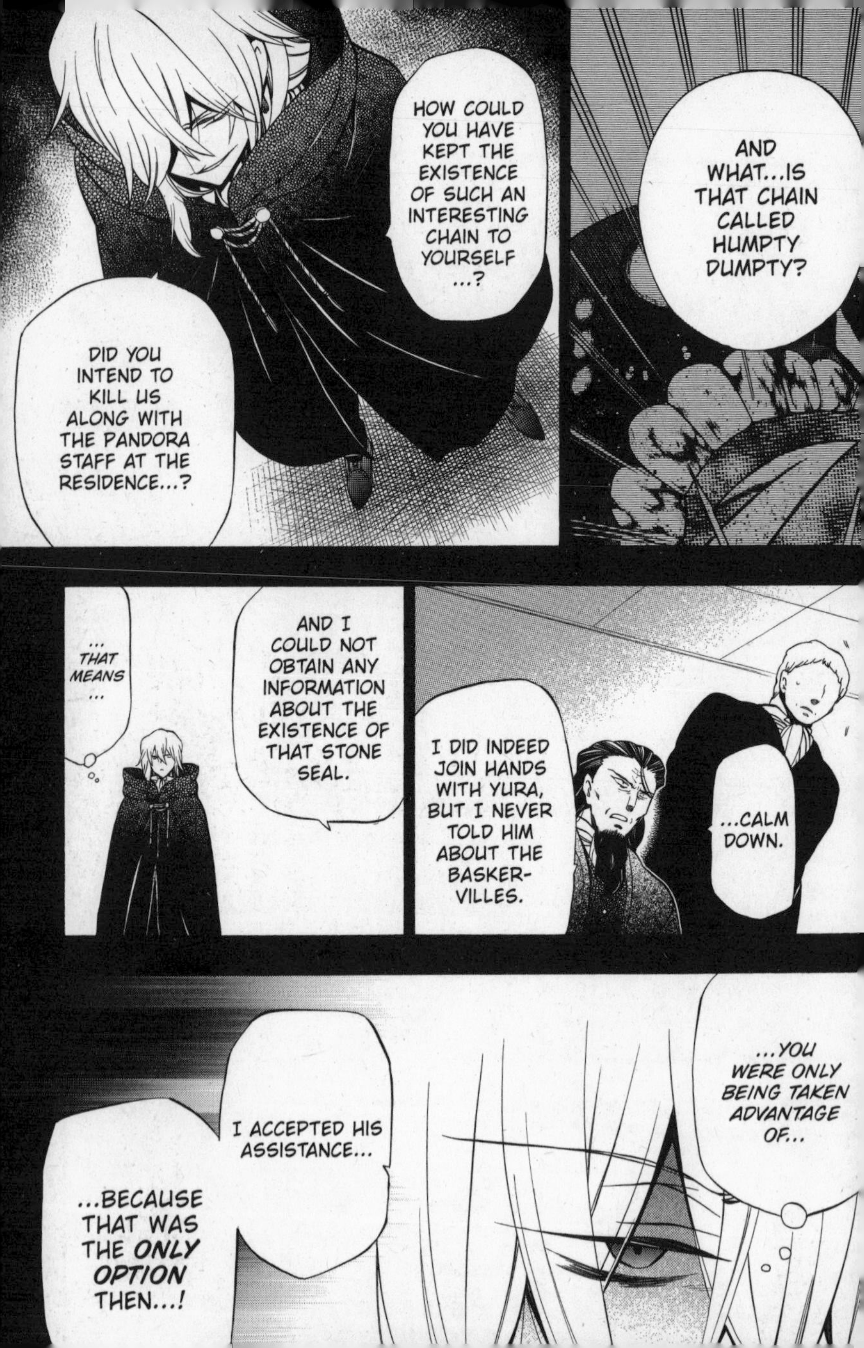
AND WHAT...IS THAT CHAIN CALLED HUMPTY DUMPTY?
HOW COULD YOU HAVE KEPT THE EXISTENCE OF SUCH AN INTERESTING CHAIN TO YOURSELF ...?
DID YOU INTEND TO KILL US ALONG WITH THE PANDORA STAFF AT THE RESIDENCE...?
...CALM DOWN.
I DID INDEED JOIN HANDS WITH YURA, BUT I NEVER TOLD HIM ABOUT THE BASKER-VILLES.
AND I COULD NOT OBTAIN ANY INFORMATION ABOUT THE EXISTENCE OF THAT STONE SEAL.
...THAT MEANS...
...YOU WERE ONLY BEING TAKEN ADVANTAGE OF...
I ACCEPTED HIS ASSISTANCE...
...BECAUSE THAT WAS THE *ONLY OPTION* THEN...!

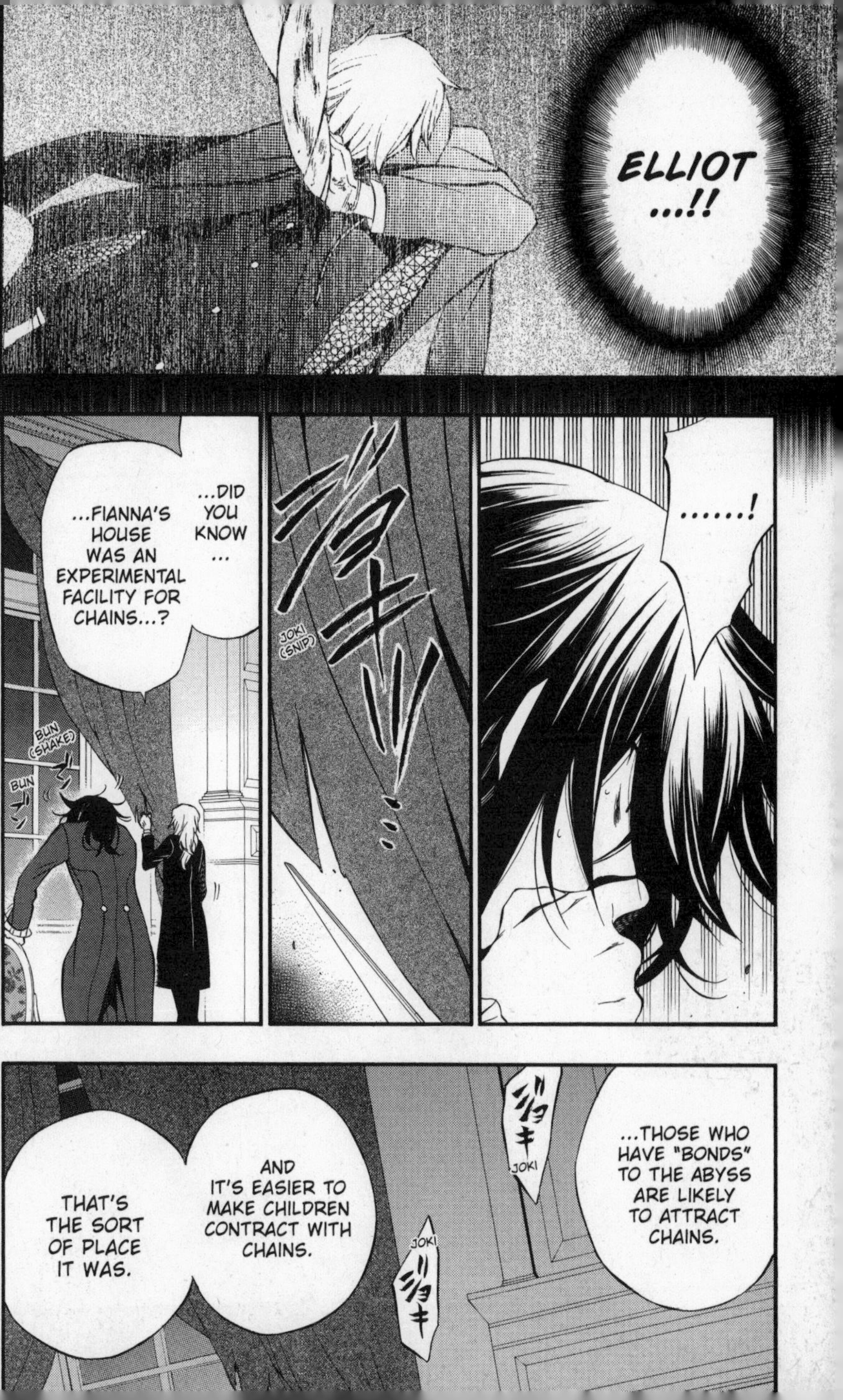
ELLIOT ...!!
......!
JOKI (SNIP)
...DID YOU KNOW ...
...FIANNA'S HOUSE WAS AN EXPERIMENTAL FACILITY FOR CHAINS...?
BUN (SHAKE)
BUN
...THOSE WHO HAVE "BONDS" TO THE ABYSS ARE LIKELY TO ATTRACT CHAINS.
JOKI
JOKI
AND IT'S EASIER TO MAKE CHILDREN CONTRACT WITH CHAINS.
THAT'S THE SORT OF PLACE IT WAS.

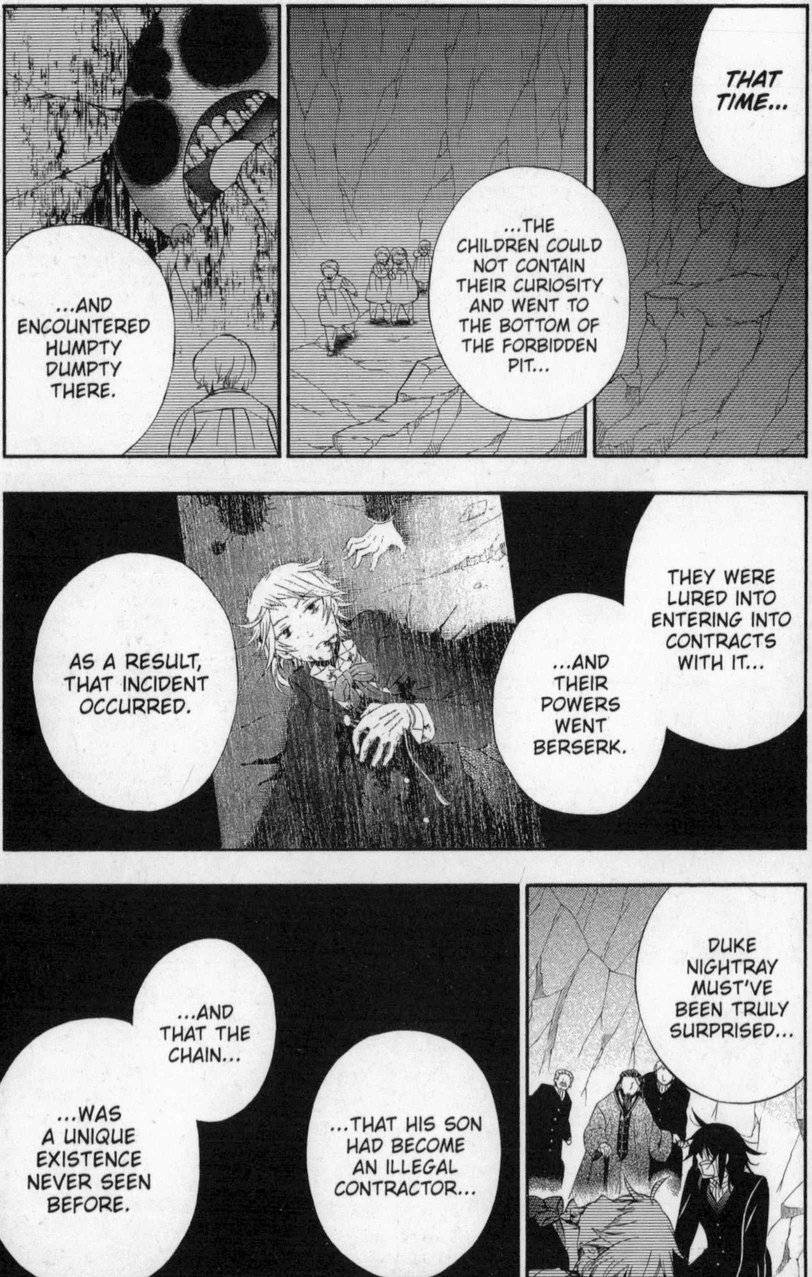
THAT TIME...
...THE CHILDREN COULD NOT CONTAIN THEIR CURIOSITY AND WENT TO THE BOTTOM OF THE FORBIDDEN PIT...
...AND ENCOUNTERED HUMPTY DUMPTY THERE.
THEY WERE LURED INTO ENTERING INTO CONTRACTS WITH IT...
...AND THEIR POWERS WENT BERSERK.
AS A RESULT, THAT INCIDENT OCCURRED.
DUKE NIGHTRAY MUST'VE BEEN TRULY SURPRISED...
...THAT HIS SON HAD BECOME AN ILLEGAL CONTRACTOR...
...AND THAT THE CHAIN...
...WAS A UNIQUE EXISTENCE NEVER SEEN BEFORE.

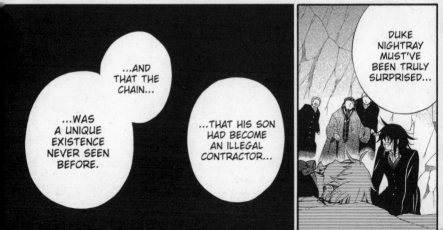

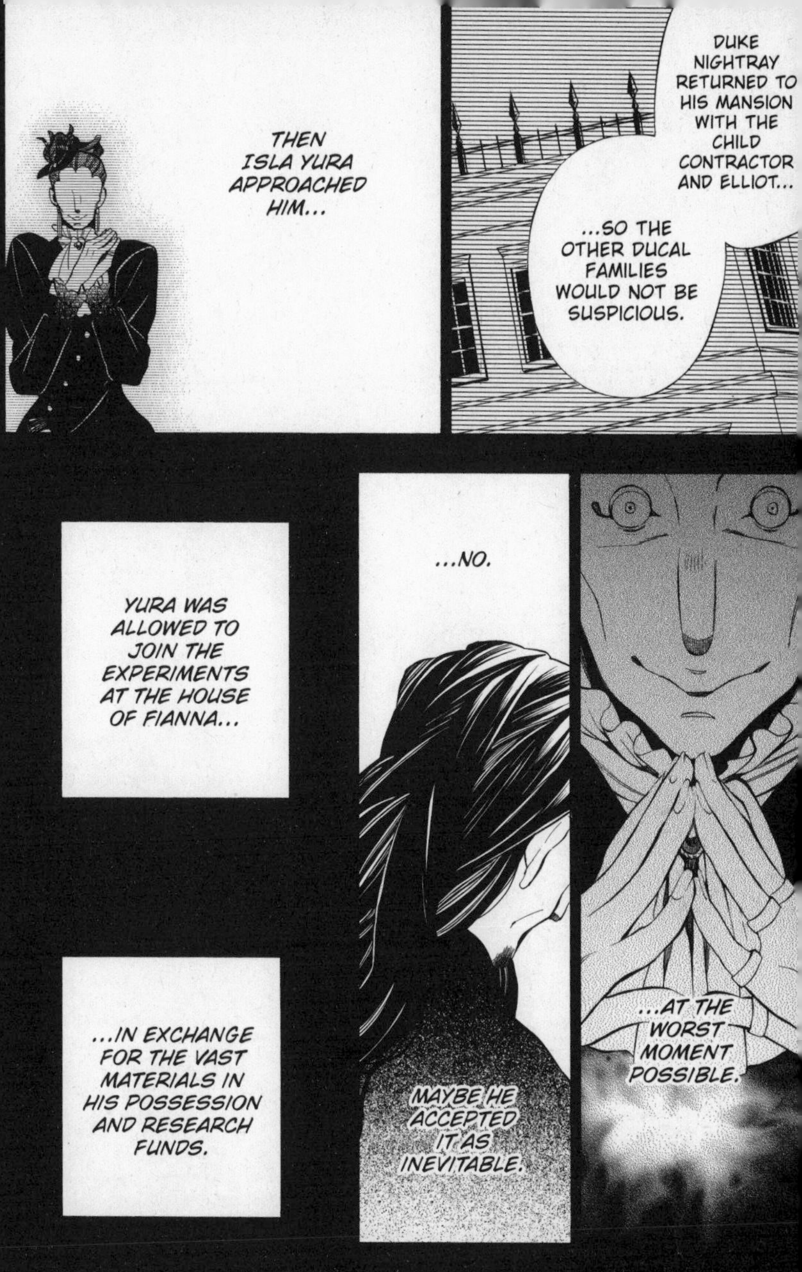
DUKE NIGHTRAY RETURNED TO HIS MANSION WITH THE CHILD CONTRACTOR AND ELLIOT...
...SO THE OTHER DUCAL FAMILIES WOULD NOT BE SUSPICIOUS.
THEN ISLA YURA APPROACHED HIM...
...AT THE WORST MOMENT POSSIBLE.
...NO.
MAYBE HE ACCEPTED IT AS INEVITABLE.
YURA WAS ALLOWED TO JOIN THE EXPERIMENTS AT THE HOUSE OF FIANNA...
...IN EXCHANGE FOR THE VAST MATERIALS IN HIS POSSESSION AND RESEARCH FUNDS.

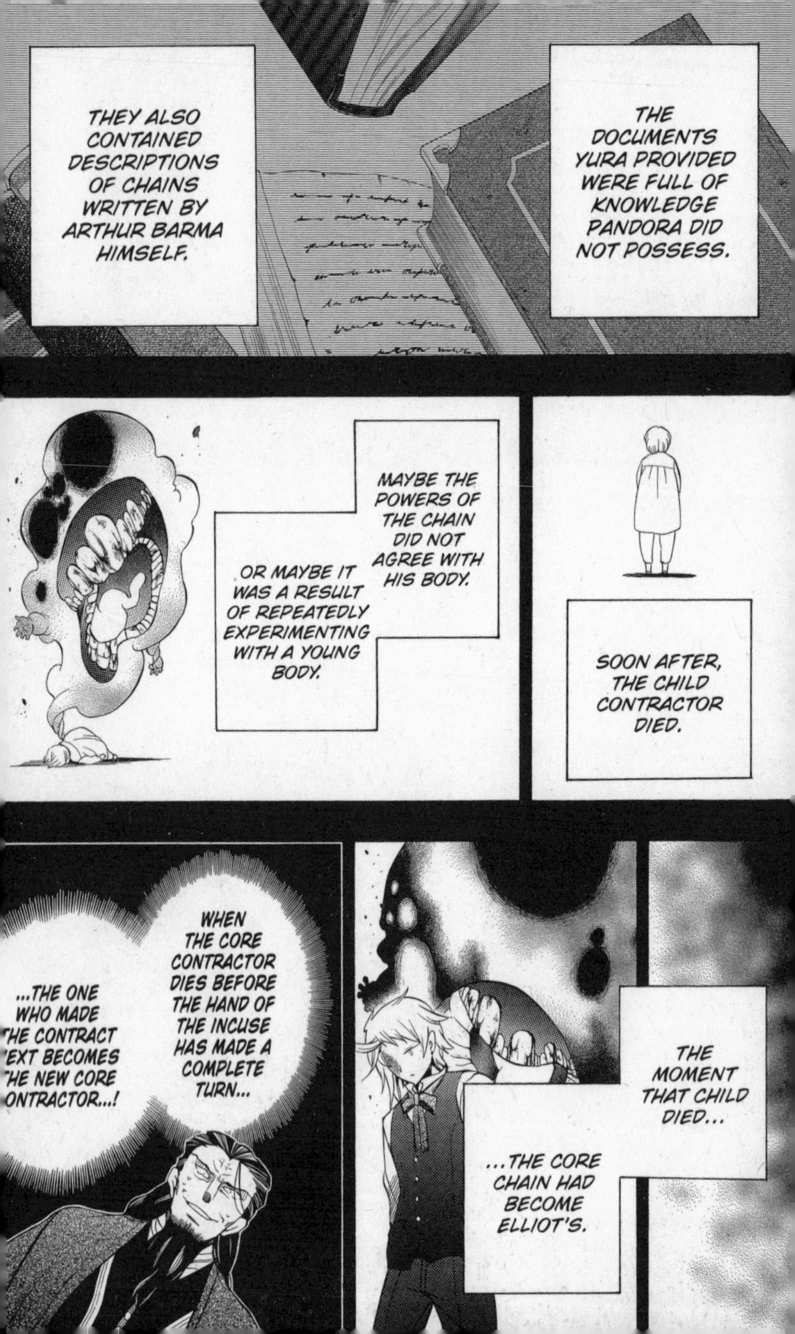
THE DOCUMENTS YURA PROVIDED WERE FULL OF KNOWLEDGE PANDORA DID NOT POSSESS.
THEY ALSO CONTAINED DESCRIPTIONS OF CHAINS WRITTEN BY ARTHUR BARMA HIMSELF.
SOON AFTER, THE CHILD CONTRACTOR DIED.
MAYBE THE POWERS OF THE CHAIN DID NOT AGREE WITH HIS BODY.
OR MAYBE IT WAS A RESULT OF REPEATEDLY EXPERIMENTING WITH A YOUNG BODY.
THE MOMENT THAT CHILD DIED...
...THE CORE CHAIN HAD BECOME ELLIOT'S.
WHEN THE CORE CONTRACTOR DIES BEFORE THE HAND OF THE INCUSE HAS MADE A COMPLETE TURN...
...THE ONE WHO MADE THE CONTRACT EXT BECOMES HE NEW CORE ONTRACTOR...!

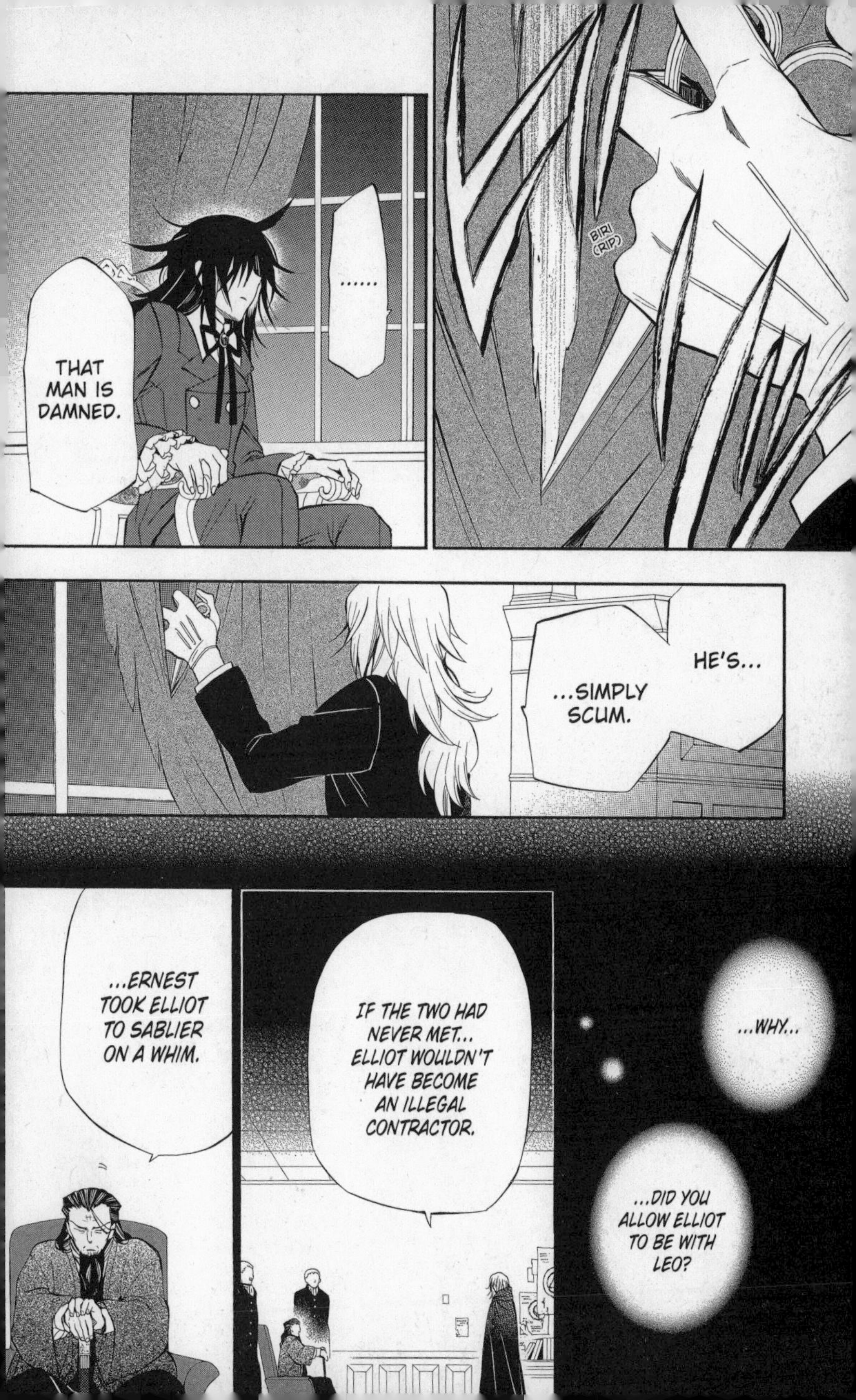
BIRI (RIP)
......
THAT MAN IS DAMNED.
HE'S...
...SIMPLY SCUM.
...WHY...
...DID YOU ALLOW ELLIOT TO BE WITH LEO?
IF THE TWO HAD NEVER MET... ELLIOT WOULDN'T HAVE BECOME AN ILLEGAL CONTRACTOR.
...ERNEST TOOK ELLIOT TO SABLIER ON A WHIM.

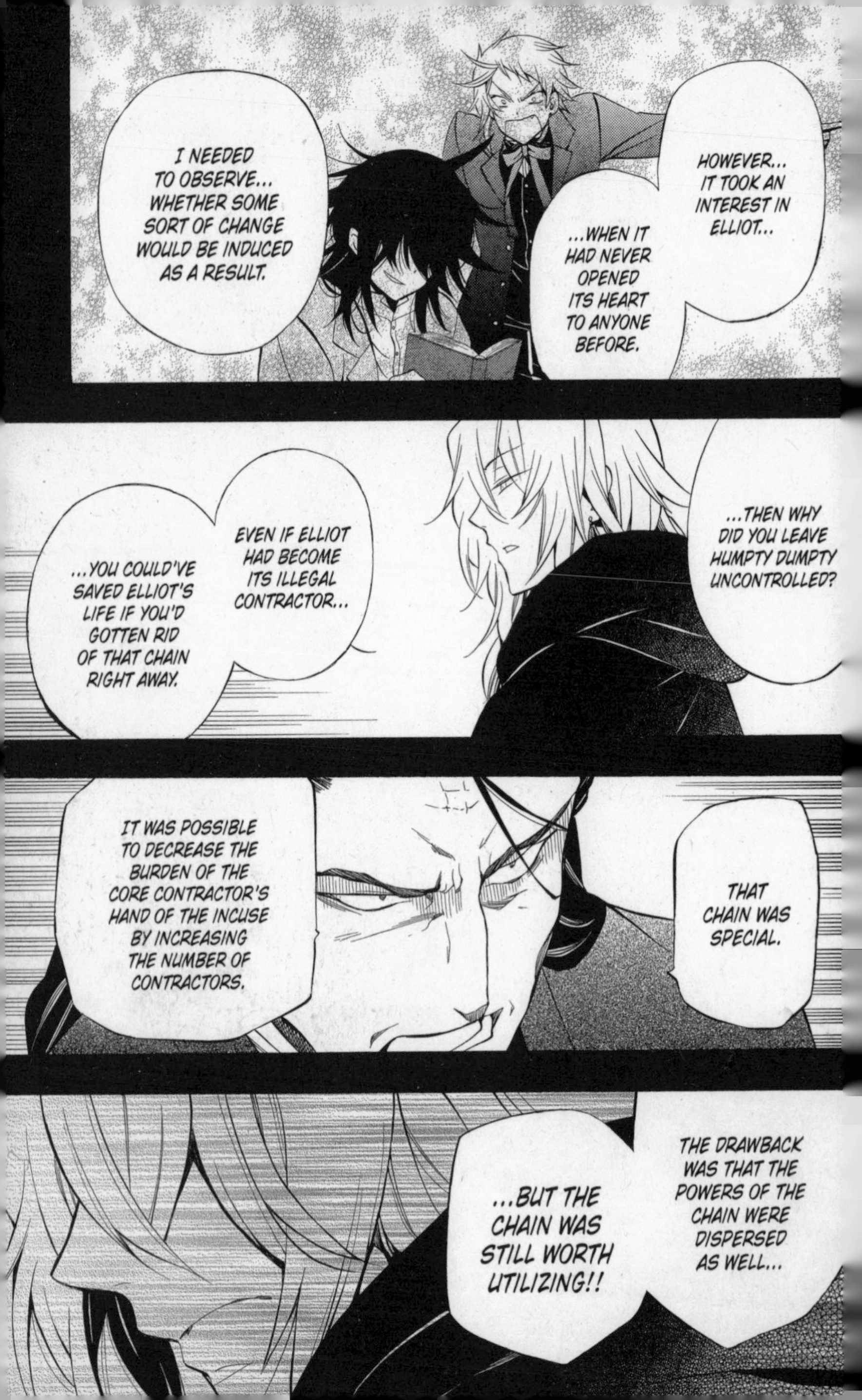
HOWEVER... IT TOOK AN INTEREST IN ELLIOT...
...WHEN IT HAD NEVER OPENED ITS HEART TO ANYONE BEFORE.
I NEEDED TO OBSERVE... WHETHER SOME SORT OF CHANGE WOULD BE INDUCED AS A RESULT.
...THEN WHY DID YOU LEAVE HUMPTY DUMPTY UNCONTROLLED?
EVEN IF ELLIOT HAD BECOME ITS ILLEGAL CONTRACTOR...
...YOU COULD'VE SAVED ELLIOT'S LIFE IF YOU'D GOTTEN RID OF THAT CHAIN RIGHT AWAY.
THAT CHAIN WAS SPECIAL.
IT WAS POSSIBLE TO DECREASE THE BURDEN OF THE CORE CONTRACTOR'S HAND OF THE INCUSE BY INCREASING THE NUMBER OF CONTRACTORS.
THE DRAWBACK WAS THAT THE POWERS OF THE CHAIN WERE DISPERSED AS WELL...
...BUT THE CHAIN WAS STILL WORTH UTILIZING!!

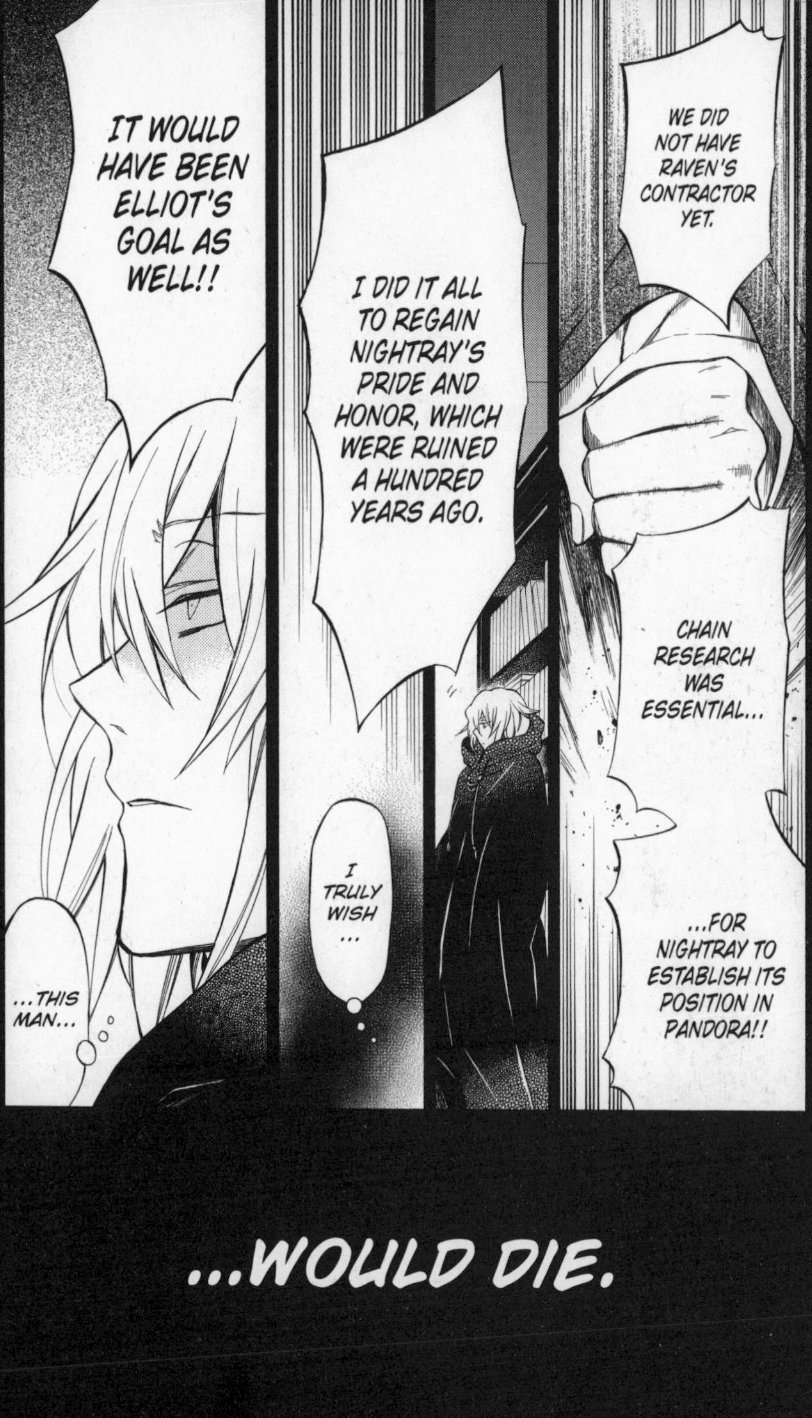
WE DID NOT HAVE RAVEN'S CONTRACTOR YET.
CHAIN RESEARCH WAS ESSENTIAL...
...FOR NIGHTRAY TO ESTABLISH ITS POSITION IN PANDORA!!
I DID IT ALL TO REGAIN NIGHTRAY'S PRIDE AND HONOR, WHICH WERE RUINED A HUNDRED YEARS AGO.
I TRULY WISH...
IT WOULD HAVE BEEN ELLIOT'S GOAL AS WELL!!
...THIS MAN...
...WOULD DIE.

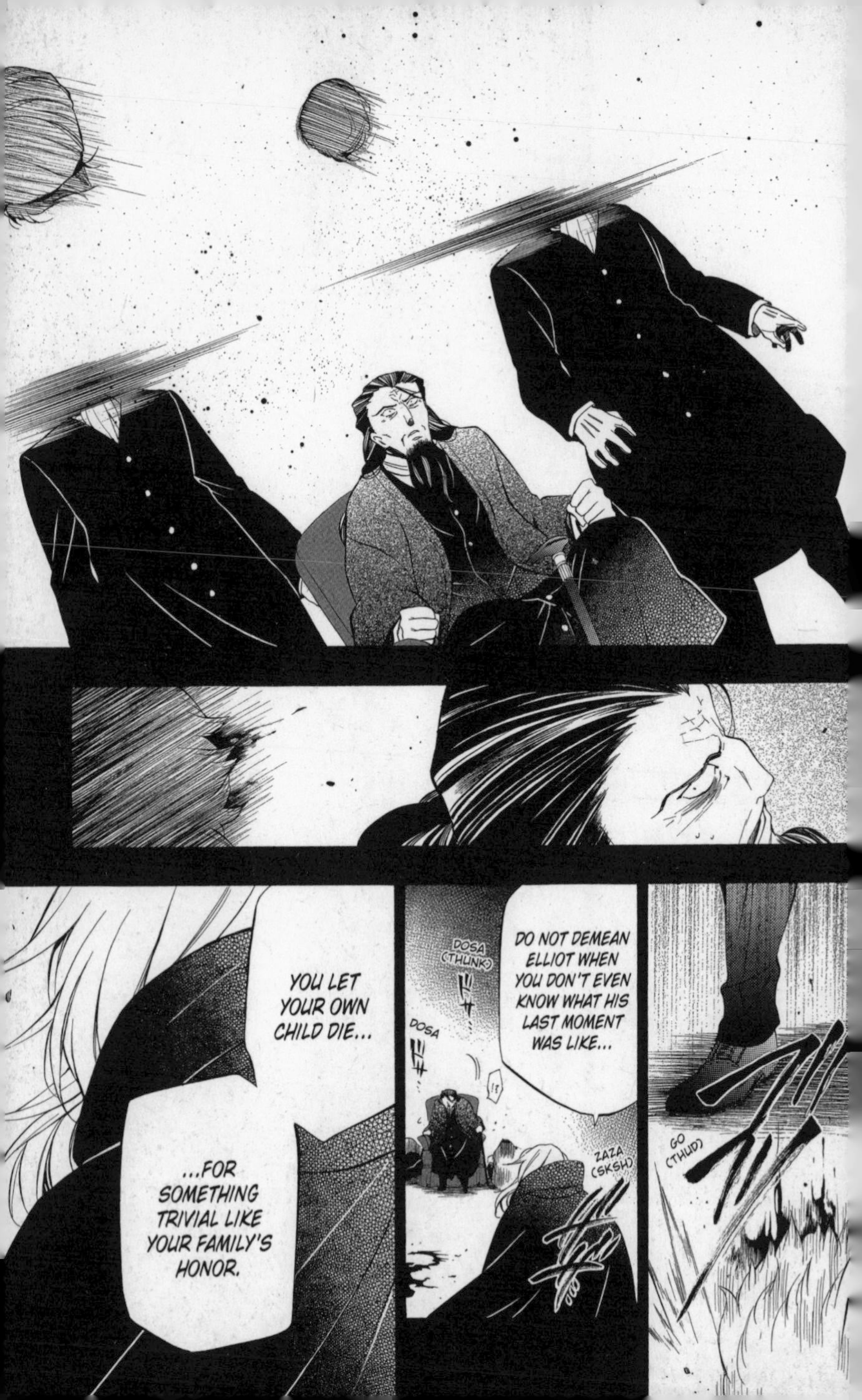
GO (THUD)
DO NOT DEMEAN ELLIOT WHEN YOU DON'T EVEN KNOW WHAT HIS LAST MOMENT WAS LIKE...
DOSA (THUNK)
DOSA
!?
ZAZA (SKSH)
YOU LET YOUR OWN CHILD DIE...
...FOR SOMETHING TRIVIAL LIKE YOUR FAMILY'S HONOR.

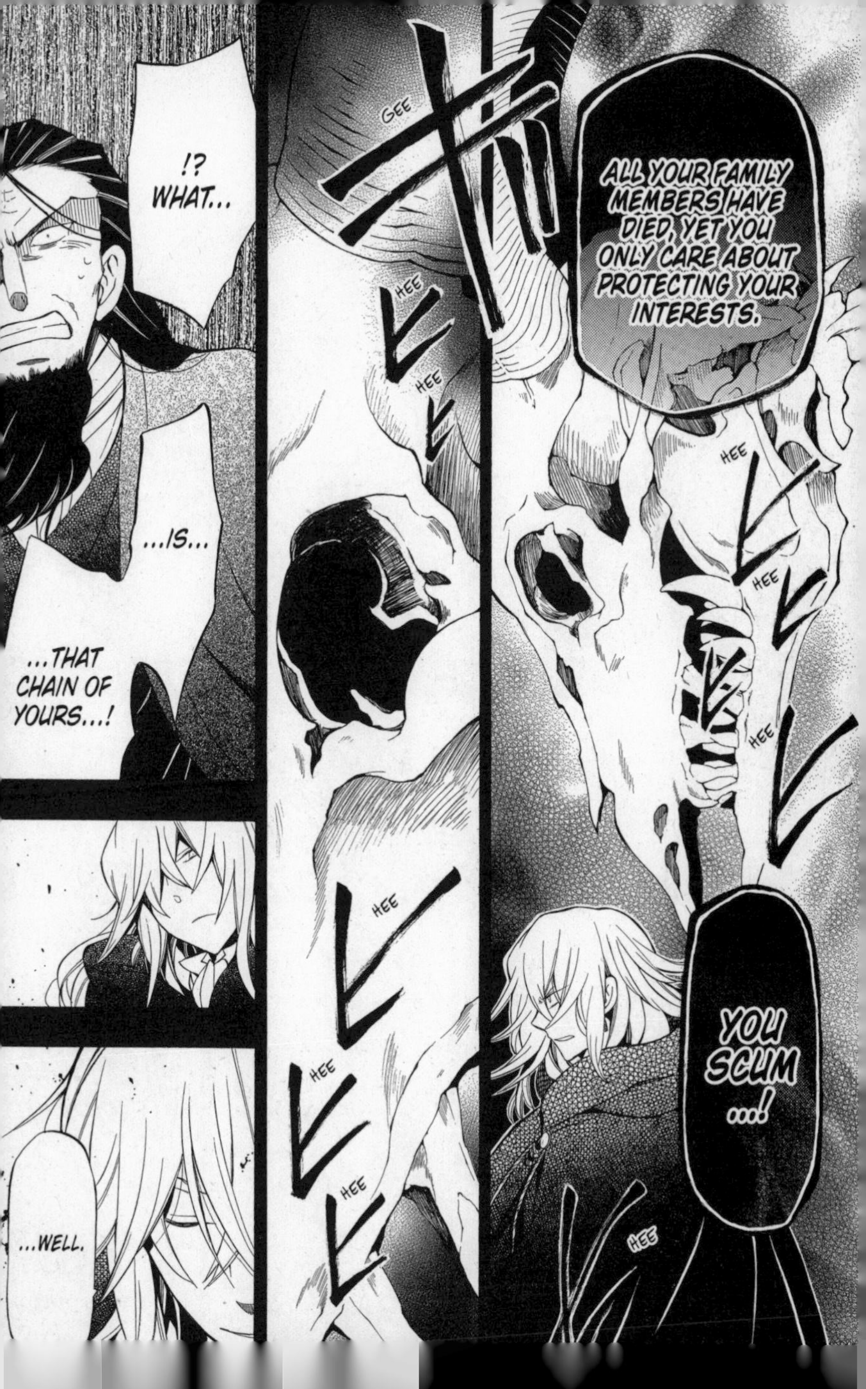
ALL YOUR FAMILY MEMBERS HAVE DIED, YET YOU ONLY CARE ABOUT PROTECTING YOUR INTERESTS.
HEE
HEE
HEE
YOU SCUM ...!
HEE
GEE
HEE
HEE
HEE
HEE
HEE
!? WHAT...
...IS...
...THAT CHAIN OF YOURS...!
...WELL.

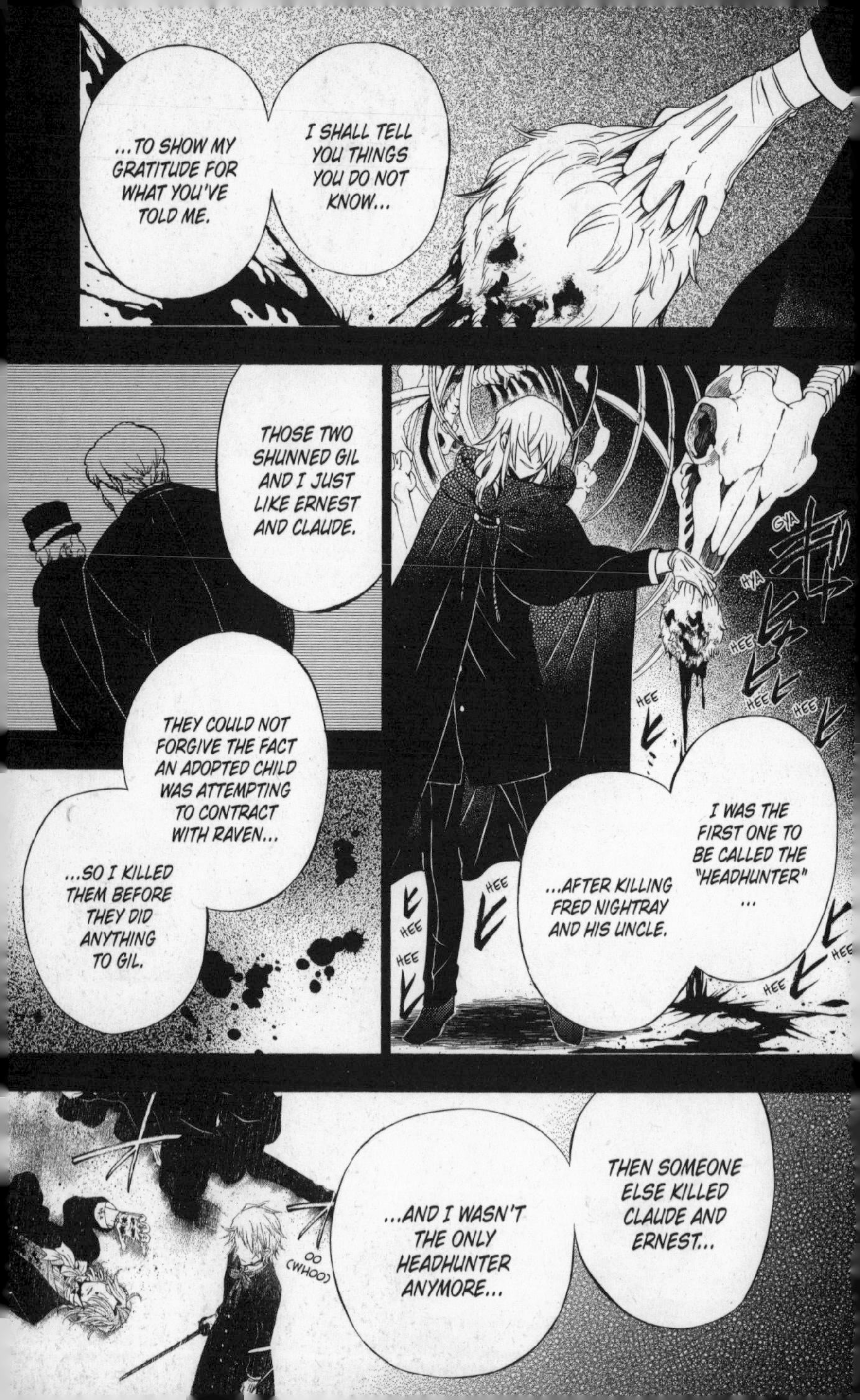
I SHALL TELL YOU THINGS YOU DO NOT KNOW...
...TO SHOW MY GRATITUDE FOR WHAT YOU'VE TOLD ME.
GYA
HYA
HEE HEE HEE HEE
I WAS THE FIRST ONE TO BE CALLED THE "HEADHUNTER"...
...AFTER KILLING FRED NIGHTRAY AND HIS UNCLE.
HEE HEE HEE HEE HEE HEE
THOSE TWO SHUNNED GIL AND I JUST LIKE ERNEST AND CLAUDE.
THEY COULD NOT FORGIVE THE FACT AN ADOPTED CHILD WAS ATTEMPTING TO CONTRACT WITH RAVEN...
...SO I KILLED THEM BEFORE THEY DID ANYTHING TO GIL.
THEN SOMEONE ELSE KILLED CLAUDE AND ERNEST...
...AND I WASN'T THE ONLY HEADHUNTER ANYMORE...
OO (WHOO)

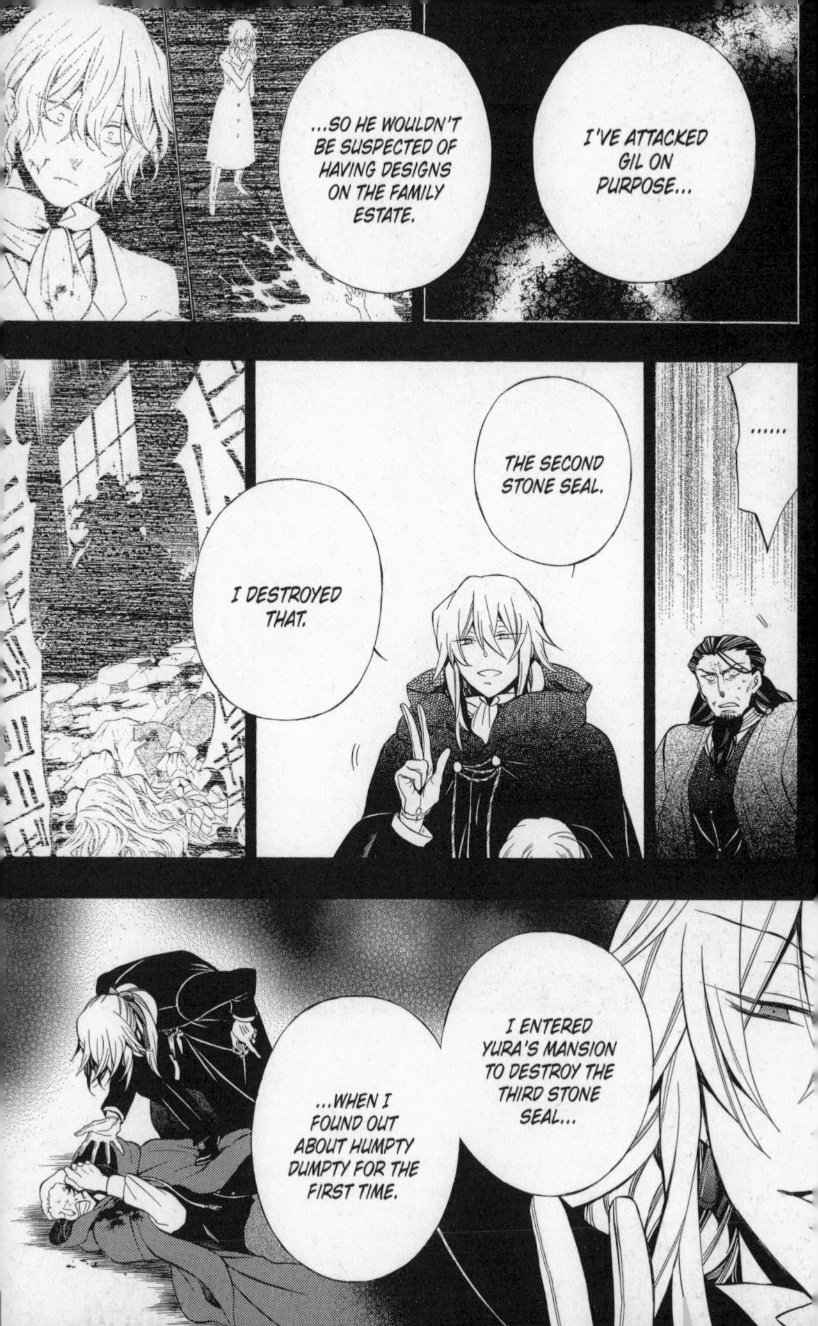
I'VE ATTACKED GIL ON PURPOSE...
...SO HE WOULDN'T BE SUSPECTED OF HAVING DESIGNS ON THE FAMILY ESTATE.
......
THE SECOND STONE SEAL.
I DESTROYED THAT.
I ENTERED YURA'S MANSION TO DESTROY THE THIRD STONE SEAL...
...WHEN I FOUND OUT ABOUT HUMPTY DUMPTY FOR THE FIRST TIME.

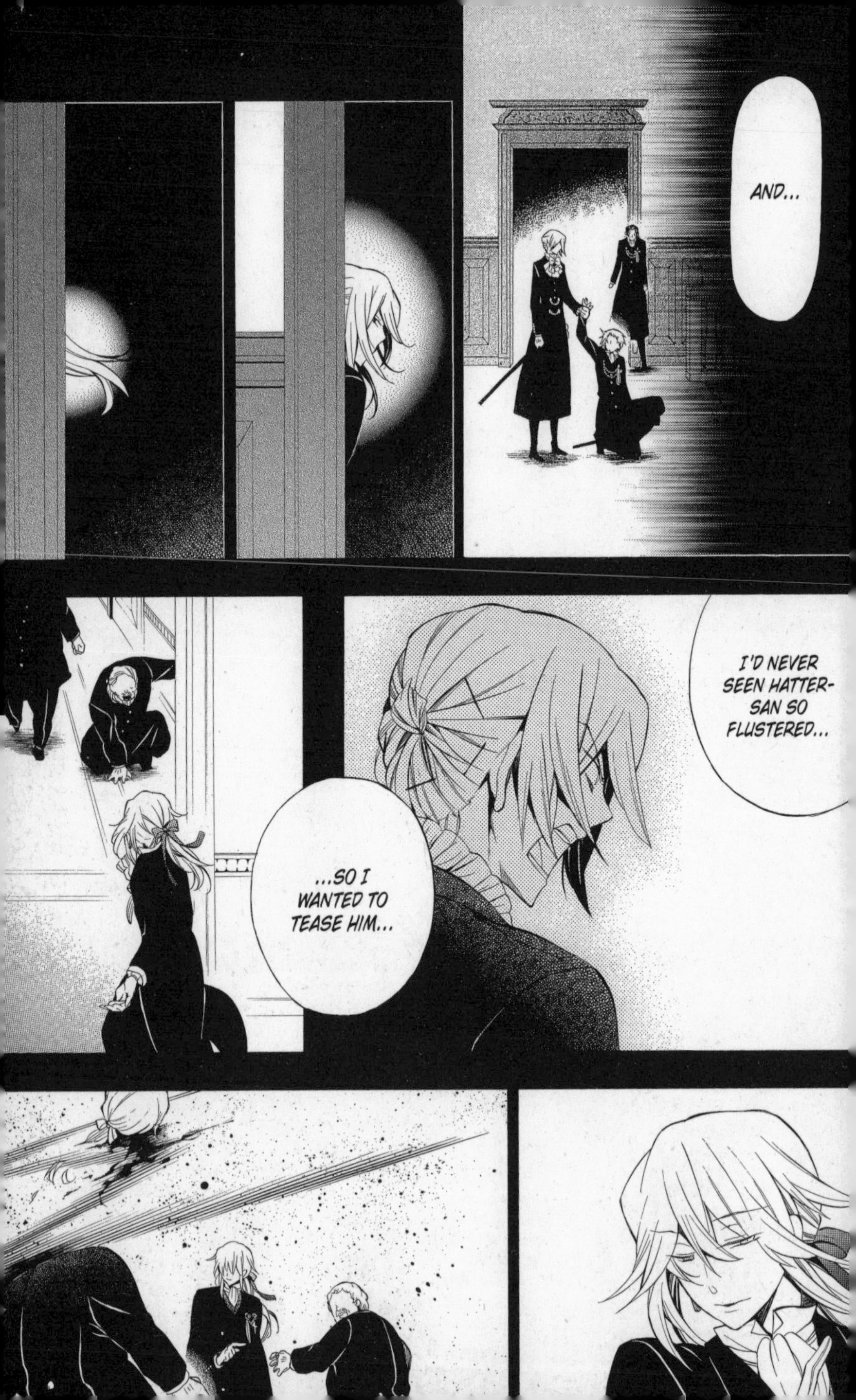
AND...
I'D NEVER SEEN HATTER-SAN SO FLUSTERED...
...SO I WANTED TO TEASE HIM...

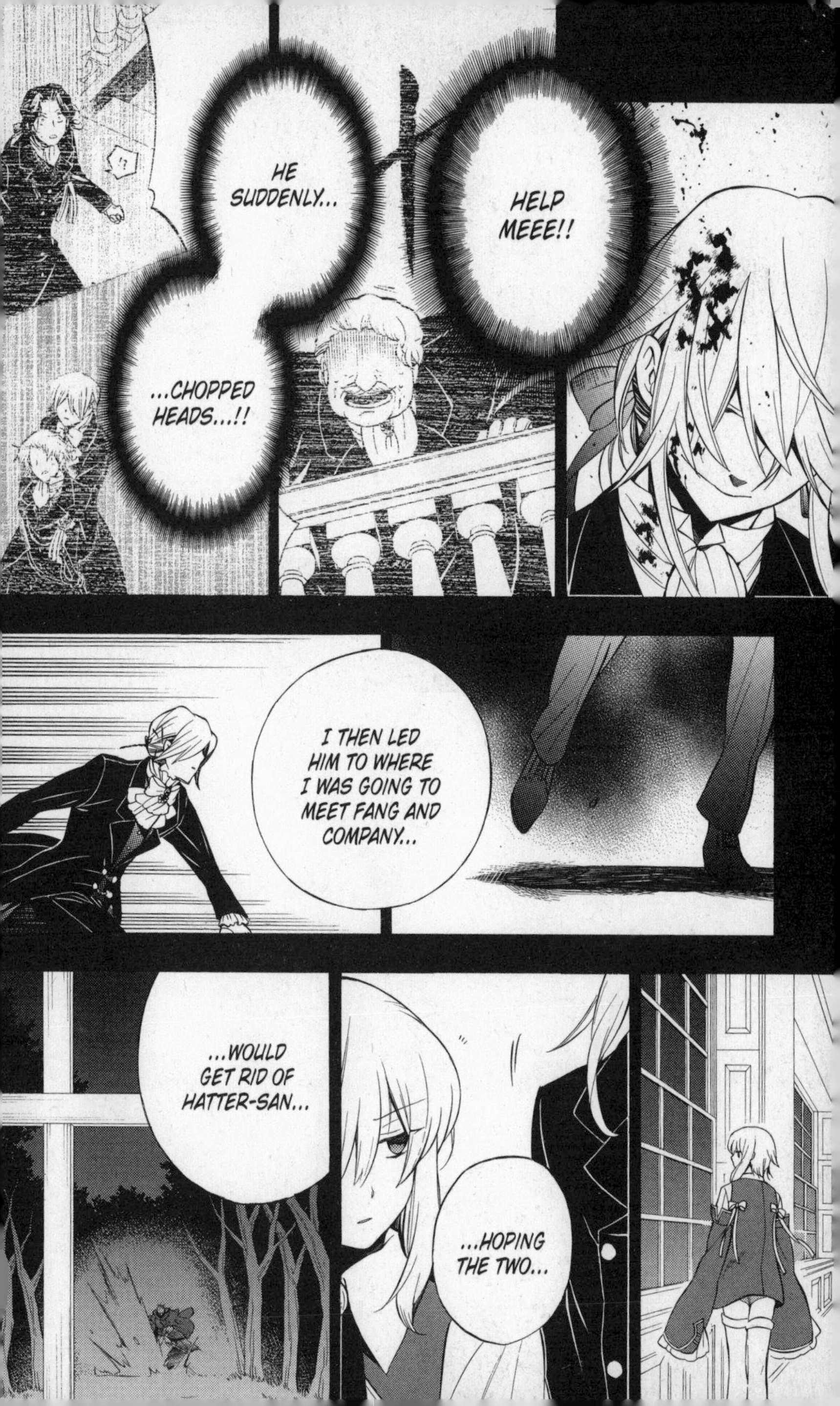
HELP MEEE!!
HE SUDDENLY...
...CHOPPED HEADS...!!
!?
I THEN LED HIM TO WHERE I WAS GOING TO MEET FANG AND COMPANY...
...HOPING THE TWO...
...WOULD GET RID OF HATTER-SAN...

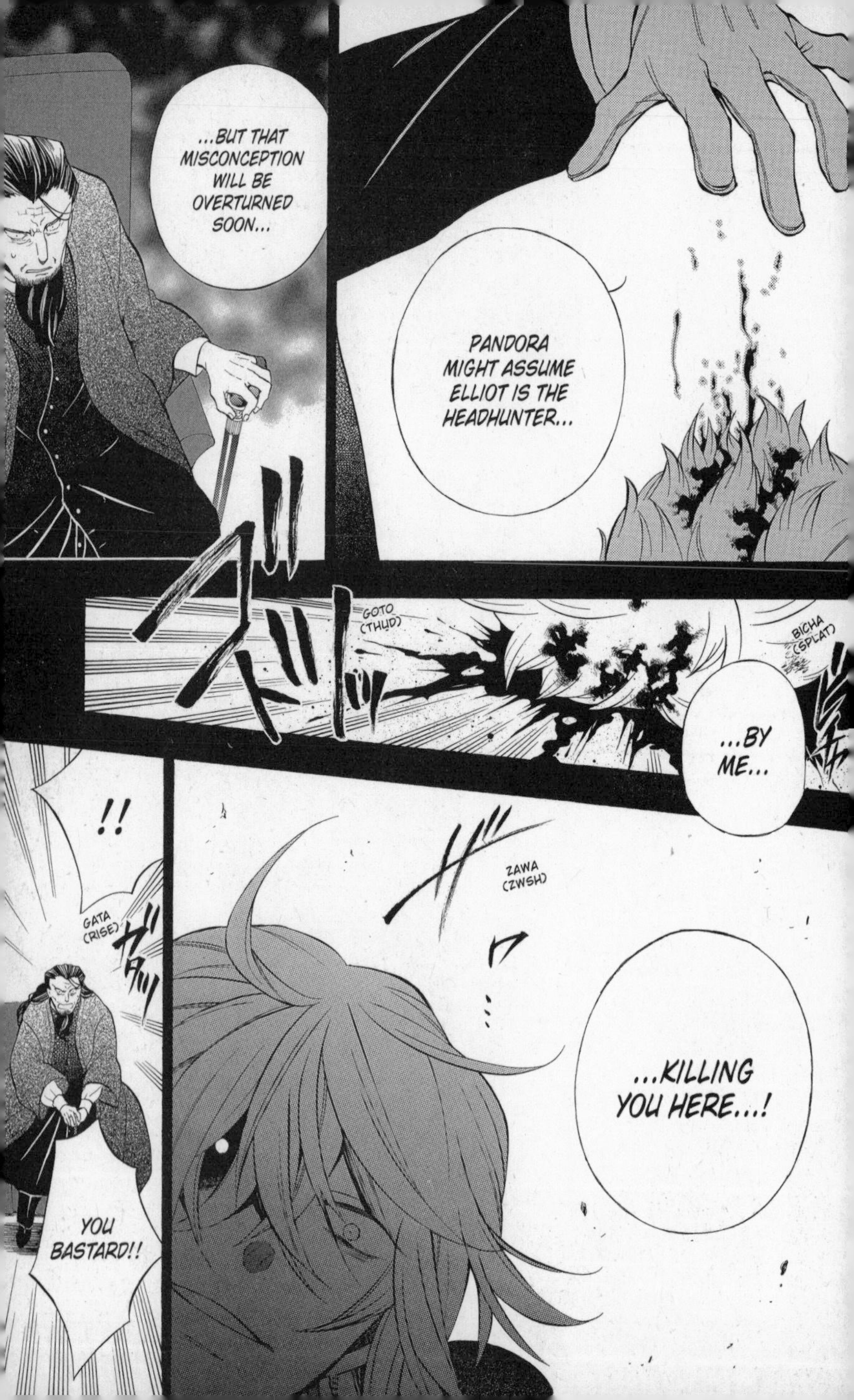
PANDORA MIGHT ASSUME ELLIOT IS THE HEADHUNTER...
...BUT THAT MISCONCEPTION WILL BE OVERTURNED SOON...
BICHA (SPLAT)
...BY ME...
GOTO (THUD)
ZAWA (ZWSH)
...KILLING YOU HERE...!
!!
GATA (RISE)
YOU BASTARD!!

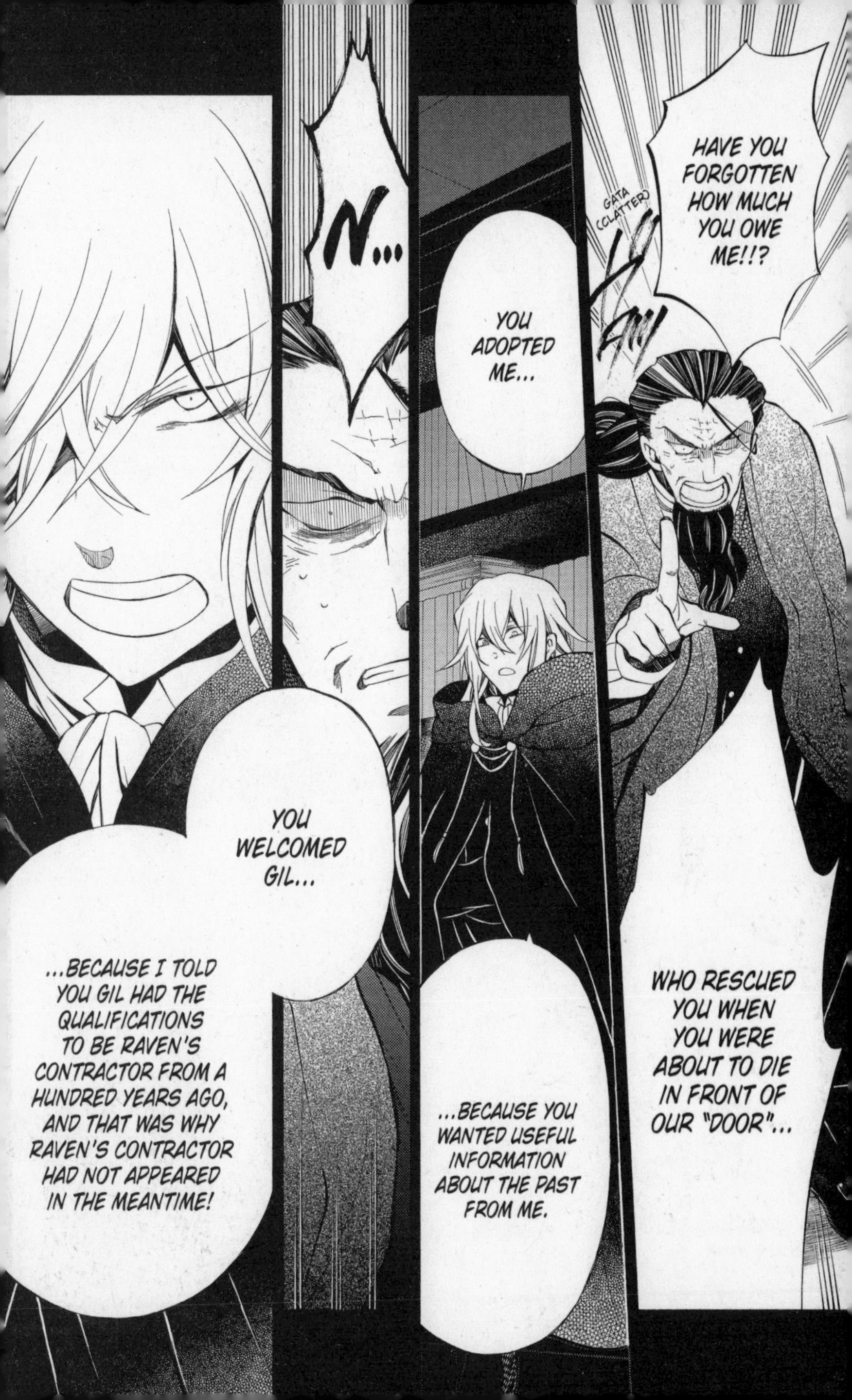
HAVE YOU FORGOTTEN HOW MUCH YOU OWE ME!!?
GATA (CLATTER)
WHO RESCUED YOU WHEN YOU WERE ABOUT TO DIE IN FRONT OF OUR "DOOR"...
YOU ADOPTED ME...
...BECAUSE YOU WANTED USEFUL INFORMATION ABOUT THE PAST FROM ME.
N...
YOU WELCOMED GIL...
...BECAUSE I TOLD YOU GIL HAD THE QUALIFICATIONS TO BE RAVEN'S CONTRACTOR FROM A HUNDRED YEARS AGO, AND THAT WAS WHY RAVEN'S CONTRACTOR HAD NOT APPEARED IN THE MEANTIME!

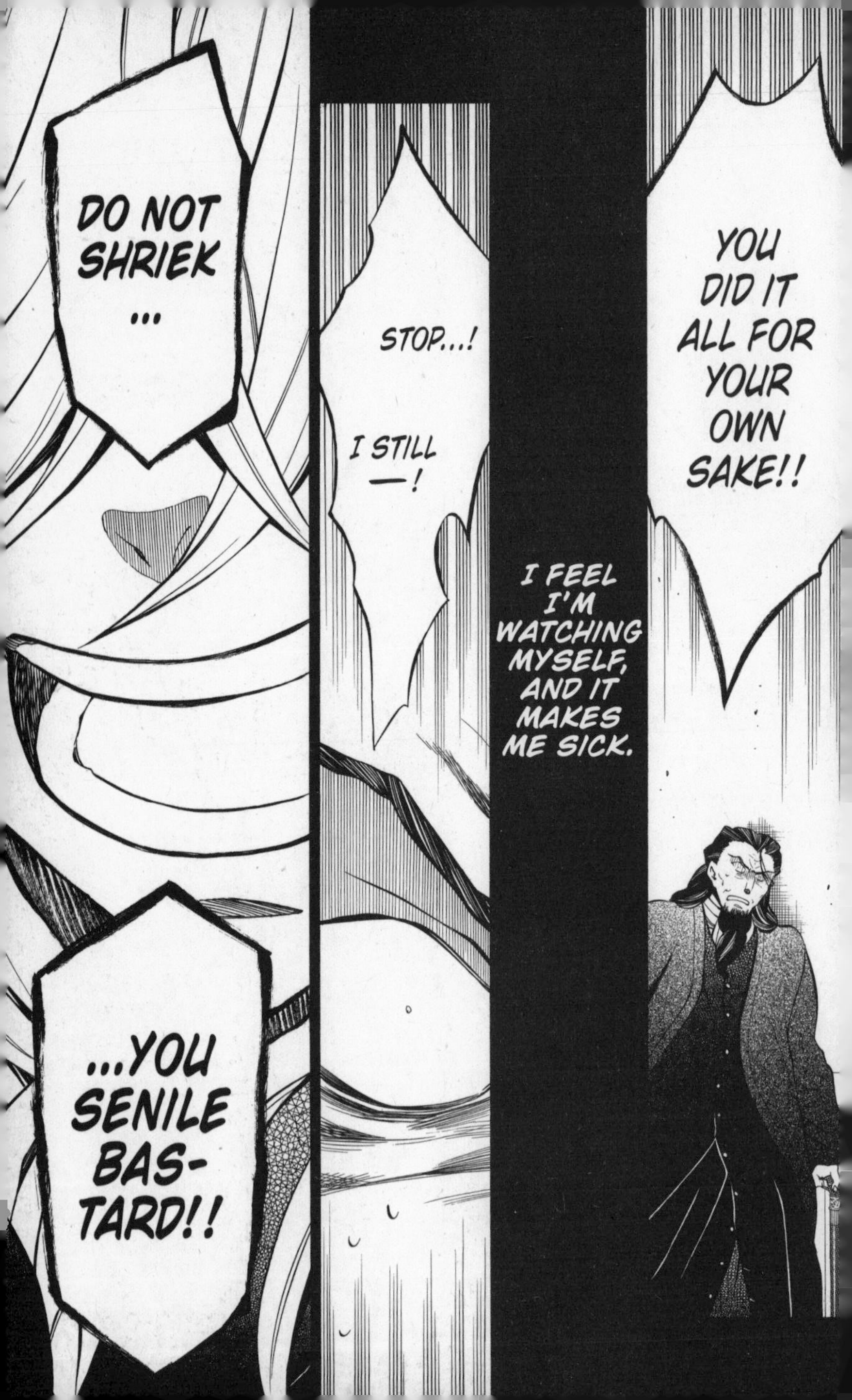
YOU DID IT ALL FOR YOUR OWN SAKE!!
I FEEL I'M WATCHING MYSELF, AND IT MAKES ME SICK.
STOP...!
I STILL —!
DO NOT SHRIEK ...
...YOU SENILE BAS-TARD!!

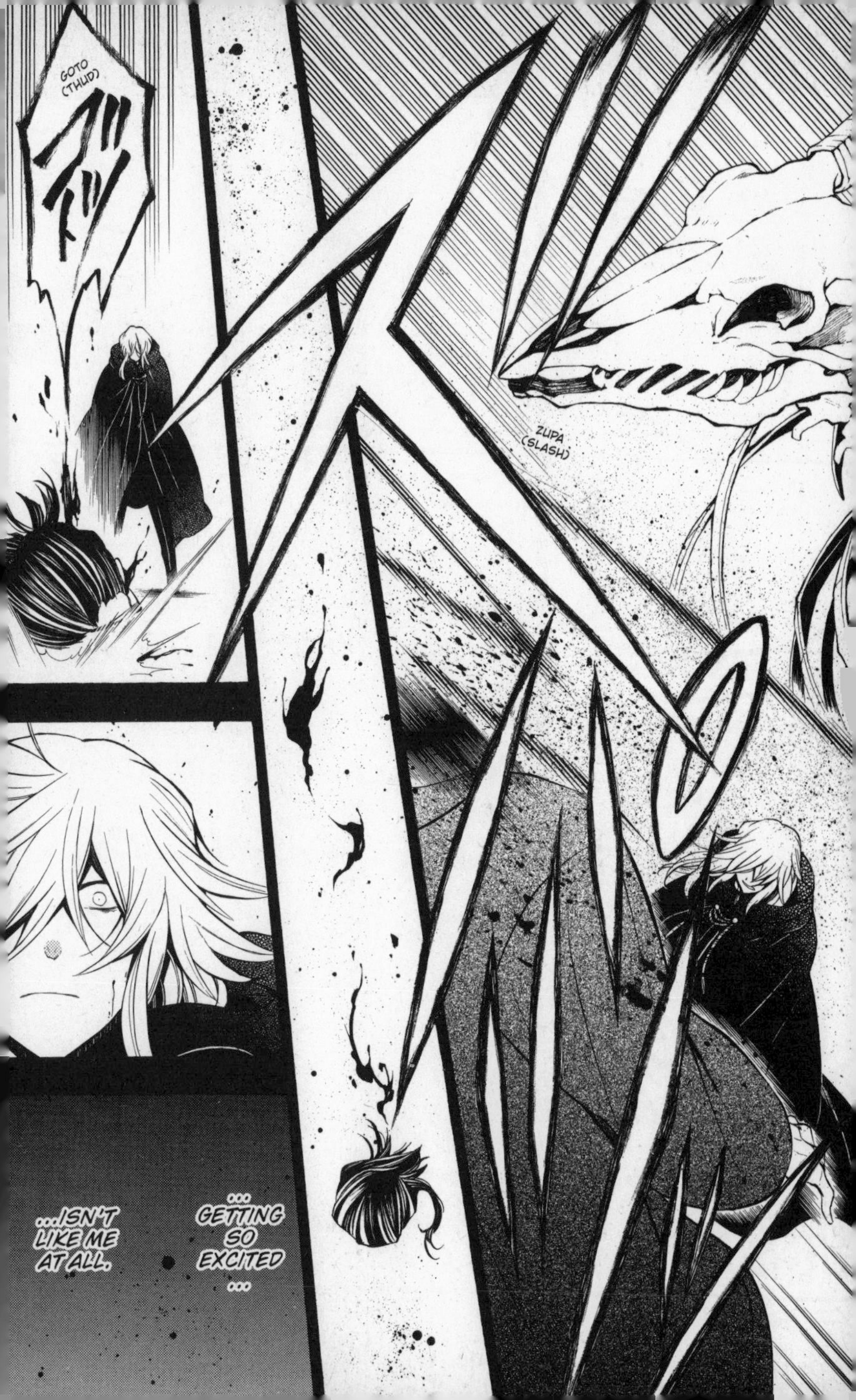
ZUPA (SLASH)
ゴトッ
GOTO (THUD)
...GETTING SO EXCITED...
...ISN'T LIKE ME AT ALL.

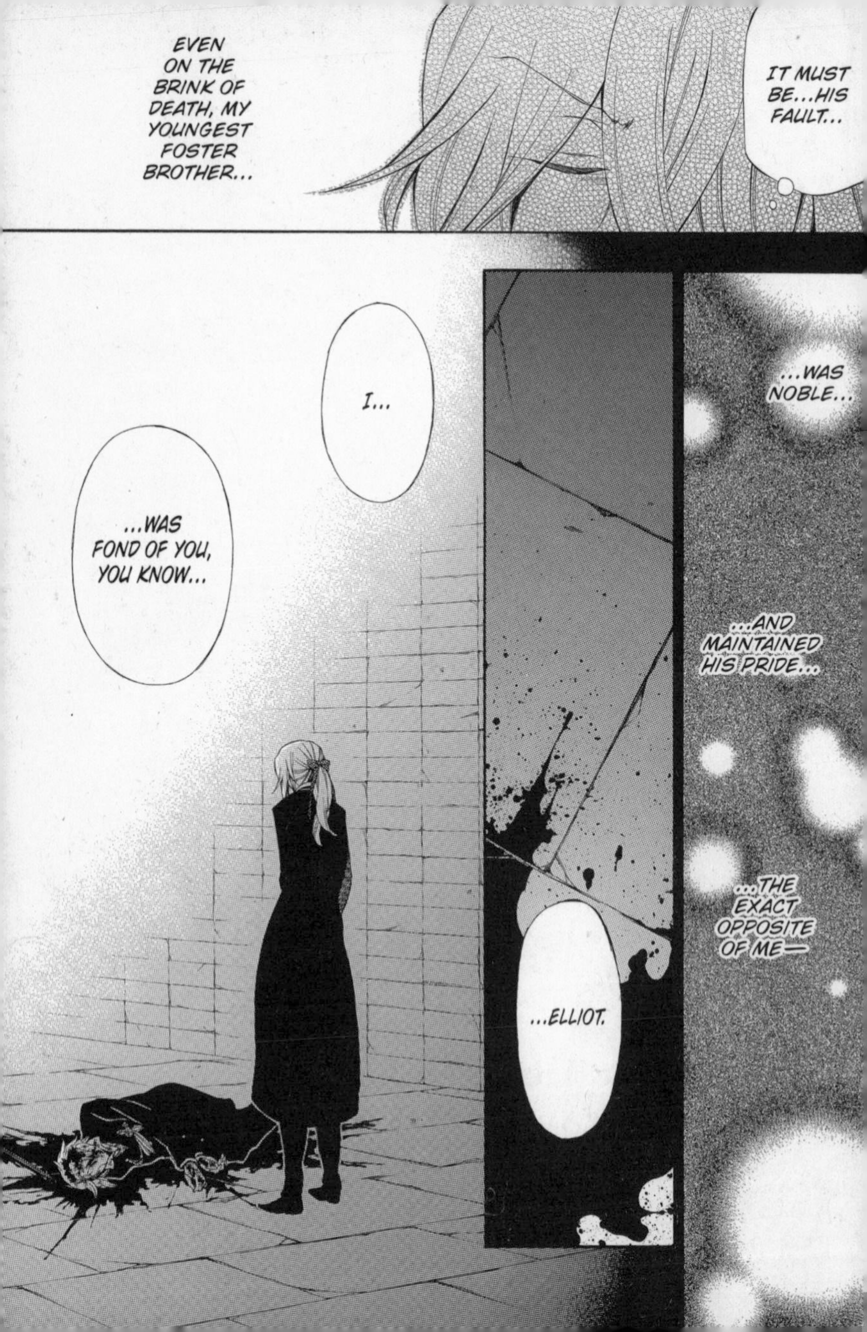
IT MUST BE...HIS FAULT...
EVEN ON THE BRINK OF DEATH, MY YOUNGEST FOSTER BROTHER...
...WAS NOBLE...
...AND MAINTAINED HIS PRIDE...
...THE EXACT OPPOSITE OF ME—
...ELLIOT.
I...
...WAS FOND OF YOU, YOU KNOW...

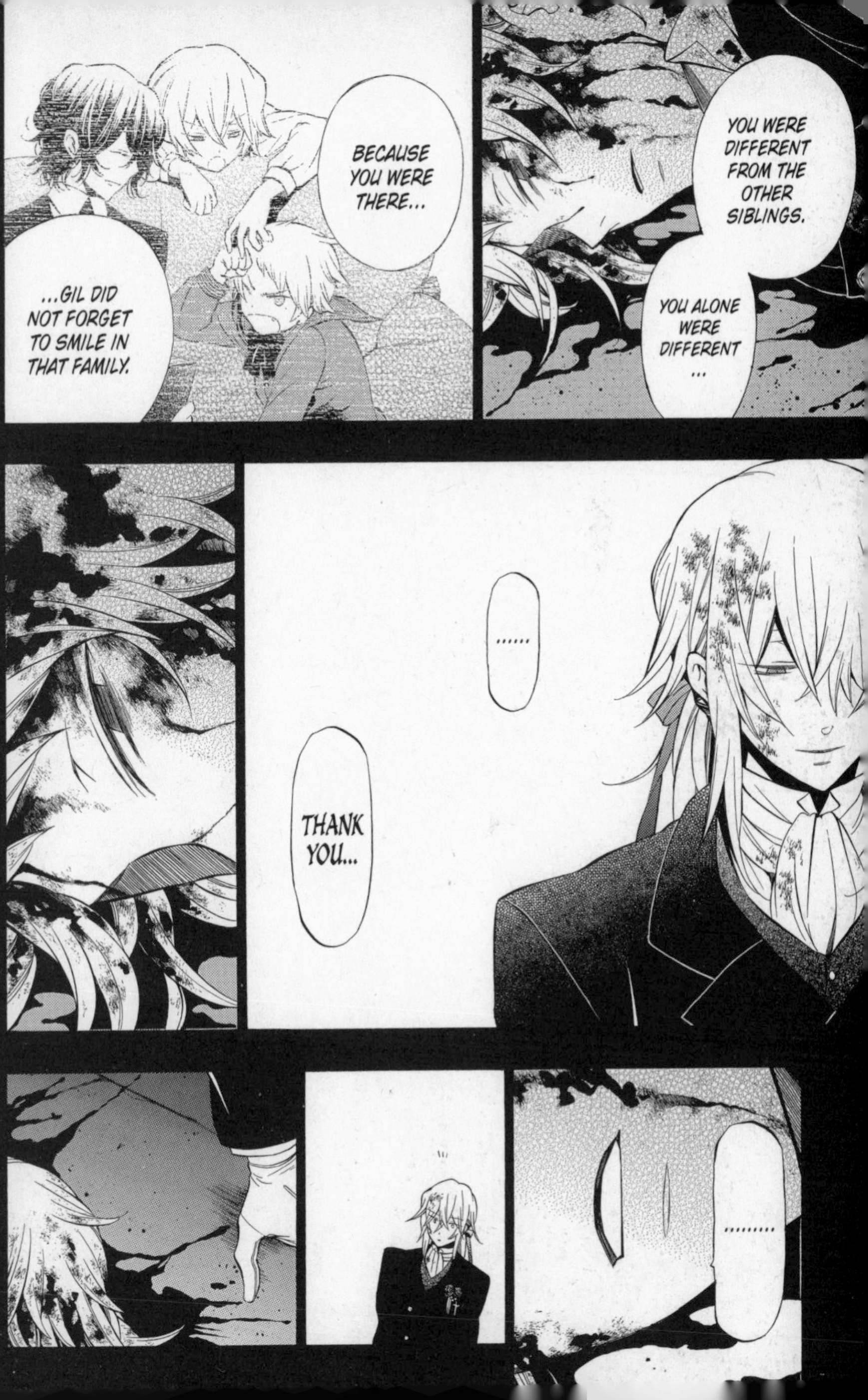
YOU WERE DIFFERENT FROM THE OTHER SIBLINGS.
YOU ALONE WERE DIFFERENT...
BECAUSE YOU WERE THERE...
...GIL DID NOT FORGET TO SMILE IN THAT FAMILY.
......
THANK YOU...
....

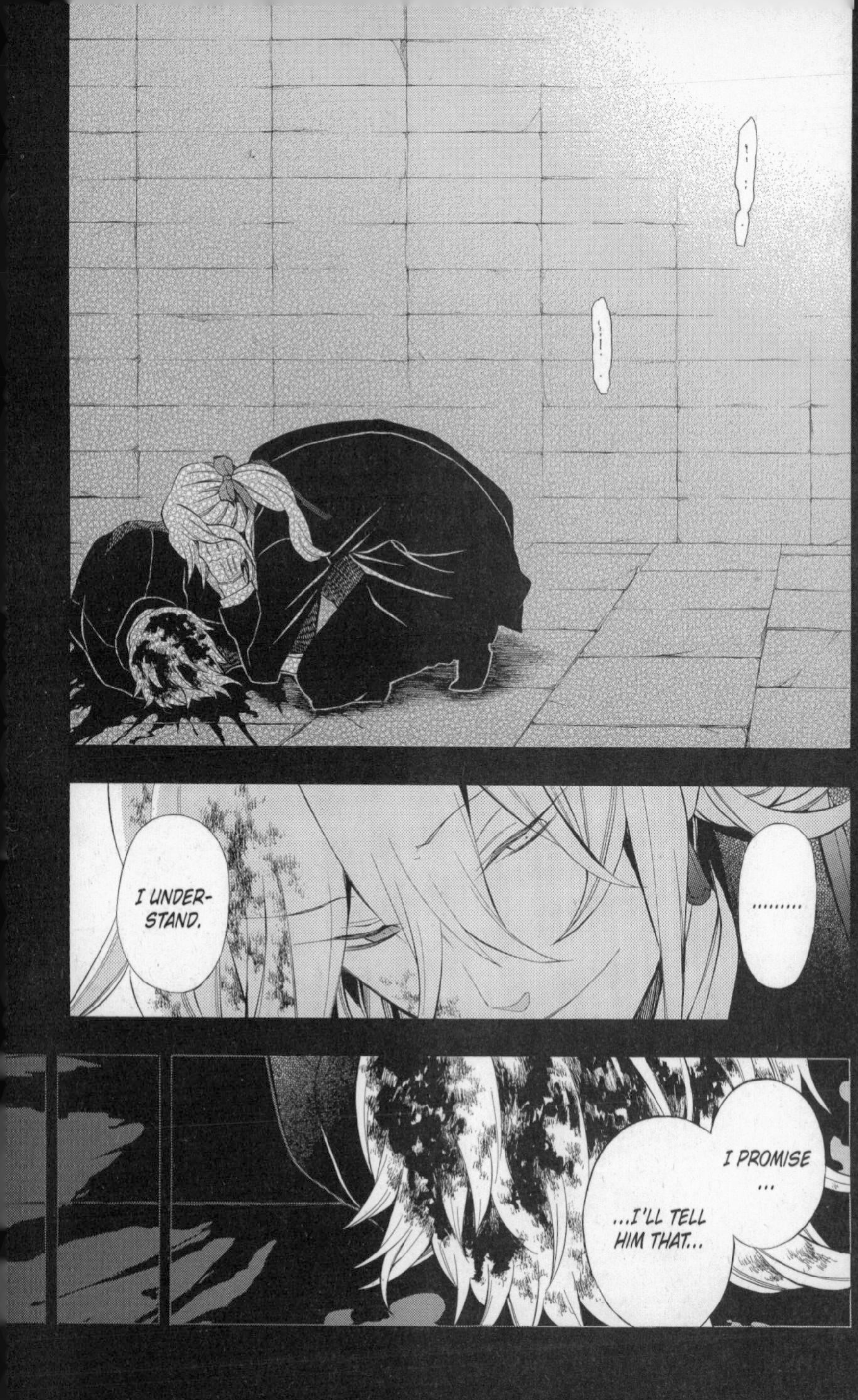
....
I UNDER-STAND.
I PROMISE ...
...I'LL TELL HIM THAT...

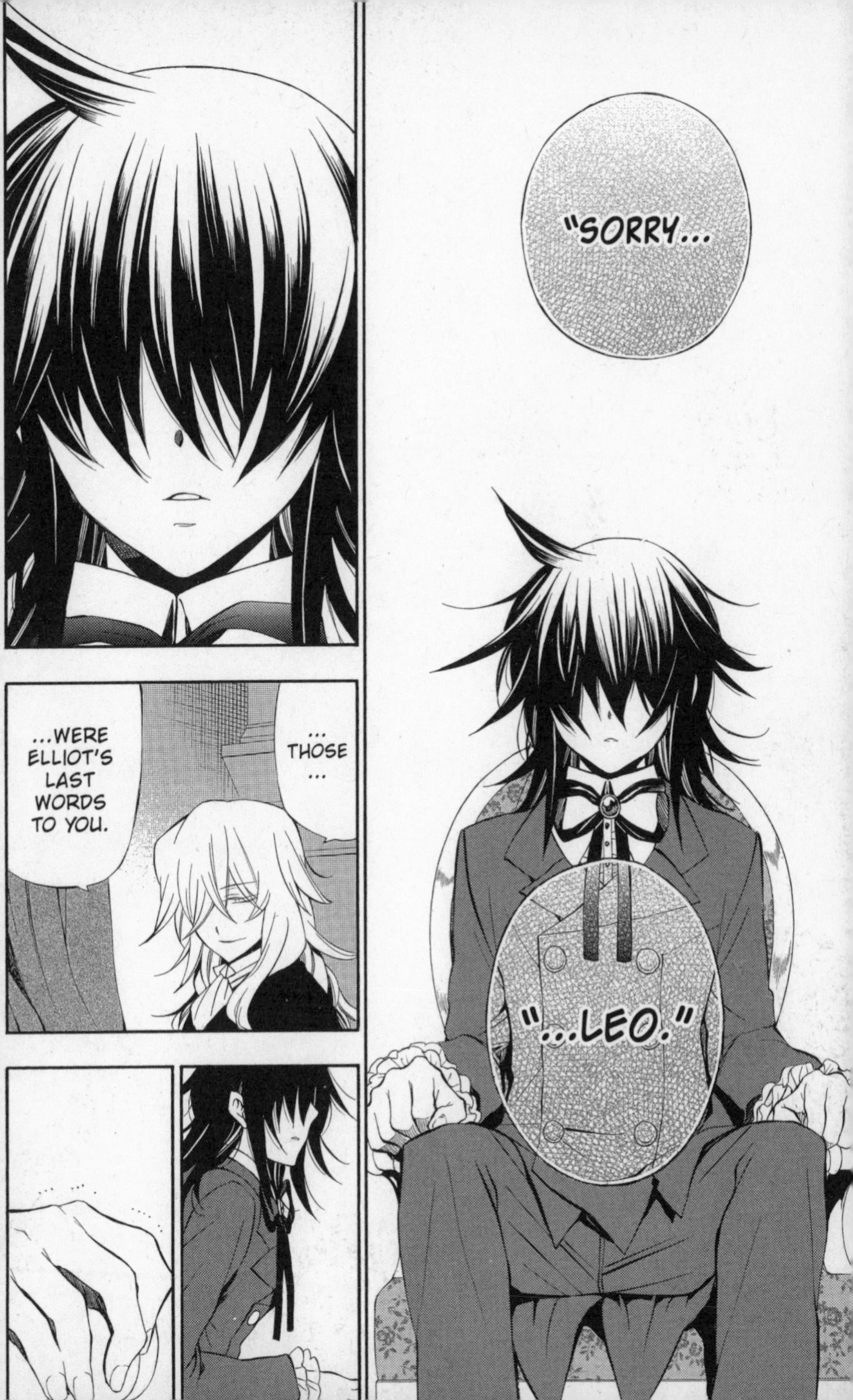
"SORRY...
"...LEO."
...THOSE...
...WERE ELLIOT'S LAST WORDS TO YOU.

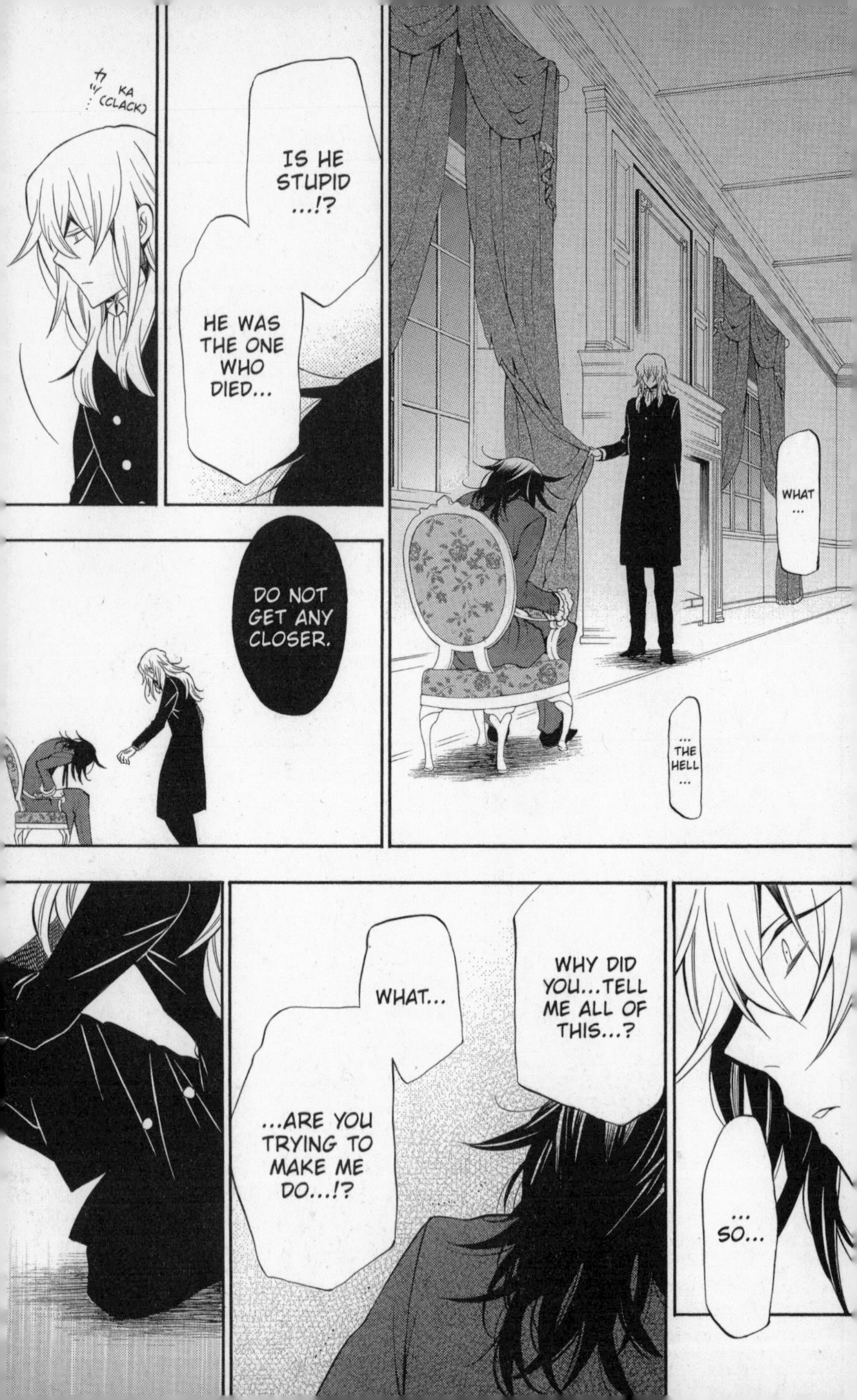
WHAT...
...THE HELL...
IS HE STUPID...!?
HE WAS THE ONE WHO DIED...
カッ
KA (CLACK)
DO NOT GET ANY CLOSER.
...SO...
WHY DID YOU...TELL ME ALL OF THIS...?
WHAT...
...ARE YOU TRYING TO MAKE ME DO...!?

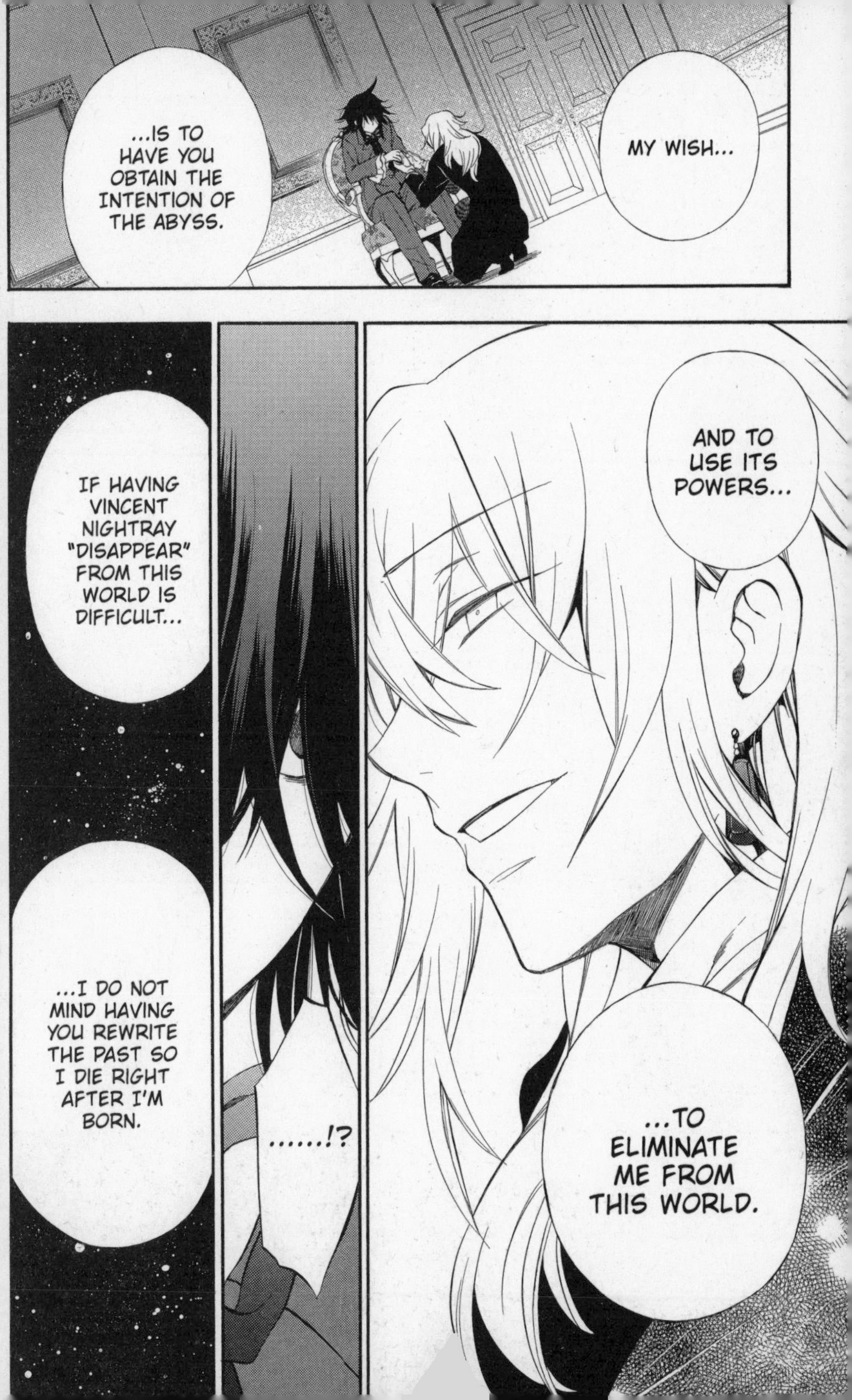
MY WISH...
...IS TO HAVE YOU OBTAIN THE INTENTION OF THE ABYSS.
AND TO USE ITS POWERS...
...TO ELIMINATE ME FROM THIS WORLD.
......!?
IF HAVING VINCENT NIGHTRAY "DISAPPEAR" FROM THIS WORLD IS DIFFICULT...
...I DO NOT MIND HAVING YOU REWRITE THE PAST SO I DIE RIGHT AFTER I'M BORN.

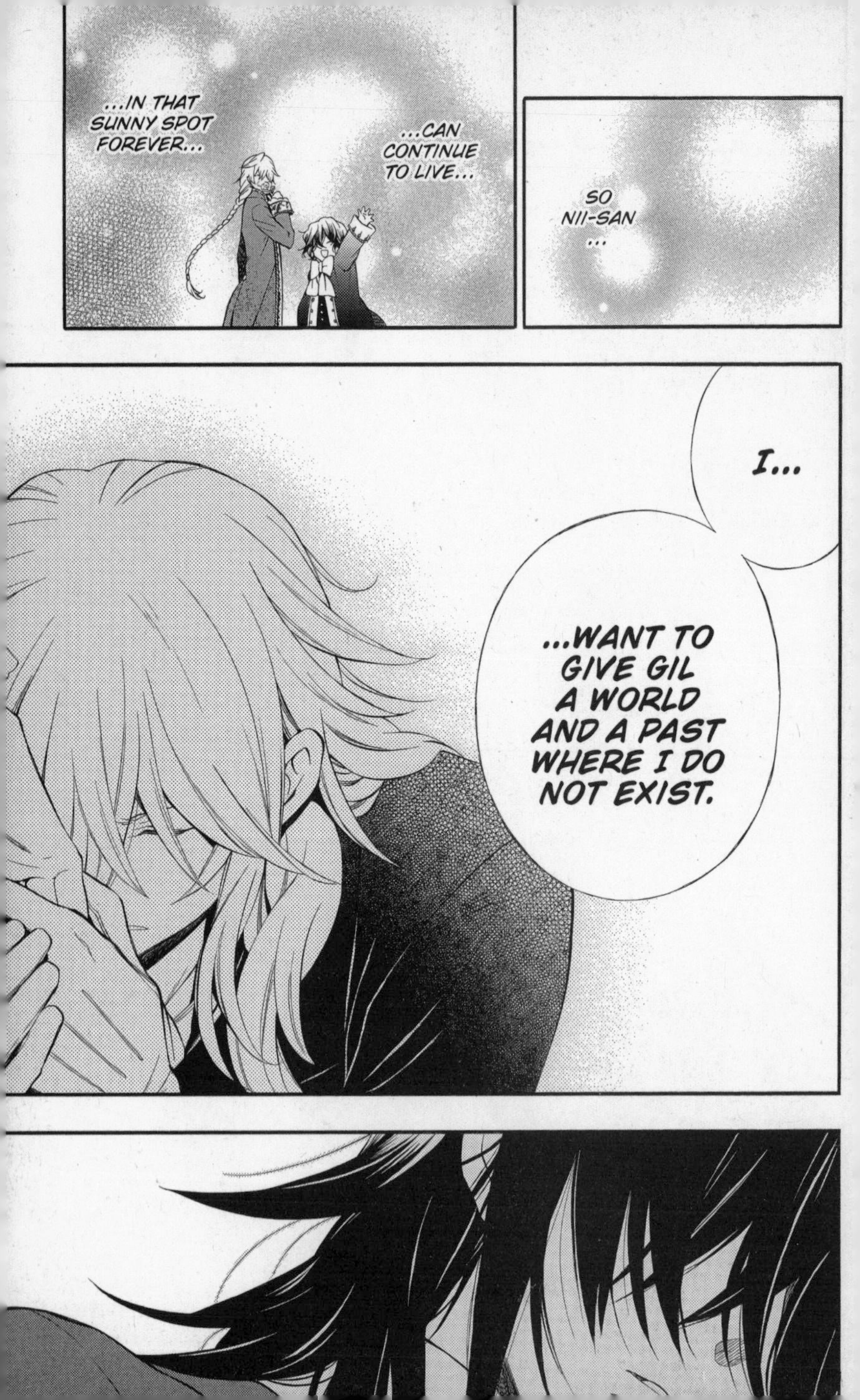
SO NII-SAN ...
...CAN CONTINUE TO LIVE...
...IN THAT SUNNY SPOT FOREVER...
I...
...WANT TO GIVE GIL A WORLD AND A PAST WHERE I DO NOT EXIST.

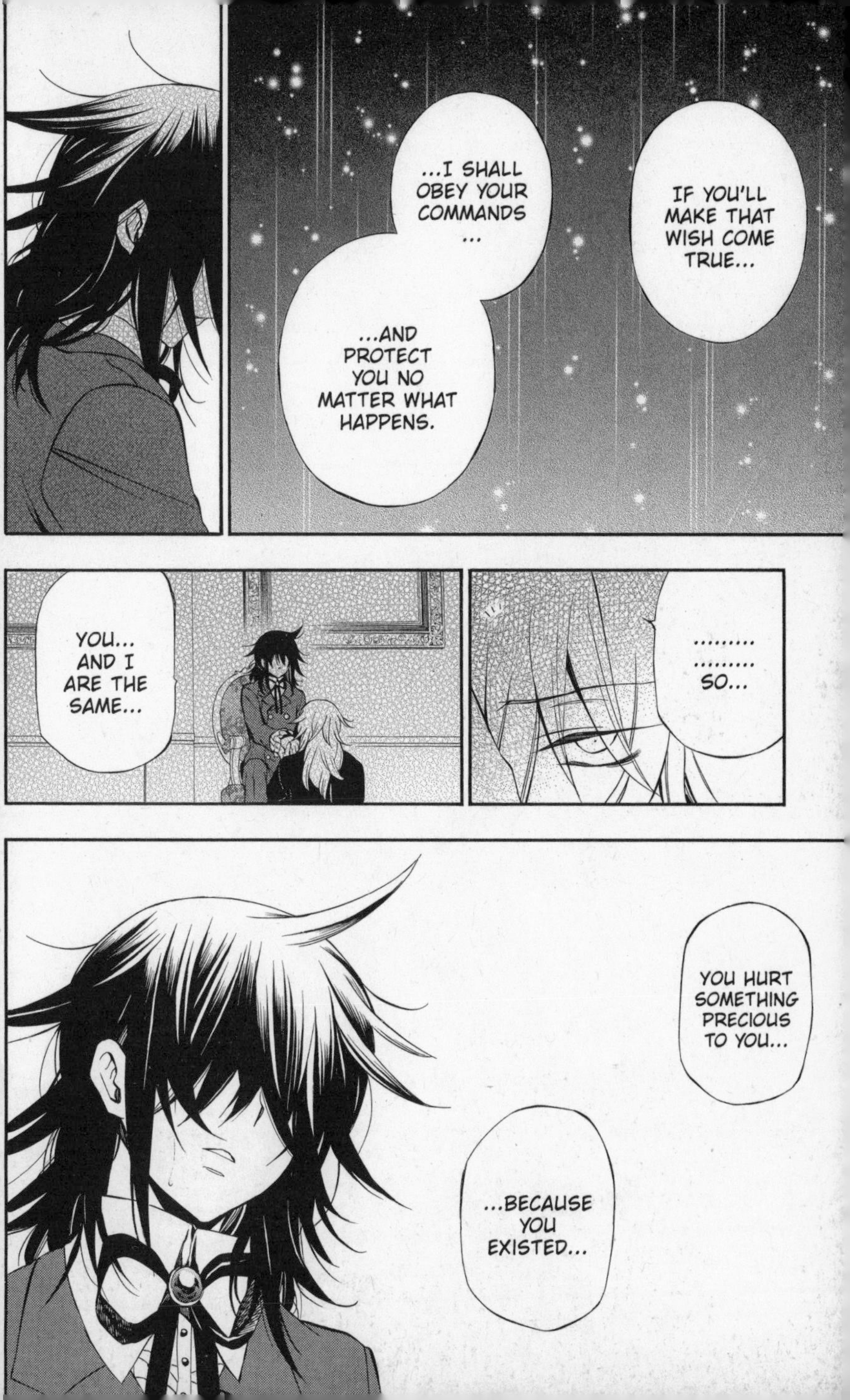
IF YOU'LL MAKE THAT WISH COME TRUE...
...I SHALL OBEY YOUR COMMANDS ...
...AND PROTECT YOU NO MATTER WHAT HAPPENS.
.... SO...
YOU... AND I ARE THE SAME...
YOU HURT SOMETHING PRECIOUS TO YOU...
...BECAUSE YOU EXISTED...

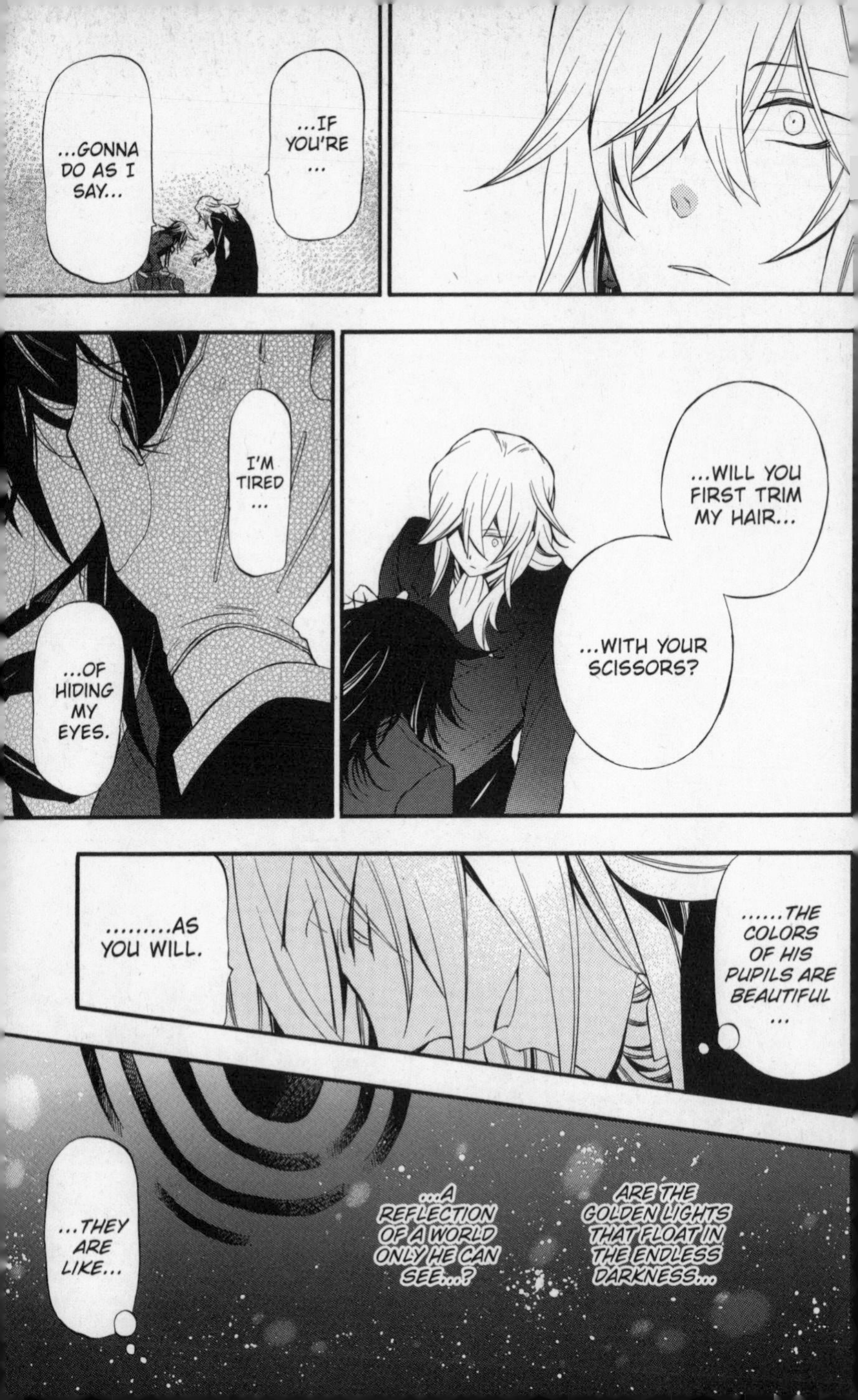
...IF YOU'RE ...
...GONNA DO AS I SAY...
...WILL YOU FIRST TRIM MY HAIR...
...WITH YOUR SCISSORS?
I'M TIRED ...
...OF HIDING MY EYES.
.........AS YOU WILL.
......THE COLORS OF HIS PUPILS ARE BEAUTIFUL ...
ARE THE GOLDEN LIGHTS THAT FLOAT IN THE ENDLESS DARKNESS...
...A REFLECTION OF A WORLD ONLY HE CAN SEE...?
...THEY ARE LIKE...

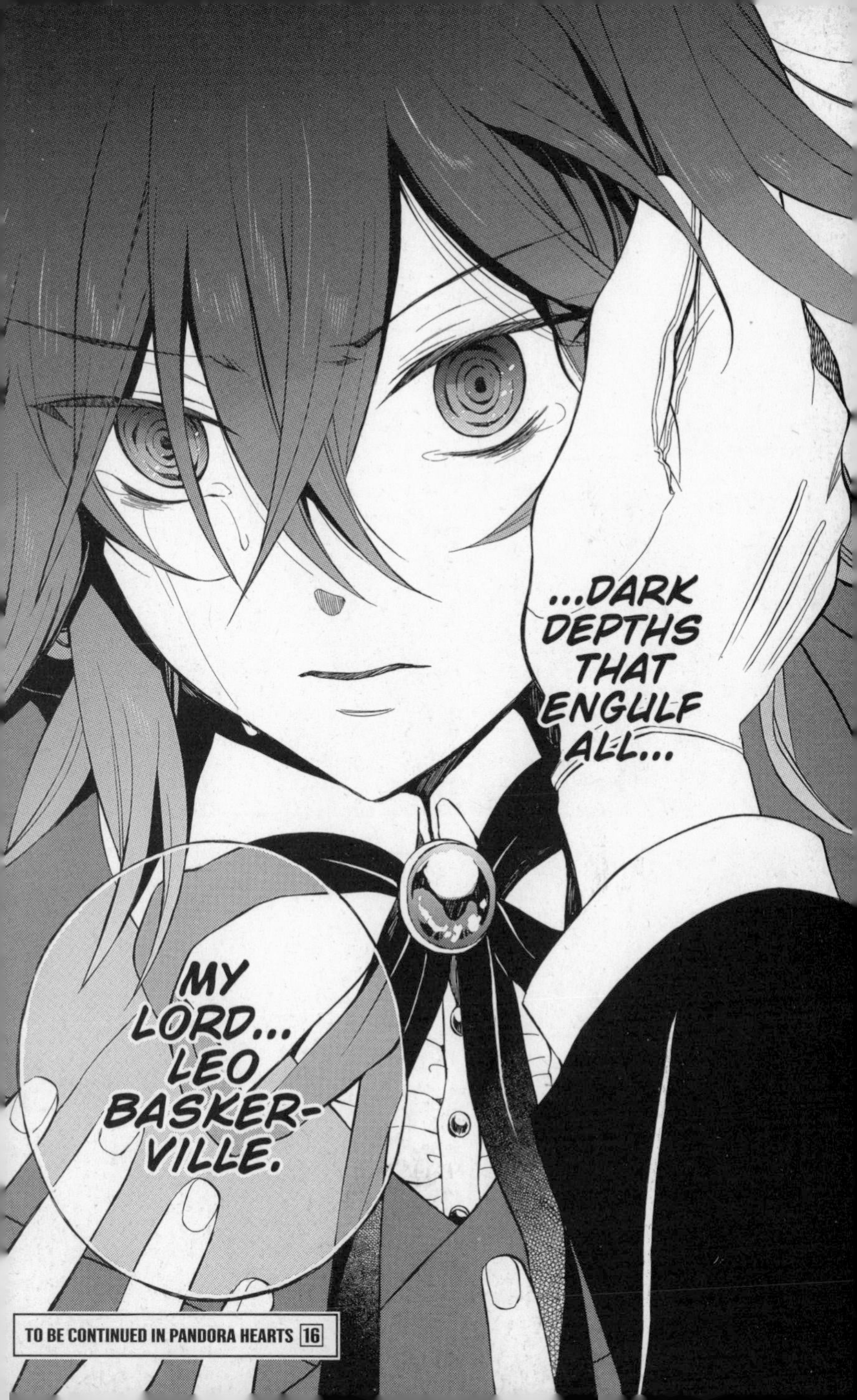
...DARK DEPTHS THAT ENGULF ALL...
MY LORD... LEO BASKER-VILLE.

TO BE CONTINUED IN PANDORA HEARTS 16

Special Thanks!!

THE NUMBER OF PEOPLE INCREASE, DECREASE, INCREASE, DECREASE....

FUMITO YAMAZAKI	GREEN CURRY IS DELICIOUS, DELICIOUS. // GIMME MORE! \\
SAEKO TAKIGAWA	QUEEN OF NICKNAMES AT THE WORKPLACE. FULL OF ENERGY.
SEIRA MINAMI	WE BOTH LOOK FORWARD TO THE ODEN SEASON.
KANATA MINAZUKI	BE CAREFUL SO YOU DON'T GET KIDNAPPED!! I'M SERIOUS!
MIDORI ENDO	I'M ROOTING FOR YOU! DO YOUR BEST!
YUKINO	THANKS FOR ALWAYS INKING THE MOST DIFFICULT PARTS. (MOCHIZUKI & YAMAZAKI)
RYOOOO	HAPPY WEDDIIIING!! ♥♥♥
YAJI	SNAG A BOYFRIEND IN GERMANY!! KYAH.
ASAGI	COME AGAIN WHEN YOU'VE GOT TIME!
YUMI NASHIGASA	HOW TO SAY, YUMI QUALITY I COULD DEPEND ON.
MIZU KING	I'LL START MAKING YOU DRAW LOTS OF BACKGROUNDS.♥(SMILE)
TADUU	OH, HAVEN'T YOU BEEN AROUND FOR ABOUT A YEAR NOW? (A STRANGE ONE WHO MAKES ME FEEL THAT WAY.)
AYANA SASAKI	I WANTED TO LISTEN TO YOU SING KARAOKE...!
NUTMEG HARUNA	THE MATERIALS I RECEIVED WERE ALL BEAUTIFUL, I WAS A LITTLE JEALOUS.

BIG BROTHER (2) & YUKKO-SAN

ALWAYS SOOTHES US. (ALL OF US.)

FATHER, MOTHER, BIG SISTER, BIG BROTHER (1) ETC. ETC.

YOUR YOUNGEST CHILD IS DOING FINE THANKS TO ALL OF YOU.

MY EDITOR TAKEGASA-SAMA

NOWADAYS, I'VE GIVEN UP ON MANY THINGS.....FU. FU-FU-FU-FU-FU-FU-FU-FU.....

— AND YOU!!

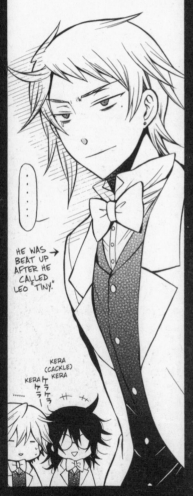

Q. OZ AND LEO ARE ABOUT THE SAME HEIGHT. THEN WHY DOES ELLIOT ONLY CALL OZ "SHORTY"?
......
HE WAS BEAT UP AFTER HE CALLED LEO "TINY."
KERA (CACKLE) KERA
KERA
......

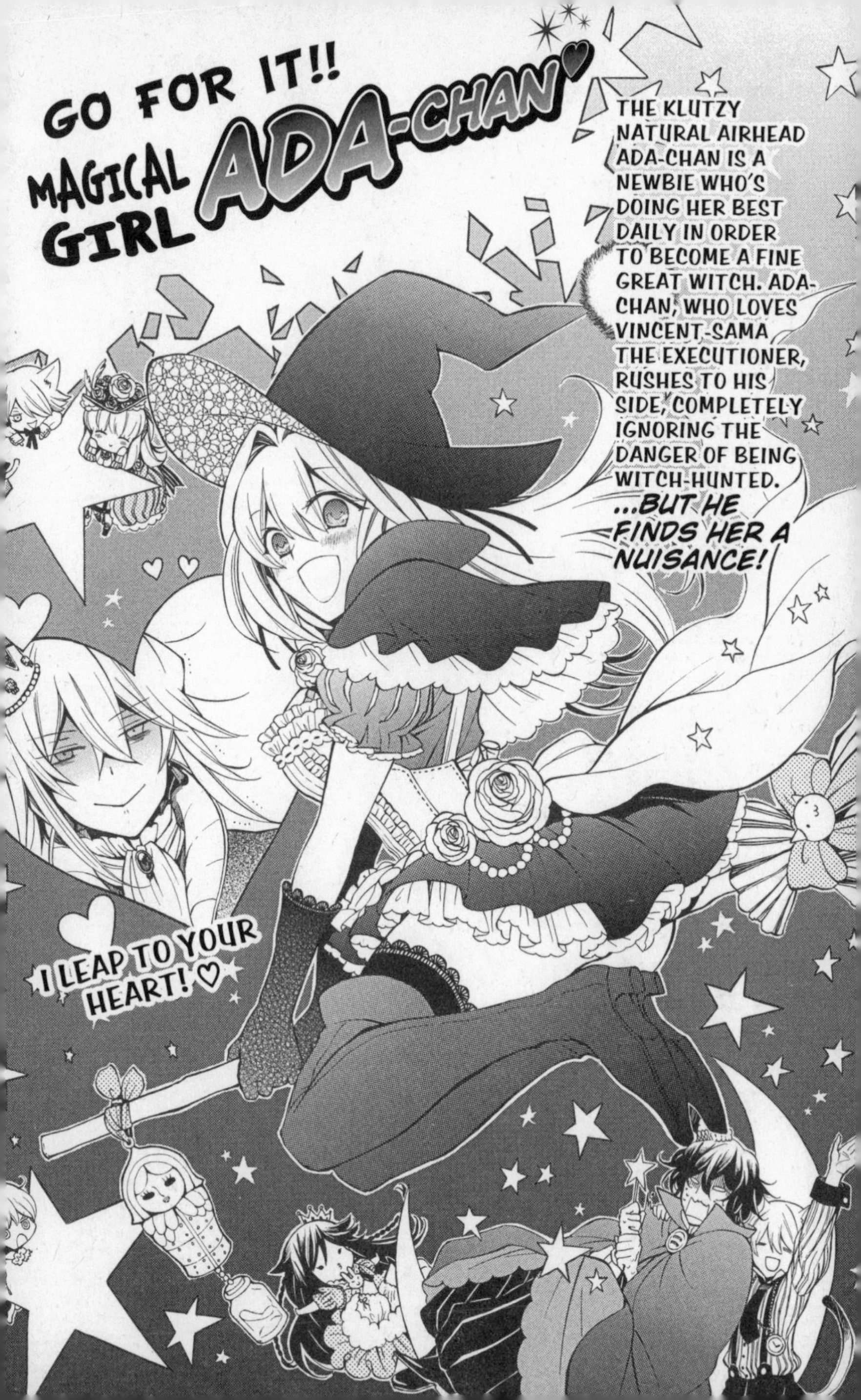
GO FOR IT!! MAGICAL GIRL ADA-CHAN♥
THE KLUTZY NATURAL AIRHEAD ADA-CHAN IS A NEWBIE WHO'S DOING HER BEST DAILY IN ORDER TO BECOME A FINE GREAT WITCH. ADA-CHAN, WHO LOVES VINCENT-SAMA THE EXECUTIONER, RUSHES TO HIS SIDE, COMPLETELY IGNORING THE DANGER OF BEING WITCH-HUNTED.
...BUT HE FINDS HER A NUISANCE!
I LEAP TO YOUR HEART! ♡

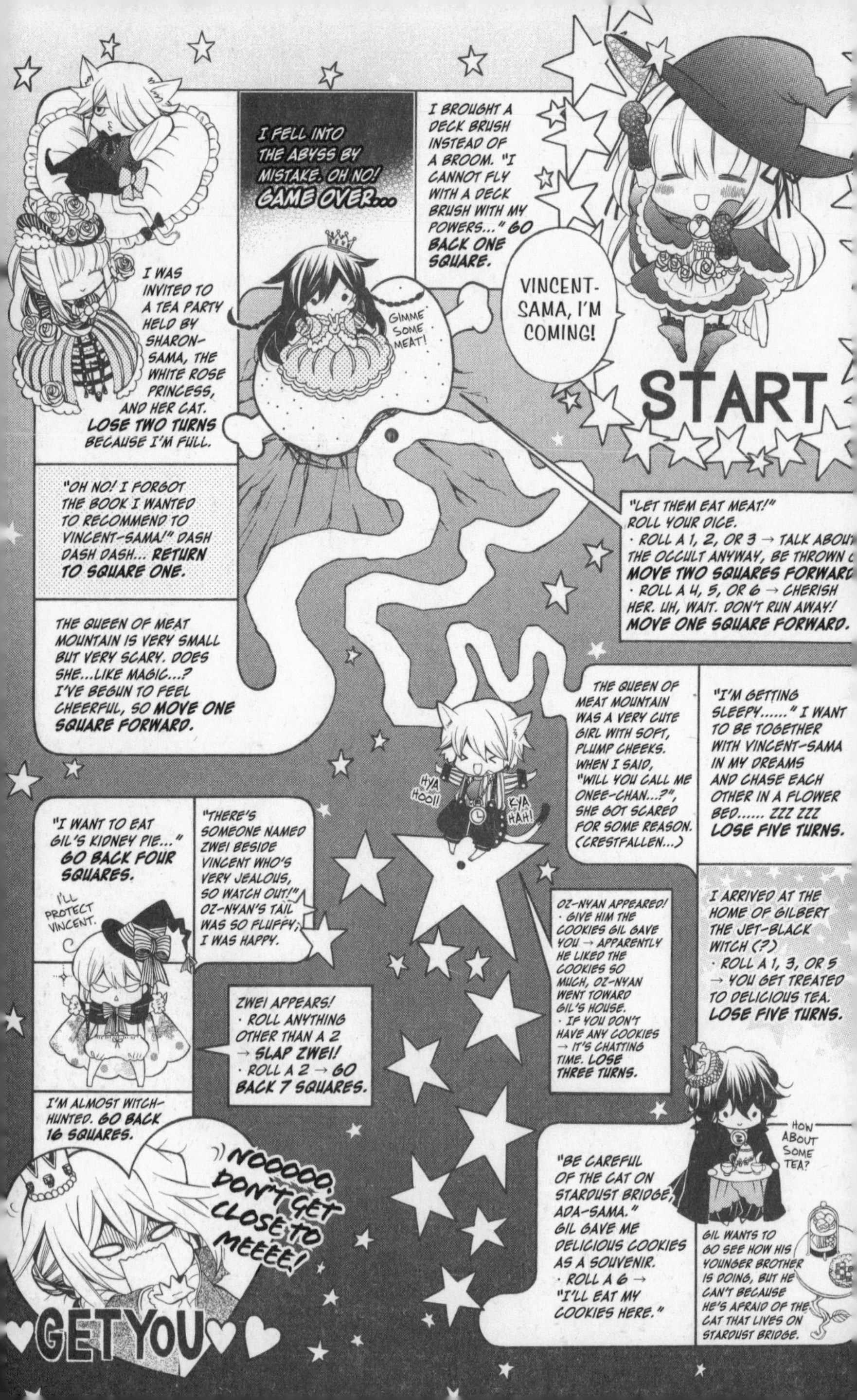

VINCENT-SAMA, I'M COMING!
START
I BROUGHT A DECK BRUSH INSTEAD OF A BROOM. "I CANNOT FLY WITH A DECK BRUSH WITH MY POWERS..." GO BACK ONE SQUARE.
I FELL INTO THE ABYSS BY MISTAKE. OH NO! GAME OVER...
I WAS INVITED TO A TEA PARTY HELD BY SHARON-SAMA, THE WHITE ROSE PRINCESS, AND HER CAT. LOSE TWO TURNS BECAUSE I'M FULL.
GIMME SOME MEAT!
"LET THEM EAT MEAT!" ROLL YOUR DICE.
· ROLL A 1, 2, OR 3 → TALK ABOU
THE OCCULT ANYWAY, BE THROWN O
MOVE TWO SQUARES FORWARD
· ROLL A 4, 5, OR 6 → CHERISH HER. UH, WAIT. DON'T RUN AWAY! MOVE ONE SQUARE FORWARD.
"OH NO! I FORGOT THE BOOK I WANTED TO RECOMMEND TO VINCENT-SAMA!" DASH DASH DASH... RETURN TO SQUARE ONE.
THE QUEEN OF MEAT MOUNTAIN IS VERY SMALL BUT VERY SCARY. DOES SHE...LIKE MAGIC...? I'VE BEGUN TO FEEL CHEERFUL, SO MOVE ONE SQUARE FORWARD.
"I'M GETTING SLEEPY......" I WANT TO BE TOGETHER WITH VINCENT-SAMA IN MY DREAMS AND CHASE EACH OTHER IN A FLOWER BED...... ZZZ ZZZ LOSE FIVE TURNS.
THE QUEEN OF MEAT MOUNTAIN WAS A VERY CUTE GIRL WITH SOFT, PLUMP CHEEKS. WHEN I SAID, "WILL YOU CALL ME ONEE-CHAN...?", SHE GOT SCARED FOR SOME REASON. (CRESTFALLEN...)
KYA HAH!
HYA HOO!!
"THERE'S SOMEONE NAMED ZWEI BESIDE VINCENT WHO'S VERY JEALOUS, SO WATCH OUT!" OZ-NYAN'S TAIL WAS SO FLUFFY, I WAS HAPPY.
"I WANT TO EAT GIL'S KIDNEY PIE..." GO BACK FOUR SQUARES.
I ARRIVED AT THE HOME OF GILBERT THE JET-BLACK WITCH (?) · ROLL A 1, 3, OR 5 → YOU GET TREATED TO DELICIOUS TEA. LOSE FIVE TURNS.
OZ-NYAN APPEARED! · GIVE HIM THE COOKIES GIL GAVE YOU → APPARENTLY HE LIKED THE COOKIES SO MUCH, OZ-NYAN WENT TOWARD GIL'S HOUSE. · IF YOU DON'T HAVE ANY COOKIES → IT'S CHATTING TIME. LOSE THREE TURNS.
ZWEI APPEARS! · ROLL ANYTHING OTHER THAN A 2 → SLAP ZWEI! · ROLL A 2 → GO BACK 7 SQUARES.
I'LL PROTECT VINCENT.
HOW ABOUT SOME TEA?
GIL WANTS TO GO SEE HOW HIS YOUNGER BROTHER IS DOING, BUT HE CAN'T BECAUSE HE'S AFRAID OF THE CAT THAT LIVES ON STARDUST BRIDGE.
"BE CAREFUL OF THE CAT ON STARDUST BRIDGE, ADA-SAMA." GIL GAVE ME DELICIOUS COOKIES AS A SOUVENIR. · ROLL A 6 → "I'LL EAT MY COOKIES HERE."
I'M ALMOST WITCH-HUNTED. GO BACK 16 SQUARES.
NOOOOOO. DON'T GET CLOSE TO MEEEE!
GET YOU

COMMON HONORIFICS

no honorific: Indicates familiarity or closeness; if used without permission or reason, addressing someone in this manner would constitute an insult.

-san: The Japanese equivalent of Mr./Mrs./Miss. If a situation calls for politeness, this is the fail-safe honorific.

-sama: Conveys great respect; may also indicate that the social status of the speaker is lower than that of the addressee.

-kun: Used most often when referring to boys (though it can be applied to girls as well), this indicates affection or familiarity. Occasionally used by older men among their peers, but it may also be used by anyone referring to a person of lower standing.

-chan: An affectionate honorific indicating familiarity used mostly in reference to girls; also used in reference to cute persons or animals of either gender.

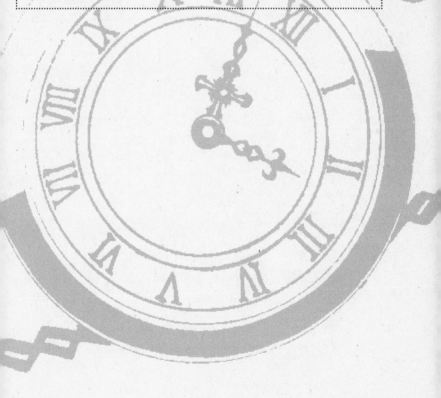

PandoraHearts

The studio I've been renting since about Volume 6 is finally getting cramped.

I have so many books that they're in piles all over... but I don't have the room to add bookshelves anymore... I want a huuuge library like the ones you see in the mansions of the aristocracy. E-books are good too, but I feel at home in a space with lots of books stacked up everywhere.

MOCHIZUKI'S MUSINGS

VOLUME 15

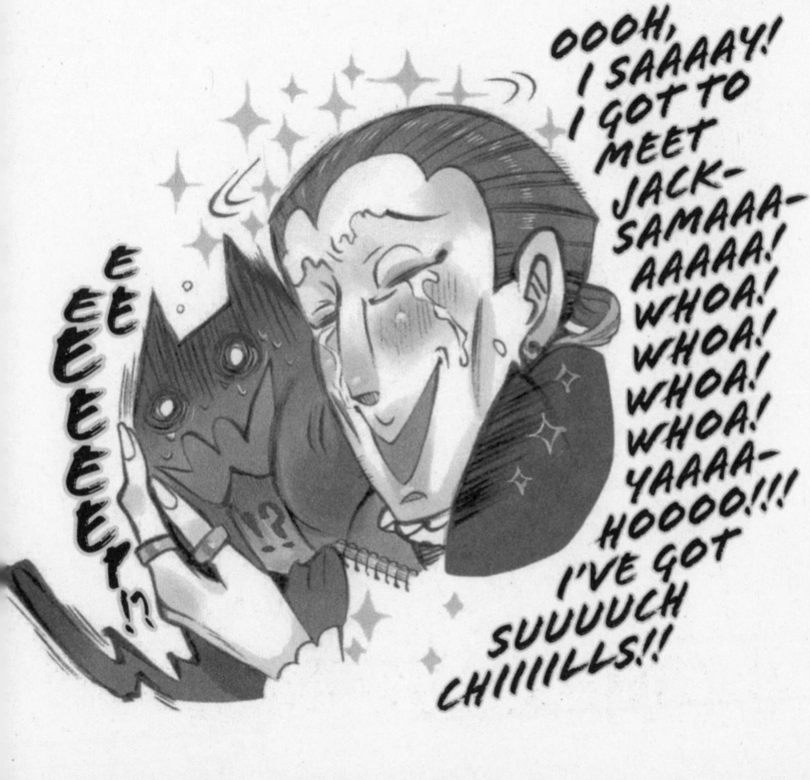
OOOH, I SAAAAY! I GOT TO MEET JACK-SAMAAA-AAAAA! WHOA! WHOA! WHOA! WHOA! YAAAA-HOOOO!!!! I'VE GOT SUUUUCH CHIIIILLS!!
EEEEEEEE!?

Pandora Hearts

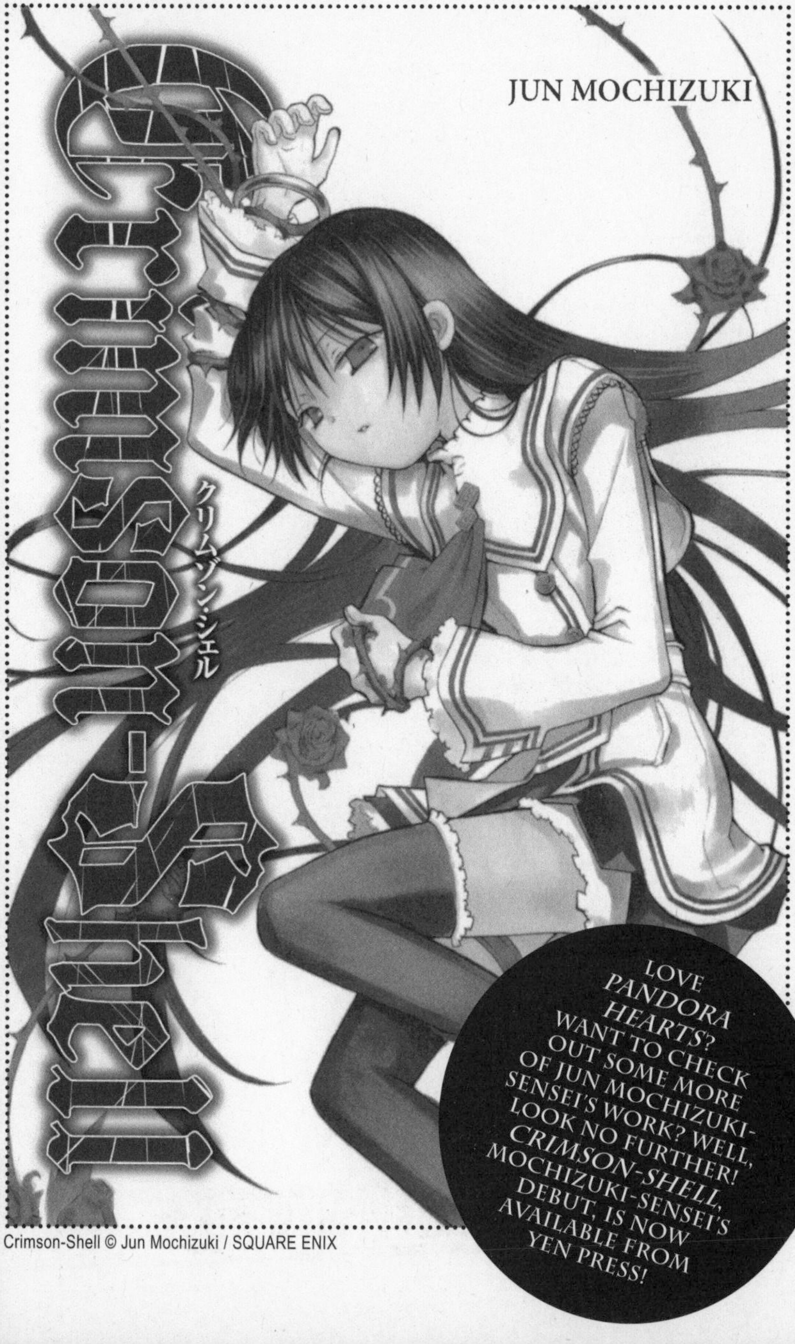
Crimson-Shell
クリムゾン・シェル
JUN MOCHIZUKI
LOVE *PANDORA HEARTS*? WANT TO CHECK OUT SOME MORE OF JUN MOCHIZUKI-SENSEI'S WORK? WELL, LOOK NO FURTHER! *CRIMSON-SHELL*, MOCHIZUKI-SENSEI'S DEBUT, IS NOW AVAILABLE FROM YEN PRESS!

PandoraHearts

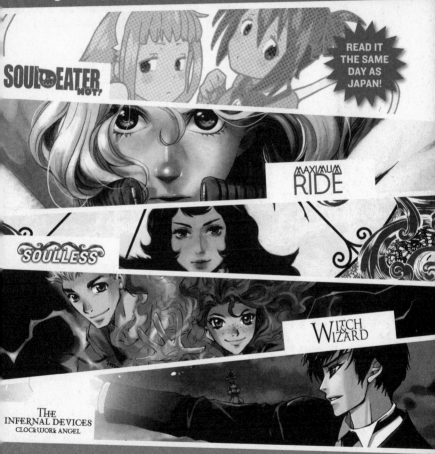
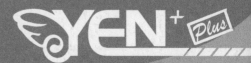

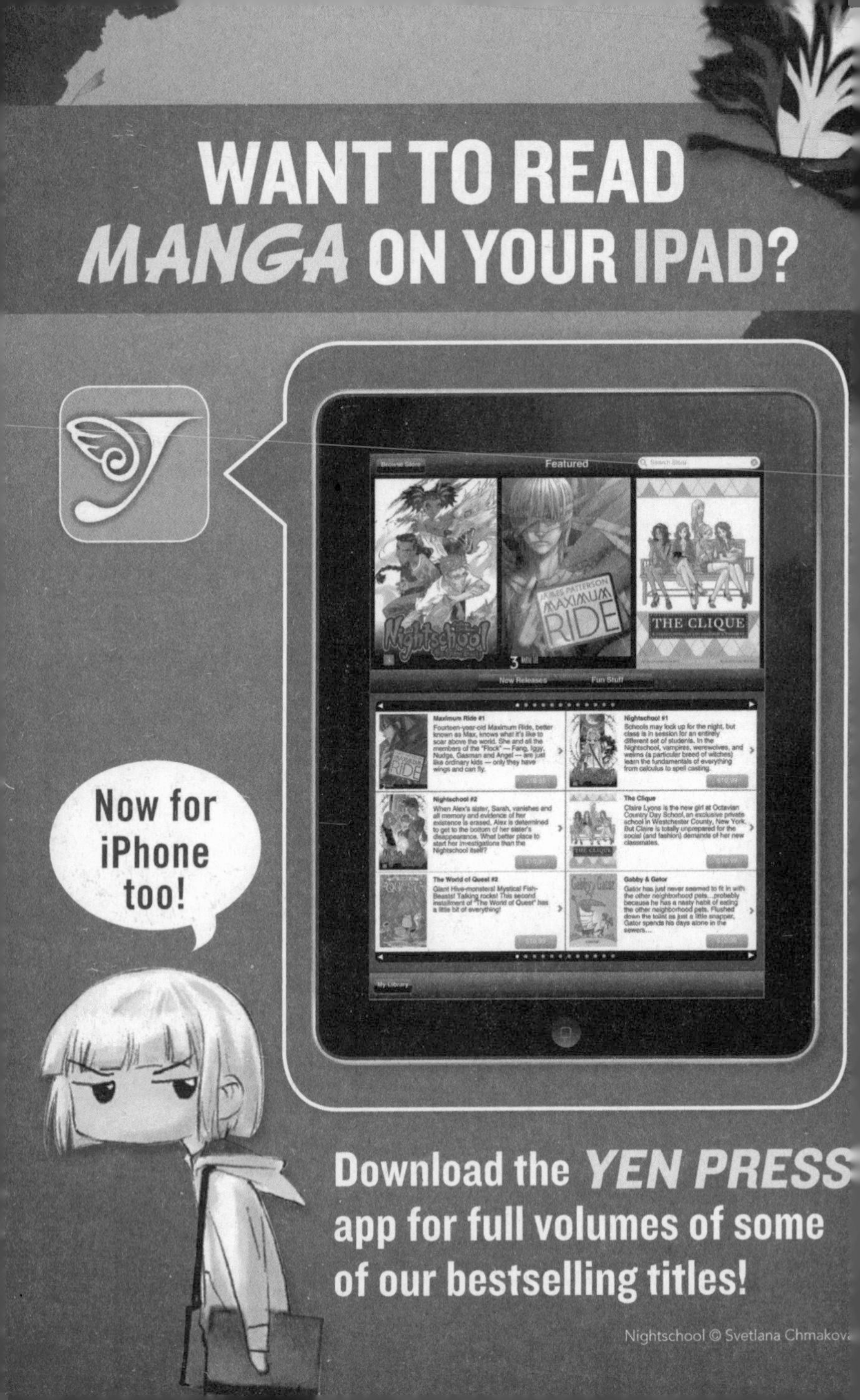
WANT TO READ
MANGA ON YOUR IPAD?
Featured
Nightschool
JAMES PATTERSON MAXIMUM RIDE
THE CLIQUE
Now for iPhone too!
Download the YEN PRESS app for full volumes of some of our bestselling titles!
Nightschool © Svetlana Chmakova

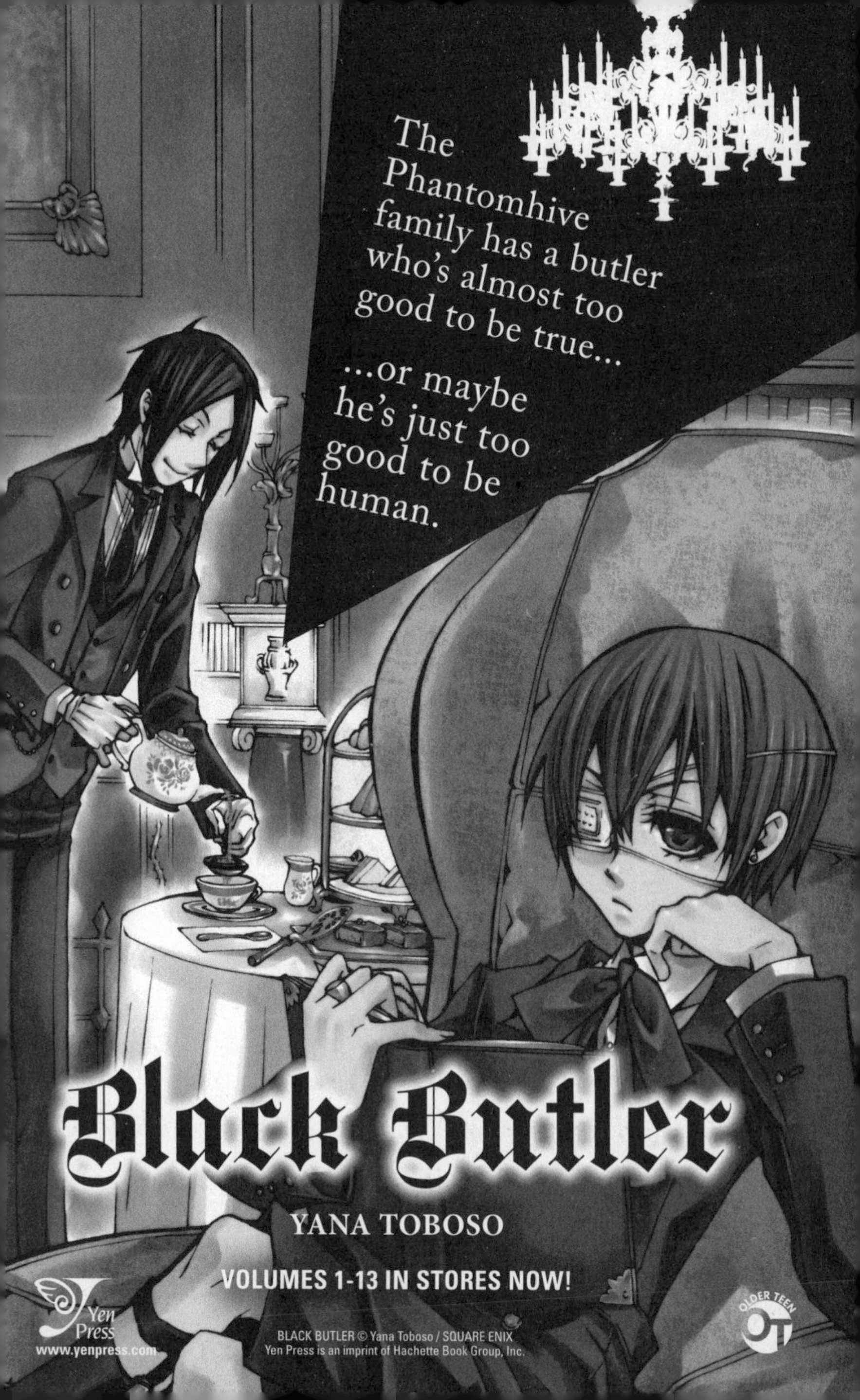
The Phantomhive family has a butler who's almost too good to be true...
...or maybe he's just too good to be human.
Black Butler
YANA TOBOSO
VOLUMES 1-13 IN STORES NOW!
Yen Press
www.yenpress.com
BLACK BUTLER © Yana Toboso / SQUARE ENIX
Yen Press is an imprint of Hachette Book Group, Inc.
OLDER TEEN
OT

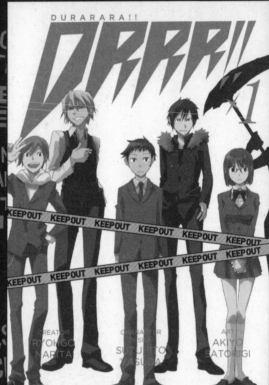

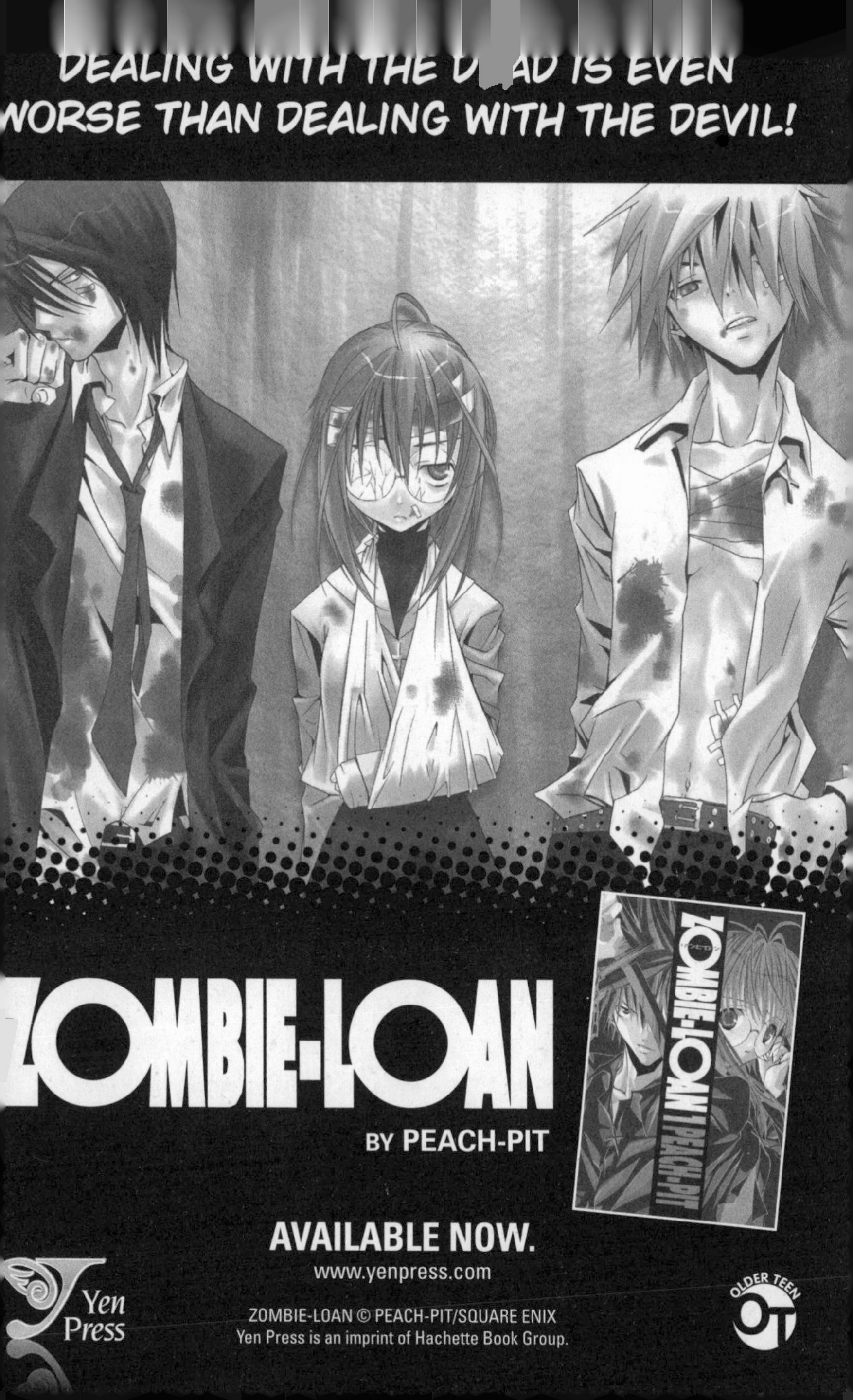
DEALING WITH THE DEAD IS EVEN
WORSE THAN DEALING WITH THE DEVIL!
ZOMBIE-LOAN
BY PEACH-PIT
ZOMBIE-LOAN 1 PEACH-PIT
AVAILABLE NOW.
www.yenpress.com
Yen Press
ZOMBIE-LOAN © PEACH-PIT/SQUARE ENIX
Yen Press is an imprint of Hachette Book Group.
OLDER TEEN
OT

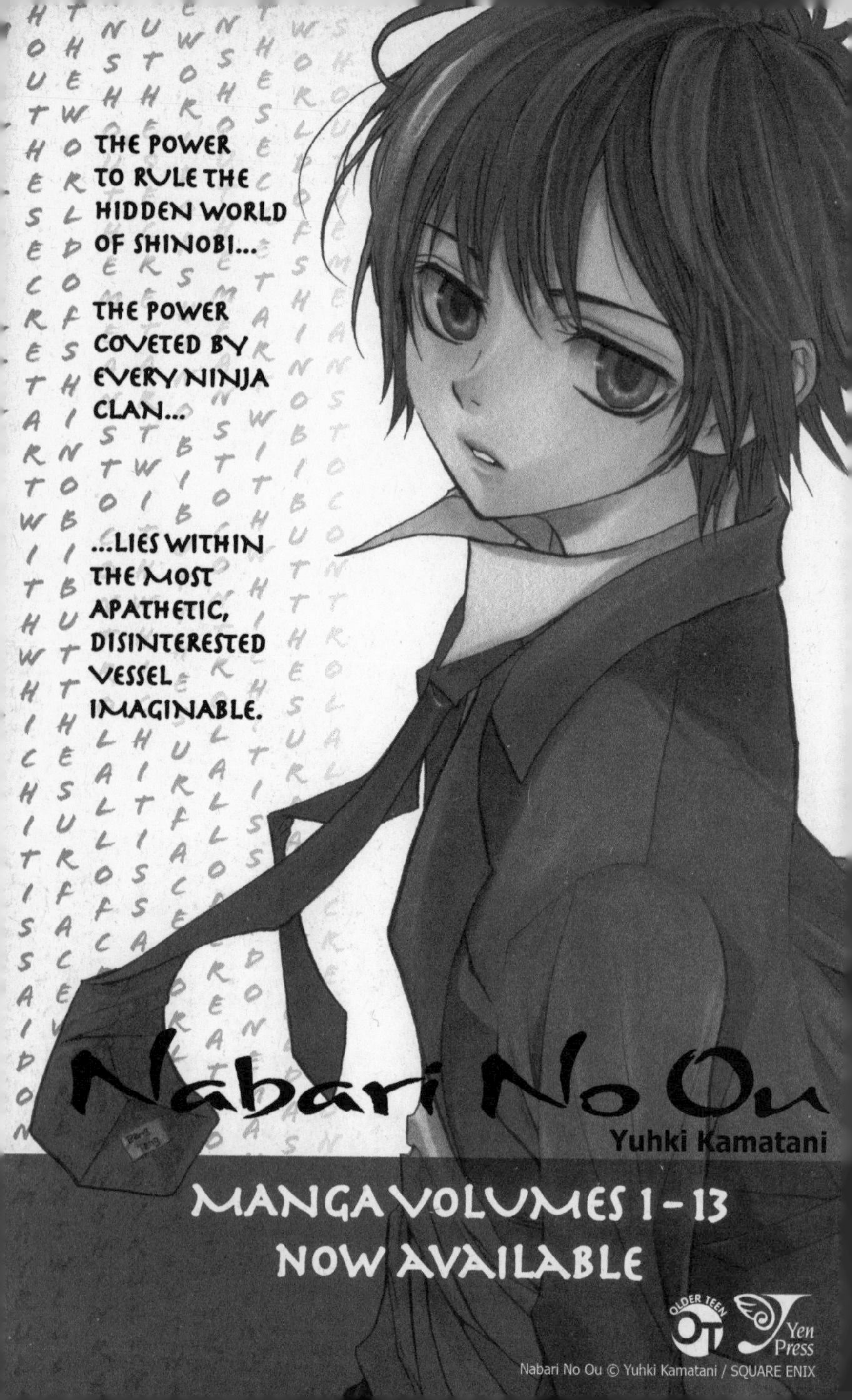
THE POWER TO RULE THE HIDDEN WORLD OF SHINOBI...
THE POWER COVETED BY EVERY NINJA CLAN...
...LIES WITHIN THE MOST APATHETIC, DISINTERESTED VESSEL IMAGINABLE.
Nabari No Ou
Yuhki Kamatani
MANGA VOLUMES 1–13
NOW AVAILABLE
OLDER TEEN OT
Yen Press
Nabari No Ou © Yuhki Kamatani / SQUARE ENIX

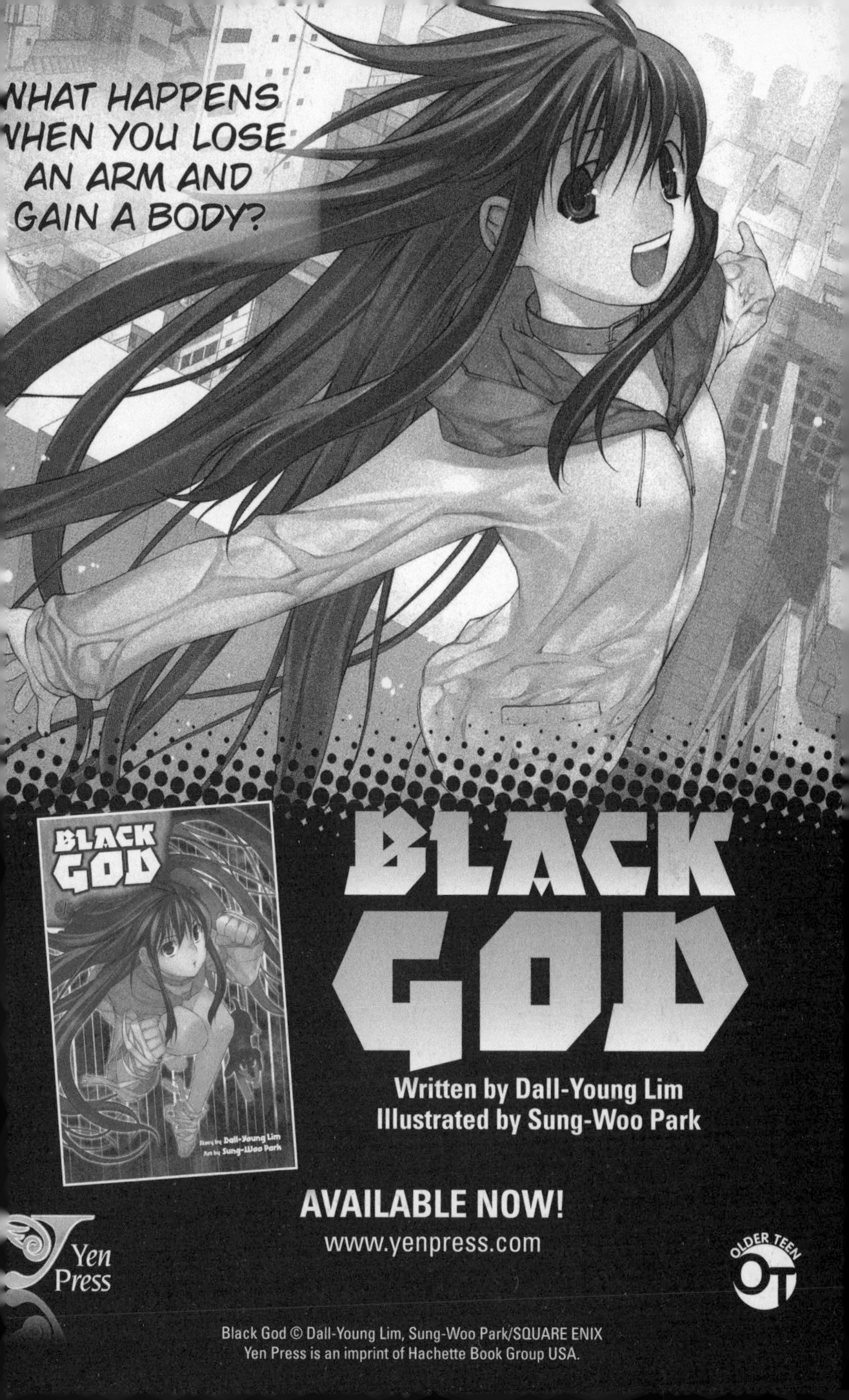
WHAT HAPPENS
WHEN YOU LOSE
AN ARM AND
GAIN A BODY?
BLACK GOD
Story by Dall-Young Lim
Art by Sung-Woo Park
BLACK GOD
Written by Dall-Young Lim
Illustrated by Sung-Woo Park
AVAILABLE NOW!
www.yenpress.com
Yen Press
OLDER TEEN
OT
Black God © Dall-Young Lim, Sung-Woo Park/SQUARE ENIX
Yen Press is an imprint of Hachette Book Group USA.

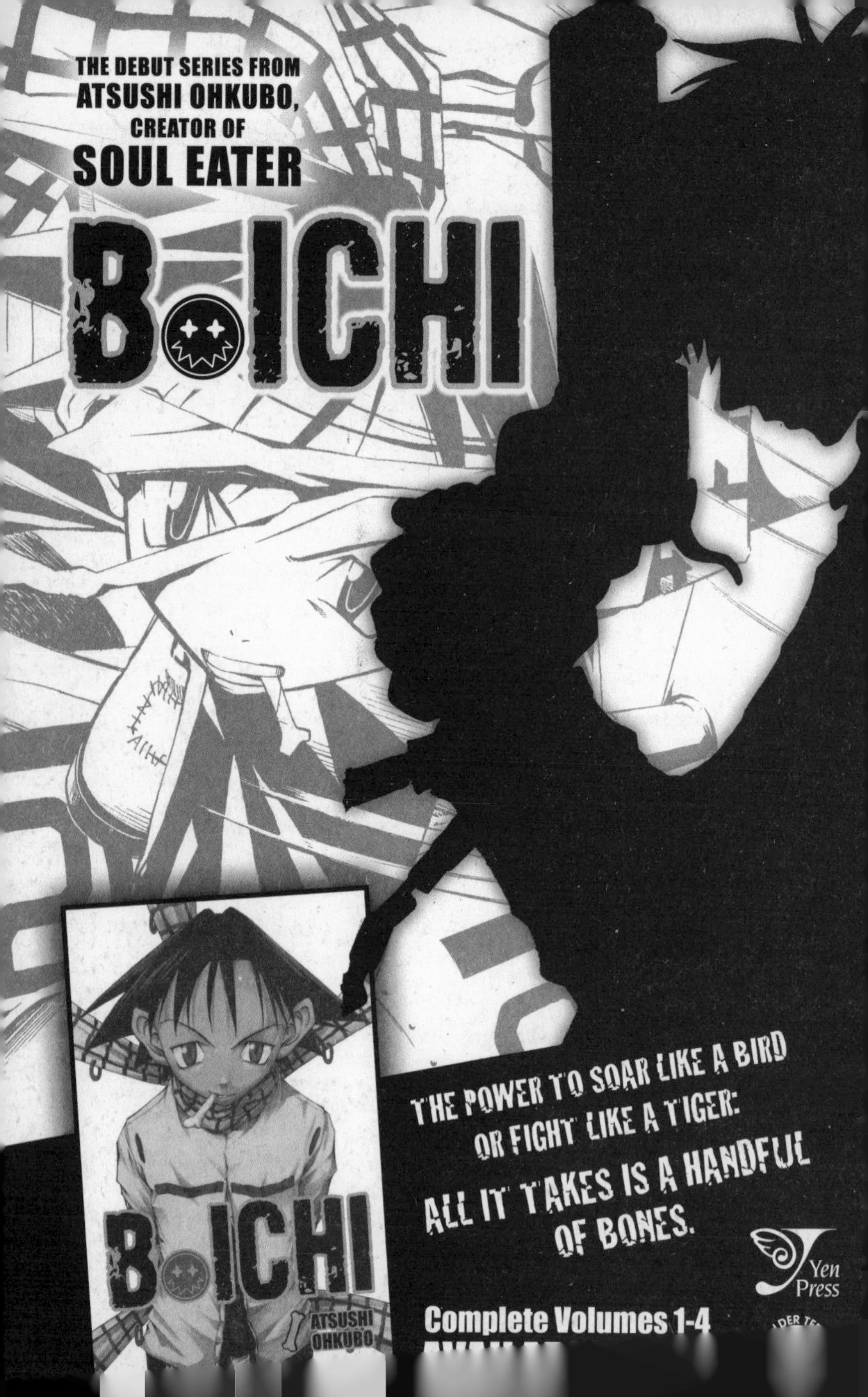

THE DEBUT SERIES FROM
ATSUSHI OHKUBO,
CREATOR OF
SOUL EATER
B ICHI
B ICHI
ATSUSHI OHKUBO
THE POWER TO SOAR LIKE A BIRD
OR FIGHT LIKE A TIGER:
ALL IT TAKES IS A HANDFUL
OF BONES.
Yen Press
Complete Volumes 1-4

PANDORA HEARTS ⑮

JUN MOCHIZUKI

Translation: Tomo Kimura   •   Lettering: Alexis Eckerman

PANDORA HEARTS Vol. 15 © 2011 Jun Mochizuki / SQUARE ENIX CO., LTD. All rights reserved. First published in Japan in 2011 by SQUARE ENIX CO., LTD. English translation rights arranged with SQUARE ENIX CO., LTD. and Hachette Book Group through Tuttle-Mori Agency, Inc.

Translation © 2013 by SQUARE ENIX CO., LTD.

Yen Press
Hachette Book Group
237 Park Avenue, New York, NY 10017

www.HachetteBookGroup.com
www.YenPress.com

Yen Press is an imprint of Hachette Book Group, Inc. The Yen Press name and logo are trademarks of Hachette Book Group, Inc.

First Yen Press Edition: April 2013

ISBN: 978-0-316-22537-3

10 9 8 7 6 5 4 3 2 1

BVG

Printed in the United States of America